Aging and Work

Aging and Work

Issues and Implications
in a Changing Landscape

Edited by

SARA J. CZAJA

Professor, Department of Psychiatry and Behavioral Sciences,
and Co-Director, Center on Aging
University of Miami Miller School of Medicine

and

JOSEPH SHARIT

Professor, Department of Industrial Engineering
University of Miami

The Johns Hopkins University Press
Baltimore

The Johns Hopkins University Press
2715 North Charles Street
Baltimore, Maryland 21218-4363
www.press.jhu.edu

Library of Congress Cataloging-in-Publication Data
Aging and work : issues and implications in a changing landscape /
edited by Sara J. Czaja and Joseph Sharit.
p.   cm.
Includes bibliographical references and index.
ISBN-13: 978-0-8018-9273-8 (hardcover : alk. paper)
ISBN-10: 0-8018-9273-2 (hardcover : alk. paper)
1. Older people—Employment. 2. Age and employment.
3. Health promotion. I. Czaja, Sara J. II. Sharit, Joseph.
HD6279.A334 2009
331.3'98—dc22   2008050562

A catalog record for this book is available from the British Library.

Special discounts are available for bulk purchases of this book.
For more information, please contact Special Sales at
410-516-6936 or specialsales@press.jhu.edu.

Contents

Contributors

Richard V. Burkhauser, Ph.D., Professor, Policy Analysis and Management, Cornell University, Ithaca, New York

Peter Cappelli, Ph.D., Professor, Wharton School, University of Pennsylvania, Philadelphia, Pennsylvania

Neil Charness, Ph.D., Professor, Department of Psychology, Florida State University, Tallahassee, Florida

Gwenith G. Fisher, Ph.D., Assistant Research Scientist, Institute for Social Research, University of Michigan, Ann Arbor, Michigan

James W. Grosch, Ph.D., Research Psychologist, Centers for Disease Control and Prevention, National Institute for Occupational Safety and Health, Division of Applied Research and Technology, Cincinnati, Ohio

Dennis J. Hanseman, Ph.D., Researcher, Department of Environmental Health, University of Cincinnati, Cincinnati, Ohio

Vicki L. Hanson, Ph.D., Manager, Accessibility Research, IBM T. J. Watson Research Center, Hawthorne, New York

Juhani Ilmarinen, Ph.D., Professor, Department of Physiology, Finnish Institute of Occupational Health, Vantaa, Finland

Richard W. Johnson, Ph.D., Senior Research Associate, The Urban Institute, Washington, D.C.

Ruth Kanfer, Ph.D., Professor, Department of Industrial/Organizational Psychology, School of Psychology, Georgia Institute of Technology, Atlanta, Georgia

Karl H. E. Kroemer, Ph.D., Professor, Virginia Polytechnic Institute and State University, Blacksburg, Virginia

Eric Lesser, M.B.A., Associate Partner, Global Human Capital Management Research Leader, IBM Institute for Business Value, Cambridge, Massachusetts

Lynn M. Martire, Ph.D., Associate Professor, Department of Psychiatry, University of Pittsburgh, Pittsburgh, Pennsylvania

Marcie Pitt-Catsouphes, Ph.D., Director, The Center of Aging and Work, Boston College, Chestnut Hill, Massachusetts

Glenn S. Pransky, M.D., M.Occ.H., Director, Center for Disability Research, Liberty Mutual Research Institute for Safety, Hopkinton, Massachusetts

Edward G. Rogoff, Ph.D., Professor of Management, Baruch College, New York, New York

Ludmila Rovba, Ph.D., Economist, Analysis Group, Inc., Montreal, Quebec, Canada

Steven L. Sauter, Ph.D., Senior Scientist, Division of Applied Research and Technology, Centers for Disease Control and Prevention, National Institute for Occupational Safety and Health, Cincinnati, Ohio

Richard Schulz, Ph.D., Professor of Psychiatry and Director, University Center for Social and Urban Research, and Associate Director, University of Pittsburgh Institute on Aging, University of Pittsburgh, Pittsburgh, Pennsylvania

Michael A. Smyer, Ph.D., Provost, Bucknell University, Lewisburg, Pennsylvania

Jessica M. Streit, M.S., Psychologist, National Institute for Occupational Safety and Health, Cincinnati, Ohio

Fernando M. Torres-Gil, Ph.D., Associate Dean, UCLA School of Public Policy and Social Research, and Director, Center for Policy Research on Aging, University of California, Los Angeles, Los Angeles, California

Pamela S. Tsang, Ph.D., Associate Professor, Psychology Department, Wright State University, Dayton, Ohio

Robert B. Wallace, M.D., Professor, Department of Epidemiology, College of Public Health, University of Iowa, Iowa City, Iowa

Foreword

At the time that this volume on work in the context of population aging was conceived, the case for its importance and timeliness was already strong. The premise was that decreasing worker-retiree ratios associated with population aging, coupled with the macroeconomic circumstances, would increase pressure on people to postpone retirement and continue working. As a consequence of the current global financial meltdown, its significance and relevance have increased by an order of magnitude. While the full impact of current financial woes on retirement savings is not yet known, it seems safe to predict that many older workers will delay planned retirements and that many retirees who suffer reduced incomes may try to return to the labor force in the midst of growing unemployment. When the editors described the demographic and economic forces combining to force a lengthening of worklife as "a perfect storm," they were perhaps all too prescient.

This volume is a comprehensive, multidisciplinary, and multifaceted treatment of the many issues related to the future of work in an aging population. The seventeen chapters cover an extensive array of topics, including the following: changes in employment patterns due to the demographic and economic consequences of population aging, aging and job performance, motivation, skills and cognition, ergonomics, health and health promotion in the workplace, and managerial attitudes toward older workers. It ends with an effective synthesis. Given the current and projected demographic and economic trends, I expect that the volume will be widely consulted.

These current trends point toward a central fact—many workers will have to retire later to finance the private (if any) and public components of their retirement income. Just how much later is less certain. It is not just that people are living longer and that the extra years have to be financed publically or privately. More important, the relative sizes of the retired and working populations are destined to change dramatically, with each retired person being supported by fewer workers as the baby boom generation begins to retire. There is only a limited set of options for dealing with the fiscal implications of the radically decreased number of workers paying into the Social Security Trust Fund per retiree drawing benefits. Social Security taxes could be increased, but this would depress labor demand and after-tax wages for remaining workers. Other options include reducing benefits, increasing birth rates, inviting large new waves of working-age immigrants, developing new technologies that dramatically increase productivity, thereby boosting the overall economy, or delaying retirement and increasing the average worklife. It appears that a consensus is developing among economists and policy makers that whatever mix of policy options is chosen for public pensions, working longer will probably be the major component.

The sum of demographic trends that are pushing pay-as-you-go pension systems farther out of balance, requiring adjustments such as extending working life or delaying benefits, may be even stronger than suggested by chapters in the volume. The usual pathway to population aging starts with a decline in infant mortality that tends to lead to lower birth rates, with the smaller birth cohorts serving as the driving force behind structural population aging. Increasing life expectancy kicks in at a later stage and then grows as a factor that accelerates the structural shift in the population. Small increases in life expectancy that accumulate and compound for decades result in large increases in the older population. While the enormous increase in life expectancy that has occurred in high-income countries is acknowledged to be one of the crowning achievements of mankind and the extra years of life expectancy are highly valued, they are not free. The added years must be financed, whether privately or publicly.

What are the prospects for longevity? While some have argued that life expectancy must soon reach an asymptote, Oeppen and Vaupel (2002) reported a remarkable, nearly linear increase in life expectancy in the best-performing country at any one time, and that trend has remained linear seven years after the publication of the article. While life expectancy in the United States has been significantly lagging behind almost all other high-income countries since about 1980 (especially among women), there is strongly suggestive evidence that increases in life expectancy may soon begin to accelerate as the effect of heavy smoking over the last two or three decades plays out (Wang and Preston, 2009). While obesity plays a major factor in disability, surprisingly, in some analyses, it appears to have less effect on mortality than it may once have had. This may be attributed to some of the intensive treatments for associated diabetes, hypertension, and hyperlipidemias. On a more speculative note, it is also possible that some biological innovation might produce substantial increases in life expectancy (Sierra et al., 2009). Such speculative occurrences are not included in any official demographic forecast because there is no way to place any probability on such an event, but one can still imagine and model the enormous impact that a change in the slope of long-term increases in survival at older ages would have on the retirement system.

A parallel debate has revolved around the course of health and functioning in the context of lengthening life expectancy. Would there be, as most believed in the 1970s and well into the 1990s, an inexorable accumulation of chronic disease-induced disability as people were saved from early death but chronic diseases could not be prevented or cured? One of the largest upsets in gerontological thinking came when a group of researchers at Duke discovered in the National Long-Term Care Survey that disability appeared to have been declining since at least the early 1980s. Many were skeptical, but the trend has been confirmed in several different surveys (Freedman, Martin, and Schoeni, 2002). Recent results suggest that there may also have been a reduction in the prevalence of dementia (Langa et al., 2008). In contrast, increases in obesity and related diabetes have raised concern that they could neutralize or even reverse the positive trend of improving levels of functioning in the older population (Lakdawalla et al., 2004). Initial analyses (Weir, 2007) find support for a lack of any improvement in functioning in the Health and Retirement Study (HRS)'s preretirement age group. How the trends in health and functioning play out, most especially in relation to the substantial increase in obesity levels, will affect the capacity to remain in the labor force at older ages. However, the increased number of healthy years spent in retirement already provided a store of healthy years available for work, especially among the better educated.

To these long-term trends we must now add the impact of the current financial crisis. Beyond anecdotal reports, it is too early to know much about the effect of the financial meltdown that started in late 2007 will have on older workers and retirees. Numerous companies have announced reduced or eliminated employer matches to 401(k) accounts. We can expect severe losses in the value of 401(k)s and other retirement savings, an inability to easily sell houses in connection with retirement moves, and adult children losing jobs and becoming dependent on their older parents. It is probably safe to predict that in response to these losses, many older workers will postpone retirement, while retirees with severe savings losses or reductions in retirement income might attempt to return to the labor force. Given that data collection in the HRS and the English Longitudinal Study on Ageing occurred before and during the current economic crisis, these studies should soon provide initial representative data. But, as the full consequences become clearer, the need to improve the capacity of older workers to maintain effective functioning in the workplace will become even more apparent and compelling. It would therefore be a significant benefit if research could lead to enhanced capacities of older workers to remain highly productive, as well as making older workers more attractive to employers.

Increasing the capacity of older people to remain at work, should they so desire, has been an important goal of the National Institute on Aging's (NIA) Division of Behavioral and Social Research (BSR), almost since its founding. BSR maintains a significant interest in work and the life course and has sponsored a wide range of research on the topic. Some years ago, BSR cosponsored (with the National Institute for Occupational Safety and Health) a National Academy of Sciences report on the health and safety of older workers (Wegman and McGee, 2004). Based on the report, BSR has launched several initiatives, including using the workplace as a context for health promotion and developing interventions (with the Child Health Institute) to improve the family friendliness of the workplace for low-income workers. BSR's grant portfolio includes studies on the impact of occupational hierarchies, job conditions, and stress on health, finding the best ways to train older persons to use computer technology, and numerous studies on the determinants of retirement. BSR recently launched an initiative on forecasting retirement patterns.

NIA has also sponsored intervention studies designed to make the workplace more family friendly for low-wage workers, such as those employed in nursing homes. It has also encouraged attempts to use the workplace for interventions that encourage healthier lifestyles while also reducing health costs. Looking to the future, we may expect to see more intervention studies, but, given how costly well-powered interventions are, the interventions will have to be carefully selected. To fully understand and then alter the dynamics within the workplace, we will also need to find ways to integrate and coordinate findings from representative observational studies with those of interventional studies. Given the increasing cognitive component of many jobs, progress in maintaining cognitive functioning with age is of paramount importance, and this is a topic accorded a high priority by the NIA. As new and more successful approaches to preventing and remediating age-related cognitive declines are developed, it is conceivable that the workplace could become a successful venue for the delivery of the cognitive interventions.

There is a growing interest in using the workplace to improve physical health. There are scattered accounts of successful employment-based interventions to reduce health risks and decrease health costs. Health costs of older workers can become a significant negative factor in determining employer attitudes toward older workers that might affect employer motivation to increase the capacity of older workers to remain in the labor force. To develop lower-cost and more-effective behavioral interventions related to health, the NIA has cooperated with at least sixteen other institutes and centers at the National Institutes of Health to begin an effort to understand the basic science of behavior change. One especially promising line of research derived from behavioral economics involves remodeling the physical and institutional environment to encourage people to act in their own best interests (e.g., Loewenstein, Brennan, and Volpp, 2007; Thaler and Sunstein, 2008). The workplace may be an ideal platform for these types of intervention experiments. As successful interventions multiply, we may eventually be in the position to compare multiple interventions directed at a specific outcome, in terms of both effectiveness and relative economic cost.

This volume supplies a useful introduction and essential guide for any researcher entering the field and is likely to provide a much-needed stimulus to the area. Much remains to be done; for example, the evidence on productivity and work capacity and age is absent for most occupational groups. Additional information is needed on how advances in computer and other technologies, for example, might compensate for declines in abilities. Successful workplace interventions that both improve health and reduce costs need to be replicated to evaluate generalizability and should be followed by competitive comparisons to evaluate comparative effectiveness and relative cost-effectiveness before widespread adoption. Knowledge in these fields has often been surprisingly localized and balkanized, and many research areas still seem to be the domain of single disciplines. Collaboration with parallel European efforts in these areas could bring significant benefits in the trade of ideas and successful technologies, and there are likely to be significant spin-offs for home use. Over the longer term, it is easy to imagine that skilled worker shortages will increase the need for research that enables older workers to remain productively employed well past current ages of retirement.

Richard Suzman

Director, Division of Behavioral and Social Research

National Institute on Aging, National Institutes of Health

REFERENCES

Freedman, V. A., Martin, L. G., and Schoeni, R. F. 2002. Recent trends in disability and functioning among older adults in the United States: A systematic review. *JAMA* 288: 3137–46.

Lakdawalla, D. N., Bhattacharya, J. and Goldman, D. P. 2004. Are the young becoming more disabled? *Health Affairs* 23 (1): 168–76.

Langa, K. M., Larson, E. B., Karlawish, J. H., Cutler, D. M., Kabeto, M. U., Kim, S. Y., et al. 2008. Trends in the prevalence and mortality of cognitive impairment in the United States: Is there evidence of a compression of cognitive morbidity? *Alzheimer's and Dementia* 4 (2): 134–44.

Loewenstein, G., Brennan, T., and Volpp, K. G. 2007. Asymmetric paternalism to improve health behaviors. *JAMA* 298 (20): 2415–17.

Oeppen, J., and Vaupel, J. W. 2002. Broken limits to life expectancy. *Science* 296 (5570): 1029–31.

Sierra, F., Hardey, E., Suzman, R., and Hodes, R. 2009. Prospects for life span extension. *Annual Review of Medicine* 60: 457–69.

Thaler, R. H., and Sunstein, C. R. 2008. *Nudge: Improving Decisions about Health, Wealth and Happiness.* New Haven: Yale University Press.

Wang, H., and Preston, S. H. 2009. Forecasting United States mortality using cohort smoking histories. *Proceedings of the National Academies of Science* 106 (2): 393–98.

Wegman, D. H , and McGee, J. P., eds. 2004. *Health and Safety Needs of Older Workers.* Washington, DC: National Academies Press.

Weir, D. R. 2007. Are baby boomers living well longer? In *Redefining Retirement,* ed. O. S. Mitchell and B. J. Soldo, pp. 95–112. New York: Oxford University Press.

Acknowledgments

We thank all of our authors for their contributions, especially Richard Schulz and David Eckert for their advice and editorial insights. We also extend our deepest appreciation to Chin Chin Lee, who has been instrumental in the production of this book; to Adrienne Goldberg, Carl Eisdorfer, and Sharon Purcell for their effort; and to all of the researchers and personnel at the Center on Aging at the University of Miami. Finally, we would like to thank our families for their continued support.

This book represents the work of the Center for Research and Education on Aging and Technology Enhancement (CREATE). CREATE is sponsored by the U.S. National Institutes of Health/National Institute on Aging (Grant P01-AG17211). In addition to support from the NIH/NIA, we acknowledge support from U.S. National Institute for Occupational Safety and Health (NIOSH) and AARP. We also acknowledge support from the Center on Aging and the Center for the Advanced Studies on Aging at the University of Miami.

Aging and Work

Introduction

Emerging Challenges for Organizations and Older Workers in the Twenty-first Century

SARA J. CZAJA, PH.D., AND JOSEPH SHARIT, PH.D.

The focus of this book is the changing landscape of work in the twenty-first century. The aging of the baby boomers, increases in life expectancy, and the decline in fertility rates in the United States will result in an increase in the number of older Americans who qualify for publicly financed retirement and health benefits in coming years and a decrease in the number of younger adults who typically work and pay taxes. From an economic and social perspective, if current employment patterns that favor early retirement continue, the shrinking labor pool will threaten economic growth, living standards, Social Security and Medicare financing, and funding for all other government programs. Current changes in Social Security and pension policies favor extending working life. In addition, many industries are looking to older workers to address the problem of labor and skill shortages that is emerging because of the large number of older employees leaving the workforce and the smaller pool of available workers. Finally, many adults in their middle and older years are choosing to remain in the workforce longer or to return to work because of concerns about retirement income, health care benefits, or a desire to remain productive and socially engaged. Together, these trends suggest an increase in the number of older workers in the coming decades.

Current demographic projections indicate that by 2010 the number of workers in the United States age 55+ will be about 26 million, a 46 percent increase since 2000, and that by 2025 this number will increase to approximately 33 million (U.S. General Accounting Office, 2003). There will also be an increase in the number of workers aged 65+. These trends are being paralleled in other developed countries throughout the world. In response, in many countries within the

European Union, for example, a great deal of ongoing effort is directed at the employment of older workers. We can learn much from the data collected in the EU countries about policies and strategies to foster the productivity of older adults.

Traditional models of working life portray three distinct life stages through which people progress: (1) childhood, an education period in which one prepares for work; (2) adulthood, the time of one's working career; and (3) retirement, the time of leisure and departure from paid employment. However, this model is no longer consistent with the experience of most workers. The trend of "early retirement," whereby people permanently leave the workforce in their mid-60s, has reversed. Instead, people are making many more transitions throughout their working life and moving into and out of the workforce in a variety of ways and at a variety of ages. Rather than take up full-time leisure, workers and retirees in their 50s, 60s, and 70s are increasingly seeking more work options, such as reduced hours or days per week, more time off over the year, special project or contract work, part-time work, and even the opportunity to start second (or third) careers, including unpaid community service. Entrepreneurial endeavors such as starting new businesses are also increasing among older adults.

In addition to changes in demographics, we are witnessing changes in the structure of work organizations. One movement is a change from vertically integrated business organizations to less vertically integrated, specialized firms; another is decentralized management and collaborative work arrangements and team work; and a third is the paradigm of knowledge-based organizations in which intellectual capital is an important organizational asset. These changes in work structures and processes will have a pronounced impact on work and worker requirements. There will be an increased demand for more highly skilled workers who have a broader scope of knowledge and skills in decision making and knowledge management. Workers will also have to communicate and collaborate in new ways with people of varying backgrounds, expertise, and work locations.

Another concern in many organizations is that the exodus of the baby boomers from the workforce will result in a depletion of skills and knowledge needed to compete in today's business market. Unfortunately, few organizations today are implementing strategies to address issues of knowledge transfer. Increased global competition will also require organizations to consider alternative work arrangements such as contractual work, part-time work, and self-employment to reduce operational costs. Demands for flexible part-time work are also likely to increase as many older adults prefer these work arrangements in order to pursue nonwork activities or need these types of work arrangements because of health or mobility restrictions or the obligations of caregiving. At present, about 21 percent of adults in the United States are involved in some type of caregiving. Most informal caregivers currently work either full-time (48%) or part-time (11%), and these caregivers are typically women in their 40s and 50s. The majority of these caregivers report that caregiving has affected their work and that they have to make adjustments to their work schedule such as working fewer hours or taking time off to provide care.

Ongoing developments in technology are reshaping work processes, the content of jobs, the place where work is performed, and the delivery of education and training. The introduction of automation and computer technologies into the workplace has dramatically changed the nature of jobs and work situations for many workers. These changes in job demands will continue as technology evolves and as we continue to move toward a service-sector economy. Workers are continually confronted with the need to learn to interact with these new technologies and new ways of performing jobs. In particular, older workers, once relatively secure in their jobs as they approached retirement, will now have to consider new careers and ventures, including the possibility for entrepreneurship; and many will need to learn new skills at a time when they were once able to rely on the accumulation of expert knowledge in their job domains. Furthermore, workers will need to continually engage in lifelong learning to accommodate changes in job demands brought about by technology throughout the course of their working life. The responsibility for the burden of continuing education is being shifted to the individual worker, and technology-mediated learning formats are being promoted as a way to help meet training challenges and lifelong learning.

Although the literature generally suggests that the ability to learn new skills shows some decline with age, research also shows that if older people are trained using effective techniques, they usually can learn a new skill. Thus, understanding factors that foster skill acquisition in older adults is critical to the development of strategies to help an aging workforce successfully adapt to new work environments. Worker motivation has a big impact on skill acquisition and learning, and older workers need to perceive that it is beneficial for them to invest time and effort in worker training programs. Training and development opportunities also need to be available to older workers. Current data indicate that attitudes held by managers are associated with a range of employment practices, such as training opportunities, that affect older workers. Unfortunately, negative stereotypes about older workers are still pervasive in many work settings.

Telework is an increasing option for many workers, and although this type of work arrangement may be beneficial for older adults, the increased incidence of telework raises a number of interesting questions regarding training, workplace design, and worker benefits and regulations. Although the federal sector and a few companies in the private sector have acknowledged the benefits of alternative work arrangements such as telework for both their organizations and their workers, companies require more guidance concerning which of their work activities can be performed as telework, how to select and train workers for these jobs, including those older workers who may lag behind in job-relevant technological skills, and how to manage these workers in the absence of face-to-face communication.

In essence, the workplace of the twenty-first century will be shaped by numerous factors resulting in many emerging challenges for employers and workers that require changes in government and organizational policies, work procedures, and educational and training systems. Organizations will need to accommodate an increasingly diverse older workforce and be prepared to focus considerably more attention on factors such as design of both traditional workplaces and home workplaces to avoid exacerbating sensory and musculoskeletal problems that many older workers are at least beginning to experience. Issues regarding worker wellness are also of paramount importance. Equally important is understanding how the work affects the health and general well-being of older adults.

New measures of work performance are needed to reflect the demands of current jobs. Retirement policies and worker benefit packages will need to be reconsidered, and appropriate mechanisms for guiding the large numbers of people who will be forced, through necessity, to consider alternative careers later in life need to be formulated. We also need to recognize that the workforce is becoming more diverse; and in our efforts to think about organizational and worker well-being, we need to accommodate not only workers of different ages but also workers with varying skills, attitudes toward work, and cultural and ethnic backgrounds.

Through contributions from leading scholars and practitioners across the many disciplines that underlie the complex domain of aging and work, this edited volume addresses the importance and multifaceted nature of the challenges confronting an aging workforce and the implications for the work sector and society overall, providing a comprehensive and multidisciplinary treatment of current and future issues regarding work and an aging population. The book is unique in the range of topics addressed and in the collection of authors, who represent a variety of disciplines and perspectives. The topics encompass demographic and policy issues, the changing nature of jobs and workplace design issues, skill acquisition and training, telework, worker wellness and health, and trends in late-life entrepreneurial endeavors.

This book is intended for a broad variety of readers, including researchers and practitioners in academia, government, and industry and managers in the private and public work sectors. The overall goal is to summarize what we know about aging and work, to forecast challenges and issues for the future, and to highlight policy and research questions that need to be addressed to prepare for the workplace of the future. We have attempted to address a broad spectrum of issues that have relevance to the workplace of the twenty-first century since, as noted throughout this volume, older workers represent an invaluable resource to economic growth and development.

REFERENCE

U.S. General Accounting Office. 2003. *Older Workers: Policies of Other Nations to Increase Labor Force Participation.* Report to the Ranking Minority Member, Special Committee on Aging. Washington, DC, U.S. General Accounting Office.

PART I

Employment Patterns
and Demographics

CHAPTER ONE

Institutional and Individual Responses to Structural Lag

The Changing Patterns of Work at Older Ages

RICHARD V. BURKHAUSER, PH.D.,
AND LUDMILA ROVBA, PH.D.

Matilda White Riley and her collaborators conceptualize structural lag as a way of considering the speed and manner by which societies adjust to exogenous change (Kahn, 1981; Riley, 1988; Riley, Kahn, and Foner, 1994).[1] They use this model both to explain why institutional structures change and how individuals effect these changes and are affected by them. But their overarching message, for those interested in how public policies evolve, is that considerable lags occur between the exogenous changes that influence individual wants in a society and the responses of social institutions established to satisfy them. Over her long career, Riley used this general model to focus on aging issues from a life-course perspective. In the spirit of that work, we consider the long-term social responses to the demographic forces affecting the social institutions established in the middle half of the twentieth century to provide retirement and health insurance to future generations of Americans.

This chapter reviews the current controversy over the long-term financial stability of the "Social Security system"—Old-Age, Survivors, Disability, and Health Insurance (OASDHI)—as part of the necessary process for reducing structural lag; that is, the process that will close the gap between the needs of increasingly healthier, longer living, and more productive cohorts of the U.S. population and the inertial tendency of public and private retirement and health insurance systems, which are only belatedly responding to their changing desires. We will discuss changes in both the public and the private retirement insurance systems that began in the 1980s in response to these demographic forces and will show that they have already begun to change individual retirement decisions. These changes will in turn mitigate, to some degree, the looming OASDHI financial crises. But additional structural changes will be necessary before these systems have completely adapted to the needs of twenty-first-century America.

DEMOGRAPHIC CHANGE

The U.S. age distribution at the start of the twentieth century could be described as a pyramid, its youngest members forming a broad base on which rested increasingly narrower older age groups, with the oldest and narrowest at the top. But beginning in the second half of the twentieth century, a dramatic transformation began to take place.[2] By 2030, this familiar age pyramid will be fully transformed into an age structure better described as a column, as the share of the population at older ages grows at the expense of younger age groups (Himes 2001).

The U.S. older population, those aged 65 or older, grew more than tenfold over the twentieth century, from just over 3 million in 1900 to nearly 35 million in 2000, and is projected to continue to grow as a share of the total population well into the twenty-first century. This is in part because of the aging of the baby boom generation (those born 1946–64). But it is also because of increasing life expectancy at all ages together with an overall decline in U.S. fertility rates. Hence, while the emergence of the baby boom generation caused a bulge in the age structure at ages 5 to 24 in 1970, at ages 35 to 54 in 2000, and is projected to do so at ages 65 to 84 in 2030, its demise will not lead to a return of the traditional age pyramid after 2030. Rather, the projected rise in life expectancy, together with the projected continuation of low fertility rates, will result in a permanent change in both the age distribution and the collective needs of what will be a very different U.S. population over the twenty-first century. This in turn will have major long-term implications for our retirement and health insurance systems.[3]

The major federal retirement/disability program, Old-Age, Survivors and Disability Insurance (OASDI), and health program, Medicare and to a lesser extent Medicaid, are funded by a pay-as-you-go system in which current payments by a large population of workers are used to fund current benefits for a much smaller older population of retirees. The transformation of our society to one in which the population is evenly spread across the age distribution is bringing increasing financial pressure on our shrinking share of younger workers to fund the retirement and health care of our growing older nonworking population.

Current projections by the Social Security actuaries (Board of Trustees, 2007) show that, while there were approximately four workers per beneficiary in 1965, this will fall to approximately three workers per beneficiary in 2010 and to approximately two workers per beneficiary by 2030. Current projections also show that, while OASDI revenues exceed benefits and will continue to do so until 2027, OASDI payroll taxes will be less than benefits by 2017 and interest from U.S. Treasury bonds held in the Social Security Trust Fund will have to be used to make up the difference. Beginning in 2027, the Social Security Trust Fund will be required to begin to cash in these bonds to make up the growing difference between payroll tax revenues and benefits paid. By 2041, all funds in the Social Security Trust Fund will be exhausted, and projected taxes will fund only about 75 percent of projected benefits (Board of Trustees, 2007).[4]

Numerous proposals have been made to bring the OASDI system into actuarial balance by lowering future benefits, raising future taxes, or a combination of both.[5] Rather than discuss the relative merits of tax increases or benefit decreases and the generational cohorts who would be required to bear their burden to return the system to actuarial balance, we will focus on how these efforts relate to fundamental system changes and their impact on individual behavior. But before doing so, it is important to put the OASDI financial crises in perspective.

Currently, 4.3 percent of the gross domestic product (GDP), the sum of all goods and services produced in the United States, is committed to OASDI payments. Another 4.2 percent is committed to the medical side of Social Security. Medicare Hospital Insurance payments amount to 1.5 percent of GDP. Medicare Supplemental Medical Insurance, which is in part paid by retirees but is heavily subsidized (about 75%) by general federal tax revenues, claims another 1.2 percent of GDP. And the means-tested program Medicaid, funded by general federal tax revenues, claims 1.5 percent of GDP. In total, these social insurance and social welfare payments, primarily targeted on the current nonworking older population and paid for by the current younger wo rking population, amounted to nearly $1 trillion in 2004, or 8.5 percent of GDP (see Palmer, 2006).

The dramatic shift in the age structure will have serious consequences for the future costs of these programs. Figure 1.1 shows that the costs of OASDI, Medicare, and Medicaid will increase dramatically over the next 70 years as a share of GDP. Most discussion of the future crises in government funding of programs for older persons have focused on projected OASDI increases from current lev-

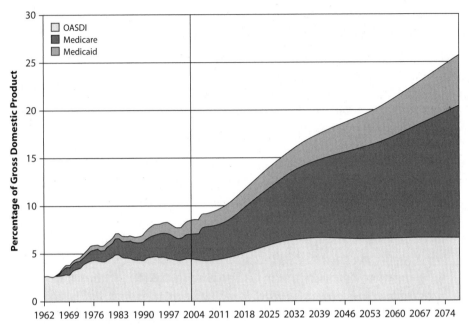

Figure 1.1. Outlays for Old-Age, Survivors, and Disability Insurance (OASDI), Medicare, and Medicaid (federal only) as a proportion of GDP. *Source*: Palmer, 2006, based on Congressional Budget Office and Social Security projections. Reprinted by permission of Sage Publications.

els to 6 percent of GDP by 2030. But as can be seen in figure 1.1, after 2030 OASDI expenses are then projected to increase at about the same rate as GDP and hence to grow only to about 6.2 percent by 2075. In stark contrast, while Medicare and Medicaid expenses are projected to increase from their current level to 10 percent by 2030, they are projected to grow much faster than GDP, rising to nearly 20 percent of GDP by 2075. Together, these programs (OASDI, Medicare, and Medicaid) are projected to consume more than twice as much of GDP in 2030 as they did in 2004 and more than 25 percent of GDP by 2075.

These sobering projections are based on current demographic assumptions about the future age structure and on assumptions about long-term economic growth. Economic growth has primarily been responsible for the increased living standard of the typical American. That growth has also been the engine that has funded the increased economic well-being of older Americans, even as their retirement ages fell and their years in retirement grew over most of the twentieth century.

But economic growth depends on two underlying forces. The first is the individual productivity of workers, which is in turn affected by increases in the capital stock, the quantity of machines and infrastructure available for each worker, and technological improvement in both the capital stock and the quality of the workforce—that is, in each worker's human capital (e.g., education, work skills, health, etc.). Historically, investments in both physical and human capital, together with technological innovation, have transformed agriculture in the United States from a labor-intensive industry dominated by small farms to a highly capital-intensive industry dominated by large farms primarily operated by highly skilled workers. Whereas a century ago it took the majority of the U.S. workforce to feed its people, we are now able to do so with a small fraction of our workforce. Hence, over generations of the nineteenth and twentieth centuries, this infusion of labor-saving capital in agriculture allowed the movement of workers out of agriculture and into manufacturing. A similar but subsequent transformation process in the twentieth and twenty-first centuries is leading to the movement of workers out of manufacturing and into the service sector. The net result is an overall labor market that increasingly puts a premium on highly skilled workers but in which physical strength and endurance are less important. Social Security projections continue to predict improvements of this sort in the capital stock over the twenty-first century.

A willing and able labor force is still required to effectively use this larger and improved capital stock. It is here that current demographic projections suggest a problem. The second part of economic growth is the growth in workers. The projected decline in the growth of workers over the twenty-first century is the primary concern with respect to future economic growth. Social Security projections (Board of Trustees, Federal Old-Age and Survivors Insurance and Disability Trust Funds, 2004) show that increases in the labor force after 1970, fueled primarily by the baby-boom generation, reached a peak of more than 2.5 percent in 1980 but then steady declined through 2000. While labor force growth is expected to hold steady until 2010, it is then expected to decline once again as the baby-boom generation exits the workforce. Thus, by 2030 and beyond, the labor force is expected to increase at only about 0.3 percent.

If these projected declines in labor force growth actually occur, we will not have the workers necessary to maintain past levels of economic growth. Painful decisions will be required to balance the gap between the retirement and health benefits promised to a growing nonworking older population and the taxes available to pay for them from a relatively smaller working younger population. But such projections are based on the assumption that the aging baby-boom genera-tion—and their children—will exit the labor force much like their parents' gen-erations did. This need not happen.

Retirement age has been and will continue to be importantly affected by so-cial institutions. The decline in the age of retirement, despite substantial im-provements in health over the twentieth century, was in large part a response to a public and private retirement system that encouraged workers to retire at age 65 or earlier. Those incentives have begun to change. The long-term decline in the labor force participation rates of older men ended in the mid-1980s. Pro-work changes in the OASI system in the 1990s—reductions in the earnings test tax on work as well as an increase in the earnings test exempt amount at ages 65–69—when added to the gradual increase to actuarially fair levels of adjust-ment for postponing acceptance of OASI retirement benefits past age 65 that began in the 1980s, and the profound shift from defined benefit to defined con-tribution employer pension plans in the private sector, substantially increased work at older ages in the 1990s. Furthermore, the complete ending of the earn-ings test for those ages 65–69 in 2000 probably further increased work at older ages thereafter.

Such findings suggest that, given appropriate incentives, workers are not only capable of work at older ages but will choose to do so. For this reason, such struc-tural changes, which increase the work of future older persons, offer a real alter-native to current proposals for solving the OASDHI fiscal crises and do so in a way that is more consistent with the improved health and productivity of this and future generations of older workers.

IMPROVEMENTS IN THE HEALTH
OF OLDER AMERICANS

Improvements in the life expectancy of succeeding generations of Americans over the twentieth century are well documented. For the total population, life ex-pectancy at birth rose from 47.7 years in 1900 to 76.6 years in 2000, a 60 per-cent increase. However, most of this change occurred over the first half of the century (Technical Panel on Assumptions and Methods, 2003). These declines in the rate of improved age-specific mortality lead the Social Security actuaries (Board of Trustees, Federal Old-Age and Survivors Insurance and Disability Trust Funds, 2003) to predict that improvements in life expectancy will continue to de-cline over the next 75 years. But in fact, improvements in life expectancy at older ages grew more in the second half of the twentieth century than in the first half. At age 65, for example, life expectancy rose from 11.7 years in 1900 to 21.2 years in 2000, with most of this change occurring after 1950. The 2003 Report to the Social Security Advisory Board (Technical Panel on Assumptions and Methods, 2003) argues that, if anything, the projected improvements in life expectancy used by the Social Security actuaries *understates* likely life expectancy increases over the next 75 years. While, if accurate, this will increase OASI expenditures because, given no change in retirement ages, it will lead to greater liabilities for the system, it also suggests the possibility of greater work effort over the lives of these longer living generations if these added years of life are healthy.

Manton, Gu, and Lamb (2006) find that the percentage of older Americans (those aged 65 or older) with any kind of disability has been falling by age since 1984, using consistently collected data from the National Long-Term Care Survey (NLTCS).[6] This suggests that, given the appropriate incentives to do so, older Americans are increasingly able to work. Unfortunately, the detailed data in the NLTCS on the activity limitations of older Americans since 1984 have not been collected for younger populations. Figure 1.2 uses a measure of disability based on a single work limitation question asked of those ages 15 to 64 since 1981. This one-period work limitation-based measure, like the NLTCS measure, does not take into account the duration of the disability. One advantage of the Current Population Survey (CPS) is that a subset of its households interviewed in March are re-interviewed the following March, so it is possible to measure the percentage of respondents who report a work limitation-based disability at two points one year apart. Assuming that this is the same work limitation, this two-period work-limited population excludes those with temporary disabilities lasting less than one year.

Not surprisingly, the prevalence of disability rises with age in both populations, and at any given age the prevalence of two-period work limitations is less than those reporting a current work limitation (one-period). But unlike the decline in disability reported by Manton et al. (2006) for those over the age of 65, there is little change in the prevalence of work limitations in the older working-age population (ages 55–64) in figure 1.2, using either our one- or two-period work limitation definition. Nonetheless, even among older workers, only around 16 percent report a current (one-period) work limitation-based disability and only around 10 percent report a longer term (two-period) work limitation-based disability. Thus, the vast majority of older workers on the verge of early retirement age do not report having a work limitation-based disability.[7]

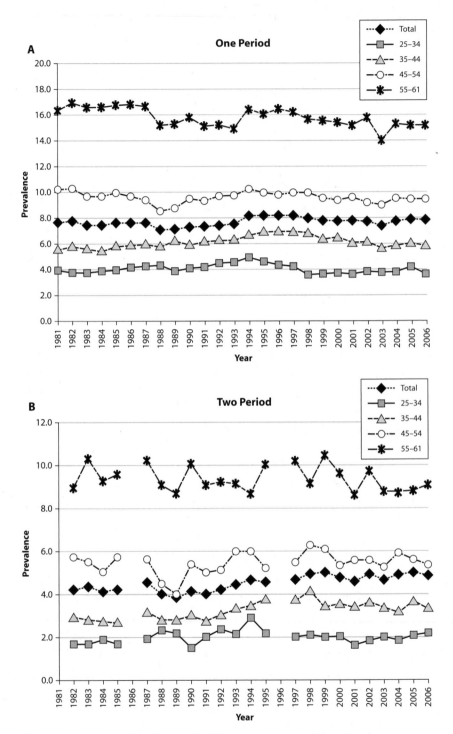

Figure 1.2. One-period (*A*) and two-period (*B*) prevalence of work limitation among working-age, noninstitutionalized civilians. *Source*: Author's calculations based on various years of the March CPS and matched March CPS

LABOR FORCE PARTICIPATION RATES
OF OLDER AMERICANS

The two greatest changes in the U.S. labor force over the second half of the twentieth century were the decline in the labor force participation rate of older men, primarily as the result of their increasingly younger age at exit, and the rise in the labor force participation rate of women.[8]

The top part of table 1.1 reports age-specific labor force participation rates for U.S. men from 1950 to 2005, using cross-sectional data from the Decennial Censes of 1950 and 1960 and from the March CPS thereafter.[9] The labor force participation rates of men aged 50 and above have fallen at all ages, but especially at ages 62 and above, the ages of first eligibility for Old-Age Insurance (OAI) benefits. For instance, the labor force participation rate for men at 62 was approximately 80 percent in both 1950 and 1960—before 1961, the first year that men were permitted to take OAI early retirement benefits. But by 1985, only about half

TABLE I.I.

Labor force participation rates of men and women, by age, United States, 1950 to 2005

Year	Age						
	50	55	60	62	65	68	70
Men							
1950[a]	—	90.6	84.7	81.2	71.7	57.7	49.8
1960[a]	—	92.8	85.9	79.8	56.8	42.0	37.2
1970	93.4	88.0	81.7	73.1	47.4	31.4	30.5
1980	92.0	83.5	74.5	60.7	35.3	27.2	24.8
1985	92.2	84.3	70.8	50.6	32.2	20.7	20.5
1990	90.9	84.9	71.5	51.8	37.2	21.5	20.3
1995	88.6	81.8	71.6	47.9	33.6	22.4	20.0
2000	88.7	78.9	69.3	53.6	38.8	25.9	20.8
2005	89.3	80.6	70.2	59.5	36.9	33.1	24.4
Women							
1970	49.4	47.7	40.3	34.0	20.2	12.5	9.8
1980	59.1	52.8	40.4	31.2	19.7	12.8	10.2
1985	63.3	59.7	41.5	32.7	16.1	13.5	8.3
1990	68.3	61.0	44.6	34.2	22.3	14.4	14.0
1995	75.1	62.5	47.2	38.4	22.3	14.7	10.5
2000	78.0	67.9	48.9	39.4	24.6	17.1	10.0
2005	77.1	70.7	55.9	43.8	27.4	21.6	19.3

Source: Labor force participation figures for 1970–2005 are author's calculations based on the CPS Annual Demographic files

[a]Based on adjusted U.S. Bureau of the Census labor force participation data. The adjustment is based on the ratio of CPS figures and census figures in 1970.

of 62-year-old men were in the labor force. At age 70, male labor force participation rates fell from 49.8 percent in 1950 to 20.5 percent in 1985.[10]

There is some evidence, however, that the long-running trends toward ever earlier retirement ages ended in the mid-1980s (Burkhauser and Quinn, 1990; Burtless and Quinn, 2001; Quinn, 2002). Table 1.1 suggests that while the labor force participation rates of men aged 50 through 61 continued to fall between 1985 and 2000, the participation rates of men at most ages 62 and above has leveled off and perhaps even reversed since 1985.[11]

Older women's labor force participation patterns are different. In each succeeding year of the post–World War II era, a larger share of women has come into the labor force. As their work histories have become more like those of men, they have increasingly faced the same social structures—private pension and OASDI—and taken on similar age-specific labor force participation patterns.

As can be seen by comparing the bottom part of table 1.1 with its top part, in 1970 the labor force participation rates of women who were less than age 62 were substantially below those of men the same ages. For instance, only 49.4 percent of women aged 50 were in the labor force compared with 93.4 percent of men. But since then, the rates of women this age in the labor force have increased dramatically. Thus, by 2000 more than three-quarters of women aged 50 were in the labor force, only about 10 percentage points below men of the same age. This same relative increase in the labor force participation rates of women can be found at all the other ages shown in table 1.1.

Like men, women's exits from the labor force increase at older ages, but the increasing percentage of women working as they approached more typical retirement ages offsets this kind of decline in labor force participation with age for the most part for those aged 62 or older (the earliest age for OAI benefits) through 1985. Thus, cross-sectional comparisons of age-specific labor force participation rates of women aged 62 or older, like the ones in table 1.1, show that these rates remained about the same through 1985, and they show that the age-specific cross-sectional labor force participation rates of women aged 62 or older have been increasing since then.[12]

The reasons for these substantial changes in the labor force participation rates of men since the mid-1980s and the changes in employment that are primarily driving them are not fully understood. The reversal of the long-run decline in labor force participation of older men beginning in 1985 is the subject of considerable debate. One possibility is that long-overdue changes in our social structures affecting retirement beginning in the 1980s—the ending of mandatory retirement, changes in Social Security OAI rules that increased the earnings allowed while receiving benefits or reduced the penalties for postponing benefits, and the longer-term shift away from defined benefit to defined contribution pension plans—permanently ended this trend and have begun to increase the labor force participation rates of older workers.[13]

Others have argued that the leveling off of labor force participation rates after 1985 might simply be an effect of a temporary business cycle, with the strong economy after 1992 explaining most of the gains in the employment and labor force participation of older men and women over that period (Costa, 1999).

But with available additional data, we are better able to see how age-specific employment rates changed over this period by comparing the behavior of two cohorts of workers age 50, one approaching retirement age at the start of the 1980s business cycle (1979–1989) and the other doing so at the start of the 1990s business cycles (1989–2000), and simulating their labor market exits.

While the initial employment rate of men age 50 in 1989 was less than that of men age 50 in 1979 and there was not much difference in their employment survival rates (the age-specific employment rates of men who were working at age 50 at subsequent ages) up to age 64, these rates are higher for the 1990s cohort at all subsequent ages. In contrast, initial employment rates of women age 50 in 1989 were much higher than those of women age 50 in 1979. But the employment survival rates of these two cohorts of working women were not much different. Hence, based on our simulations, we will argue that the employment rates of men aged 50 in 1989 will be greater at age 65 and above relative to their counterparts who were aged 50 in 1979, primarily because of their increased survival rates after age 64. The employment rates of women aged 50 in 1989 will be greater at age 65 and above relative to their female counterparts who were aged 50 in 1979, primarily because more women were working at age 50.

Finally, changes in the level and pattern of age-specific employment exit risk driving these employment survival rate differences is consistent with the argument that changes in social structures initiated in the 1980s have begun to change the retirement behavior of men.

MEASURING THE EMPLOYMENT SURVIVAL AND EXIT RATES OF RECENT COHORTS OF OLDER WORKERS
Data and Methodology

The March demographic supplement to the CPS surveys a nationally representative sample of households each year and includes information on between 17,000 and 33,000 individuals ages 50 or older. The survey asks individuals about their basic demographic characteristics and their labor force participation in the preceding year.

The March CPS provides a representative cross-section of the U.S. population, and about half of the sample is re-interviewed the next year, so one can match information on the employment and economic well-being of this subsample over two consecutive years.[14] Our empirical analysis is based on the matched consecutive March CPS data files from 1980 to 2001.[15] Short panel data sets constructed by matching individuals across monthly files of the CPS have been used to study a wide range of questions in labor economics.

Our matching technique enables us to follow the employment of the same people over two years for each age. However, small yearly sample sizes require us to pool our yearly samples. In doing so, we try to control for differences in outcomes that result from differences in the business cycle by creating our cohorts out of all years of the 1980s business cycle (1979–1989) and all years of the 1990s business cycle (1989–2000).[16]

To do so, we realign our calendar-year data into an event-history framework, where the event begins in the last year of employment (t). We then assign the age at survey interview year as the age of exit in year t. This allows us to estimate age-specific employment exit rates for men aged 50–70 during these two business cycles. We define a person to be employed if he or she performs at least 1,000 hours of non-self-employed paid work in year t. We define that person to have exited that employment if she or he does no more than 100 hours of such work in year $t+1$.

Estimation of Employment Survival and Exit Rates

Table 1.2 reports the simulated age-specific cumulative employment survival probabilities as well as predicted employment of men and women at each age for our 1980s and 1990s cohorts, assuming that those who exit employment do not return. The cumulative survival rates are estimated by following men and women who were employed at age 50 for the period of interest and then assuming that their probability of leaving employment at each age is the average exit rate for all members of their cohort.[17]

As can be seen in column 2 of table 1.2, of the men who were employed for over 1,000 hours at age 50 in our 1980s cohort, 87 percent are still employed for at least 100 hours per year at age 55. This falls to 62 percent at age 61 and to 53 percent at age 62. High employment exit rates thereafter cut the cumulative employment survival rate (employment probability) to 29 percent at age 65 and 11

TABLE I.2.
Estimated employment survival function and predicted employment rate, by gender

	Men				Women			
	1979–1989 Cohort employment		1989–2000 Cohort employment		1979–1989 Cohort employment		1989–2000 Cohort employment	
Age	Survival function	Rate	Survival function	Rate	Survival function	Rate	Survival function	Rate
50	1.00	88.50	1.00	86.19	1.00	54.33	1.00	67.57
51	0.97	86.28	0.98	84.59	0.97	52.90	0.97	65.38
52	0.95	84.38	0.96	83.15	0.93	50.68	0.93	62.70
53	0.93	85.03	0.95	81.52	0.90	48.88	0.90	60.76
54	0.91	80.32	0.93	79.75	0.86	46.65	0.87	58.58
55	0.87	77.13	0.89	76.38	0.81	43.75	0.82	55.74
56	0.84	74.62	0.84	72.71	0.77	41.85	0.78	52.74
57	0.81	72.11	0.81	69.94	0.73	39.60	0.74	50.15
58	0.78	69.24	0.77	66.76	0.69	37.50	0.70	47.20
59	0.74	65.84	0.73	62.78	0.65	35.21	0.65	44.01
60	0.69	60.71	0.68	58.92	0.60	32.81	0.61	40.89
61	0.62	55.10	0.62	53.51	0.56	30.17	0.55	37.11
62	0.53	46.70	0.51	43.63	0.48	25.81	0.47	31.94
63	0.47	41.45	0.44	37.89	0.41	22.24	0.41	27.93
64	0.39	34.51	0.38	32.52	0.35	19.27	0.36	24.32
65	0.29	25.43	0.31	26.78	0.28	15.27	0.28	19.19
66	0.23	20.57	0.26	22.42	0.24	12.99	0.24	16.29
67	0.20	17.41	0.23	19.48	0.21	11.14	0.20	13.85
68	0.15	13.66	0.18	15.94	0.17	9.45	0.18	11.95
69	0.13	11.41	0.17	14.39	0.14	7.54	0.15	10.12
70	0.11	9.78	0.14	11.87	0.11	6.16	0.12	8.16

Source: Author's calculations based on the CPS Annual Demographic files

percent at age 70. The survival functions for both cohorts of working men are about the same up through age 64 but are higher thereafter for men in the 1990s, reflecting their lower exit rates at older ages over the period. But because the employment rates (column 3) of men age 50 were higher in 1979 than in 1989, age-specific employment rates are actually lower in our 1980s cohort than in our 1990s cohort until age 65.

In contrast, the employment rates of women age 50 in the 1990s cohort are much higher than women in the 1980s cohort, but there is little change in the employment survival rates of women at older ages in these two cohorts.[18]

Figure 1.3 more clearly shows what is behind the differences we report in the cumulative employment survival rates of our two cohorts of men. There is a substantial difference in both the level and shape of their age-specific employment exit rates. While there is little difference between the level of risk of an employment exit for men in the 1990s and 1980s cohorts at ages before age 62, exit rates

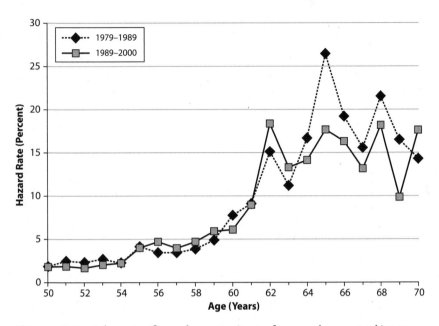

Figure 1.3. Estimated age-specific employment exit rates for men who were working at age 50, by cohort. *Source*: Author's calculations based on the CPS Annual Demographic files

are higher at age 62 but lower in all subsequent years for the 1990s cohort. Thus, given that a man in the 1990s cohort continued to work past age 62, he was less likely to exit employment at any age thereafter until age 70 than was the case for men in the 1980s cohort.

Most important with respect to changes in the age pattern of employment exit, while the highest spike in the 1980s cohort was at age 65, with a smaller spike at age 62, in the 1990s cohort the exit rate at age 65 is much reduced and is now at about the same level as exit rates at ages 62 and 68.

This change in the pattern of age-specific employment exits is suggestive evidence that policy changes are a plausible cause of this increase in exit rates after age 64 for men. A series of changes in Social Security policy over this period first reduced the earnings test tax for those aged 65–69 in 1990 and then raised the exempt amount gradually to $30,000 in 1996. In addition, the actuarial payment to workers who postponed Social Security benefits past their 65th birthday, which before 1990 increased yearly benefits by 3 percent per year, was slowly increased by one-half of 1 percent every other year over this period. By 2000 it was at 5.5 percent and will continue to increase until it reaches 8 percent in 2010—the actuarially fair amount. Finally, in 2000, the earnings test tax was ended for all workers aged 65 to 69.

Our simulation suggests that these OAI policy changes, together with the longer-term movement from defined benefit to defined contribution pensions in the private sector, no longer makes 65 the age with the highest risk of employment exit for men. Age 62 has become the highest employment exit risk age. Once past age 62, the risk of exiting is no longer centered on age 65 but is spread more evenly across post-62 ages, and in all cases is lower than was the case at these ages in the 1980s cohort.

In contrast to the substantial changes in men's employment exit patterns between the 1980s and 1990s cohorts, as seen in figure 1.4, little has changed for women in these cohorts. The highest risk employment exit age continues to be age 65. What has changed is that dramatically more women are working at age 50 in 1989 than was the case in 1979. It is this change in the number of women working at younger ages that is responsible for the rise in the employment of women at older ages rather than any change in their survival function after age 50 or pattern of age-specific employment exit risks at older ages.

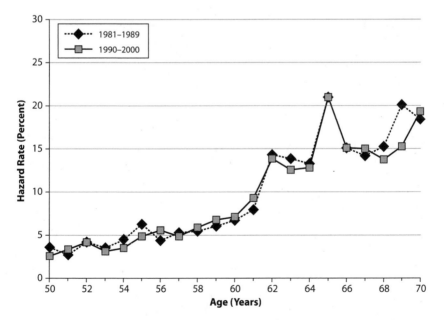

Figure 1.4. Estimated age-specific employment exit rates for women who were working at age 50, by cohort. *Source:* Author's calculations based on the CPS Annual Demographic files

Differences in Male Employment Survival
and Exit Rates by Race and Education

Table 1.3 disaggregates our simulated cohorts of employed men age 50 in 1979 and in 1989 to compare differences in their estimated employment survival function by race and education. Figure 1.5 does the same to show the age-specific employment exit rates of these subgroups of men.

We find substantial differences in the level of the age-specific employment survival rates of white and nonwhite males in the 1980s cohort but not much difference in their shape. When we compare them with their counterparts in the 1990s cohort, we find that the difference in the employment survival rates of these two cohorts of white men mirror the differences we found previously in the aggregated cohorts discussed above, with little change before age 65 and increases thereafter. Ages 62 and 68 replace age 65 as the highest risk employment exit ages.

There is a similar change in the shape of the age-specific employment exit rate curve between the 1980s and 1990s nonwhite cohorts with 62 and 67 becoming the highest risk employment exit ages in the 1990s cohort. The major difference in how white and nonwhite cohorts changed in the 1990s is that the nonwhite cohorts' employment survival function decreased substantially before age 65 and only modestly increased thereafter. How much of this difference is caused by past and current discrimination in the job market and how much is the result of poorer health and job skills is uncertain. But the result is that whites in the 1990s cohort are now even more likely to be employed at all older ages when compared with their nonwhite counterparts.

TABLE 1.3.
Estimated employment survival functions of men, by race and education

Age	White		Nonwhite		College degree		No college degree	
	1979– 1989 Cohort	1989– 2000 Cohort	1979– 1989 Cohort	1989– 2000 Cohort	1979– 1989 Cohort	1989– 2000 Cohort	1979– 1989 Cohort	1989– 2000 Cohort
50	1.00	1.00	1.00	1.00	1.00	1.00	1.00	1.00
55	0.88	0.91	0.83	0.78	0.94	0.92	0.85	0.87
60	0.70	0.71	0.60	0.55	0.78	0.75	0.66	0.66
62	0.54	0.54	0.42	0.36	0.69	0.63	0.49	0.47
65	0.29	0.34	0.25	0.20	0.41	0.48	0.26	0.26
68	0.16	0.21	0.10	0.11	0.25	0.32	0.14	0.15
70	0.12	0.15	0.05	0.07	0.16	0.26	0.10	0.11

Source: Author's calculations based on the CPS Annual Demographic files

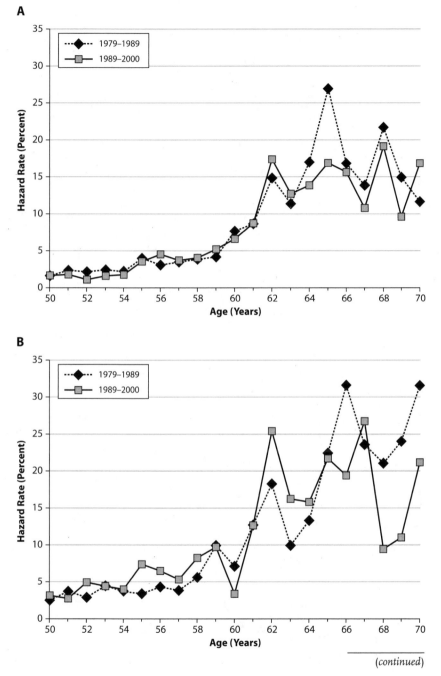

(continued)

Figure 1.5. Estimated age-specific employment exit rates for men who were working at age 50, by cohort, race, and education. *A*, white men; *B*, nonwhite men; *C*, men with at least a college degree; *D*, men with less than a college degree. *Source*: Author's calculations based on the CPS Annual Demographic files

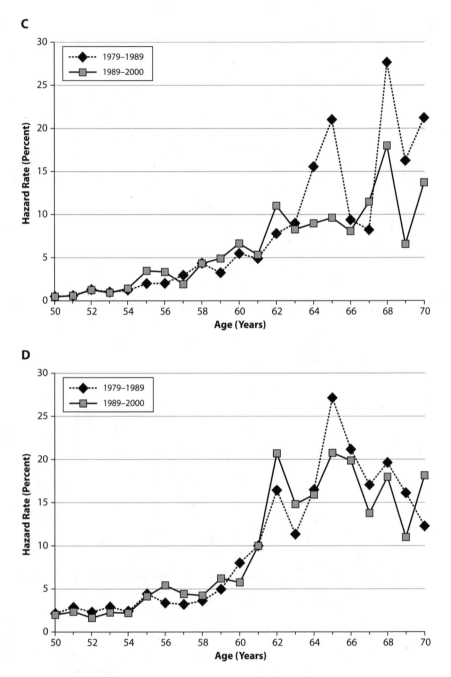

Figure 1.5. (Continued)

College graduates have experienced the greatest change in their work patterns at older ages between our two cohorts. The employment survival rates of our 1990s cohort of college graduates is somewhat lower than our 1980s cohort from age 50 to age 62, with a noticeable rise in their exit rate at age 62. But there is a substantial increase in their survival rate thereafter, with major declines in their two former peak exit ages of 65 and 68. While 68 remains the highest employment risk of exit age for college graduates, 65 is now a lower risk age than 62. In contrast, there is little difference between the employment survival functions of our 1980s and 1990s cohort of less than college graduates. There is the now-familiar increase in employment risk at age 62 and a decline in that risk at age 65.

CONCLUSION

Changes in the age distribution of the U.S. population in the twenty-first century caused by substantial declines in fertility rates and increases in age-specific mortality rates, together with the aging of the baby-boom generation, require substantial changes in the social structures created in the middle years of the twentieth century to provide retirement and health insurance in old age. Thus far, most discussions of the long-term financial stability of these structures have focused on how to preserve them either by increases in the taxes needed to finance current promises or by reducing promised benefits to future generations without raising taxes. Improvements in both the age-specific mortality and morbidity of succeeding cohorts of Americans have resulted in a structural lag between the work capacity of Americans over their increasingly healthier lives and a retirement system that still discourages work at older ages.

The decline in the employment of older men that marked most of the twentieth century ended around 1985, and changes in Social Security rules that reduced disincentives to work after age 65 are a plausible explanation for this change. Using cohorts of men and women aged 50–70 in the periods 1979–1989 and 1989–2000, we simulate and then compare the employment survival rates of men who were working at age 50 in 1979 and in 1989, using the actual age-specific employment exit experiences of all the persons in their cohort. We show:

- The estimated employment rate of men aged 65 and above in our 1989 cohort was higher than in our 1979 cohort, primarily because of reductions in their age-specific employment exit rates after age 62.
- The estimated employment rate of women aged 65 and above in our 1989

cohort was higher than in our 1979 cohort, primarily because of increases in their employment rates at age 50 and below.

- Our estimated changes in the employment exit rates of men after age 62 are consistent with those found by Friedberg (2000), who argues that relaxation of the earnings test in the 1990s increased the labor earnings of workers aged 65–69.

- Age 65, once the most likely age for men to exit the labor force, was no more likely to be the age of exit than other ages past age 62 in our 1989 cohort. For men, age 62 is now the most likely age of employment exit. This dramatic change is consistent both with Friedberg's (2000) arguments and the growing actuarial fairness of Social Security benefit increases for those who postpone benefits past age 65. It is also consistent with Engelhardt and Kumar's (forthcoming) finding that the passage of the Senior Citizens Freedom to Work Act of 2000, which abolished the OAI retirement earnings test for men aged 65–69, has significantly increased the labor force participation of men this age. This, plus the fact that additional payments for those who delay accepting Social Security benefits will become fully actuarially fair by 2010, means that age 65 should become even more irrelevant as a retirement-specific age for men.

- Age 65 remains the most likely age of employment exit for women. We found no change in the employment survival function of women who were employed at age 50 between our two cohorts.

- There is a considerable difference in the employment patterns of white and nonwhite men and of male college graduates and nongraduates within our cohorts and in the changes in their employment exit patterns between the two cohorts we simulated.

- While the risk of an employment exit at age 62 increased for both white and nonwhite men, the increase was much larger for nonwhites. Employment exit risks rose for nonwhites at all pre-65 ages, while they remained about the same for whites before age 62 and fell thereafter. The result is an even greater gap between employment rates of white and nonwhite men at older ages. How much of this gap is due to differences in the relative health and job skills of these two populations and how much is due to past and current discrimination is unclear.

- Male college graduates in the 1990s cohort had slightly higher risks of employment exit at age 62 but dramatic reductions in their employment exit rates at ages 65 and 68, the peak exit ages for the 1980s cohort, than did male college graduates in the 1980s cohort. Males who were not college graduates in the 1990s cohorts had substantial increases in their risk of exit at age 62 and declines in those risks at ages 65 to 69 as compared with our 1980s cohort. The result is an even greater gap between labor force participation rates of college graduates and nongraduates at older ages.

Our findings are consistent with the view that older men are willing and able to work at older ages when the social structures they face encourage them to do so. But this is much more so for college-educated and white men, who on average can command greater wages at these ages. Burkhauser and Quinn (1983) and more fully Quinn, Burkhauser, and Myers (1990) argued that changes in mandatory retirement rules in the 1970s and 1980s would not greatly affect the employment of workers at older ages until the disincentives to work beyond early retirement ages in defined benefit pensions plans and in Social Security were changed.

Friedberg (2000) provides such evidence with respect to OAI changes in the 1990s and Engelhardt and Kumar (2007) add to the evidence with respect to OAI changes in 2000. Friedberg and Webb (2005) provide evidence that the shift from defined benefit to defined contribution plans, which are more likely to be age neutral with respect to their pension accrual patterns, has also increased work at older ages. Our findings of survival rates past age 65 are also consistent with all of these findings.[19]

Hence, there is much to be optimistic about. Pro-work structural changes have ended the long decline in the labor force participation of older men that has been found as far back as the 1880s. Technological change, which has long enhanced the capacity of machines to replace low-skilled physical labor but increased the productivity and hence the demand for high-skilled labor, is likely to continue to make it possible for highly skilled older workers to compete for jobs even as their physical abilities decline. And a majority of older workers, based on recent AARP surveys, expect to work beyond age 65. But much remains to be done.

While mandatory retirement is no longer an issue in most occupations, mandatory retirement rules still prevail in some private and public-sector occupations: state and local police (aged 55–60) and firefighters (aged 55–60); federal firefighters (aged 57); federal law enforcement and corrections officers (aged 57); and air traffic controllers (aged 56 if hired after 1972); and commercial airline pilots (aged 60). It is long past time that these restrictions on employment at older ages are reconsidered.

However, given past experience (Burkhauser and Quinn, 1983), it is unlikely that simply lifting mandatory retirement ages on these workers, most of whom have defined pension plans, will greatly effect the age of exit from their jobs. But such changes, together with a transition from a defined benefit to a defined contribution pension plan, are likely to increase the age of exit from such a job, especially given the changes already in place for OAI.

More generally, however, an increase in the early OAI retirement age is the structural change most likely to increase employment at older ages. It is troubling that initial employment rates for men at age 50 declined between 1979 and 1989, the two peaks of the 1980s business cycle, and that age 62 is now the highest risk age of exit for men. Given the improvements in both age-specific mortality and morbidity, it is not clear why our social structures should continue to encourage retirement as early as age 62.

Raising the early-retirement age for Social Security is relatively neutral with respect to OASI program liabilities because benefits are now close to actuarially fair at all ages. But it is likely to reduce employment exits at this age, hence increasing the overall employment rate, total GDP, and overall tax revenues. Therefore, supporters of the current OAI early-retirement age should be required to justify why it still makes policy sense to offer all Americans the option to retire as early as age 62, given the dramatic improvements in both age-specific mortality and morbidity since this early OAI option was first introduced for men in 1961.

It is certainly not the case that this option is being taken primarily by those who are unable to work or who have no other sources of pension income. Burkhauser, Couch, and Phillips (1996) were the first to show that the vast majority of persons who first took OAI benefits at age 62 had neither a work limitation nor relied on OAI benefits as their sole source of retirement income. Subsequent work by Smith (1999) using a different data set confirmed this finding.

Longer-living, healthier, and more-productive Americans in the twenty-first century can work longer. Changes already put into place in the OAI system have made age 65 irrelevant with respect to employment exit. But as we struggle to further change our social structures to accommodate demographic changes in our society, it will become increasingly important to raise the earliest retirement age for OAI benefits in recognition of our collective need to increase our years of work to support our longer years of life.

ACKNOWLEDGMENT

Partial funding for the work reported in this article came from the U.S. Department of Education, National Institute of Disability and Rehabilitation Research, cooperative agreements H133B031111 and H133B040013. This work does not necessary reflect the views of the National Institute of Disability and Rehabilitation Research. We thank Andrew J. Houtenville and John L. Palmer for comments on earlier drafts of this chapter.

NOTES

1. "By structural lag, we mean the tendency of social structures and norms to lag behind people's rapidly changing lives. . . . The inertial tendency of social structures to persist rather than respond to the changing needs and characteristics of individuals, creates a continuing tension between people and the structures in which their lives are embedded" (Riley et al., 1994, vii).

2. See National Research Council (2001) for a review of projected demographic changes throughout the world and the research necessary to inform policy makers about its consequences.

3. See Technical Panel on Assumptions and Methods (2003) for a discussion of the assumptions specified by the Board of Trustees of the Old-Age and Survivors Insurance Trust Fund and the Disability Trust Fund and the methods used by the Social Security actuaries to project the future financial status of these funds.

4. These numbers are based on the intermediate assumption of the Trustees of the Social Security Trust Funds and are the ones most commonly referred to in discussions of the long-term financing of OASDI.

5. See, for instance, Cogan and Mitchell (2003) for a discussion of the President's Commission to Strengthen Social Security Report, which does so primarily by reducing benefits, and Diamond and Orszag (2005), which does so primarily by raising revenues.

6. A special working panel of demographers concluded that the weight of the evidence supported the view that age-specific morbidity rates at older ages (65 or older) have fallen over the last 20 years (Freedman et al., 2004).

7. One possible longer-term concern is that disability prevalence rates, both one- and two-period, in the total working age population (those aged 25–61) have been rising since around 1989, fueled by increases in work-limitation-based disabilities reported at younger ages.

8. Costa (1998), using data from the U.S. Decennial Census, shows that the long-term decline in the age of retirement of older men began as early as 1880.

9. The labor force participation rate at any age is defined as the number of people of that age who are either employed or are not employed but looking for work (i.e., the unemployed), divided by the total population of that age. At older ages most people who are not employed are not looking for work and hence are considered to be out of the labor force. There has not been much systematic change in the unemployment rate of older persons over the period of this analysis, so it is changes in the employment rate of older persons that have been primarily driving the changes in their labor force participation rates discussed here.

10. The causes of this dramatic decline are controversial in the economics literature. The dominant view is that the rise in the importance of defined benefit employer pension plans as well as the expansion of the OAI retirement system substantially reduced the net

compensation for workers at older ages by effectively reducing the actuarial value of their retirement benefits if they continued working. See Quinn et al. (1990) and more recently Gruber and Wise (1999). Costa (1998), however, argues that the increase in wealth of American workers provides a better historical explanation of the very long-term decline in the labor force participation of older men that began as early as 1880.

11.   Quinn (2002) shows that if the trend in early retirement for men aged 60–64 over the period 1964 through 1985 had continued at that same rate until 2001, their labor force participation rates would have been dramatically below their actual levels, which are in fact higher than they were in 1985.

12.   Quinn (2002) uses these data to show that, as was the case for men, labor force participation trend lines based on data before 1985 dramatically underestimates the actual labor force participation rates of older women between 1985 and 2001.

13.   For early evidence, see Burkhauser and Quinn (1983) and Quinn and Burkhauser (1983). For more recent evidence, see Friedberg (2000), Friedberg and Webb (2005), and Engelhardt and Kumar (forthcoming).

14.   For detailed information on matching CPS files, see Unicon Research Corporation (1999) and Welch (1993).

15.   The March 1984 and March 1985 as well as the March 1994 and March 1995 CPS data cannot be merged because of revisions in the household identifiers implemented in those paired years to protect the confidentiality of survey respondents.

16.   We define a business cycle peak as the year in which real household median income hit its highest absolute level over the cycle. Our method of choosing comparison years only approximates the official measure of business cycle peaks and troughs by the National Bureau of Economic Research (NBER) using overall economic growth. Our results do not change substantively if we choose other alternatively defined comparison years of the business cycle.

17.   We use a Kaplan-Meier nonparametric estimator of the employment survival curve to look at the percentage of men and women in each cohort who worked for at least 1,000 hours for someone else in year (t) and who worked for no more than 100 hours in the next year ($t+1$) to estimate age-specific employment exit rates. Our survival curve shows the probability that a person survives (remains employed) at the specified age. Our hazard rate of employment exit is defined as the number of persons who exit employment at the specified age, relative to the size of the employed labor force a year earlier.

18.   At older ages the difference between labor force participation outcomes discussed in the earlier tables and employment outcomes used in our analysis are small because the unemployment rate of older workers is low and relatively stable over the period of our analysis. Most older workers who face significant periods of unemployment are likely to leave the labor force. Hence, our definition of employment exit—not working for at least 100 hours in a given year—is likely to be close to a definition of complete exit from the labor force.

19.   Our view is consistent with recent surveys of older workers by AARP. Brown (2006) found that of the 1,052 workers she interviewed in 2006, 52% of those who reported an expected retirement age expect to retire past age 65. Of those ages 50 or older at the time of the survey, 64% expected to retire past age 65. In an earlier survey of 2,167 workers 50 or older in 2005, Brown (2005) found that 38% of those who expected to retire from their job

wanted to do so gradually. And of this group, 78% reported that they would work beyond their expected retirement age if given the option of phased retirement.

REFERENCES

Board of Trustees, Federal Hospital Insurance and Federal Supplementary Medical Insurance Trust Funds. 2007. *Annual Report.* Washington, DC: U.S. Government Printing Office.

Board of Trustees, Federal Old-Age and Survivors Insurance and Disability Trust Funds. 2003. *Annual Report.* Washington, DC: U.S. Government Printing Office.

———. 2004. *Annual Report.* Washington, DC: U.S. Government Printing Office.

Brown, S. K. 2005. *Attitudes of Individuals Aged 50 and Older toward Phased Retirement.* Washington, DC: AARP.

———. 2006. *Attitudes toward Work and Job Security.* Washington, DC: AARP.

Burkhauser, R. V., and Quinn, J. F. 1983. Is mandatory retirement overrated? Evidence from the 1970s. *Journal of Human Resources* 18:337–58.

———. 1990. Economic incentives and the labor force participation of older workers. In *Research in Labor Economics,* vol. 11, ed. L. S. Bassi and D. L. Crawford, 319–33. New York: JAI Press.

Burkhauser, R. V., Couch, K. A., and Philips, J. W. 1996. Who takes early Social Security benefits? The economic and health characteristics of early beneficiaries. *The Gerontologist* 36 (6): 789–99.

Burtless, G., and Quinn, J. F. 2001. Retirement trends and policies to encourage work among older workers. In *Ensuring Health and Income Security for an Aging Workforce,* ed. P. P. Budetti, R. V. Burkhauser, J. M. Gregory, and H. A. Hunt, 375–416. Kalamazoo, MI: W. E. Upjohn Institute for Employment Research.

Cogan, J. F., and Mitchell, O. S. 2003. Perspectives from the President's Commission on Social Security Reform. *Journal of Economic Perspectives* 17 (2): 149–72.

Congressional Budget Office. 2004. *The Budget and Economic Outlook, Fiscal Years 2005 to 2014.* Washington, DC: CBO and 2004 Annual Report of the Social Security and Medical Board of Trustees.

Costa, D. 1998. *The Evolution of Retirement: An American Economic History, 1880–1990.* Chicago: University of Chicago Press.

———. 1999, May. Has the trend toward early retirement reversed? Presented at the First Annual Joint conference for the Retirement Research Consortium, Washington, DC.

Diamond, P. A., and Orszag, P. R. 2005. *Saving Social Security: A Balanced Approach.* Washington, DC: Brookings Institution Press.

Engelhardt, Gary V., and Kumar, A. forthcoming. The repeal of the retirement earning test and the labor supply and health of older workers. *Journal of Pension Economics and Finance.*

Freedman, V. A., E. Crimmins, E. Schoeni, R. F., Spillman, B. C., Aykan, H., Kramarow, E. et al. 2004. Resolving inconsistencies in trends in old-age disability: Report from a technical working group. *Demography* 41 (3): 417–41.

Friedberg, L. 2000. The labor supply effects of the Social Security earnings test. *The Review of Economics and Statistics* 82 (1): 48–63.

Friedberg, L., and Webb, A. 2005. Retirement and the evolution of pension structures. *Journal of Human Resources* 40 (2): 411–34.

Gruber, J. and Wise, D. A. 1999. *Social Security and Retirement Around the World*. Chicago: University of Chicago Press for the National Bureau of Economic Research.

Himes, C. L. 2001. Elderly Americans. *Population Bulletin* 56 (4): 3–41.

Kahn, R. L. 1981. *Work and Health*. New York: John Wiley & Sons.

Manton, K., Gu, X. L., and Lamb, V. 2006. Change in chronic disability from 1982 to 2004/2005 as measured by long-term changes in function and health in the U.S. elderly population. *Proceedings of the National Academy of Sciences USA* 103 (48): 18374–79.

National Research Council. 2001. *Preparing for an Aging World: The Case for Cross-National Research*. Panel on a Research Agenda and New Data for an Aging World, Committee on Population and Committee on National Statistics, Division of Behavioral and Social Sciences and Education. Washington, DC: National Academy Press.

Palmer, J. L. 2006. Entitlement programs for the aged: The long-term fiscal context. *Research in Aging* 28 (3): 289–302.

Quinn, J. F. 2002. Changing retirement trends and their impact on elderly entitlement programs. In *Policies for an Aging Society*, ed. S. H. Altman and D. Shactman, 293–315. Baltimore: Johns Hopkins University Press.

Quinn, J. F., and Burkhauser, R. V. 1983. Influencing retirement behavior: A key issue for Social Security. *Journal of Policy Analysis and Management* 3 (1): 1–13.

Quinn, J. F., Burkhauser, R. V., and Myers, D. 1990. *Passing the Torch: The Influence of Economic Incentives on Work and Retirement*. Kalamazoo, MI: W. E. UpJohn Institute for Employment Research.

Riley, M. W. 1988. The aging society: Problems and prospects. *Proceedings of American Philosophical Society* 132:148–53.

Riley, M. W., Kahn, R. L., and Foner, A. 1994. *Age and Structural Lag: Society's Failure to Provide Meaningful Opportunities in Work, Family, and Leisure*. New York: John Wiley & Sons.

Smith, R. 1999. *Raising the Earliest Eligibility Age for Social Security Benefits*. CBO Paper. Washington, DC: Congressional Budget Office.

Technical Panel on Assumptions and Methods. 2003, October. *Report to the Social Security Advisory Board*. Washington, DC.

Unicon Research Corporation. 1999. Appendix S: Discussion regarding: Matching of CPS Files. In *CPS Utilities Annual Demographic and Income Supplement, March 1976–1998* (Disc C) CD-ROM (Manual/section5). Santa Monica, CA: Unicon Research Corporation.

Welch, F. 1993. Matching the current population surveys. *STATA Technical Bulletin* 12: 7–11.

CHAPTER TWO

Caregiving and Employment

RICHARD SCHULZ, PH.D.,
AND LYNN M. MARTIRE, PH.D.

The effects of combining work and caregiving on caregivers, their disabled relatives, and business and industry has emerged as an important research area in the caregiving literature. Middle-aged women at the peak of their earning power, many of whom are employed, provide the majority of care to older disabled relatives. The increasing labor force participation of women, along with the increasing demand for care, raises important questions about how effectively and at what cost the roles of caregiver and worker can be combined. This chapter describes and illuminates key issues in the literature on caregiving and employment, including the effects of work on caregiving and vice versa, the extent to which work moderates the caregiving experience, and the economic impact of caregiving on work and employers. We conclude with recommendations for policy and research.

One of the central questions addressed in this chapter concerns the causal link between caregiving and employment. Does employment affect caregiving or does caregiving affect employment? Taking on the caregiving role for an ill or disabled relative may depend on whether the individual is employed, the magnitude of the caregiving demands, and the flexibility of the individual's job. Employed caregivers with little flexibility in their jobs who are faced with extensive caregiving needs may be less likely to take on the caregiving role. Indeed, the fact that men are a small minority among caregivers may be due in part to their higher labor force participation rates. Once caregiving has started, caregivers may reduce work hours or stop work completely to care for an impaired elder. Thus, causal processes may operate in both directions: being employed reduces the likelihood of becoming a caregiver, and becoming a caregiver reduces the likelihood of being employed. We can anticipate that a definitive answer to this question will require longitudinal data.

A second question concerns the extent to which experiences at work spill over into caregiving and whether characteristics of employment moderate the relation between caregiving and psychosocial well-being of the caregiver. Although employment is generally beneficial to women's health (Ross and Mirowsky, 1995), is employment in the context of caregiving, where care demands may compete with work demands, beneficial or detrimental to caregiver well-being?

A third area of inquiry shifts the focus away from the caregiver to business and industry and asks, What is the economic impact of caregiving on employers? and How have employers responded to alter the workplace and job demands to accommodate the needs of caregivers? A related question concerns the effectiveness of workplace adaptations to meet caregiver needs and identifying interventions that might benefit both caregivers and employers. Before addressing any of these questions, however, we need to lay a foundation for this discussion by reviewing the prevalence of caregiving and employed caregivers.

THE PREVALENCE OF CAREGIVING
AND EMPLOYED CAREGIVERS

Families continue to be the primary sources of care and support for their older relatives. There are no exact estimates of the number of family caregivers in the United States. Prevalence estimates vary widely, depending on definitions used and populations sampled. For example, at one extreme we have estimates that 22.1 percent of the U.S. adult population or 44.4 million Americans provided unpaid care to an adult relative in 2003, with the majority (79%) of this care being delivered to persons aged 50 years or older (NAC and AARP Survey, 2004). At the other extreme, data from the National Long-Term Care Survey suggest that as few as 3.5 million caregivers provided instrumental activities of daily living (IADL) or activities of daily living (ADL) assistance to persons aged 65 and over. Intermediate estimates of 28.8 million caregivers ("persons aged 15 or over providing personal assistance for everyday needs of someone age 15 and older") are reported by the Survey on Income and Program Participation (www.nltcs.aas .duke.edu). These differences are in part attributable to when the data were collected, the age range of the potential caregiver and care-recipient populations targeted, but most importantly, to the definition of caregiving. Thus, the high-end estimates are largely a result of the broad and inclusive definitions of caregiving (e.g., "Unpaid care may include help with personal needs or household chores. It might be managing a person's finances, arranging for outside services, or visiting regularly to see how they are doing," www.sipp.census.gov/sipp); and the low-end estimates are generated by first confirming the presence of functional disability in an older person that might require assistance and then following up to ascertain the presence of a caregiver who provides ADL or IADL assistance (e.g., Wolff and Kasper, 2006).

Not surprisingly, the confusion regarding the prevalence of caregiving carries over to estimates of the number of employed caregivers. National advocacy organizations for caregivers (e.g., NAC, AARP) estimate that 59 percent of caregivers are employed for pay, while others suggest that this figure might be considerably lower depending on whether the focus is on spouse caregivers (8%), child caregivers (50%), or others (38%; Wolff and Kasper, 2006). Reconciling these differences is difficult but important. To the extent that caregiving has economic consequences for the caregiver and for American businesses, it will be essential to have accurate assessments of the number of individuals affected.

Regardless of the actual prevalence of working caregivers, we can anticipate that the challenge of providing informal care in the future will be daunting due to a variety of factors, including the rapid growth of the senior population in the United States to 70 million in 2035; the large increase in the oldest old, who have the highest need for care; the inability of existing formal care systems to handle the increasing number of older adults; changes in family size and composition; and the increased proportion of women in the labor force. Female labor force participation in the United States increased from 34 percent in 1950 to 60 percent in 1998 and is expected to continue to increase in the future (Fullerton, 1999). An additional factor is the increasing need and preference of individuals to continue working after traditional retirement years. The rate of labor force participation among individuals aged 65 to 69 has increased from 18 percent in 1985 to 28 percent in 2004 (AARP, 2005). The convergence of these factors in the decades ahead have the makings of a perfect storm that will challenge our society's ability to provide adequate care for the aging baby boomers.

DOES EMPLOYMENT AFFECT PARTICIPATION IN THE CAREGIVING ROLE?

A large number of studies have explored the effects of caregiving on employment, but relatively few studies have reversed this question to ask whether employment affects caregiving. Several studies suggest that social structural factors like employment status at least in part explain gender differences in caregiving. It is well established that adult daughters spend more time giving assistance to their parents than do adult sons, and researchers have been interested in assessing the extent to which this gap is explained by structural variation in employment rates and the kinds of jobs that women and men tend to hold. Using data from the National Survey of Families and Households, Sarkisian and Gerstel (2004) show that both employment status and job characteristics (e.g., wages and self-employment) are important factors in explaining the gender gap in help given to parents and that these operate similarly for women and men. Similar results are reported by Gerstel and Gallagher (1994), who show that the differential helping rates of wives versus husbands is in part explained by differential rates of employment. Employed wives give more help than employed husbands but less help than homemaker wives. Wives employed in jobs similar to those of men give care in ways similar to men.

The 1996 General Social Survey of Canada addressed this question by comparing whether paid employment reduces the provision and/or intensity of specific types of help offered by women to older parents and parents-in-law. Using these data, Rosenthal, Hayward, Martin-Matthews, and Denton (2004) focused on a subsample of women aged 40–64 who had at least one living parent or parent-in-law. The results showed that employment status was not significantly related to the total amount of time spent helping parents or parents-in-law, although there was some variability in the type of help provided as a function of employment status, with employed daughters and daughters-in-law less likely to help with banking or bill paying than those who were not employed. Overall, employment status did not reduce women's provision of help. Using British data, Henz (2006) also found that whether one worked part-time or full-time did not affect caregiving, nor did most aspects of job flexibility. There is some evidence that among dual-earner couples, husbands and wives strategically allocate caregiving responsibilities to accommodate their respective work roles, although the heavier caregiving load is still carried by women (Chesley and Moen, 2006).

DOES CAREGIVING AFFECT PARTICIPATION IN THE EMPLOYMENT ROLE?

The majority of research on caregiving and work has focused on the effects of caregiving on women's employment. The primary hypothesis tested in these studies is that informal care provision reduces labor force participation. Because caregiving tends to occur during peak employment years (ages 35–64), it has the potential to profoundly alter the economic well-being of women.

Early findings in this line of research were equivocal, with some studies show-ing lower rates of labor force participation among caregivers when compared to noncaregivers, while others showed no difference. For example, in a cross-sectional study, McLanahan and Monson (1990) found that being a caregiver re-duced married women's chances of being employed and lowered the number of hours they worked. Doty, Jackson, and Crown (1998) found that female employed caregivers rearranged work to manage challenges associated with being em-ployed and serving as a caregiver. Ettner (1995a, 1995b) found that caregiving re-duced women's hours worked for pay and that impact on employment status was related to the magnitude of caregiving demands. On the other hand, Wolf and Soldo (1994) found no effect of caregiving to parents on married daughters' hours worked for pay, and Moen, Robinson, and Fields (1994) found that caregiving did not interrupt women's labor force participation. Multiple factors contribute to this mixed bag of findings, including the fact that many of the early studies were cross-sectional, making it difficult to infer causality; variability in the type of help being provided (e.g., ADL versus IADL assistance); and varying definitions of who is a caregiver (e.g., some studies define caregiving as co-residence with elderly house-hold members and assume that co-residence is associated with caregiving).

Recent longitudinal studies have helped clarify this issue. Pavalko and Artis (1997) used data from the National Longitudinal Survey of Mature Women to ex-amine the causal relationship between employment and caring for an ill or dis-abled friend or relative over a three-year period. They found that employment sta-tus does not affect whether or not women start caregiving, but that women who do start are more likely to reduce employment hours or stop work. For their sample of women in late midlife, the causal relationship between employment and caregiving was largely unidirectional, with women reducing hours to meet caregiving demands. Similar findings were reported by Spiess and Schneider (2002) in analysis of midlife caregiving employment in Europe, by Kneipp, Castle-man, and Gailor (2004) and Henz (2006) in analysis of low-income caregivers, by Latif (2006) in a study of the relations between caregiving and labor market behavior among Canadian adults, and by Johnson and LoSasso (2006), showing that time spent helping parents strongly reduces female labor supply at midlife and that this effect is stronger among individuals of lower social class.

Wakabayashi and Donato (2005) used two waves of data (1987 and 1992) from the National Survey of Families and Households to examine whether and how caregiving transitions affect changes in women's labor force participation and the implications of these caregiving transitions for their earnings. They found that the initiation of parental caregiving led to a substantial reduction in their weekly hours worked and annual earnings. However, the effects were different across various subgroups of women. Younger women (aged 19–25), older women (46 years or older), and women with less than high school education experienced large declines in their hours worked and corresponding reduction in average income of $750 and $3,064 for the younger and older cohorts, respectively. These findings were extended in a subsequent study focusing on the long-term consequences of elder care by asking how caring for elderly parents affects women's subsequent risk of living in poverty (Wakabayashi and Donato, 2006). Using the Health and Retirement Study longitudinal panel data, Wakabayashi and Donato showed that being a caregiver in 1991 increased women's risks of living in households with incomes below the poverty threshold, receiving public assistance, and being covered by Medicaid in 1999. Caregivers who spent 20 hours a week assisting their parents with personal care were 25 percent more likely than noncaregivers to live in poverty, 27 percent more likely to be recipients of public assistance, and 46 percent more likely to receive Medicaid eight years later.

Overall, recent findings indicate that elder caregiving has both short- and long-term economic impacts on female caregivers. Low levels of caregiving demand (e.g., 14 hours or less per week) can be absorbed by employed caregivers with little impact on labor force participation. However, heavy-duty caregiving demands (e.g., 20 hours or more per week) result in significant work adjustment, involving either reduced hours or stopping work altogether, and in associated declines in annual incomes. Women with less than high school education are most vulnerable to these negative effects. These short-term effects increase the probability of long-term negative impacts in the form of lower economic and health status of the caregiver. The long-term impacts may in part be attributable to the difficulty of reentering the labor force once caregiving stops (Pavalko and Artis, 1997; Spiess and Schneider, 2002; Wakabayashi and Donato, 2005). An important implication of these findings is that there may be no net cost savings to federal and state governments resulting from informal caregiving to elderly people because the accrued short-term savings are offset by subsequent increases in costs associated with becoming poor and dependent on public assistance.

DOES EMPLOYMENT AFFECT CAREGIVER BURDEN AND MENTAL HEALTH?

The vast majority of the caregiving literature has focused on the nature of caregiving demands and their impact on caregiver burden and physical and mental health. This literature has documented significant psychiatric and physical morbidity among caregivers exposed to high levels of chronic caregiving stress. A subset of this literature has focused on positive and negative spillover of work into the domain of caregiving and on job characteristics that moderate the relation between caregiving demands and caregiver well-being. Two opposing models have been proposed to explain the effects of multiple roles on well-being outcomes. One perspective (scarcity hypothesis, depletion perspective, role conflict theory) argues that multiple roles deplete women's limited energy and resources, resulting in adverse health outcomes for individuals who are employed and provide care. The second perspective (expansion hypothesis, role enrichment hypothesis, positive spillover effects) asserts that benefits accrue to people who operate in multiple roles or domains because they increase opportunities for prestige, recognition, and financial reward, which in turn can bolster women's self-concept and well-being (Cannuscio et al., 2004; Bainbridge, Cregan, and Kulik, 2006; Neal and Hammer, 2007).

Support for both perspectives can be found in research on caregiving and work. Consistent with the scarcity or role conflict hypotheses, several early studies showed that caregivers who combine family care with work responsibilities report higher levels of physical and emotional stress (Brody, 1985; Enright and Friss, 1987; Steuve and O'Donnell, 1989; Meisenheimer, 1990; Neal, Chapman, Ingersoll-Dayton, and Emlen, 1993). In addition, a study of midlife women showed that, when considering their other roles (mother, wife, employee), the largest proportion of women (38%) identified the employee role as the one that conflicted most with caregiving (Stephens, Townsend, Martire, and Druley, 2001). In research focused specifically on role spillover, caregivers report that responsibilities at work frequently made them impatient or irritable when assisting a parent and also made it difficult to enjoy caregiving (Stephens, Franks, and Atienza, 1997).

On the other hand, Martire, Stephens, and Atienza (1997) found protective effects of full-time employment for women involved in parent care, consistent with the expansion hypothesis. That is, higher caregiving stress was not associated with poorer physical health and emotional well-being for daughters who worked more than 35 hours per week, and this finding was not due to less care provision by full-time workers. Skaff and Pearlin (1992) also found that caregivers who were involved in an outside work role experienced significantly less stress than caregivers who were not. The former reported greater self-worth, more personal satisfaction, and greater ability to combat fears of inadequacy. In their review of this literature, Martire and Stephens (2003) conclude that while parent care and employment often conflict with one another, occupying both roles can also be beneficial for the health of adult daughters. The positive effects of work on caregiver well-being may be due to respite or distraction from caregiving; higher pay and benefits associated with full-time work, which enables outsourcing of some tasks; and social support from work colleagues. In addition, women with highly rewarding jobs may be buffered from the stress of caregiving, and their successes at work may contribute to a more positive mood during caregiving tasks (Stephens and Townsend, 1997; Stephens, Franks, and Atienza, 1997).

The resolution of these disparate literatures likely rests with complex interactions involving the nature of the caregiving experience and the characteristics of the work role. Bainbridge, Cregan, and Kulik (2006) suggest that the type of disability (mental vs. non-mental) of the one cared for may interact with hours of work to determine caregiver stress outcomes. They found that spending more time in a work role generally had no effect on caregiver stress outcomes. However, caregivers who were caring for a person with a mental disability experienced significantly fewer stress outcomes as they spent more hours engaged in outside work. Neal and Hammer (2007), Chesley and Moen (2006), and Fredriksen and Scharlach (1997) emphasize the importance of workplace characteristics as contributors to caregiving outcomes. Factors such as job classification, work demand, work control, workplace support, and flexibility have the potential of contributing to or alleviating caregiver stress. Unraveling causal relationships between work, caregiving, and caregiver distress will require ambitious studies that not only study the association among these factors but also follow adults into and out of caregiving and work roles longitudinally.

WHAT IS THE IMPACT OF CAREGIVING ON AMERICAN BUSINESS?

Data on the effects of caregiving on business and industry are scarce. The primary resource on this topic is the Metlife Caregiving Cost Study: Productivity Losses to U.S. Business (2006, www.caregiving.org). This study combines data from the 1997 Metlife Study of Employer Costs for Working Caregivers with data from the 2004 National Alliance for Caregiving and AARP study of U.S. caregivers. Using caregiver prevalence estimates derived from the 2004 study, the authors generate cost estimates in multiple categories as illustrated in table 2.1. The total costs to employers attributable to full-time employed caregivers are estimated to be $33.6 billion annually. These costs are due primarily to absenteeism ($5.1 billion), shifts from full- to part-time ($4.8 billion), replacing employees ($6.6 billion), and workday interruptions ($6.3 billion). These cost estimates should be viewed cautiously because they are driven by caregiver prevalence estimates that may be inflated and because of the many arguable assumptions made to generate them.

TABLE 2.1
Estimated cost to employers of all full-time employed caregivers

	Cost per employee	Total employer cost
Replacing employees	$413	$6,585,310,888
Absenteeism	320	5,096,925,912
Partial absenteeism	121	1,923,730,754
Workday interruptions	394	6,282,281,750
Eldercare crisis	238	3,799,217,477
Supervisor time	113	1,796,385,842
Unpaid leave	212	3,377,082,202
Full-time to part-time	299	4,758,135,522
Total	$2,110	$33,619,070,346

Source: NAC and MetLife data

HOW HAVE EMPLOYERS RESPONDED TO THE NEEDS OF CAREGIVERS?

Employee benefit programs providing retirement and health care support have existed in the United States since colonial times (Neal and Hammer, 2007). Family-oriented support programs included child care services, day nurseries, and preschools for children of working parents. Such programs peaked in the 1920s and then declined during the Great Depression of the 1930s, when companies could neither afford extras such as family support nor was there any incentive to provide them, given the oversupply of labor. Although employee benefit programs such as pension benefits grew rapidly after World War II, family-oriented programs made few advances until the 1960s. Under the auspices of the federal government's Great Society programs, child care centers and later adult day care services became prominent features of our society. One of the first companies to focus on working caregivers was the Travelers Insurance Companies, which surveyed its employees to learn about the extent, nature, and effects of their informal elder care responsibilities in the early 1980s. IBM conducted a similar survey in 1988, and again in 1993. The first documented elder care program was begun in 1986 by Hallmark Cards and included a resource center designed to link employees with services in the community. Other notable developments included the first public-private partnership between the New York City Department on Aging and Phillip Morris, American Express, and J. P. Morgan to provide workplace elder care referral services. In 1990, AT&T and two labor unions, the Communications Workers of America and the International Brotherhood of Electrical Workers, created the Family Care Development Fund and national elder care referral program. In 1991 the *Wall Street Journal* began its "Work and Family" column as a regular feature.

At the same time, federal state governments began enacting legislation that benefited family caregivers. Notable examples are:

- The Federal Family and Medical Leave Act (1993), designed to provide unpaid leave to family members who need to care for a sick relative.
- National Family Caregiver Support Program (2000), which provides direct services (e.g., information about available services, assistance in gaining access to supportive services, individual and group counseling, caregiver training, etc.) to family members caring for an elder aged 60 or older.
- Federal and State Dependent Care Credits, which enable family members to lower income taxes to offset expenses incurred in caring for an elder.

In the last decade the landscape of workplace-based supports for employees with family responsibilities has changed dramatically. The diversity of available programs is vast, although their widespread availability is more limited. Neal and Hammer (2007) organize these programs into three broad categories: policies, benefits, and services. *Policies* provide either formal or informal guidelines for dealing with employee scheduling and leave in order to support family care. Examples included flexible work schedules, reduced work hours, options for leave, where work is done (e.g., telecommuting), relocation, and management sensitivity (e.g., management training in work/life issues). *Benefits* provide direct or indirect compensation to protect the worker against loss of earnings, payment of medical expenses, or paid release time for personal needs. Specific examples include flexible spending accounts, dependent-care assistance plans or tax credits, and various types of health insurance. *Services* include tangible forms of help, but not direct compensation, provided by the employer to address family care needs. For example, some employers provide educational seminars on caregiving or caregiving fairs, newsletters, and guidebooks; some provide case management, support groups, and wellness programs. Other direct service programs might include adult day-care centers or subsidies for elder care, employee assistance in the form of stress management, crisis intervention, and bereavement counseling. Note that many of these policies are not specifically designed to support employee elder care and may be beneficial to all workers.

How prevalent are these programs? Two of the better databases on the availability of these programs are the Families and Work Institutes Business Work-life Survey conducted in 2005, and the Society of Human Resource Management (SHRM) online survey of 3000 randomly selected SHRM members conducted in 2003 (Neal and Hammer, 2007). The former survey found that 34 percent of companies with 100 or more employees reported the provision of elder care information and resources, and 5 percent of employers provided direct financial support for local elder care programs. About 48 percent of companies reported that they provided training to supervisors with respect to responding to employees' work-family needs, and 63 percent responded "very true" to a statement concerning whether supervisors were encouraged to be supportive of employees with family problems. The SHRM survey found that 20 percent of primarily large companies with more than 500 employees were providing elder care referral services, 15 percent were providing elder care leave, 3 percent were providing emergency elder care, 2 percent were subsidizing elder care, and 1 percent was paying for elder care or had an on-site elder care center.

Even when elder care support services are available, the extent to which they are used is relatively low, with some studies reporting usage rates of 1–4 percent of the 7–12 percent of those eligible taking advantage of such programs (Neal and Hammer, 2007). These low usage rates should be interpreted cautiously for at least two reasons: first, the available data on this issue are limited, so we must be cautious in generalizing from these findings; and second, low utilization rates may be a reflection of the value of the services offered. For example, many industrialized nations other than the United States provide paid family leave to family caregivers of elders. Not surprisingly, these incentives increase use dramatically. However, data on the impact of these services are scarce. We know virtually nothing about how these programs affect outcomes such as work performance or caregiver burden and distress.

CONCLUSION

Research on caregiving and work has a rich tradition dating back more than two decades. Researchers in North America and Europe have addressed important questions regarding the impact of work on adopting the caregiving role and, conversely, the effects of caregiving on the work role. The evidence indicates causal effects in both directions—employment status affects who takes on the caregiving role, and the onset of caregiving affects hours worked and whether or not one stays employed. Overall, though, the effects of caregiving on work have stronger and more consistent support than the effects of work on caregiving. Because labor force participation for both men and women continues to change, with more women entering the labor force and both men and women increasingly working after retirement, it will be important to continue to monitor the relation between caregiving and work in the future. In particular, we need to be concerned about the possibility that caregiving demands may undermine the ability of older workers to remain in the workforce postretirement.

The traditional family model of husband as breadwinner and wife as homemaker is approaching extinction, with nearly three-quarters of women already in the labor force and the likelihood that these rates will continue to increase in the future. For dually employed married couples, this means that effective elder care will require negotiation and strategic allocation of responsibilities based in part on the demands of work, although we can anticipate that women will continue to carry the larger burden of care provision. Understanding how couples negotiate care provision and developing optimal strategies for sharing the care should be part of our future research agenda in this area.

The trend toward increasing labor force participation and longer work careers among all adults has the potential of eroding caregiving resources at the same time that the need or demand for care is increasing and the available resources for formal care are decreasing. This scenario has all the ingredients of a perfect storm, with the potential of becoming a major crisis if we do not begin to plan for it now. One solution to this problem is to maximize our ability to combine work with caregiving. The research in this chapter provides numerous examples of how work can be compatible with and even complement the caregiving experience for those individuals who stay in the workforce (e.g., respite, pay and benefits, social support, rewarding careers). What is needed are workplace programs that support caregivers at a level that allows them to remain in the workforce.

A second theme of this chapter is that there are large economic work-related costs of caregiving for both the individual and business and industry. Women who leave the workforce to care for a parent endure economic costs in the form of immediate losses in wages and benefits and long-term losses in retirement benefits. These effects are more pronounced on women of lower socioeconomic status and are difficult to reverse once initiated. For businesses, the costs are measured in terms of lost productivity due to absenteeism, replacing workers who leave the workforce, and interruptions at work. Addressing these issues will require macro-level policy based on accurate assessments of projected cost and benefit. A first step in developing such policy will require an accurate count of the number of employed caregivers. One of the lessons of this chapter is that we do not know the prevalence of work and caregiving at the population level because of the varying definitions of caregiving. As a result, estimating the cost of a program like paid leave from work or subsidized day care for older relatives is precarious. Generating the data needed to address big policy questions should be a high priority and will require thoughtful and consistent definitions of caregiving and large representative population based samples that are followed longitudinally. Coming up with the right policy questions will require creativity and daring. For example, caregiving and work are inextricably linked to the availability and cost of formal health care services. Developing policy in any one domain will inevitably spill over to the other, suggesting that a proactive strategy that simultaneously considers all three domains is essential.

A third area for future study concerns the role of work and caregiving after the age of 65 or the postretirement years. Research on work and caregiving appropriately focuses on working-age adults before retirement. However, with increasing numbers of older individuals needing or wishing to work after traditional retirement age, it is important that we gain a better understanding of how work and caregiving intersect for the older worker/caregiver. How prevalent is work and caregiving in late life? How do caregiving demands affect labor force participation in later life? What types of programs might ease the burden of care for the employed caregivers at different stages in the life course? How do economic factors affect labor force participation in late life in the context of caregiving?

Finally, we must not overlook the potential of existing and emerging technologies to play a role in work and caregiving. Telemedicine technologies have already become an important adjunct to monitoring health and functioning of older persons residing in communities. For employed caregivers, technologies that enable greater latitude in where and when one works (e.g., teleworking) have the potential of easing the burden of care provision. Technology could also play an important role in minimizing work interruptions. A frequent concern among working caregivers is knowing whether a relative at home alone is performing routine tasks during the day such as eating and taking medications at appropriate times. Monitoring these activities requires frequent phone calls and sometimes emergency visits home. Technology has the potential of providing systematic reminders to the care recipient about important tasks that need to be carried out, monitoring whether and how the tasks were completed, and communicating information to both the caregiver at work and the care recipient at home. Applications such as these could make the difference between remaining employed or becoming a full-time caregiver.

ACKNOWLEDGMENTS

Preparation of this article was supported in part by grants from the National Institute of Nursing Research (NR08272, NR0009573); the National Institute on Aging (AG024827,

AG13305, AG015321, AG20677, AG19180); the National Institute of Mental Health (MH 071944); the National Center on Minority Health and Health Disparities (MD000207); the National Heart, Lung, and Blood Institute (HL076852, HL076858); and the National Science Foundation (EEEC-0540865).

REFERENCES

AARP. 2005. *Reimagining America: AARP's Blueprint for the Future.* Washington, DC: AARP.

Bainbridge, H. T. J., Cregan, C., and Kulik, C.T. 2006. The effect of multiple roles on caregiver stress outcomes. *Journal of Applied Psychology* 91 (2): 490–97.

Brody, E. M. 1985. Parent care as a normative family stress. *The Gerontologist* 25:19–29.

Cannuscio, C. C., Colditz, G. A., Rimm, E. B., Berkman, L. F., Jones, C. P., and Kawachi, I. 2004. Employment status, social ties, and caregivers' mental health. *Social Science and Medicine* 58 (7): 1247–56.

Chesley, N., and Moen, P. 2006. When workers care—dual-earner couples' caregiving strategies, benefit use, and psychological well-being. *American Behavioral Scientist* 49 (9): 1248–69.

Doty, P., Jackson, M. E., and Crown, W. 1998. The impact of female caregivers' employment status on patterns of formal and informal elder care. *The Gerontologist* 38 (3): 331–41.

Enright, R. B., and Friss, L. 1987. *Employed Caregivers of Brain-Impaired Adults.* San Francisco: Family Survival Project.

Ettner, S. L. 1995a. The opportunity costs of elder care. *Journal of Human Resources* 31 (1): 189–205.

———. 1995b. The impact of "parent care" on female labor supply decisions. *Demography* 32 (1): 63–80.

Fredriksen, K. I., and Scharlach, A. E. 1997. Caregiving and employment: The impact of workplace characteristics on role strain. *Journal of Gerontological Social Work* 28 (4): 3–22.

Fullerton, H. N., Jr. 1999. Labor force participation: 75 years of change, 1950–98 and 1998–2025. *Monthly Labor Review* 122 (12): 3–12.

Gerstel, N., and Gallagher, S. 1994. Caring for kith and kin: Gender, employment, and the privatization of care. *Social Problems* 41 (4): 519–39.

Henz, U. 2006. Informal caregiving at working age: Effects of job characteristics and family configuration. *Journal of Marriage and Family* 68:411–29.

Johnson, R. W., and LoSasso, A. T. 2006. The impact of elder care on women's labor supply. *Inquiry* 43 (3): 195–210.

Kneipp, S. M., Castleman, J. B., and Gailor, N. 2004. Informal caregiving burden: An overlooked aspect of the lives and health of women transitioning from welfare to employment? *Public Health Nursing* 21 (1): 24–31.

Latif, E. 2006. Labour supply effects of informal caregiving in Canada. *Canadian Public Policy-Analysis de Politiques* 32 (4): 413–29.

Martire, L. M., and Stephens, M. A. P. 2003. Juggling parent care and employment responsibilities: The dilemmas of adult daughter caregivers in the workforce. *Sex Roles* 48 (3–4): 167–73.

Martire, L. M., Stephens, M. A. P., and Atienza, A. A. 1997. The interplay of work and caregiving: Relationships between role satisfaction, role involvement, and caregivers' well-being. *Journals of Gerontology: Psychological Sciences and Social Sciences* 52 (5): S279–89.

McLanahan, S. S., and Monson, R. A. 1990. *Care for the Elderly: Prevalence and Consequences.* NSFH Working Paper 18. Center for Demography and Ecology, University of Wisconsin, Madison.

Meisenheimer, J. 1990. Employee absences in 1989: A new look at data from the CPS. *Monthly Labor Review* 113 (8): 28–33.

Metlife. 2006. *Metlife Caregiving Cost Study: Productivity Losses to U.S. Business.* www.care giving.org/data/Caregiver%20Cost%20Study.pdf.

Moen, P., Robinson, J., and Fields, V. 1994. Women's work and caregiving roles: A life course approach. *Journal of Gerontology: Social Sciences* 49: S176–86.

National Alliance for Caregiving (NAC) and AARP. 2004. *Caregiving in the U.S.* www.care giving.org/data/04finalreport.pdf.

Neal, M. B., Chapman, N. J., Ingersoll-Dayton, B., and Emlen, A. 1993. *Balancing Work and Caregiving.* Newbury Park, CA: Sage

Neal, M. B., and Hammer, L. B. 2007. *Working Couples Caring for Children and Aging Parents: Effects on Work and Well-being.* Mahwah, NJ: Lawrence Erlbaum Associates.

Pavalko, E. K., and Artis, J. E. 1997. Women's caregiving and paid work: Causal relationships in late midlife. *Journal of Gerontology: Social Sciences* 52B (4): S170–79.

Rosenthal, C. J., Hayward, L., Martin-Matthews, A., and Denton, M. 2004. Help to older parents and parents-in-law: Does paid employment constrain women's helping behaviour? *Canadian Journal on Aging* Supplement: S97–112.

Ross, C. E., and Mirowsky, J. 1995. Does employment affect health? *Journal of Health and Social Behavior* 36 (3): 230–43.

Sarkisian, N., and Gerstel, N. 2004. Explaining the gender gap in help to parents: The importance of employment. *Journal of Marriage and the Family* 66 (2): 431–51.

Skaff, M. M., and Pearlin, L. I. 1992. Caregiving: Role engulfment and the loss of self. *The Gerontologist* 32:656–64.

Spiess, C. K., and Schneider, U. 2002. Midlife caregiving and employment: An analysis of adjustments in work hours and informal care for female employees in Europe. *European Network of Economic Policy Research Institutes Working Paper* 9:1–36.

Stephens, M. A. P., Franks, M. M., and Atienza, A. A. 1997. Whether two roles intersect: Spillover between parent care and employment. *Psychology and Aging* 12:30–37.

Stephens, M. A. P., and Townsend, A. L. 1997. The stress of parent care: Positive and negative effects of women's other roles. *Psychology and Aging* 12:376–86.

Stephens, M. A. P., Townsend, A. L., Martire, L. M., and Druley, J. A. 2001. Balancing parent care with other roles: Inter-role conflict of adult daughter caregivers. *Journals of Gerontology: Psychological Sciences* 56:24–34.

Steuve, A., and O'Donnell, L. 1989. Interactions between women and their elderly parents: Constraints of daughters' employment. *Research on Aging* 11 (3): 331–53.

Wakabayashi, C., and Donato, K. M. 2005. The consequences of caregiving: Effects on women's employment and earnings. *Population Research and Policy Review* 24:467–88.

———. 2006. Does caregiving increase poverty among women in later life? Evidence from the Health and Retirement Survey. *Journal of Health and Social Behavior* 47: 258–74.

Wolf, D. A., and Soldo, B. J. 1994. Married women's allocation of time to employment and care of elderly parents. *Journal of Human Resources* 29 (4): 1259–76.

Wolff, J. L., and Kasper, J. D. 2006. Caregivers of frail elders: Updating a national profile. *The Gerontologist* 46 (3): 344–56.

CHAPTER THREE

Aging and Work

An International Perspective

JUHANI ILMARINEN, PH.D.

The aging of the population and the workforce is due to both an increase in life expectancy and lower birth rates. The proportion of people over 60 years of age was 8 percent of the population in 1950 and 10 percent in 2000, and it is predicted to increase up to 21 percent by the year 2050. Aging represents an unprecedented, pervasive, profound, and enduring change in population structures. Aging affects everyone: individuals, organizations, and societies. Aging is also a global phenomenon, and both developed and less developed countries are searching for strategies to help successfully manage an increasing number of older people. In the European Union, the situation for each country and its strategies for managing older people are significantly influenced by the public policies of the country.

The workforce will age with the aging of the population. This trend poses serious economic, social, and political implications for individuals and communities. It is important to redesign worklife and support the work ability of older workers so that they are able and willing to work longer than before. This chapter (1) describes the employment situation of older workers from an international perspective; (2) evaluates our knowledge base of aging and work; (3) introduces the concept of work ability and demonstrates how it can be used to promote employment for older workers; and (4) recommends actions to facilitate the ability of older workers to successfully adapt to today's work environments.

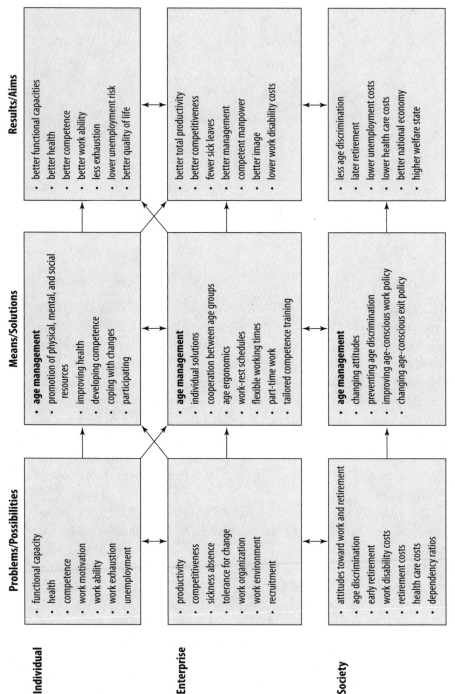

Problems/Possibilities　　　**Means/Solutions**　　　**Results/Aims**

Individual

Problems/Possibilities:
- functional capacity
- health
- competence
- work motivation
- work ability
- work exhaustion
- unemployment

Means/Solutions:
- **age management**
- promotion of physical, mental, and social resources
- improving health
- developing competence
- coping with changes
- participating

Results/Aims:
- better functional capacities
- better health
- better competence
- better work ability
- less exhaustion
- lower unemployment risk
- better quality of life

Enterprise

Problems/Possibilities:
- productivity
- competitiveness
- sickness absence
- tolerance for change
- work organization
- work environment
- recruitment

Means/Solutions:
- **age management**
- individual solutions
- cooperation between age groups
- age ergonomics
- work-rest schedules
- flexible working times
- part-time work
- tailored competence training

Results/Aims:
- better total productivity
- better competitiveness
- fewer sick leaves
- better management
- competent manpower
- better image
- lower work disability costs

Society

Problems/Possibilities:
- attitudes toward work and retirement
- age discrimination
- early retirement
- work disability costs
- retirement costs
- health care costs
- dependency ratios

Means/Solutions:
- **age management**
- changing attitudes
- preventing age discrimination
- improving age-conscious work policy
- changing age-conscious exit policy

Results/Aims:
- less age discrimination
- later retirement
- lower unemployment costs
- lower health care costs
- better national economy
- higher welfare state

Figure 3.1. Aging and work, a challenge for the individual, enterprise, and society

CHALLENGES CREATED BY CHANGES
IN AGE STRUCTURES

The great generation of baby boomers that followed World War II from 1945 into the 1950s has been the backbone of today's workforce in many countries. It has enabled these countries to develop into prosperous, and in many ways exemplary, welfare states. In 2005, the majority of baby boomers were 55 to 60 years of age. In the 15 years that will follow, about 40 percent of the current workforce, represented by the baby boomers, will retire. As a consequence, large numbers of jobs will become available in the private, municipal, and governmental sectors. At the same time, the proportion of people over 65 years of age will increase to 25 percent of the population by 2020. The workforce is also predicted to decrease in developed countries due to new technology, economic overdrive of businesses, and lack of manpower in several sectors. The growth of the economy is threatened because there will not be enough younger workers to replace those workers that retire. We may be facing a workforce shortage in many countries that could threaten future economic growth and development. One solution is the development of strategies to extend the worklife of older adults.

As shown in figure 3.1, problems or impediments facing older workers and associated solutions vary according to the target entity: the individual, organizations (enterprise), or society. Solutions represent forms of age management. From the point of view of the individual, age management means managing oneself and participating in the realization of age management. From the point of view of organizations, age management involves sets of actions to accommodate the needs of people of different ages. From the point of view of society, age management means creating social structures that enhance the success of strategies that extend the working life of older adults.

Official statements and the setting of mutual goals between individuals and organizations are necessary but insufficient with respect to the promotion of successful age management. If the appeal of worklife is to be enhanced for older adults, worklife must be remodeled. In this regard, the most important objectives are to increase the years of active worklife and to make work more attractive. For these objectives to be achieved, changes that are taking place in worklife must be better managed, well-being of worklife must be enhanced, equality must be promoted, and the demands of work and the other sectors of life must be integrated.

Individuals, organizations, and society are therefore all responsible for the successful consolidation of aging and worklife. Even though the barriers for the different parties may seem to differ, they are nevertheless part of the same phenomenon. There are no shortcuts to an improved society comprising people of different ages. Progress is generated by changes in the work cultures of organizations that create a new type of worklife better suited for workers of all ages and by changes in society regarding attitudes about older adults.

For the situation of older workers to be improved, a new common understanding about the collaboration among individuals, organizations, and society is needed. A change in the mindset toward aging is also crucial. Otherwise, the possibilities to improve the employment opportunities of older workers are limited.

In the next section the employment rates of older workers in the European Union (EU) will be described. In this discussion the EU15 refers to the first 15 countries to join the European Union (Belgium, France, Germany, Italy, the Netherlands, Luxembourg, Denmark, Finland, Ireland, the United Kingdom, Greece, Portugal, Spain, Austria, and Sweden). The EU25 includes these countries and Cyprus, the Czech Republic, Estonia, Hungary, Latvia, Lithuania, Malta, Poland, Slovakia, and Slovenia; and the EU27 includes Bulgaria and Romania.

THE EMPLOYMENT RATE OF OLDER WORKERS IN THE EUROPEAN UNION

The employment rate of older workers is calculated here by dividing the number of persons aged 55–64 who are employed by the total population of the same age group. The indicator is based on the recent EU Labor Force Surveys. The employed population consists of those persons who worked during the reference week, did any work for pay or profit for at least one hour, or were not working but who had jobs from which they were temporarily absent. The total population covers people living in private households and excludes those in collective households such as boarding houses, halls of residence, and hospitals. The entire population for EU27 countries was 493 million in year 2006. One objective of the European Union is to increase the employment rate of those aged 55–64 to 50 percent before 2013 and to 59 percent by 2025. In addition to the target employment rates for older workers, the target rate for female employment rate is 65 percent and for overall employment rate 70 percent by the year 2020. It should be noted that the European Union will reach the current U.S. employment level by 2020.

In 2005, the employment rate for older workers was 42.3 percent in the EU27 countries. Thus, there was still a gap of 7.7 percentage points between reality and the goal. However, the differences between EU27 countries were substantial. Altogether, eight countries (Sweden, Denmark, United Kingdom, Estonia, Finland, Ireland, Cyprus, and Portugal) exceeded the 50 percent target in 2005. In contrast, the employment rate of older workers in 2005 was 84 percent in Iceland and more than 60 percent in Norway, Switzerland, Japan, and the United States. Overall, the EU27 was substantially behind these countries, and the newest member countries of the European Union had slightly lower employment rates of older workers than the original member countries (figure 3.2).

The employment rate of older men was higher than that of older women in 2005. More than 70 percent of older men were working in Iceland, Japan, Switzerland, and Norway. In contrast, only slightly more than 50 percent of older women were working in these countries. In the EU27, the employment rates were 51.5 percent for older men and 33.5 percent for older women.

There were also differences in retirement patterns between members of the European Union and other developing countries. The average retirement age was several years higher in Iceland ($M = 66.3$ years) and Norway ($M = 63.1$ years) than in the EU25 ($M = 60.9$ years). Women tend to leave the labor force about one year earlier than men. With respect to other age groups, the employment rate is the

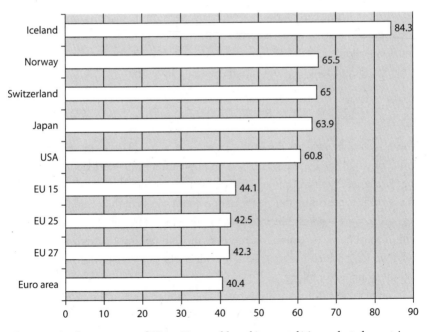

Figure 3.2. Employment rate of 55- to 64-year-old working population, selected countries, 2005

lowest among the youngest age groups (15- to 24-year-olds) and the highest among 25- to 54-year-olds, with seniors being in a slightly better situation than younger people. Employment rates also vary according to educational level such that the rates increase when the level of education is higher. The difference in employment between people in the lowest educational level and the highest educational level is almost triple among young people and double among older people. Among those aged 55–64, 62 percent of those with a high level of education were employed in contrast to 32 percent of those with low levels of education.

A lower level of education also seems to have a greater impact on the employment of women than on that of men. Among those with low education, there was a difference of almost 20 percentage points in the employment rates of men and women in the oldest age group. Therefore, special attention is being given to increasing the employment rates of women with low levels of education in the EU25 countries (European Communities, 2004).

This section has highlighted the large differences between the employment rates of older workers among the European Union and other developed countries. Older workers themselves do not differ significantly from country to country, so the different levels in employment rates largely reflect differences in attitudes about aging, enterprise practices toward older workers, and societal infrastructures and policies. Early retirement options, pension regulations, and Social Security models play an important role in the employment patterns of older workers. To develop strategies to foster extended worklife it is important to have an understanding about the implications of aging for work.

WHAT DO WE KNOW ABOUT AGING AND WORK?

There is vast knowledge about the process of aging. However, until recently, much of what was known was based on populations who were no longer working. To a large extent gerontology and geriatrics have focused on people in the last phases of life, providing little information about adults in their middle and older years who were working. In response to this gap in knowledge, there has been, within the European Union, an increase in funding and research focusing on older workers, which has increasingly bridged the gap between gerontology and "occupational gerontology."

A large variety of research information is available about the potential implications of aging for work and older workers (e.g., Kumashiro, 1995; Spirduso, 1995; Ilmarinen, 1999; Costa, Goedhard, and Ilmarinen, 2005; Ilmarinen, 2006). This information encompasses topics such as health, functional capacities, skills and knowledge, learning and competence, attitudes, values, and motivation. There is also information available regarding age-related changes in working capacity, work performance, and work ability. In addition, there are data regarding the work patterns and preferences of older workers as well as information pertaining to community, organization, and management views about older workers.

International and national employment, exiting worklife, and retirement policies are well documented (Reday-Mulvey, 2005). There are also international recommendations from the United Nations, the International Labor Organization, the World Health Organization (WHO, 1993), and the European Union (Ilmarinen, 2006) regarding older workers. These recommendations state that the employment of older workers should be part of strategic planning among organizations and that governments should strive to reach full employment for all age groups. The recommendations also focus on the prevention of age discrimination. The most important aspect of these recommendations was the acknowledgement of the need for worklife to change so that the circumstances of older workers can be improved. Many measures have been taken in the European Union to promote the situation of older workers, including retirement and Social Security changes, workplace modifications, and support for lifelong learning. To this end, a collection of examples of good practices in age management that span more than 130 organizations was published by the European Foundation for the Improvement of the Living and Working Conditions (Naegele and Walker, 2006).

Despite this increased emphasis on older workers, more recently updated information about age and work is continuously needed because of trends toward increased globalization and the emergence of new technologies. Continuous changes in business environments and technology demand the creation of new paradigms and concepts for aging and work that are evidence based. The Life Course and Work and Age-Integrated Work Life models (Ilmarinen, 2006; Reday-Mulvey, 2005) provide good examples of paradigms that are evolving in the European Union. Life course approaches emphasize the roles and needs of different generations. These models suggest that young people are not engaged enough in worklife, while older people tend to leave employment too early as a result of having to take a disability pension or because of corporate restructuring. Long absences due to sickness and exclusion from the labor market are risks that can affect workers of all ages. According to this approach, for longer and better work careers, the entire span of worklife should be taken into consideration, including critical transitions that occur with aging.

In different cultures, people are guided into different statuses and roles according to their age, and their benefits, rights, and responsibilities are also age-based. Long-term age-specific phases of life related to family, education, or professional career are called life trajectories. In contrast to life trajectories, short-term changes or transitions are changes that include transitions to a life trajectory (e.g., first job), changes along a life trajectory (e.g., changing jobs), or from a life trajectory (e.g., retirement).

Transitions can have long-term effects but should be differentiated from crises. A transition can be normative (graduation, retirement), whereas a crisis is typically non-normative (dropping out of school, unemployment). A transition, therefore, contains both opportunity and risk. A typical life-course transition, whether it is examined from the biological, psychological, or sociological point of view, is nonlinear. In some way, each transition changes how we see ourselves and how others view us (Heikkinen and Tuomi, 2001). Therefore, transitions require attention during life trajectories. Life-course approaches attempt to account for life-course transitions. However, this is still a new approach in the European Union because its adoption requires a large, multidisciplinary knowledge base about human development that encompasses school-age to the third age.

The "Age-Integrated Worklife" approach focuses on the parallelism that occurs during life's phases, and use of this approach requires a change of paradigm. The previous categorization of life's phases into separate periods of training, work, and retirement can be illustrated as parallel periods of life where other events, such as building families, enjoying socialization, and leisure time, are occurring simultaneously. Furthermore, these phases and events can shift in emphasis and take on different forms. For example, with respect to work, training has become lifelong learning, and work schedules have become more flexible and encompass part-time work and other flexible work hour schemes, which in turn enable new types of leisure time. Using this paradigm, "retirement" takes on a new meaning and is viewed differently from the previous "guillotine models," which view retirement as worklife "cut off in one stroke." Instead, it represents a period of transition to alternative work roles, engagement in learning or development activities, or participation in volunteer or leisure pursuits.

In general, successful aging at work forms the base for successful aging and longer lives in general. However, the demands and contents of worklife that support successful aging are not well known.

Pension reforms have pushed people to work longer than ever before. However, many employers are unwilling to hire older workers because of myths about aging and productivity. We need more knowledge about how worklife among 60+ or 70+ people should be designed so that both personal and corporate goals can be reached. Other knowledge gaps include understanding the effects of the work on the "third age" (60–80 years of age) and, if there are such effects, what happens after people are no longer working. Are longer work careers a risk for health and longevity, or does the opposite occur? Other important questions relate to the work ability of voluntary workers, who will play a growing role in coming societies as service providers.

Globalization and new technologies offer both possibilities and threats for older workers. Therefore, identification of positive and negative aspects of these two mega-phenomena is urgently needed. One of the most enduring problems at work has been age discrimination. Although direct discrimination is rare and prohibited by law, the prevention of indirect age discrimination at work is more or less an impossible mission. Yet the reasons for age discrimination are not sufficiently known. On the one hand, there is a large and increasing data base about aging and work, but on the other hand, there is a continuous need for new research information due to the rapid and marked changes in worklife. New approaches like Life Course models need intensive research. In addition, large amounts of evidence-based research information have not been transferred or used in worklife settings. Clearly, we need to pay more attention to the usability of the existing research findings.

GAPS BETWEEN KNOWLEDGE AND PRACTICE: THE "KNOWING-DOING GAP"

An important challenge is successfully combining research information and the implications for work practices into formats that are useful to and understandable by managers and policy makers. There is an abundance of information available on aging, and it increases yearly at such a rapid pace that tracking, understanding, and integrating it requires a great deal of time and effort. Information from research is not automatically converted into meaningful knowledge, and knowledge is not automatically transferred into practice. This paradox is illustrated by "the knowing-doing gap" (Pfeffer and Sutton, 2000). This gap between knowledge and action is manifested in three ways: first, the problem of information not being converted into useful knowledge; second, the challenge of applying the knowledge derived from research to applications in work settings; and third, the amount of time it takes to transfer and implement knowledge in real world contexts (figure 3.3).

The core of the problem in business organizations is that all of the gaps between knowledge and action will expand rapidly if processes for transferring, integrating, and using knowledge are not developed and improved. Especially

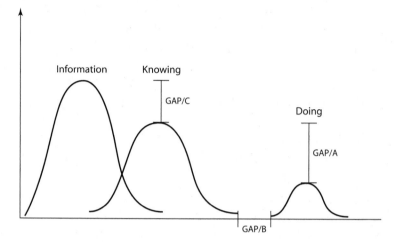

Figure 3.3. The gap between knowledge and action in the transfer of age information to new practices in worklife. *A,* gap between knowledge and action; *B,* delay between knowledge and action; *C,* gap between an increase in information and the emergence of knowledge.

alarming is the time gap between knowledge and its practical application. Knowledge often remains in an unsuitable format or fails to be accepted as part of everyday practice. Closing these gaps requires new innovations and many kinds of expertise as well as different actors working together to change and develop behaviors, procedures, or everyday practices.

Increasing the attraction of worklife (i.e., developing worklife to suit and encourage aging employees) is a concrete challenge for knowledge transfer and the subsequent implementation of new everyday practices in the workplace. For this task, individuals, organizations, worklife services and support systems, labor market parties, and society's decision makers are required to work together toward the achievement of a common goal. Changes in worklife can be achieved only if this goal is supported by the will of everyone (Ilmarinen, 2006).

One good example of transforming the research findings into practice is the "work ability" concept based on follow-up studies at 4, 11, and 16 years of 6,500 municipal employees from 1981 to 1997 in Finland. The study identified factors that deteriorated or improved the work ability of workers 45–58 years old. A promotion concept of work ability (PWA) was created and tested in practice, and social partners agreed to use and support the model. Also, a method for measuring work ability, the Work Ability Index (WAI) was transformed into a practical tool for occupational health services. Today the use of WAI and PWA has been tested in several countries, and plans for further implementation into the EU strategies for older workers are under way.

THE WORK ABILITY APPROACH

The work ability approach is an enterprise-level strategy that has been employed since 1990s in Finland. Since 2000 several other countries in Europe and in Asia (Japan, South Korea, China) as well as Brazil and Australia have started research activities with the work ability model. It has been shown to address the situation and needs of older workers as well as to help formulate plans for the actions needed to promote their work ability during aging. Presently, the work ability model is an evidence-based approach that results in a win-win situation for both employers and employees in worklife.

Work ability is a new concept describing a holistic approach to human potential in worklife (Ilmarinen, 2006; Ilmarinen and Tuomi, 2004). Work ability is predicated on a balance between a person's resources and work demands. A person's resources consist of health and functional capacities, education and competence, values, and attitudes. Work, on the other hand, covers the work environment and community as well as the actual contents, demands, and organization of work. Management (i.e., supervision) is also associated with work (figure 3.4).

Work ability can be conceptualized as a building with several floors. Health and physical, psychological, and social functional capacity occupy the ground floor on which the entire weight of the remaining floors of the building rests. For example, changes in functional capacity and health can affect work ability such that deterioration of health is a threat to work ability, whereas improved functional capacity makes the development of work ability possible. The second floor of the building represents professional knowledge and competence (skill). Knowledge and competence and their continuous development are needed to meet the demands of worklife. Changes in work challenges and demands imply that the continuous development of professional skills become an even more important prerequisite for work ability. Ability to interact in different work communities is also an aspect of competence.

The third floor represents values, attitudes, and motivation. This floor relates to the balance between work and personal resources, as well as the relationship between work and personal life. It is relatively open to different influences. Changes in society or legislation (e.g., pension reform) are also reflected in the third floor. The fourth floor represents work and its related factors. It is the largest and heaviest floor of the work ability building, and its weight is supported

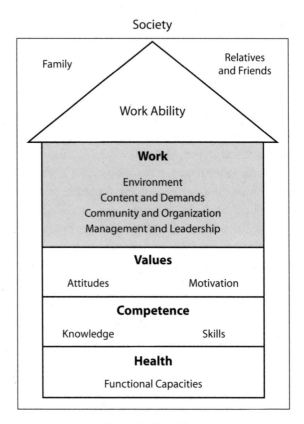

Figure 3.4. Work ability and related factors

by the lower floors. The demands and organization of work, as well as the functioning and management of the work community, make the work floor an entity that is multidimensional, difficult to understand, and hard to measure. On the work floor, special attention needs to be given to supervision and management, because supervisors are responsible for the maintenance of the fourth floor and have a mandate to organize and change the floor if necessary.

Work ability (the top of the building) is primarily a question of balance between work and personal resources, attitudes and values, and so forth. In practice, people search for the optimal balance throughout their entire worklife. This optimal balance may be very different in different phases of worklife. To create a balance, work and personal resources need to be continuously evaluated. Personal resources change with age, for example; and, with globalization and new technology, work demands also change. The factors affecting work ability are therefore continuously changing and must be balanced.

The maintenance and promotion of work ability requires cooperation between supervisors and employees. However, neither can ensure that work ability will not change; instead, the responsibility must be shared between the employer and employee. Nevertheless, the promotion of work ability is not only a matter of effective employer-employee cooperation; the work community is also an important factor in supporting the work ability of its members.

Central roles are also played by the occupational health care and the occupational safety organizations. For example, tasks regulated by law for occupational health care can include the maintenance of employees' work ability. The occupational safety organization can prevent work risks that threaten work ability. However, combining the professional knowledge about health with changes occurring in the demands of work is a challenging task.

It is also important to note that work ability is not separate from life outside work. Family and a person's close community (relatives, friends, and acquaintances) can also affect a person's work ability in many different ways throughout life. Making work and family life compatible is becoming increasingly more important. In addition, society creates the infrastructure, services, and rules according to which organizations and employees' work ability can be supported.

The importance of the different dimensions of work ability was studied using the representative national data from the Health 2000 project in Finland, which gathered data through interviews, questionnaires and health examinations. The work ability of persons aged 18–74 years was studied, although the emphasis was on persons aged 30–64. The number of persons of this age range who participated in home interviews was 5,199 (89 percent of the sample). The results showed that, among people of all ages, health, functional capacity, and the characteristics of one's work are statistically the most significant factors influencing work ability (Ilmarinen, Tuomi, and Seitsamo, 2005).

THE WORK ABILITY OF OLDER WORKERS

Follow-up studies of work ability among people over 45 years of age showed that for about 60 percent of these workers work ability remained good or excellent, it decreased for a little less than 30 percent, and it increased for a little under 10 percent over a period of 11 years. The results were similar for both the men and women. The changes in work ability among different occupations were relatively similar. However, the work ability of the women in physically demanding jobs improved more often than that of the men, whereas work ability improved more often among the men in mentally demanding work. The improvement among women can be explained both by the promotion of work ability (PWA) activities in their physical jobs and the healthy worker effect. A decrease in work ability seemed to be more common for men who perform mixed mentally and physically demanding tasks (primarily transport) and for women in, for example, nursing work (Ilmarinen, Tuomi, and Klockars, 1997; Tuomi, 1997). In nursing, the stress and pace of work have increased due to decreased manpower in hospitals.

A cross-section of the work ability of people of different ages in 20 small and middle-size organizations illustrates both the differences between age groups and the increase in individual differences as a function of age (figure 3.5). It is important to note that the work ability of most of the people was good or excellent, regardless of age. Young people, however, were more homogeneous in relation to work ability than those over 45 years of age. There were more people whose work ability was moderate or poor among the older employees. Among the senior workers of the same age, work ability varied from one extreme to the other.

It is also important to note that poor work ability does not necessarily mean "poor employee." The reasons for poor work ability can be found on any floor of the work ability building (figure 3.4), and according to some studies the reason is

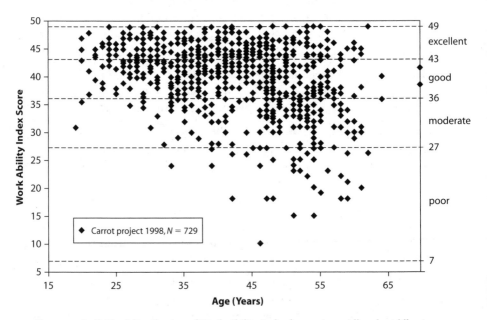

Figure 3.5. Individual distribution of Work Ability Index by age in small and middle-size enterprises, Finland, 2000. The Work Ability Index ranges from 7 to 49 points; the greater the number of points, the better the perceived work ability. Each diamond represents an individual.

often located on the fourth floor (work floor). Reasons for poor work ability may be poor work organization or work demands that do not correspond to the resources of the employee. Poor work ability can also be caused by poor management or a poor work community. The reasons for poor work ability can also derive from other floors of the work ability building. Therefore, it is important to determine the reasons for poor work ability in order to identify the necessary corrective actions. The order of and schedule for the corrective actions must be planned. Balanced work ability can be achieved for a person's entire worklife, but this requires good planning and long-term implementation of good work practices and maintenance of knowledge, skill, and functional abilities on the part of the worker.

STRATEGIES TO PROMOTE WORK ABILITY

Promotion of work ability (PWA) has a long tradition in Finland and is spreading to other countries. Activities to help employees in Finland maintain their work ability began in the early 1990s. It started with an agreement between labor market organizations, which unanimously promoted the necessity of work ability maintenance. The practices and methods devised for work ability maintenance have become more sophisticated and versatile ever since. Today, they cover the development of both the work environment and the work community as well as the strengthening of individual resources of employees. Occupational health care services and human resource departments have often planned and implemented activities to help workers maintain their work ability. The PWA has been set by legislation as one important duty of Occupational Health Services (OHS) in Finland and has proven to be operational. The OHS´s annual plan includes the measurement of work ability index and targets for improvement (figure 3.6).

A critical component of work ability promotion must involve understanding prevailing work situations and characteristics of the workforce. In this regard, any survey of the needs for work ability maintenance must cover the many different dimensions of work ability. Actions are then planned according to the results of this survey. Work ability maintenance requires good management and perseverance. The results must also be continually evaluated so that success can be defined and methods developed for further improvement. Successful work ability promotion needs the commitment and good collaboration of several actors in the company. Usually, the OHS indicates the needs for PWA through corporate surveys and plans together with the company's human resource department. Management evaluates the plan and, if feasible, finances the PWA programs.

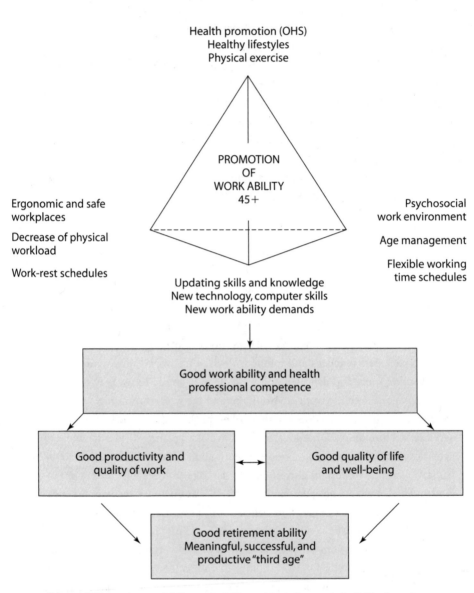

Figure 3.6. Promotion model for work ability and its influence in individuals and enterprises. OHS = Occupational Health Service (Finland)

For example, the Finnish Institute of Occupational Health has developed and tested different methods for work ability maintenance in organizations. Overall, the results indicate that the effects of work ability promotion are initially manifest as improved health and work ability among employees and the work community. There is also improvement both in the quality and productivity of work and in quality of the life, functional capacity, and well-being of personnel. The effects of work ability maintenance also last until retirement, with health status, functional capacity, and quality of life remaining high. Investing in work ability maintenance therefore improves the "third age" (60–80 years of age; Tuomi, Huuhtanen, Nykyri, and Ilmarinen, 2001). This result is an important example of the effects that the stages of life have on each other. Good worklife ensures a good "third age."

A cost-benefit analysis of PWA in 200 small and midsize companies showed that the return of investments on PWA ranged from three- to tenfold, and at least a threefold return on investment was realized in a few years. Half of the return came from the decrease of sickness/absence rates and early retirement costs, and the other half came from higher productivity in the companies. Besides the improvement in productivity, the managers felt that people were better able to continue working and that the work atmosphere had improved. Interventions studies in workplaces represent the most reliable evidence that work ability can be modified. The cost-benefit analyses of PWA have been successful in convincing other managers to institute programs to promote work ability.

RESEARCH INTERVENTIONS TO IMPROVE WORK ABILITY

Research has focused on the contributory factors of work ability such as health and functional capacity, competence, attitudes, worklife properties, and age-awareness of managers.

Interventions that simultaneously target several factors contributing to work ability and in which an external researcher participates in the planning, implementation, and follow-up of the organization's strategies produce good results but are both complex and demanding in practice. They require a long time span and may be expensive. On the other hand, an intervention of limited scope, though intense, may not initiate permanent improvements in work ability, and the results may depend on several factors, such as the nature of the organization and the root causes of the problems (Ilmarinen and Tuomi, 2004).

Several research intervention studies in the early 1990s tested the effect of increased physical activity on work ability (Ilmarinen and Louhevaara, 1999). The results of these studies showed that increased physical activity improved the work ability of police officers over a period of eight months and that of personnel in a small metal-working organization in six months. In addition, these studies showed that these interventions resulted in improvements in the health and physical functional capacity of the policemen and a decrease in their psychosomatic symptoms. In some cases improving health and functional capacity, which are the basis of work ability, may be enough to increase work ability.

An important question in these efforts is determining how much regular physical activity needs to be increased to affect work ability. In a randomized controlled study, the effects of versatile workplace physical activity on the work ability of women in physically semi-demanding textile work was studied. The 8-month, supervised, and versatile physical activity intervention improved the 2-year work ability prognosis for the textile workers and increased the proportion of women receiving a "good work ability" rating at the 12-month follow-up. The average work ability index did not improve, however, nor did sick leaves decrease as anticipated. Overall, the results indicate that supervised workplace exercise (1 hour/week) had a positive but relatively small effect on the work ability of women in semi-demanding physical work.

The work ability of women in semi-demanding, basic service occupations has also been assessed. In a study of female cleaning workers, an 11-month intervention that focused on work methods and equipment, combined with increased physical activity, improved the work ability of cleaners by about 10 percent (Hopsu, Leppänen, and Klemola, 2003). The combined effects of ergonomic improvements and physical activity have also been studied among home help personnel. In this study, improvements in ergonomics were targeted toward solving problems related to work content and to workload. A challenge in this study was that the improvements had to be partially made according to the terms of the clients and in the clients' homes. The results indicated that the intervention prevented work ability from decreasing with age. Moreover, when the results were compared with those of a control group whose members did not participate in the intervention, the data indicated that work ability actually decreased for the control group during the follow-up (Pohjonen, 2001).

These personnel and their work ability were monitored for five years after the intervention. The results showed that work ability decreased in all of the groups; however, the deterioration of work ability was lowest in the groups that had participated in the interventions. Although the long-term effects of the research interventions were evident when the results were compared with the changes in the control group, the prior interventions did not prevent deterioration of work ability. Overall, these findings demonstrate that work ability maintenance in workplaces should be continuous (Pohjonen, 2001).

An example of a multidimensional intervention in one workplace, the so-called Mahis program, was conducted in an organization that manufactured low voltage equipment. About 700 people participated in the 3-year program, which consisted of a total of 16 different activities (e.g., physical examinations, health care, seminars on the maintenance of work ability, health education, improvement of functional capacity, workplace ergonomics, teamwork and management, strategies for managing work-related stress, excursions, and cultural activities). The personnel participated in different parts of the program according to their job descriptions and interests, and the results were therefore analyzed in relation to employee participation. The active participants improved their work ability when compared with baseline values three years earlier, whereas the work ability of the passive participants decreased (Louhevaara, Leppänen, and Klemola, 2003).

Similar results were obtained in an intervention in which the development of both the work community and management were targeted as mechanisms to improve worker well-being. This study was carried out in a municipal technical office, and about 1,800 persons, of which 77 percent were men, participated in the program. The goal of this program was to change the operational culture to include more worker participation and to improve the psychosocial work environment. The participation of personnel in different development interventions was recorded. The results showed that the psychosocial work environment improved and fatigue decreased but work-related stress increased. Familiarity with work objectives, beliefs about ability to affect work, communication, and management improved. Overall, active participation in the intervention activities improved participants' work ability as well as their understanding of the organization's goals (Ilmarinen and Tuomi, 2004). In all of the aforementioned research interventions, work ability was measured using the work ability index, a method developed and validated by the Finnish Institute of Occupational Health to measure subjective work ability (Tuomi et al., 1998).

Overall, this discussion demonstrates that work ability can be improved through multidimensional interventions in the workplace. To be effective, the interventions should include at least three dimensions of work ability, such as health promotion of employees, improving the ergonomics in the workplace, and age-awareness training for the managers. The cost-benefit analyses of work ability promotion have shown that the return of investments is at least threefold after an intervention period of two to three years. A successful promotion of work ability requires a commitment of several key actors in the company: the executive group, line managers and foremen, human resources and administration, Occupational Health and Safety bodies, and representatives of the personnel groups. These key actors should agree with the plan and share and carry out assignments and program components. In addition, interventions require active, long-term commitments.

CONCLUSION

The aging of the population presents a great challenge for worklife worldwide. Life expectances have improved markedly, and fertility rates are decreasing. In the European Union the proportion of older workers will increase during the next decades: workers 50+ years will represent about one-third of the EU27 workforce in the year 2025, and the younger generations will represent less than one-fifth of the workforce. There will also be a shortage of skilled manpower. Organizations will need older workers more than ever, as does society, to keep the dependency ratios tolerable and help finance the longer lives of the citizens.

Actions aimed at extending the careers of aging workers in the European Union primarily focus on retirement policies, exiting worklife, and employment policies. However, actions such as the institution of flexible retirement ages, reduction of early retirement pensions, and information and educational campaigns about older workers have created significant changes in some countries. These reforms in policy levels need to be combined with reforms in worklife. Strategies for extending the careers of older workers need to be more comprehensive and intensive and include actions at the organizational level.

Projections for the future also need to include programs for the simultaneous development of the well-being of older workers and the productivity of organizations. Promotion of work ability is a new, evidence-based model that can produce a win-win situation for both organizations and workers. In this regard, recommendations for future policies and research are as follows:

1. *Changes are needed in conceptualization of aging.* Instead of emphasizing the aging of the population, a more correct expression would be the lengthening of middle age. Whereas early and late middle age previously was positioned between the ages of 40 and 60 years, the definition of middle age could, in the future, last until 65 or even 70 years. Naturally, including people 40 and 70 years of age in the same age period will increase variation in middle age. Thus, the new definition of middle age also needs to include a more accurate description of what constitutes aging as well as more positive descriptors of aging. The words "aged," "older," and "old" have negative connotations in our contemporary language.

2. *New conceptualizations of retirement are also needed.* Retirement is not just a point in human life; it is a process during which people change their work role and exit the workforce gradually. This conceptualization of retirement is the opposite of the general "all or nothing" model in which working stops suddenly. The sudden stopping of work has been compared to falling off a cliff ("cliff retirement") or having an accident ("guillotine retirement"). Instead, thinking of retirement as a gradual transition opens up many more opportunities for older workers.

3. *Planning the shift to retirement and the implementation and management of the process of retirement should be included as a component of worklife.* Training for managers and older workers should include preparation for retirement.

4. *Worklife must be extended in various ways.* In most occupations, an extended career is based on decreasing work hours or workload. Part-time work and flexible work hour arrangements are among the most potentially successful methods of adjusting workload. Full-time work is not an option for extending worklife for most workers. Part-time work should be available and voluntary, and it must enable a decent living and pension security. Achieving these conditions will require legislative action in several countries and new ways of thinking in some organizations.

5. *Lifelong learning must become everyone's right.* The right to education, improving one's expertise, and vocational training should be a part of work, and it should also extend to retirement. Appropriate methods that support the learning needs of seniors must be identified and used in training systems.

6. *Building and finding a suitable job may require re-education or moving.* Telework may offer one opportunity to achieve this goal. There is a need for more research to help define what constitutes a suitable job for older workers and to define guidelines for telework. New methods and procedures to evaluate jobs are also needed.

7. *It must be possible to retire from heavy and consuming occupations with good functional capacity.* Therefore, workloads must be adjusted and individuals must be provided with opportunities to switch to a less-demanding job, or retirement must be made available earlier for workers in these occupations without the label of work disability being applied. The implementation of this principle requires legislative action. The fair criteria for retirement age must be partly adjusted according to the total workload of different occupations. Participation in a so-called second career as part of career planning is a good alternative for many people in physically demanding occupations.

8. *The costs to organizations of employing seniors must be decreased.* Accomplish-

ing this requirement may mean setting salaries more directly to productivity. The indirect workforce costs of senior employees must also be decreased. This would serve to decrease age discrimination and enable senior employment.

9. *Economic factors represent the greatest challenge to extending and improving worklife.* Increasing demands on productivity, tight schedules, and changes in worklife caused by economic decline alienate people of all ages from worklife, especially seniors. Everyone is entitled to be treated with human dignity in his or her work. Globalization and moving production elsewhere to benefit faceless owners will not lengthen the careers of baby boomers, for example, but will likely have the opposite effect. Bad work practices and human mistreatment, however, will remain a burden for the image of the organization for a long time. This silent negative information is easily transferred from one generation to another.

10. *Future research on the topic of aging and work should cover the whole life course.* Longitudinal studies are needed to clarify the critical transition phases from school to retirement. Cohort studies would help explain the roles and needs of these phases and their modifying factors among different generations. A better understanding of changes in values and attitudes toward work is also needed. The "real" reasons for age discrimination need to be identified; otherwise, zero-tolerance against direct and indirect age discrimination cannot be achieved. In the organizations, comprehensive intervention studies are needed. These studies need to demonstrate which intervention strategies are the most effective to promote the work ability of younger, middle-aged, and older workers in the changing business environment. Finally, to bridge the gap between knowing and doing, researchers and practitioners need to create a new common paradigm that enables a better implementation of evidence-based models in organizational practices.

REFERENCES

Costa, G., Goedhard, W. J. A., and Ilmarinen, J., eds. 2005. *Assessment and Promotion of Work Ability, Health and Well-being of Ageing Workers.* International Congress Series 1280. Amsterdam: Elsevier.

European Communities. 2004. *Eurostat Yearbook, 2004: The Statistical Guide to Europe. Data 1992 2002.* Luxembourg: Eurostat.

Heikkinen, E., and Tuomi, J. eds. 2001. *Suomalainen elämänkulku. Kustannusosakeyhtiö Tammi.* Helsinki: Vantaa.

Hopsu, L., Leppänen, A., and Klemola, S. 2003. A program to support and maintain the work ability and well-being of kitchen workers. In *Aging and Work,* ed. M. Kumashiro, 117–84. London: Taylor & Francis.

Ilmarinen, J. 1999. *Ageing Workers in the EU: Status and Promotion of Work Ability, Employ-*

ability and Employment. Helsinki: Finnish Institute of Occupational Health, Ministry of Social Affairs and Health, Ministry of Labour.

————. 2006. *Towards a Longer Worklife: Aging and Worklife Quality in the European Union.* Helsinki: Finnish Institute of Occupational Health, Ministry of Social Affairs and Health.

Ilmarinen, J., and Louhevaara, V., eds. 1999. *FinnAge—Respect for the Aging: Action Programme to Promote Health, Work Ability and Well-being of Ageing Workers in 1990–96.* People and Work, Research reports 26. Helsinki: Finnish Institute of Occupational Health.

Ilmarinen, J., and Tuomi, K. 2004. Past, present and future of work ability. In *People and Work, Research Report,* ed. J. Ilmarinen, and S. Lehtinen, 65:1–25. Helsinki: Finnish Institute of Occupational Health.

Ilmarinen, J., Tuomi, K., and Klockars, M. 1997. Changes in the work ability of active employees over an 11-year period. *Scandinavian Journal of Work, Environment, and Health* 23 (Suppl 1): 49–57.

Ilmarinen, J., Tuomi, K., and Seitsamo, J. 2005. New dimension of work ability. In *Assessment and Promotion of Work Ability, Health and Well-being of Ageing Workers,* ed. G. Costa, W. J. A. Goedhard, and J. Ilmarinen, 3–7. International Congress Series 1280. Amsterdam: Elsevier.

Kumashiro, M., ed. 1995. *The Paths to Productive Aging.* London: Taylor & Francis.

Louhevaara, V., Leppänen, A., and Klemola, S. 2003. Changes in the work ability index of aging workers related to participation in activities for promoting health and work ability: A 3-year program. In *Aging and Work,* ed. M. Kumashiro, 185–92. London: Taylor & Francis.

Naegele, G., and Walker, A. 2006. *A Guide to Good Practice in Age Management.* Dublin: European Foundation for the Improvement of the Living and Working Conditions.

Pfeffer, J., and Sutton, R. I. 2000. *The knowing-Doing Gap: How Smart Companies Turn Knowledge into Action.* Boston: Harvard Business School Press.

Pohjonen, T. 2001. Perceived work ability and physical capacity of home care workers: Effects of the physical exercise and ergonomic intervention on factors related to work ability. Academic dissertation. Kuopio University Publications D. Medical Sciences 260, Kuopion yliopisto, Helsinki.

Reday-Mulvey, G. 2005. *Working beyond Sixty: Key Policies and Practices in Europe.* Basingstoke, United Kingdom: Palgrave Macmillan.

Spirduso, W. W. 1995. Job performance of the older worker. In *Physical Dimensions of Aging,* ed. W. W. Spirduso, 367–87. Champaign, IL: Human Kinetics.

Tuomi, K., ed. 1997. Eleven-year follow-up of aging workers. *Scandinavian Journal of Work, Environment, and Health* 23:1.

Tuomi, K., Huuhtanen, P., Nykyri, E., and Ilmarinen, J. 2001. Promotion of work ability, the quality of work and retirement. *Occupational Medicine* 51 (5): 318–24.

Tuomi, K., Ilmarinen, J., Jahkola, A., Katajarinne, L., and Tulkki, A. 1998. *Work Ability Index,* 2nd ed. Helsinki: Finnish Institute of Occupational Health.

World Health Organization. 1993. *Aging and Working Capacity.* Report of a WHO study group. WHO Technical Report Series 835. Geneva, Switzerland: World Health Organization.

PART II

Implications of an Aging Workforce

CHAPTER FOUR

The Politics of Work and Aging

Public Policy for the New Elders

FERNANDO M. TORRES-GIL, PH.D.

This book examines the future of work for an aging population and the myriad issues facing people as they near retirement age, including demographic shifts, health care concerns, savings and pensions, family caregiving, and the changing nature of occupational expectations, opportunities, and demands. Many of these issues will be debated and addressed in the public policy arena. How the public and private sectors and society at large respond to the unique needs of older workers will determine the quality of life of an aging population—defining the extent to which frustration and conflict may become hallmarks of the post–World War II baby boom generation in their "golden years." The inability or unwilling-ness of public policy or the private sector to effectively respond to these chal-lenges may lead to a politics of aging in which the need or desire for employment and economic security cannot be met. The vicissitudes of longevity, coupled with potential economic and work insecurity, frustrations from a changing job mar-ket, and a diminished social safety net may conspire toward a politics of aging that presses society to use public policy to facilitate work in old age, a politics of aging not unlike one seen during the previous century.

THE STAGE IS SET

Growing attention is focused on the extent to which older people can, will, or should continue working as they near and pass traditional retirement age. The general aging of the population, increased life expectancy, and the pending retirement of the baby boomers is forcing the public and private sectors to reckon with a host of issues related to work and aging. The image of the past, albeit illusionary for many, in which people work in one company for thirty years, garner a lifetime pension, and retire to a life of leisure and contentment, has clearly changed. So, to some extent, has the ability to find meaningful, fulfilling work that allows for financial security in old age. Today we are living longer, the economy and technology are dramatically changing, the workplace is more fluid and less predictable, and the ability of individuals to have choices about when, how, and where to work in their later years is increasingly uncertain. We are in the midst of a contradictory set of labor force patterns: many want to retire early, but more and more are working later in life. Public policies have alternated between incentives to leave the workforce early and incentives to stay in it longer.

Since World War II, major changes in workforce patterns have emerged, including more women, minorities, and older workers in the labor force, a shifting from early retirement to working longer, dramatic changes in the U.S. economy affected heavily by globalization and technological advancement, declining fertility rates, a serious decline in the power of labor unions, and greater demands for occupational and educational skills. Certain to add to this transformation is the entry of up to 75 million baby boomers into middle and old age and their potential need to keep working. Can they find meaningful, well-paying work? And even if they can, will it meet their expectations?

The central questions among researchers and policy analysts appear to be: Will these individuals want or need to work as they approach retirement? Can the labor force accommodate increasing ranks of older workers? Will baby boomers work more years than their parents? The question of "to work or not to work" depends heavily on answers to questions regarding employers' willingness to hire older workers, the ability of older adults to adapt to the changing nature of workforce skills and job performance requirements, training and education issues, job placement issues, and workplace receptivity to older workers. Within these macro-level issues are a deeper set of questions that revolve around particular scenarios: What if employers do not want older workers? What if ageism and age discrimination inhibit job opportunities? What if older workers and retirees do not have the requisite job and technological skills, education, or health and mobility necessary to obtain well-paying work? What if the available jobs offer low wages and require low skills and thus force older workers to compete with young people, immigrants, and the economically vulnerable? And should a sufficient segment of the older population find that their economic circumstances are worsened because of the inability to find decently paying jobs, who will advocate for them and represent their interests in the public and private sectors?

One scenario is sanguine, with the decline in fertility rates leading to labor market scarcities and, in turn, creating a "worker's market." Baby boomers would then be in a powerful position, able to negotiate favorable conditions as they are sought after by employers in government and the private sector. For example, Burkhauser predicts that labor shortages will characterize the aging of baby boomers, leading to public policy and private sector focus on reintegrating older workers and providing the job training, skills, and education necessary to meet the needs of new industries, technologies, and employer requirements (Wolfe, 2007). Others focus on the opportunities for "encore careers" and refashioning a more meaningful and fulfilling work role in later years (Freedman, 2007).

But what if a less rosy scenario emerges? What if worker shortages and declining fertility rates do not open job opportunities for aging baby boomers? What becomes of those individuals shut out of jobs or forced to take ones that lower their standard of living? This chapter focuses primarily on the second scenario, in which we may find rising frustrations and a growing number of older persons dissatisfied with their economic, social, and employment circumstances. If that scenario emerges, public policy will be forced to intervene to meet the challenge of ensuring that elderly people live long, healthy, and secure lives with opportunities to continue working. This activist scenario rests on the premise of our democratic system of politics and government, with its history of and penchant for interest-group politics and self-correcting instances of public interventions when social problems reach a crisis point.

The response to the challenges associated with an increasing aging population has short- and long-term implications for the country's future economic and social stability and for the next generation of elderly people and retirees. To gain insights into these implications, we can review the current state of U.S. public policy regarding older workers and the historical preconditions for public- and private-sector response. The United States has a legacy of using laws, legislation, regulations, and tax incentives and disincentives to promote or inhibit employment among those classified as "old." These public policies (e.g., Social Security, disability and worker's compensation, guaranteed pensions, age discrimination lawsuits) have historically served to encourage or discourage workers and employers vis-à-vis aging workers. The question remains: To what extent might we once again draw on public policy to respond to these challenges in the future? What contemporary issues illuminate the possibility of a politics of aging that presses government and the private sector to respond to the employment needs of an older population?

This chapter explores the public policy implications of work and aging by examining the historical role of public policy, identifying the issues that may require the government to step in, and speculating on the pressures that may lead to a politics of aging, with older persons pressing the government, private sector, and broader society to find policy solutions to their need for employment and security in their later years.

HISTORICAL CONDITIONS IN PUBLIC POLICY

Examining the use of laws, regulations, legislation, administrative mandates, and judicial requirements to influence work and employment in the United States reveals an eclectic role for public policy. There have been no overarching, comprehensive, rational, or "big picture" approaches using public policy to influence or manage the nature of work and employment. And that is even truer when we examine the nature of public policy as it relates to older workers. Instead, we find a history of disparate, categorical, and opportunistic responses, each based on a particular concern rather than an overarching political, ideological, or policy consensus. To the extent that a political direction exists in the general field of work and aging, two eras emerge. The first, between 1935 and 1990, revolved around encouraging workers to move out of the workforce and into retirement. The second, after 1990, entails encouraging older workers to stay in the labor force and employers to retain and hire them.

Hudson and Gonyea (2007), in their seminal piece on the "evolving role of public policy in promoting work and retirement," find that public policy has both influenced and been influenced by changes in U.S. labor markets and families. The economic depression of the 1930s led to the Social Security Act of 1935, which has since become the prime lever in influencing the nature of work and employment. The Old Age and Survivors Insurance program (OASI), an integral feature of the Social Security Act, for example, provided a basic income floor that allowed eligible individuals 65 years and over the option to leave the workforce (and, for a large proportion of beneficiaries, became the primary "retirement program"). Other components of Social Security—including Supplemental Security Income (SSI) and the Disability Insurance program (DI)—provide a safety net of income support for those unable to work due to injury, disability, or chronic illness. Thus, although Social Security may not have been intended as the overarching policy approach to work and aging, it has become the primary policy tool influencing how and when older workers elect to work or retire. Social Security, along with pension plans, retiree health care coverage, and Medicare, are now the major public policies allowing workers to retire before becoming physically unable to work. In fact, a major political rationale for the passage of the Social Security Act was to move the elderly out of the workforce and make room for others, with its various provisions reinforcing this underlying premise.

Among its most powerful features are the early retirement provisions. These benefits, which are available at age 62, were introduced in 1956 for women and in 1962 for men. The earnings test served as an additional incentive for early retirement by creating limits to what one could earn in retirement without an offset in monthly benefits. The two provisions served as powerful inducements for early retirement; and even today, a major question facing aging baby boomers will be whether to "grab" the early retirement benefits at age 62, even if it means lower lifetime benefits, or wait until the Social Security normal retirement age (NRA), modified in 1983 to 66 by 2009 and 67 by 2027. That decision was ameliorated to some extent by the passage of H.R. 5, the Senior Citizens Freedom to Work Act of 2000 (Friedland, 2000). The bill repealed the retirement earnings limit for Social Security beneficiaries age 65–70 (once reaching the NRA, workers could now have unlimited wage and salary earnings without offsets in Social Security benefits) and began to shift the "work paradigm" from leaving early to staying in the workforce longer.

Another powerful set of public/private policies affecting trends in work and aging has been the evolving nature of defined benefit (DB) and defined contribution (DC) plans. Pensions and retirement guarantees have existed since the Civil War, with former Union soldiers receiving modest retirement support (Blanck and Song, 2007). Subsequently, corporations began to institute versions of a guaranteed pension, though their real impetus grew during and after World War II as the rise of labor unions forced pension coverage as an essential aspect of labor-management negotiations. These defined benefit plans were revolutionary in ensuring lifelong retirement income with an amount generally based on the employee's earnings and length of service (Schulz and Binstock, 2006). A primary feature was placing the onus on employers to set aside the necessary funds and to manage and invest them with financial acuity. Its overriding rationale, however, was not income security in old age but maintenance of worker loyalty and providing enticement for workers to retire.

In 1975 there were 20.1 million participants in traditional pension plans in the United States, rising to a peak of 24.2 million in 1984. By 2008, projections were that only 11 million participants would be in these pension plans (Gosselin, 2007). Problems with DB plans, including the lengthy vesting period, bankruptcies, and unfunded liabilities, led to the enactment of the Employee Retirement Income

Security Act (ERISA) of 1974. This legislation attempted to strengthen safeguards for DB plans through minimum vesting standards (e.g., 5 years) and the creation of the Pension Benefit Guarantee Corporation (PBGC) to insure partial coverage of insolvent DB Plans. The dramatic downgrading of DB plans has undermined the effectiveness of ERISA and PBGC, which face a large unfunded liability for the growing number of companies shifting DB liability to PBGC. Recent congressional decisions on funding requirements, together with the defaulting of many large pension plans (e.g., steel industry, auto supplies, and airlines), have only amplified these concerns. Even "new tech" companies such as IBM and Verizon are shedding their DB plans.

Into the void left by their decline has been a dramatic increase in defined contribution (DC) plans. The primary difference between the two plans is that DC plans place the responsibility on individuals for their own saving, including the amount they contribute and the management and investment of that money. Put simply, if employees save and invest wisely, they will have substantial retirement income, but if they squander the opportunity, they may need to work longer or find alternative sources of support. Some employers add a supplement to DC plans (matching or profit sharing), and a variety of offshoots have evolved, including so-called hybrid pension plans that combine features of DB and DC plans. A major impetus for the shift to DC plans has been changes to tax laws, particularly the Revenue Act of 1978 that added section 401(k) to the tax codes, allowing employees to make tax-deferred contributions to employer-sponsored plans (Schulz and Binstock, 2006).

A dramatic shift has thus occurred over the last thirty years, with DB plans decreasing and DC plans increasing, essentially moving the onus for retirement from employers to employees. Hudson and Gonyea (2007) report that defined contribution plans in fact increased from 26 percent in 1975 to 58 percent in 1998, with an average 401(k) accumulation of $42,000. Yet only about half of the labor force is currently covered by some form of pension plan. The result is that, with lower accumulation and retirement income, retirees will be at increased risk, providing a strong impetus for staying in the workforce longer. Recent public policy changes have thus clearly affected incentives to stay employed longer, whether by choice or necessity.

A combination of regulatory, legislative, and public mandates further complicates the picture, exerting subtle pressures to encourage workers to keep working. The passage of the Age Discrimination in Employment Act (ADEA) in 1967 protects workers 40 or older from workplace ageism, indirectly allowing them to stay in their jobs longer if they wish. Some exemptions do exist for police officers, air traffic controllers, and airline pilots; and there are concerns that the potential for litigation might in fact discourage employers from retaining or hiring older workers. Another issue is the EEOC (Equal Employment Opportunity Commission), which is charged with enforcing provisions of the ADEA. It tends to match its enforcement with the ideology of a presidential administration—with those who favor strong government oversight and regulation being more aggressive, and those who support limited government and weak enforcement being less inclined to pursue instances of workplace discrimination. Republican administrations from Reagan forward have thus been lax in enforcing the rules, undermining the potential to benefit older workers.

More tangential to work and aging are two other major civil rights safeguards: Title VII of the Civil Rights Act, and the Americans with Disabilities Act (ADA), which are both designed to allow compensatory or punitive damages to those unfairly discriminated against (Dennis and Thomas, 2007). More recent policy developments include the Pension Protection Act of 2006, intended to strengthen defined benefit plans by allowing those aged 62 or older to receive benefits while working (Hudson and Gonyea, 2007), and automatic enrollment features that make it easier for workers to take advantage of DC plans and diversified employer stock holdings in 401(k) plans. These features aid workers in saving more and, if they wish, working longer, while the shift to DC plans, the strains on Social Security and Medicare, increasing health care costs, and general decline in economic security all serve to force workers to stay in the labor force longer than they used to and potentially longer than they want to.

WORK AND AGING: POLITICAL AND POLICY IMPLICATIONS

What are the implications of this assortment of public policies, based on tax codes, regulations, laws, legislation, or civil rights safeguards? As mentioned earlier, we have no overarching or comprehensive public policies designed to explicitly oversee or influence the nature of work and aging. What does emerge from this picture is the redefinition of the nature and role of retirement and work, with clear trends toward working longer and later into old age. There will always be some segments of the workforce that can and will be able to retire at relatively younger ages, say between 50 and 55, and have the health care and pension coverage to maintain a good quality of life in their retirement. Successful entrepreneurs, public sector employees, and academics in well-funded universities will still be able to leave the workforce at a younger age. They will become the new privileged class, reinforcing a stereotype of older retirees off to their second or third vacation homes, to see the country in their RVs (while anecdotal, this stereotype was featured on a cover of a national magazine), and generally enjoying a life of leisure and recreation. Some will want to reenter the workforce on their own terms for extra discretionary income, socialization, to keep busy, or to remain vibrant in new careers and endeavors. They will be the lucky ones who can use early retirement for their benefit, and in large measure they will find little need for public policy assistance.

However, in reviewing the historical preconditions to work and aging, we find that the incentives to retire early, whether via Social Security provisions, defined benefit plans, or tax incentives to private employers, has existed for a relatively short period of time. The expectation of retirement with some guarantee that one could enjoy leisure and recreation with adequate income and security has in fact only existed for the 60 or so years since the end of World War II. This expectation remains strong today, even as a host of factors coalesce to create a situation where individuals will have fewer protections, fewer guarantees of alternative retirement income, and a diminished social safety net in retirement. For example, health considerations have always been an important factor influencing retirement decisions (Friedland, 2000). The prevalence of retiree health care coverage and Medicare provided an important element of security in knowing that one could leave the workforce and retain medical coverage through the employer, private insurance companies, or government. With the dramatic evisceration of retiree health care coverage in the private sector, growing unfunded liabilities among public agencies, and the fiscal pressures facing Medicare, that protection is diminishing. For an increasing number of workers, a default policy appears to be arising: forcing them to stay in the workforce as long as possible to maintain health care coverage and to account for diminished retirement security.

UNFORESEEN CONSEQUENCES

By 2004, up to 43 percent of working-age households were financially unprepared for retirement, compared with 31 percent in 1983 (Hacker, 2007). This "risk shift" increases the number of retirees that may be forced to work in retirement. If this scenario is accurate and if it becomes the case for growing numbers of baby boomers, then we must ask whether there will be increased pressure and demands from future retirees for government or the private sector to intervene and ameliorate this growing sense of insecurity and vulnerability. What might be the issues and pressure points that would lead toward a renewed spirit of political activism and public policies? Might we see a renewed civil rights movement emerge in the next twenty years predicated, in part, on work and aging?

A number of issues compound and complicate this potential scenario. They include ageism (e.g., assuming negative attributes based on a given age, such as that older workers are unable to use new technology) and age discrimination, globalization, diversity and immigration, and growing retirement insecurity. Ageism and age discrimination are subtle yet effective barriers to employment and work options. Few conclusive data exist to measure the extent of ageism and age discrimination, with the EEOC, at least in Republican administrations, generally considered an ineffective tool for tracking and enforcement. For example, according to Dennis and Thomas (2007), the EEOC filed only 29 lawsuits out of 19,921 age discrimination charges brought to them in 2002. Thus, to the extent that employers, especially in the private sector, subtly or overtly create barriers for older workers based on being too slow, too expensive, or perceived as unable to effectively perform their jobs, they may be building a legion of disgruntled older workers anxious but unable to find or retain employment. The case of Circuit City, which laid off 3,400 of its older workers in 2007 because they were too expensive while offering them the opportunity to apply for their positions at entry-level wages, may be the tip of a proverbial iceberg. It remains to be seen if ageism and age discrimination exacerbate frustrations and resentments among future retirees.

Globalization and the internationalization of work and business has brought great benefits to the U.S. economy and world trade. Yet this trend may also create additional barriers to older workers. Outsourcing, including telemarketing in India and the Philippines, low-wage manufacturing in China and Indonesia, and auto plants in Mexico, clearly benefits other nations and our own consumers, but it simultaneously reduces the number of low-skilled jobs in this country. On the other hand, better jobs are created here that require a higher level of skills, education, and technological abilities, though it is unclear whether aging baby boomers and other retirees can meet those needs. Again, the extent to which globalization complicates the work options for older persons is an open question.

Diversity, immigration, and fertility rates are a third factor in the equation. The growing diversity of the United States and the growing populations of black, Latino, and Asian Americans as well as immigrants from other countries is amply chronicled, and the United States is moving toward a majority of minorities (as already seen in California and other regions). How might the growing numbers of migrants and immigrants affect a society where there are also growing numbers of older person and retirees? What might that mean for work and aging? Two related questions emerge: the extent to which aging minorities have a unique set of issues and challenges that complicate the story—including larger families, longer life expectancy (for Latinos), lower retirement savings and health care coverage, less education, and lower economic security—and the ways that immigrant populations may delimit the availability of jobs traditionally filled by elderly or semi-retired people.

BLOWBACK AND PUBLIC ANXIETY

A case study of long-term care facilities gives one set of clues. In places like California, nursing homes, assisted living facilities, and long-term care agencies (e.g., home health) demonstrate a dramatic visual display of age-race stratification. It is not uncommon to enter a nursing home and find that the owners are white males; the top administrators, white male and females; the RNs, diverse females; and the lower-paid and "hands-on" staff (e.g., CNAs, aides, janitors) are non-English speaking and often from Mexico, the Philippines, and the Caribbean. The residents, in turn, are primarily English-speaking white females, while the available caregivers, willing to work for minimum wage and no health insurance or transportation allowance, are invariably recent immigrants (generally with limited English-speaking skills).

Much research and debate has surrounded the decline in defined benefit plans; the inadequacy and insecurity of defined contribution plans; abysmal saving rates, especially among baby boomers; and the decline in retiree health care coverage. Of course, Medicare and Medicaid programs continue to provide substantial health care coverage to those over 65 years of age, low-income, or totally disabled. Yet those important health entitlement programs are facing serious financial problems, and state and federal governments continue to struggle to meet the escalating costs of health and medical care for eligible recipients. There are real questions about the extent to which Medicare, in particular, will provide at least the same level of coverage and costs to the next generation of Medicare beneficiaries, particularly as it now draws on its trust fund. And there are growing frustrations among state governments regarding the huge share of their revenue going to Medicaid costs (often persisting as one of the two largest state expenditures along with education). Assuming a terminal prognosis for Medicare and Medicaid, further declines in retiree health care coverage, and the increased reliance on defined contributions plans, where does that leave older generations? To what extent will increasing numbers of retirees be forced to work, even if in low-wage, nonbenefit jobs (e.g., retail, service, fast food), assuming that future entrepreneurs and businesses will desire older workers?

Before addressing this admittedly negative scenario, one must acknowledge that a substantial segment of the population will not face these dilemmas. Government workers, for example, particularly those in municipal, county, state and federal occupations, are blessed with generous pensions and retiree health care coverage. There are retirees with multiple sources of pension coverage (government, military, academic, Social Security). And of course there are private sector workers whose 401(k) plans, severance pay, dividend and stock accumulations, and windfall profits make them immune to these dilemmas. To add to their good fortune, many maintain good health and mobility, have acquired higher education or continuing education, and are in well-compensated industries that welcome the wisdom, experience, and work history that older workers can bring. To this group, using public policy to address issues of work and aging makes little sense. However, is this outlook unduly optimistic? Might even the privileged and secure retirees and older workers face surprises in their expectations of an active and secure retirement?

One clue lies with publicly funded pensions and government retirees. A substantial proportion of the labor force participates in some form of government retirement program. Yet these funds are facing growing unfunded liabilities. The penchant for elected officials and labor unions to negotiate expanded benefits and compensations has led to promises unfunded with current dollars. The Financial Accounting Standards Board in 2003 issued regulations requiring details about their defined benefit plans as well as projections about what they may owe in future outlays and how much of that amount is prefunded. Not surprisingly, most public pension plans and retiree health care benefits are inadequately funded. These unfunded liabilities are leading to an interesting blowback, as conservative and even moderate legislators are alarmed and are proposing to scale back benefits or create two-tier retirement plans (future workers no longer receive DB guarantees and must rely on DC plans). Liberal legislators (those relying on government and taxes to resolve these dilemmas) and their labor and union allies, on the other hand, argue either that these unfunded liabilities are not a serious financial risk or that all individuals should enjoy guaranteed pensions and retiree health care coverage and that public workers should not be penalized for protecting their social safety net. In either case, as voters and taxpayers become increasingly aware that these escalating costs may result in reduced services and programs, a voters' revolt may occur (not unlike proposition 13 in California). Why, individual citizens may reason, should I see longer lines at the Department of Motor Vehicles, higher property and sales taxes, and higher tuition in public colleges to pay for generous benefits to government workers when

I cannot afford health insurance myself and I must work hard without the cushy jobs and retirement benefits accrued to public employees? Whether or not this simplistic and superficial view of a complex policy problem has merit, what is likely to occur on the street level are citizen initiatives to roll back government benefits and promises. Such is often the nature of a pluralistic democracy when a critical mass of citizens feels discriminated against or believes they are unfairly burdened by others.

CONCLUSION

This broad overview of issues, concerns, and trends may not directly address the more technical question of whether older workers will want to work, can find work, will be hired, and have the qualification and skills to meet the needs of the twenty-first-century global economy. Yet the larger concern for public policy may well be whether government will be forced to step in and legislate, regulate, and otherwise mandate how the public and private sector should accommodate older persons who need to work. The historic public policy response has been fragmented and opportunistic, with the workforce and employment largely influenced by one major public program: Social Security.

One possible response to the challenge is a renewed political activism among older and aging workers organizing to pressure government to intervene on their behalf. What this may entail in terms of legislative proposals, civil rights safeguards, employer mandates, and job and training programs is uncertain. Yet the first vestiges of this potential movement are evident within the baby-boomer population. They will represent a large retiree population faced with growing disparities between those doing well in old age and those vulnerable to economic and health setbacks. This cohort was raised with a heightened sense of entitlement and expectations of a good old age, at least as good as that of their parents, who enjoyed financially robust entitlements with Medicare and Social Security. At the same time, these "aging boomers" are beginning to show a desire to "give back" and contribute to their communities and the larger society. The return to volunteerism and service is a positive resource, given their numbers and the higher educational levels of the cohort. Whether that correlates to changing skill requirements remains to be seen.

Many baby boomers will need to do more than volunteer work to supplement their retirement income and pay for their medical and long-term care costs. The traditional three-legged stool envisioned by the proponents of the Social Security Act of 1935 (savings, pension, Social Security) no longer applies to the new economics of aging. With little savings and fewer pension guarantees, for large numbers of elderly people, especially women, minorities, and disabled people, Social Security is their retirement program. For others, their new retirement stool is composed of four parts: (a) whatever pension contributions and savings they have amassed, (b) assistance from children and others, (c) the equity in their homes (if they own a home), and (d) continued employment. The new four-legged stool will depend most heavily on the availability of jobs and work, and we can thus expect a level of political and policy attention to this issue unlike anything seen since the 1930s.

Herein lies the seeds of a new potential politics of aging and work. Given the diverse array of factors and trends lending themselves to this scenario, it appears that public policy will once again play a central role in determining how the workforce and the workplace adjust to the competing demands of aging, longevity, vulnerability, and retirement security. Without some intervention by the government and the private sector, a whole generation of future retirees stands in jeopardy of great economic peril. The current trend toward working longer may lead to demands that public policy regulate the workplace. The nature of this political and policy intervention is uncertain, but it may well be comparable in scope to what occurred in the 1930s and 1960s.

REFERENCES

Blanck, P., and Song, C. 2007. Never forget what they did here: Civil War Pensions for Gettysburg Union Army Veterans and Disability in nineteenth-century America. *William and Mary Law Review* 44 (3): 1109–71.

Dennis, H., and Thomas, K. 2007. Ageism in the workplace. *Generations* 31 (1): 84–89.

Freedman, M. 2007. In search of an encore career. *San Jose Mercury News: Perspective,* 3 June, 1, 3.

Friedland, R. 2000. Will baby boomers work more years than their parents did? National Academy on an Aging Society, Washington, DC.

Gordon, M., Johnson, R., and Murphy, D. 2006. *Why Do Boomers Plan to Work So Long?* www.urban.org/urs.cfm?ID=311386.

Gosselin, P. 2007. Study says more employers doing away with pensions. *Los Angeles Times,* 11 July, A16.

Hacker, J. 2007. The great risk shifter: Issues for aging and public policy. *Public Policy and Aging Report* 17 (2): 1–7.

Hudson, R., and Gonyea, J. 2007. The evolving role of public policy in promoting work and retirement. *Generations* 31 (1): 68–75.

Schulz, J., and Binstock, R. 2006. *Aging Nation.* Westport, CT: Praeger.

Wolfe, W. 2007. Job search ahead as boomers retire. (Minneapolis) *Star Tribune,* 7 June.

CHAPTER FIVE

Implications of an Aging Workforce

An Industry Perspective

VICKI L. HANSON, PH.D.,
AND ERIC LESSER, M.B.A.

In much of the developed world, the increase in the number of older workers and the slowing of birthrates have many companies concerned about the current and future state of the workforce. In countries ranging from the United States to Germany, France, Australia, and Japan, much has been recently written about the impact of the retiring baby boom generation and the corporate and societal impacts of such a shift. In our work with companies, we are seeing organizations in a number of industries begin to consider the implications of these demographic shifts on their workforce. While not every company will be facing significant challenges associated with these changes, a number of industries have already started to feel their impact. This chapter will highlight some of the industries in which this issue has started to have an effect and describe how various organizations are dealing with it. In addition, it will outline some next steps for organizations beginning to address this unique situation and will identify additional areas for further research.

AN INDUSTRY VIEW OF CHANGING
WORKFORCE DEMOGRAPHICS

Challenges associated with changing workforce demographics are starting to manifest themselves across a number of industries. While some industries, such as media and entertainment, have been less affected by the increasing numbers of older workers, others are dealing with turnover of experienced professionals whose judgment and experience significantly contribute to their personal effectiveness and organizational performance. Consider the following three examples.

Health Care

In the nursing industry, the average age of nurses is expected to continue to rise. In 1983, half of the nursing workforce was under the age of 35; today that number is less than 22 percent (Cohen, 2006). The average age of nurses is expected to climb to 45.4 years by the year 2010, and the U.S. nursing shortage is expected to increase from 6 percent today to 29 percent in 2020. Given the increasing demands for health care professionals as the result of the aging population, the increasing age of the nursing population represents a significant challenge from both demand and supply perspectives.

Electric Utilities

The electric utility industry is facing significant demographic issues. According to Michael Ashworth, a researcher at Carnegie Mellon University, about half of the country's 400,000 electric utility workers will be eligible to retire within the next five years (Greene, 2005). A 2002 Electric Power Research Institute (EPRI) survey of utility management and supervisory staff indicated that while nearly 92 percent of respondents believed that losing unique, valuable expertise would pose a problem for them within the next five years, only 30 percent said they had a plan in place to capture knowledge from experienced personnel that could be made available to new hires (Hylko, 2005).

The problems facing the electric utility industry are being magnified in the nuclear power industry. Demographic challenges have taken on increasing importance as companies are looking to revisit nuclear power as an alternative source of power. For example, today there are two dozen proposals for new reactors in the United States alone. However, the average age of individuals in the nuclear power sector is 48, with almost 30 percent of the workforce eligible to retire by 2010 (Aston, 2007).

A Nuclear Energy Institute (NEI) survey of current nuclear power generation staffing levels estimated that about 20,000 positions (approximately 45% of the current workforce) will need to be filled over the next five years. Retirements are expected to account for more than 60 percent of attrition in this time frame, which represents approximately a 150 percent increase over current levels. Even if only the most likely retirees leave the workforce, an estimated 16,000 employees will be lost to retirement alone (Juliano and Valocchi, 2003).

Even the Nuclear Regulatory Commission, the overseeing body of the nuclear industry, is facing demographic challenges (Beattie, 2007). According to a 2007 GAO report, "If overall workforce and resource allocations are not balanced, NRC risks overextending its available workforce, undermining its employee satisfaction and potentially increasing its attrition. . . . if so, reviewing mission critical activities within estimated time frames could become more difficult and could adversely affect NRC's ability to ensure a safe and secure nuclear power industry" (44).

Mining

The aging population and the rising demand for raw materials coming from growing economies such as China have created unique labor shortages in the mining industry. The demand for additional workers exists in key mining export countries such as Canada, which is predicting a shortage of between 3,600 and 7,000 positions a year for the next ten years, according to a report by the Government of Canada's Sector Council Program (Leung, 2006). In Australia the figures are even more dramatic: it is estimated that by 2015, the industry will require an additional 70,000 employees compared with their staffing today (Minerals Council of Australia, 2006). Tom Albanese, the CEO of Rio Tinto, one of the largest mining companies in the world, noted in an interview that "as we look ahead, particularly over the next 20 to 30 years, we have an aging demographic within the sector, and we're probably seeing even more (professionals) retiring, even adding to this challenge" (Kosich, 2007).

As is clear from these examples, a number of industries are being significantly affected by workforce demographics. The full extent of the problem in some cases has yet to be acknowledged. Some companies, however, are taking innovative steps to address the issues.

STRATEGIES FOR ADDRESSING
THE MATURING WORKFORCE

Given the challenges that industries are encountering, we see four strategies that companies are employing to mitigate risks associated with mature workers. These strategies, summarized in table 5.1, take a multipronged approach to addressing issues related to maturing workers.

TABLE 5.1
*Four strategies for addressing issues
of a maturing workforce*

Strategy 1: Workforce management
    Attracting and retaining older workers
Strategy 2: Knowledge transfer
    Preserving and transferring critical knowledge
Strategy 3: Training
    Providing appropriate opportunities for updating of skills
Strategy 4: Addressing needs and preferences
    Job options and technology accommodations

Strategy 1: Adjusting Workforce Management Strategies

Recognizing both the number of employees who are leaving the organization and the potentially smaller pools of workers entering the workforce, companies are starting to look for new sources of labor. One of the primary sources is mature workers themselves, and companies are looking for means to both attract and retain older workers. Many older workers, motivated either by financial need or simply by the desire to remain active, are looking for opportunities to remain in the workforce, at least in a part-time capacity. For example, a study from Rutgers University indicates that nearly seven out of every ten workers report that they plan to continue to work for pay following retirement from their primary job (Reynolds, Ridley, and Van Horn, 2005).

Organizations are finding that mature workers bring a significant amount of benefit to their employers. For example, in 1999 Harris Interactive conducted a U.S. survey of 774 human resource directors in which 80 percent reported that older workers had lower turnover and lower absenteeism; 75 percent indicated that older workers had higher levels of commitment; and 74 percent thought that older workers were more reliable (Peterson and Spiker, 2005).

In addition, mature workers may be valuable in helping companies service their older customer base, which for many industries has been steadily increasing. For example, Westpac, a major financial services institution based in Australia, found that its older customers were more likely to feel comfortable discussing financial issues with advisors from a similar demographic. To address this issue, it recruited and trained approximately 900 persons who were over 55 years of age and looking to establish a second career as financial planners (Nixon, 2002). Similarly, the YMCA of Rochester found that many of its newer fitness members were older baby boomers who had little or no experience in working with weight and aerobics machines. In 2004 it began to target older workers, and today 20 percent of its employees are older than 50. They found that these mature employees were not only able to relate better to older customers but their attrition rate was less than 2 percent, compared with 20 percent overall (Schwinn, 2007).

As a result of the opportunity presented by an increase in maturing workers, there has been a rise in the number of recruitment firms that have started to cater to this demographic. Firms such as Experience Works, YourEncore, Retirement jobs.com, and ContinuingCareers.com serve as intermediaries in a secondary labor market for recent retirees. YourEncore, for example, serves as a marketing and contracting agent for retired scientists and product designers looking for project-based work, matching them with companies such as P&G, Eli Lilly, and Boeing.

The opportunity for many companies is not only the attraction of mature workers from the outside but the retention of older workers within the organization. Organizations such as The Aerospace Corporate, a defense contractor; Stanley Consultants, an engineering firm; and Mitre, a consulting firm focused on the public sector, have been seen as a successful in allowing mature workers to work either on a part-time or a project-by-project basis. These part-time arrangements not only give organizations the flexibility to cover peaks in their demand but also allow them to retain critical experience along the way. As George Paulikas, a retired executive vice president and a program participant, stated, "The Retiree Casual program keeps expertise around and helps transfer it to others. People often remark that we don't have many consultants around here. Actually, we do, but they are called retirees, and they already know the business inside out" (Dychtwald, Erickson, and Morison, 2004).

For organizations that recognize the impact that changing workforce demographics will have, workforce analytics can be used to better understand the magnitude of the risks of retirement and attrition in the organization. Before any companies begin to address the challenges of a maturing workforce, their first step is to understand where their organizations are currently at risk for key employees walking out the door. We have found that few if any companies have done an effective job at segmenting their workforce and identifying positions that are most vulnerable in their organization. In fact, a survey by the Boston College Center on Aging at Work indicated that only one-third of employers reported that their organization had made projections about retirement rates of their workers to either a moderate (24%) or great (10%) extent (Pitt-Catsouphes, Smyer, Matz-Costa, and Kane, 2007).

Firms need to address three areas of analysis. First, organizations should understand the dynamics of their internal and external labor markets. Firms must be able to disaggregate their workforce to identify the positions that are most at risk with respect to retirement eligibility and strategic importance to the firm. Then they need to better understand the dynamics of when retirement-eligible personnel actually decide to retire and understand the forces that influence that decision. Also, firms need to be able to determine the need for the skills of those who are retiring, including how long it will take to train replacements and enable them to become productive in their new roles. For roles that require formal training or certification, this process could be measured in months, if not years. Finally, companies should also consider employing techniques such as social network analysis to better understand the connections and relationships of specific employees that are leaving and their jobs, and the impact of those departures on other employees within the organization.

Strategy 2: Preserving and Transferring Critical Knowledge

While numerous strategies can be enacted to retain employees, eventually individuals leave the organization. With their departure, they take a career's worth of documents, contacts, and experiences that are difficult to replicate. The subject of knowledge transfer has taken on significant importance in many organizations. In a survey of learning executives conducted by IBM and the American Society for Training and Development (ASTD), knowledge transfer issues were the highest rated challenge associated with changing workforce demographics, cited by almost 30 percent of participants (Lesser and Rivera, 2006). As one respondent noted, "We need to develop the preoccupation for knowledge transfer and information sharing at all levels of the organization, and not only when employees are leaving. It should be considered at all times." Despite this concern, less than half of the organizations surveyed are specifically addressing knowledge transfer as part of their overall learning strategy, with more than one-quarter indicating they are not addressing the issues at all.

For those who are involved in promoting knowledge transfer, several techniques have been used. Mentoring has been one of the more frequently used approaches to knowledge transfer. According to the IBM/ASTD study, 60 percent of companies use some form of mentoring as a way of transferring knowledge between workers of different generations (Lesser and Rivera, 2006). Mentoring has the advantage of developing the one-to-one relationships that facilitate the transfer of experiential, or tacit, knowledge. Research conducted by Dorothy Leonard at Harvard Business School and Walter Swap at Tufts University suggests that the most effective mentoring relationships focus on "learning while doing," where the mentor provides guidance to the student that is specifically geared to situations the student is facing (Leonard and Swap, 2005). However, mentoring represents a fairly time- and labor-intensive activity that requires ongoing interaction between both parties who need to develop a mutual sense of trust toward one another.

Relatively few companies are incorporating knowledge transfer into their more traditional learning programs. For example, only 30 percent are using mature workers to deliver classroom content, 29 percent are fostering the development of communities of practice, and 29 percent are capturing and embedding the lessons from mature workers into existing learning programs. For some companies, a lack of urgency has not placed this issue high on the corporate agenda; for others, the learning function has not had the mandate or the necessary skills to make a contribution in this area. However, a number of organizations have seen value in building mature workers' experiences directly into their training and community development programs. For example, Los Alamos Nuclear Laboratory brought back retired workers to teach in their postgraduate university on nuclear technologies. Much of the instructors' focus is on passing along experiential knowledge around nuclear tests that had been conducted even before the birth of many of the program's participants (Ratliff, 2002).

Several companies have focused their knowledge transfer efforts around the orientation process. Siemens, for example, has developed a "4 by 6" integration process, where new employees have four defined points of knowledge transfer. During the first six hours, there is an initial job orientation. Within the first six days, there is a thorough discussion between the new employee and the manager to develop a mutual agreement for integration into the new job based on information outlined in the job profile. For the next six weeks, there is a close working relationship between the new and departing employees. Finally, after six months, there is a feedback session between the new employee and the manager to discuss the results of the knowledge transfer (American Productivity and Quality Center, 2002).

Similarly, when West Australian Petroleum Proprietary Limited identifies an employee who is about to retire, the company attempts to find a replacement approximately three months before the planned retirement date. For the retiring employee's last three months, he or she is able to work at a reduced schedule while drawing full salary. During this time, however, the retiree is expected to "diligently apply himself or herself to instructing their successor until they are capable of assuming full responsibility for the job." This transition period provides the incumbent with the opportunity to share with their replacement some of the critical knowledge that might not be easily captured or stored (Government of Western Australia, 2004).

Both organizations have found that building knowledge transfer into the orientation process can be a valuable, cost-effective tool in ensuring the proper handoff between incumbents and newcomers. However, this approach can only be effective when the retirements are planned and replacements can be identified with a sufficient lead time so that overlaps can occur. Furthermore, the process requires a reasonable amount of time for both parties to interact because it will take the new employee time to build sufficient context necessary for the knowledge transfer to occur.

Strategy 3: Providing Appropriate Opportunities for Updating of Skills

Today's rapid advances in technology can lead to skill obsolesce. Market competition demands that workers stay up-to-date, thus requiring continuous learning. The issue of how best to address the need for updating skills requires an understanding of the learning needs of older workers and, increasingly, how these needs can be addressed in a multigenerational workforce that has a diversity in learning styles.

Surveys indicate that older workers typically receive less training than their younger counterparts (Lesser and Rivera, 2006). It is unclear whether this is due primarily to resistance on the part of older workers or reluctance on the part of employers to invest. It may also have to do with perceived differences in learning styles for older and younger workers. The previously mentioned IBM/ASTD study found that executives who oversee learning initiatives in their company believe that older and younger workers learn by very different means. The perception is that older workers learn best from classroom or directed instruction, find training an arduous process, and are not completely comfortable with technology (Lancaster and Stillman, 2003). In contrast, the perception is that younger workers are collaborative learners, consider skill updating to be an ongoing process, and expect technology to be fully integrated into their environment. Research with older workers themselves, however, has found them receptive to the use of technology and wishing to get the training they need to be able to use technology (Czaja and Moen, 2004; Lesser and Rivera, 2006; Convertino et al., 2007). Demands to drive down training costs have lead to technology-mediated training by some employers. This is a Catch-22 situation if the employee needs training on the technology itself.

It may be the case, however, that in many technology-driven industries traditional distinctions between working and learning are evaporating (Vicente, 2000; Convertino et al., 2007). That is, the work situation and work tools may foster continuous learning on the job. Specifically, given rapid changes in technology and services, job demands will require workers to respond to novel situations that were not anticipated during training. Workers will need to be appropriately flexible to make decisions for which they were not specifically trained. Vicente argues: "The global knowledge-based economy will continue to transform the landscape of modern work. Changing and unpredictable circumstances will be the norm. As a result, there is an increasing need for workers, managers, and organizations to become more flexible and adaptive than in the past. These trends suggest that the requirement to design for adaptation will only increase in the future" (Vicente, 2000, 270). In this analysis, adaptation is considered a case of continuous learning.

Continuous learning and requirements for workers to use technology in unanticipated ways will be a consideration in the training needs of older adults. For workers re-entering the labor force or updating skills for current employment, procedural training techniques will not be sufficient in many cases. Technology that can support continuous learning on the job may prove to be an important design point in the coming years.

Not all training needs to be technology-mediated, however. As previously discussed, mentoring can also provide an opportunity for meeting training requirements. Unfortunately, negative stereotypes sometimes held by younger workers about their older counterparts—and vice versa—could undermine the success of mentoring programs. Pairing older and young workers, however, has the potential to allow each to benefit from the strengths of others and, as discussed earlier, can be extremely valuable for knowledge transfer (Convertino, Farooq, Rosson, and Carroll, 2005; Lahey, 2007).

Consider an interesting twist on traditional mentoring in which General Electric sought to improve the technology skills of older workers by having younger workers mentor them (Breen, 2001). In this case, they paired senior managers with younger employees, and the younger employees taught the managers about Web technologies. The managers gained skills needed for successful business in the Internet age. As an added bonus, the younger workers made valuable contacts with executives that otherwise would have been unlikely to have happened.

We are also starting to see employers partner with community colleges and other third parties to provide retraining services for older workers. For example, the states of Michigan and North Carolina have brought together companies and educational institutions to provide retraining for manufacturing workers who are interested in pursuing second careers in the health care field (Marquez, 2007). "Older workers are more loyal and a much more stable workforce," says Robyn Stone, senior vice president for research at the American Association of Homes and Services for the Aging, a not-for-profit nursing home association based in Washington. "The potential to recruit these workers is great for areas that have been heavy in manufacturing as they transition into a service-sector economy."

Strategy 4: Addressing the Needs and Preferences of Older Workers

The needs and preferences of older adults can be seen both in job choices and in accommodations that may be needed to perform the job.

One example of job choices is in flexible or alternative work arrangements, some of which have been mentioned previously. The attraction of alternative work arrangements is not limited to older workers. Options such as part-time work, flexible hours, and telecommuting are prevalent throughout the workforce and have been found to provide many benefits (Bond, Galinsky, Kim, and Brownfield, 2005; McGuire, Kenney, and Brashler, n.d.). Approximately one quarter of the working-age population have jobs with some type of flexibility, either formally or informally. Flexibility in the number of hours and the scheduling of hours are two of the more common arrangements. Less common are options for telework and commuting, although these appear to be highly industry specific, with few telecommuters in public administration or armed forces, but as high as 20 percent telecommuters in some scientific and professional occupations (McGuire et al., n.d.). Benefits of alternative work arrangements include less (particularly unscheduled) absenteeism, greater job satisfaction, more inclination to stay with the job, and greater engagement with the job. The 2005 National Study of Employers concludes:

> In the seven years since we last conducted this study, the economy has been quite volatile and common wisdom would have it that employers would cut back on the work life assistance they offer employees. Except for reductions in how much employers pay toward benefits that cost money (their contribution to health care, disability programs, and pension plans), we did not find this to be the case. Employers have largely maintained or increased the support they provide to employees in managing their personal and family lives, probably because, as they report, these are increasingly seen as strategic business tools for recruitment, retention, commitment, and productivity—and for making work "work" for both employers and employees. (Bond et al., 2005, 28)

This conclusion bodes well for many older workers who are looking for flexible job arrangements as they seek employment or plan to remain in the workforce.

Another example of job choices is that of older workers seeking jobs that rely more on mental than physical abilities. In part, this can be considered the result of technological change in industries that make knowledge, rather than labor, an important job qualification. With increasing reliance on technology, however, the abilities of older workers to use these technologies must be considered.

Aging can bring about the need for accessible technology as new disabilities arise and existing mild impairments become more severe. Many of these changes in perception, movement, and cognition can affect ability to use technology. The Americans with Disabilities Act (ADA) requires employers to make reasonable accommodations for workers with disabilities. One aspect of this is the provision of assistive technology when needed to do the job.

Designers of software for the workplace have not tended to address the needs of older workers. Critically, little attention has been paid to the current multigenerational aspect of workforce and the software and technology demands this imposes (Gregor, Newell, and Zajicek, 2002; Hanson, Snow-Weaver, and Trewin, 2006; Czaja and Lee, 2007). Differences in use of technology are widespread. With the emergence of collaborative tools designed to support a variety of business needs such as e-mail, instant messaging, shared editors, and calendars, it is important to understand the requirements for these tools in supporting the interaction of different generations of workers. Notably, collaboration tools may be emerging not only as a way to facilitate contact among employees but also as a means of knowledge transfer for retiring employees.

RESEARCH DIRECTIONS

Given the enormous impact that changing demographics will create in the workplace, it is important to consider areas in which industry could benefit from research. As summarized in table 5.2, we suggest important research topics for each of the strategies discussed.

With respect to *workforce management*, companies need to develop the capability to effectively predict the skills and capabilities they currently need and to anticipate future needs. Specific topics that could be explored include: (1) predictive modeling techniques that would anticipate the supply and demand for various key skills and capabilities; (2) the use of "knowledge marketplaces" to identify and bring together relevant skills on a global basis; and (3) the corporate capabil-

TABLE 5.2.
Areas of research related to industry needs in the face of a maturing workforce

Strategy 1: Workforce management
  Capability that allows companies to effectively predict the skills and capabilities they
  currently need and anticipate needing in the future
Strategy 2: Knowledge transfer
  Contingency models; effectiveness of various techniques; techniques for rapid transfer;
  social networks
Strategy 3: Training
  Effectiveness of training methods, especially the role of technology
Strategy 4: Addressing needs and preferences
  Understanding interactions with experience; appropriate collaboration tools

ities (i.e., people, processes, and tools) necessary to effectively manage the current and future workforce needs of a global organization.

The effectiveness of *knowledge transfer* is an area in which there is a significant amount of anecdotal evidence but little academic research. Among the issues that could be explored are: (1) the development of a contingency model approach to knowledge capture and transfer that incorporates elements such as the content domain, the expected lifecycle of the knowledge, and the personal characteristics of the knowledge sender and receiver; (2) the effectiveness of multimedia capturing techniques (such as videotaping) in the transfer of experiential knowledge; (3) methods for quickly being able to transfer knowledge and reducing time-to-competence for employees replacing older workers; and (4) understanding the value of the social networks of older employees and developing techniques to influence social network development in the absence of older workers.

Better understanding of *training* is also needed. Research is needed regarding training methods that can be successfully used by older as well as younger workers—investigations of the potential for technology's role will be key.

Addressing the needs and preferences of workers of various ages is another area needing further research. The experience that older workers bring to a job is critical. However, perceptual and cognitive changes that accompany aging may require certain accommodations, particularly in a multigenerational workplace. Some topics for requiring further research include: (1) better data about the relationship between physical declines and experience as they factor into job performance; (2) better understanding of inclusive designs that will enable older adults to more easily use technology; and (3) improved collaborative workplace tools to facilitate communication between younger and older workers.

In general, the collaboration of industry and universities is a valuable approach to addressing these issues. At IBM, the importance of industry working with university researchers is highlighted by a recent partnership between IBM researchers and university researchers at the University of Miami and the University of Dundee. The goal of this work is to find innovative solutions to technology issues that allow maturing workers to remain in the workforce.

CONCLUSION

The changing demographics of the workforce are a fact that industry cannot ignore. While some companies have considered approaches to this problem, many have not yet come to grips with the need to retain and train older workers and to provide a working environment that accommodates their needs. We have given an overview of some solutions considered in different industries, highlighted areas in which employers can begin to deal with the issues, and suggested research that must be addressed to meet industry needs in the coming years.

ACKNOWLEDGMENT

Portions of this chapter were written as part of a Leverhulme Visiting Professorship at the University of Dundee for the first author.

REFERENCES

American Productivity and Quality Center. 2002. Retaining Valuable Knowledge: Proactive Strategies to Deal with a Shifting Workforce. *APQC Best Practice Report.* Houston: American Productivity and Quality Center.

Aston, A. 2007. Who will run the plants? As the nuclear industry starts to expand again, it faces a graying workforce. *Business Week,* January 22. Retrieved September 23, 2007, from www.businessweek.com/magazine/content/07_04/b4018079.htm?chan=search.

Beattie, J. 2007. NRC facing massive manpower problems—GAO. *Energy Daily,* January 22, 1.

Bond, J. T., Galinsky, E., Kim, S. S., and Brownfield, E. 2005. *2005 National Study of Employers.* Retrieved September 23, 2007, from http://familiesandwork.org/site/research/reports/2005nse.pdf.

Breen, B. 2001. Trickle-up leadership. *Fast Company Magazine* 52:70. Available at www.fastcompany.com/magazine/52/useem.html.

Cohen, J. D. 2006. The aging nursing workforce: How to retain experienced nurses. *Journal of Healthcare Management* 51:233–45.

Convertino, G., Farooq, U., Rosson, M. B., and Carroll, J. M. 2005. Old is gold: Integrating older workers in CSCW. *Proceedings of the 37th Hawaii International Conference on System Sciences,* 1–10.

Convertino, G., Farooq, U., Rosson, M. B., Carroll, J. M., and Meyer, B. J. F. 2007. Support-ing intergenerational groups in computer-supported cooperative work (CSCW). *Behav-iour and Information Technology* 26:275–85.

Czaja, S. J., and Lee, C. C. 2007. Information technology and older adults. In *The Human-Computer Interaction Handbook: Fundamentals, Evolving Technologies and Emerging Ap-plications*, 2nd ed., ed. A. Sears and J. A. Jacko, 413–27. Mahwah, NJ: Erlbaum.

Czaja, S. J., and Moen, P. 2004. Technology and employment. In *Technology and Adaptive Aging*, ed. R. Pew and S. Van Hamel, 150–78. Washington, DC: National Research Council.

Dychtwald, K., Erickson, T., and Morison, B. 2004, March. It's time to retire retirement. Re-trieved from http://harvardbusinessonline.hbsp.harvard.edu/b02/en/hbr/hbr_mckinsey_awards_2004.jhtml.

Government Accountability Office. 2007, January. *Human Capital: Retirements and Antici-pated New Reactor Applications Will Challenge NRC's New Workforce*. GAO Report #07-105. U.S. Government Accountability Office. Retrieved October 3, 2007, from www.gao.gov/new.items/d07105.pdf.

Government of Western Australia. 2004. *Phased Retirement in the Western Australian Public Sector*. 2003, March (amended March 2004). Department of the Premier and Cabinet. Retrieved October 3, 2007, from www.dpc.wa.gov.au/psmd/pubs/stremp/retirement/phasedretire.pdf.

Greene, K. 2005. Bye bye boomers? *Wall Street Journal*, September 20. Retrieved Septem-ber 23, 2007, from http://online.wsj.com/article/0,,SB112718141602545779,00-search.html?KEYWORDS=%22Carnegie%2BMellon%22&COLLECTION=wsjie/archive.

Gregor, P., Newell, A. F., and Zajicek, M. 2002. Designing for dynamic diversity: Interfaces for older people. *Proceedings of the Fifth international ACM Conference on Assistive Tech-nologies*, 151–56.

Hanson, V. L., Snow-Weaver, A., and Trewin, S. 2006. Software personalization to meet the needs of older adults. *Gerontechnology* 5:160–69

Hylko, J. 2005. Thanks for the memories: Capturing expert knowledge. *Power*, May 15. Retrieved September 23, 2007, from www.powermag.com/ExportedSite/Archives/Archives.htm.

Juliano, J., and Valocchi, M. 2003, December. The aging workforce: What can you do about it? *Electric Light and Power*. Retrieved September 23, 2007, from http://uaelp.pennnet.com/display_article/195622/34/ARTCL/none/none/The-aging-workforce:-What-can-you-do-about-it?/

Kosich, D. 2007. Building the future for Rio Tinto: Mineweb interviews Tom Albanese, February 5. *Mineweb*. Retrieved from www.mineweb.com/mineweb/view/mineweb/en/page15831/?oid=167388sn=23tail.

Lahey, L. 2007. *Social networking in the workplace proving to be a valuable tool. ConnectIT*. Available at www.connectitnews.com/usa/story.cfm?item=1185.

Lancaster, L. C., and Stillman, D. 2003. *When Generations Collide: Who They Are. Why They Clash. How to Solve the Generational Puzzle at Work*. Wheaton, IL: Harper Business.

Leonard, D., and Swap, W. C. 2005. *Deep Smarts: How to Cultivate and Transfer Enduring Business Wisdom*. Harvard Business School Publishing Corporation.

Lesser, E., and Rivera, R. 2006. *Closing the Generational Divide: Shifting Workforce Demographics and the Learning Function.* Retrieved February 23, 2007, from www.935.ibm .com/services/us/gbs/bus/pdf/g510-6323-00_generational_divide.pdf.

Leung, W. 2006. Industry scrambles for workers: New exploration and aging workforce fuel demand, experts say. *Vancouver Sun,* January 24. Retrieved September 23, 2007, from http://working.canada.com/components/print.aspx?id=e2586ff7-7957-49d9-be8e-b2c42f00e8c6.

Marquez, J. 2007. Retrained for the next career. *Workforce Management,* May 7. Retrieved September 15, 2007, from www.workforce.com/archive/article/24/89/80.php.

McGuire, J. F., Kenney, K., and Brashler, P. n.d. Flexible work arrangements: The fact sheet. *Workplace Flexibility 2010, Georgetown University Law Center.* Retrieved September 23, 2007, from www.law.georgetown.edu/workplaceflexibility2010/definition/gener al/FWA_FactSheet.pdf.

Minerals Council of Australia. 2006. August. *Staffing the Supercycle: Labour Force Outlook in the Minerals Sector, 2005–2015.* Retrieved September 23, 2007, from www.minerals.org .au/__data/assets/pdf_file/17120/Staffing_the_Supercycle.pdf.

Nixon, S. 2002. Looming labour crisis puts the focus on grey force. *Sydney Morning Herald,* October 2. Retrieved September 23, 2007, from www.smh.com.au/articles/2002/10/ 02/1033283493451.html.

Peterson, S. J., and Spiker, B. K. 2005. Establishing the positive contributory value of older workers: A positive psychological perspective. *Organizational Dynamics* 34:153–67.

Pitt-Catsouphes, M., Smyer, M. A., Matz-Costa, C., and Kane, K. 2007, March. Phase II of the National Study of Business Strategy and Workforce Development. Retrieved September 23, 2007, from http://agingandwork.bc.edu/documents/RH04_NationalStudy _03–07_004.pdf.

Ratliff, E. 2002, March. This is not a test. *Wired.* Retrieved September 23, 2007, from www .wired.com/wired/archive/10.03/nukes.html.

Reynolds, S., Ridley, N., and Van Horn, C. E. 2005, August. *A Work-filled Retirement: Workers' Changing Views on Employment and Leisure.* New Brunswick, NJ: John J. Heldrich Center for Workforce Development, Rutgers University.

Schwinn, E. 2007. A charity's mature vision. *Chronicle of Philanthropy,* March 8. Retrieved September 23, 2007, from http://philanthropy.com/subscribe/login?url=/premium/ articles/v19/i10/10002601.htm.

Vicente, K. J. 2000. HCI in the global knowledge-based economy: Designing to support worker adaptation. *ACM Transactions Computer-Human Interaction* 7:263–80.

PART III

The Changing Nature of Jobs

CHAPTER SIX

Trends in Job Demands and the Implications for Older Workers

PETER CAPPELLI, PH.D.

The dramatic changes in the workplace that took place during the second half of the twentieth century have created an idea of work and career that is virtually unrecognizable to the classic American workplace that emerged full-steam after World War II. Lifetime employment is all but dead, while job insecurity is alive and kicking. No one in the workforce has been untouched by these changes, but minorities—whether women or African Americans or older workers—tend to be affected more dramatically. Interestingly, today's economy, which relies more than ever before on contingent workers, offers some definitive advantages to older workers. This chapter looks at how trends in job demands are affecting older workers, specifically, how the skill sets of older workers match up to the needs of today's employers. Before looking toward the future, however, it is appropriate to put today's workplace into a larger context.

THE GOOD OLD DAYS

The Organization Man, the famous book about corporate careers written in 1955 by *Fortune* editor William H. Whyte, defined for a generation the career experience of managers entering the business world and the effects of that experience on society. It provided the details for practical issues such as how corporations made hiring decisions (even detailing how to "cheat" on personality tests), how executives thought and acted, and how they got ahead in their careers. In those days, virtually all the good jobs in business were in large corporations.

When *The Organization Man* was published and for the generation that followed, business careers began with college recruiting, where employers looked for candidates who could be molded into executives with the values and characteristics appropriate for their company. They looked for potential, and the key component of potential was personality. Once hired, the company set about training and developing the skills of the young manager—not just business skills, but social and interpersonal skills. Pressures to conform were considerable, and those pressures extended to their families and to their life outside of work. Managers were groomed to see their interests and identity as defined by their organization, hence "The Organization Man." The defining attribute of careers was that they were governed by the company's rules and interests.

All senior positions were filled by promotions from within, which made it essentially impossible to quit because no other company would hire managers from the outside. The company decided who would advance, often based on elaborate assessment exercises, when they would move, and where they would go. The hierarchy of authority and the rewards associated with it were clear, as was the path through which one got there. Candidates climbed well-defined ladders of advancement, and no deviations were allowed. This included relocations, which were frequent; and the failure to accept them was a "career-ending move." The skills crucial to getting ahead involved good performance but also managing internal politics—especially, fitting in and cultivating superiors. But the companies also took care of their managers. No one was laid off, and virtually no one was ever fired. Managers who were passed over were shunted to marginal positions and retired with generous pensions. For non-managers, union-based systems provided job security and income stability for blue-collar workers. Seniority-based systems for promotions and for pay schedules made the workplace more attractive for workers as they grew older.

THE COLLAPSE OF THE OLD MODELS

Workforce planning, succession planning, and the Organization Man approach to careers began to fall apart when the ability to forecast the overall level of demand in the economy collapsed following the oil price shocks, first in 1973 and then in 1979. The economy grew far more slowly than anticipated. The gross national product, which had been growing at a rate of about 5 to 6 percent in real terms during most of the 1960s, actually declined in 1974, 1975, and again in 1980. The 1970s became known as the decade of "stagflation," low economic growth despite inflation.[1] Companies that planned on growth of 6 percent per year on average suddenly discovered that their business demand not only failed to meet that target but actually declined. Talent management arrangements ran into trouble because of the long lead time inherent in a system of internal development. The number of managers who were ready for director positions, for example, was set in motion by decisions made ten years or more earlier and based on forecasts of much higher demand. Overshooting demand even by only a few percent soon begins to add up: 3 percent per year over a decade like the 1970s would lead to having one-third too many managers in the pipeline at the end of the decade.

What should companies do with all those excess managerial candidates, especially in the context of lifetime employment for white-collar workers, which virtually all companies practiced?

THE ERA OF DOWNSIZING

Facing the internal glut of talent, the sharp recession of 1981, and the changes in the economic environment noted above, employers moved aggressively to break the lifetime employment arrangements with their employees. As late as the end of the 1970s, survey evidence from the Conference Board indicated that management's priorities in setting employment practices were to build a loyal, stable workforce. But a decade later, by the end of the 1980s, that priority had clearly shifted to increasing organizational performance and reducing costs (these surveys are discussed in Belous, 1989). The most powerful evidence in this regard is another Conference Board survey that found more than two-thirds of the large employers in the sample reporting that they had changed their practice and no longer offered employment security: only 3 percent in the mid-1990s said that they still offered job security to employees (Conference Board, 1997). Declining seniority for older workers is consistent with greater job losses for older workers, although there can be other explanations as well.

The most important manifestation of this new relationship was "downsizing." The term was at first a euphemism for layoffs, but it later came to mean something different. Whereas layoffs had been seen as a temporary response to downturns in business resulting from recessions (and focused mainly on hourly workers), downsizing was a permanent reduction in jobs, and it did not appear to differentiate between levels in the organization. The U.S. Bureau of Labor Statistics did not even measure permanent job losses (as distinct from recession-based and temporary ones) until after 1984, because the assumption was that workers who had lost their jobs would get them back once business recovered. Similarly, the level of "contingent work," defined by the Bureau of Labor Statistics as jobs that are expected to end soon, was not measured before the 1990s. Contingent work by this definition remained roughly constant at about 4.3 percent of the employed workforce through the late 1990s, even as the overall unemployment rate fell and the labor market tightened (Hipple, 2001).

When the American Management Association (AMA) surveyed its member companies about downsizing during the 1990s, they found that the incidence of downsizing increased virtually every year through 1996, despite the economic expansion of the 1990s. Roughly half of the companies reported downsizing, and 40 percent had downsizing in two or more separate years over the previous six (AMA, 1996). Other surveys report roughly similar rates of downsizing. The scale of these job cuts was unprecedented in a period of economic expansion.

Data on workers who have been permanently displaced from their jobs since 1981 confirm that job security declined. The overall rate at which workers were permanently displaced backed down a bit in the late 1980s from the peak of the recession period (1981–83), but it then rose again—despite the economic recovery—and jumped sharply through 1995. The rate at which workers were thrown out of their jobs was about the same in 1993–95, a period of significant economic expansion and prosperity in the economy as a whole, as compared to the 1981–83 recession, the worst downturn since the Great Depression (Farber, 1998). It is difficult to find more compelling evidence that the nature of the employment relationship changed. About 15 percent of the workforce saw their jobs go forever during that 1993–95 period of growth. The cause of the job losses reported in these surveys of individual workers mirrors the developments in the firm surveys—shifting away from economy or company-wide reasons such as downturns in business or plant closings toward eliminating particular positions associated with restructuring. Furthermore, the costs of job loss (i.e., the declines in earnings when finding a new job) since the 1980s actually increased, especially for older workers who otherwise find it difficult to locate new jobs, even as the improved economic picture saw it decline for other workers (Farber, 2003).

REENGINEERING TO SHED TALENT

Companies began to find new ways to get work done with fewer people after the 1981 recession and to get rid of the management roles that had been created during the 1970s, a process that became known as reengineering. Work systems that empower employees, such as cross-functional teams, eliminated supervisory positions and widened spans of control. Information systems eliminated many of the internal control functions of middle management positions, and decentralizing operations through the creation of profit centers and similar arrangements further reduced the need for central administration. Corporate hierarchies flattened in the 1990s (Rajan and Wulf, 2006), and with them job and career ladders in part, as headquarters were deflated and power was decentralized.

The net consequence of these developments was to reduce the need for managers just at the time that companies had an excess supply of managerial talent still carried over from the 1970s. As a result, the priority inside companies shifted from developing talent to getting rid of talent. New companies that started in this period found a plentiful supply of managerial skills and talent available on the outside market. There was no need to develop talent when it could easily be acquired ready to go. Manpower planning was not exactly a challenging exercise when companies were cutting back jobs. Nor was it even necessary when companies had the option of bringing in experienced hires from the outside: Just wait and see what was needed and then go get it. Most employers moved to something like a "just in time" workforce, hiring any skilled worker when the need arose and laying off as soon as needs changed.

EVIDENCE OF DECLINING ATTACHMENT
BETWEEN EMPLOYER AND EMPLOYEE

The churning of employees note above, based on layoffs and outside hiring, has important implications for career issues by shortening the length of time that the employee and employer are together. Shorter tenure makes it much more difficult to do long-term planning and to recoup developmental investments in employees. It may also increase the uncertainty of those attachments, an issue that is harder to measure but just as important.

Tenure is driven by layoffs and dismissals—but also by quits. The last of these accounts for about two-thirds of all job changes, hence the concern about employees being hired away. Most observers are surprised to find that roughly 40 percent of the U.S. workforce has been with their current employer less than two years, a figure that has not changed much in recent decades. This topic has been studied extensively for the United States, and the early studies found reasonable stability in employment when comparing the 1980s with earlier periods (layoffs were higher but quits were lower because jobs were scarce). More recent results, using data from the mid-1990s, find declines in average tenure, especially for managerial employees, but even for the workforce as a whole.[2] They also find large declines in tenure for older white men in particular, the group historically

most protected by internal labor markets. For example, for men approaching retirement age (58 to 63) only 29 percent had been with the same employer for ten
years or more as compared to a figure of 47 percent in 1969 (Ruhm, 1995). The
percentage of the workforce with long-tenure jobs, ten years or more, declined
slightly from the late 1970s through 1993 and then fell sharply through the mid-
1990s (Farber, 1997). The rate of dismissals also increased sharply for older workers with more tenure, doubling for workers age 45 to 54.[3] The finding that tenure
declined for managerial jobs is especially supportive of the arguments for the erosion of internal career systems (Neumark, Polsky, and Hansen, 1999). Unfortunately, we don't know how much of the decline in tenure is due to quits or layoffs.

Figure 6.1 shows the changes in tenure across the economy as a whole through
the 1990s. This chart includes all workers. Managers and corporate employees in
general represent only a small part, perhaps less than 10 percent. While tenure
for men declined noticeably, tenure for women has not declined—indeed, it appears to have increased, because women are now less likely to quit their jobs when
they have children, in part because of legislated protections (Wellington, 1993).

Changes in tenure for men are more dramatic when one examines the changes
within age groups (figure 6.2). Because older men quit jobs less frequently, the

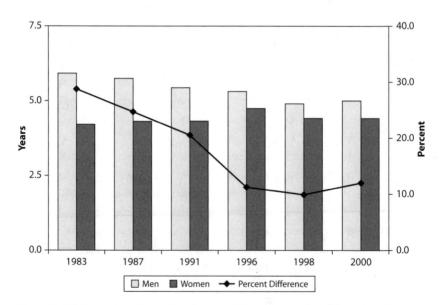

Figure 6.1. Median tenure for employed men and women age 25 or older, selected years,
1983–2000. *Source*: Bureau of Labor Statistics, www.bls.gov/opub/ted/2000/aug/wk4/
art03.htm

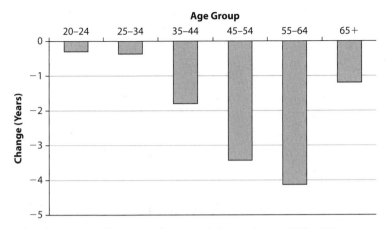

Figure 6.2. Change in median years of tenure, adult men, by age, 1983–1998.
Source: Bureau of Labor Statistics. Median tenure declines among older men, 1983–2000.

aging of the workforce over the past decade or so should have worked to *increase* average tenure in the workforce as a whole. Comparing levels within age groups over time controls for that effect (figure 6.3). The striking point is that tenure is declining most specifically among those older age groups that have historically had the highest attachment to their employers, especially the cohort just before retirement.

The most persuasive evidence of a change in the employment relationship comes from studies that follow a cohort of individuals over time. A recent longitudinal study of workers born from 1957 to 1964 indicates how unstable jobs are, even for what we think of as the "prime age" workforce. By the 1990s, when these workers were well into middle age, a large percentage of them were still experiencing the type of job insecurity that decades ago we associated with teenage workers. Of those who started a new job in the 1990s, for example, 40 percent saw that job end in less than a year; only 30 percent who started a new job saw it last more than five years.[4]

The most powerful of these studies compares the experience of (initially) young men from 1966 to 1981 with a later group from 1979 through 1994. In the earlier period, about 16 percent of workers had stable job histories, as defined by having one or two employers over their career; in the later period, it fell to 11 percent. Fifteen percent of the workforce had seven or more employers in the earlier period, a figure that rose to 21 percent in the later period. When comparing equivalent workers, the odds of leaving a job—being dismissed or quitting—after two

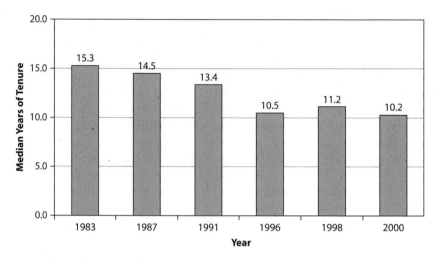

Figure 6.3. Median years of tenure with current employer, men age 55 to 64, 1983–2000
Source: Bureau of Labor Statistics. Median tenure declines among older men. *Monthly Labor Review,* September 1, 2000.

years was 43 percent greater in the latter cohort (Bernhardt, Morris, Handcock, and Scott, 2001). Another study indicates that the more recent cohort experienced considerably greater changes in their jobs and occupations than did the previous generation even when they remained with the same employer (Hollister, 2006). A third study finds workers in the more recent period changing industries and occupations more frequently than in the previous generation (Kambourov and Manovskii, 2004).[5]

We cannot easily tell from these studies whether the changes were instituted by the employer or the employee. Either way, though, they suggest the instability that makes long-term investments in employees and in career planning difficult to achieve. For example, older workers who were being hired traditionally have had shorter employment lives than younger workers (because they were closer to retirement). Thus, one could surmise that a reduction in long-term investments to employees might make older workers less attractive to employers. The most recent data from the U.S. Bureau of Labor Statistics suggest that tenure has increased somewhat from 2000 to 2006, by approximately six months for the average employee.[6] But whether that simply reflects the slowdown in the economy from the red-hot labor market in 2000 or the beginning of a more structural change is difficult to know.

THE ROLE OF COMPENSATION AND BENEFITS

Evidence of the breakdown of the Organization Man model can also be found in data on compensation. The most important effect is that the earnings of individuals have become much more variable, and the variation cannot be accounted for by the usual set of individual and job characteristics (Gottschalk and Moffitt, 1994). The instability of unemployment, specifically the growing incidence of job loss, also contributes in important ways to an overall instability of earnings, especially for older workers (Stevens, 2001).

One of the important attributes of the systems of jobs in traditional employment models was the fact that wage levels were set in such a way as to form distinct and clear hierarchies. The technique of "job evaluation" described the tools used to fashion wages across jobs so that more senior positions in promotion ladders always paid more than lower positions, encouraging upward mobility. The steady progression of wages based on seniority or tenure was one of the hallmarks of internal systems. But by the early 1990s, there was no longer any advantage to inside moves as compared to those across employers (Wilk and Craig, 1998). The apparent decline in the return to tenure with the same employer is further evidence of the decline of more traditional pay and employment relationships. Researchers studying the semiconductor industry, for example, found a decline in the wage premium paid to more experienced workers. Among the explanations are that new technical skills are becoming more important, and those skills are learned, not inside the firm but outside, typically in higher education (Brown, 1997). In aggregate data, the returns to seniority—that is, tenure with the same employer—have collapsed in recent years (Chauvin, 1994). Studies find a sharp decline in returns to seniority of about $3,000 annually from the 1970s to the 1980s for workers with ten years of seniority.

Another way to describe this effect is that the costs of job changing dropped dramatically. Workers who changed employers every other year saw almost the same earnings rise in the late 1980s as did those who kept the same job for ten years (Marcotte, 1994). Moreover, the probability that employees who quit would find a job that offers a large pay raise has increased by 5 percent, while the probability that those who were dismissed will suffer a large decline in their pay has risen by 17 percent over the previous decade (Polsky, 1999). These results suggest that a good lifetime match between an employee and a single employer is becoming less important in determining an employee's long-term success. By default, what must be becoming more important are factors outside of the relationship with an individual employer, factors associated with the outside market, such as whether we are experiencing a tight or a slack labor market.

Pension plans have been the aspect of compensation benefit with the most important implications for the employment relationship since they represent a continuing obligation to employees even if employment ends (at least for vested employees) and as such are an indication of a more permanent obligation by employers to employees. While pension coverage has declined over time, more important has been the shift in the nature of pensions from defined benefit plans, where workers earn the right to predetermined benefit levels according to their years of service, toward defined contribution plans, where employers make fixed contributions to a retirement fund for each employee—especially 401(k) programs where employees contribute directly to their retirement fund (Ippolito, 1995). With this shift, the employer no longer bears the risk of guaranteeing a stream of benefits. The employee does. Employees no longer have an incentive to stay with the company long enough to gain access to those pension contributions (although employees with existing illnesses who receive health insurance coverage through their employer tend to stay "locked in" to their current employer). The employer's obligations to the employee end with the end of employment, signaling a move away from long-term obligations and relationships. In 1980, 84 percent of full-time workers in the United States were covered by a defined benefit pension plan; but by 2003, the figure was down to 33 percent (EBRI 2005).

Finally, it is worth noting that an increasing percentage of the workforce are not employees at all. In 2006, 7.4 percent of the workforce were independent contractors, up from 6.4 in 2001 (Monthly Labor Review, 2006). It might be reasonable to include contracting out and vendors in this category of independent contracting, at least from the perspective of the original firm, because they represent the movement of work that had been done inside the firm as a fixed cost to work that is now done outside the firm at variable cost.

THE NEW EMPLOYMENT STRUCTURE
AND OLDER WORKERS

From this long progression starting in the 1950s, we move from lifetime employment (The Organization Man) to what might be characterized as an era defined by job insecurity, shorter tenures, declining attachment between employer and employee, and contingent work. I have described this as "The New Deal at Work," but it would also be reasonable to think of it as the era of "Everyone for Themselves."

The changes noted above suggest that employers are relying much more on outside hiring and a more contractual relationship with workers. The dominance of contingent (i.e., part-time, temporary, seasonal) work is, in general, good news for older workers. While women, minorities, and teens traditionally served as America's contingent workforce, older workers are increasingly adding to this labor pool (Schultz, 2001). According to the U.S. Census Bureau, an increasing proportion of older workers in industrialized nations are making the transition from full-time work to retirement via a period of part-time work. Part-time work as a proportion of total employment among older workers generally held stable for men during the 1970s and early 1980s but increased for women. In the late 1980s and early 1990s, more men and women were working part-time, while the share of full-time workers declined (U.S. Census Bureau, 2002). Part of the reason for this shift is voluntary, as many older individuals express an interest in creating a bridge between full-time work and retirement (Schultz, 2001). A 2002 AARP study of the needs of workers aged 45–74 found that these workers don't necessarily want to continue in the same career or with the same hours or even the same daily schedule. Many are trying new careers, consulting or working part-time, and starting their own businesses—just because they want to or in order to hold onto health benefits (AARP, 2004). Specifically, the study showed that 84 percent would work even if they were financially set for life, and 69 percent plan to work into their retirement years. But a vast majority (70%) is looking for ways to better balance their work and personal lives, since many of them are dealing with major life challenges that pull them away from work. Not surprisingly, flexibility in their jobs was among the top needs of this age group (AARP, 2004).

CHANGING SKILLS REQUIREMENTS

Not surprisingly, as the structure of work has changed, so too have the skills necessary to compete in the workplace. Since companies are much less interested in making long-term investments in developing the competencies of employees, they instead expect employees to bring the skills and competencies that are needed to the job. This development would clearly seem to favor experienced workers, and experience is correlated with age. It also disadvantages new entrant workers, again correlated with age, who will struggle to get the skills and experience that employers want.

Many researchers point to the growth in wage inequality in the United States during the past 20 years as an indication that skills in the labor force do not match the requirements of jobs. If indeed there is a skills gap, one must wonder whether the gap is driven by the supply side (human capital is lagging due to educational failures and lagging test scores) or the demand side (employers need more highly skilled workers to manage in the high-tech knowledge economy). Anecdotally, one hears about the skills gap and the difficulty of finding good talent, but research on the existence or extent of the problem is still quite limited. What we do know is that in general there is a shift toward jobs requiring higher skills.

The most obvious shift in the past 60 years has been the move away from the hard physical labor of an agrarian and industrial society to the complex thinking skills needed in today's knowledge economy. Howell and Wolff (1991) found that between 1960 and 1985 employment trends (the loss of some jobs, the growth in others) led to an overall upgrading of cognitive and interactive skill requirements. Not surprisingly, they found that demand for motor skills stayed relatively the same during this period, most likely due to changes in the mix of production jobs. Yet even within the production jobs that remained, there was greater demand for higher skills. A study of skills requirements for production jobs in 93 manufacturing facilities between 1978 and 1986 (Cappelli, 1993) found strong evidence of system-wide "upskilling" in job requirements, combined with some tendency to shift the composition of employment toward job families with greater skill growth.

While Handel (2003) finds evidence in the literature of the same kind of upskilling across a number of industries, he does not agree that it is impeding companies from finding qualified candidates. Instead, the trouble appears to be finding workers with the kinds of "soft" skills employers are seeking. Handel cites, for example, a survey of rural manufacturers showing that 30 percent of employers reported that their biggest problem was finding workers with a "reliable and acceptable work attitude" (2003, 152). He cites many studies showing that "employers place as much or greater weight on noncognitive factors, such as work effort and cooperative attitudes" (155). He goes on to say that "difficulties in finding workers with desired social skills, attitudes, and motivation were often ranked as high, or higher, than dissatisfaction with cognitive skill levels" (156).

Cappelli (1995), looking primarily at the academic skills gap and focusing mainly on high school education, also found that attitudes tend to trump skills. He cited numerous studies suggesting the importance of work-related attitudes to employers:

- A 1983 survey of executives by Research and Forecasts found that "character" was the applicant characteristic most often given primary importance in hiring decisions (48%); only 5 percent ranked "education" first.

- The Committee for Economic Development's survey of small employers concluded that their top priority in seeking applicants was "a sense of responsibility, self-discipline, pride, teamwork, and enthusiasm."
- A 1989 employer survey by Towers Perrin found that the most common reason for rejecting applicants (other than a lack of prior work experience) was the belief that they did not have the work attitudes and behaviors to adapt successfully to the work environment. The most common reasons for firing new hires were absenteeism and failure to adapt to the work environment; only 9 percent of workers were dismissed because of difficulties in learning how to perform their jobs—the category most suggestive of a basic skills deficit.
- A 1990 survey of the National Association of Manufacturers (NAM), conducted by Towers Perrin, found that the belief that applicants would not have the work attitudes and behaviors needed to adapt to the work environment was almost twice as common a reason for rejecting applicants as the next most important factor.
- The Commission on the Skills of the Workforce found in its 1990 employer survey that more than 80 percent of employers were more concerned with worker attitudes and personalities than about basic academic skills in new hires.
- A 1991 Committee for Economic Development survey conducted by Louis Harris found that dedication to work and discipline in work habits were the biggest deficits that employers saw in high school graduates who were applying for jobs.
- The National Center on the Educational Quality of the Workforce's 1995 establishment survey conducted by the Bureau of the Census saw employers ranking applicant attitudes as the most important criterion among a list of 11 items in making hiring decisions.

These surveys suggest that employers saw the most important consideration in hiring and the biggest deficit among new workforce entrants as being the attitudes concerning work that they bring with them to their jobs. It is difficult to say whether older workers have better attitudes or a greater sense of responsibility than their younger counterparts, but there is anecdotal evidence for it. A report published by AARP (2000) lists the seven qualities desired by employers alongside the top qualities of older workers as reported by HR managers. According to the report (see table 6.1), older workers do indeed possess the kinds of soft skills most desired by employers.

TABLE 6.1.
Older workers' "soft" skills (according to HR managers)

Employee qualities most desired	Top qualities of older employees
1. Commitment to doing quality work	1. Loyalty and dedication to the company
2. Getting along with coworkers	2. Commitment to doing quality work
3. Solid performance record	3. Someone you can count on in a crisis
4. Basic skills in reading, writing, and arithmetic	4. Solid performance record
5. Someone you can count on in a crisis	5. Basic skills in reading, writing, and arithmetic
6. Willing to be flexible about doing different tasks	6. Solid experience in job and/or industry
7. Loyalty and dedication to the company	7. Getting along with coworkers

This is further reinforced at the industry level. An interview with Vic Buza-chero, vice president of human resources at Scripps Health System, a multi-hospital health system in southern California (conducted by L. Selhat, March 19, 2007), reinforces the notion that mature workers bring valuable soft skills that are not easily taught in school. Scripps, which has regularly been among the AARP's "Best Employers," has made a strong commitment to mature workers, says Buzachero, but not simply because they are desperate for bodies in the face of the crushing nursing shortage. Buzachero believes that the experience that comes from "multiple seasons" makes mature workers "more highly produc-tive," in particular because of their "resident knowledge" and "their ability to mo-bilize resources and handle complex tasks." To hold on to older workers, Scripps has instituted a phased retirement program that allows workers over age 55 to hold onto benefits despite a drastically reduced work schedule. Because many older workers would end up quitting otherwise, it is more financially advanta-geous to hold on to these workers—even on a part-time schedule—than to recruit and train new nurses. They have also created a new position, clinical mentor, which is mainly a teaching position for older workers to share their experiences with younger nurses in the clinical setting.

The CVS drugstore chain is also turning to older workers to fill many of its workforce needs. In the past ten years, after an aggressive recruiting campaign, CVS has more than doubled its over-55 workforce, which now makes up 16 per-cent of the company. According to a study conducted by CVS, older workers were much less likely to call in sick than their younger counterparts. They also displayed a stronger work ethic and sense of civility than did the younger employees, ac-cording to the company's director of government programs (Mullich, 2003).

One of the factors that has increased the importance of "work attitudes," broadly defined, is changes in the structure of organizations and jobs. As noted above, work groups come apart—and also come together—more frequently now as employers churn their workforces through layoffs and outside hiring; as flattening hierarchies reduce the level of supervision and control; and as teamwork transfers responsibility and decision making to frontline workers. All of these developments require that employees make decisions and work out problems along with their coworkers. Interpersonal skills in this context become much more important. Older workers at least have more experience addressing such problems, and we might expect that, other things being equal, they would be better at doing so.

THE RELATIONSHIP BETWEEN AGE AND JOB PERFORMANCE

The likelihood that the older population will benefit from the trends discussed thus far depends in large part on perceptions about our abilities as we age. There appears to be widely held perceptions that job performance decreases with age, despite the lack of solid evidence to back up that perception. Schultz (2001) looked at several recent meta-analytic studies and found no relationship between decreased job performance and age.

That is not to say that aging has no bearing on work outcomes, but it is most likely an indirect relationship. Schultz suggests that "while age may be positively related to increased job knowledge (which in turn leads to increased job performance) it may also be negatively related to physical abilities (which in turn is positively related to job performance" (2001, 251). In a study of computer usage and older workers, Friedberg (2003) found that age alone did not explain why older workers use computers less. She suggests that "impending retirement, which reduces the time horizon to recoup an investment in new skills, appears to play a major role" (511).

The journal *Neurology* reported on research that took up the question of age and performance by studying older and younger pilots over a three-year span. They found that "expert knowledge may compensate for age-related declines in basic cognitive and sensory-motor abilities in some skill domains" (Taylor, Kennedy, Noda, and Yesavage, 2007, 648). Pilots aged 40 to 69 were tested annually on performance, using data from flight simulators that measured, among other things, traffic avoidance, executing air-traffic controller communications, performing an approach to a landing, and scanning cockpit instruments. Results showed that although older pilots initially performed worse than younger pilots, over time older pilots showed less decline in flight summary scores than younger pilots. Secondary analysis showed that the oldest pilots did well over time because their traffic avoidance performance improved more than did that of the younger pilots.

An Australian study (Brooke, 2003) suggests that the ideal is to have an "age-balanced" workforce, where the complementary strengths of younger and older generations are recognized and used within human resource planning. Brooke says that "the increased human resource costs of the younger workforce may potentially be countered by their currency of technical skills, which may in turn be balanced by the experience and stability that older workers bring to their employment" (280). The Clinical Mentor program at Scripps mentioned earlier is the embodiment of the age-balanced workforce. It recognizes that older nurses find it more and more difficult to do the hard physical labor of nursing but have a great deal of resident experience and knowledge. The role of clinical mentor allows them to transfer that knowledge to younger nurses who are better able to do the physical labor but lack the intuitive skills that come from years of experience.

RESEARCH DIRECTIONS AND
POLICY IMPLICATIONS

One of the areas holding back change on the policy front is the lack of data on the association between age and performance. The pilots study mentioned earlier is one of just a few that actually quantifies the relationship. Generalizing the pilots study across a number of other domains such as medicine, law enforcement, and air traffic control would make sense, but more studies are needed to confirm this. Such studies could, for example, lead to changes in current regulations on forced retirement in certain fields.

Similarly, beyond the anecdotal information coming out of industry regarding older workers' "soft" skills, we need more qualitative studies that measure this. A study by Mayer, Caruso, and Salovey (1999) on emotional intelligence found, as predicted, that adults performed at higher ability levels than did adolescents. In addition, emotional intelligence was shown to grow from early adolescence to young adulthood. Another study (Fox, Tett, and Palmer, 2003) looking at whether emotional intelligence is a valid predictor of job performance found that women scored higher on Emotional Appropriateness, Recognition of Emotion in the Self, and Empathy (the women in the study tended to be older), and that older workers scored higher on Empathy, Emotional Appropriateness, and Mood Redirected Attention. Clearly, more work needs to be done to measure soft skills specifically among older people.

Finally, we need to know more about the changing skill requirements in the workplace. This information is critical to educational institutions as well as to policymakers who must decide how much government resources to invest in training programs. Unfortunately, we have yet to develop a standard methodology for rating job skill demands. In all, however, the news appears to be positive for older workers, for today's work environment has many opportunities for the skills and qualities found among the aging population.

NOTES

1. Data on gross national product over time are available from the Department of Commerce's Bureau of Economic Analysis at www.bea.gov/bea/dn/gdpchg.xls.

2. A good survey of the results, at least through the 1990s, is in Neumark (2000).

3. See Polsky (1999) for this result. The other two studies are Bernhardt, Morris, Handcock, and Scott (1999) and Valetta (1996).

4. U.S. Bureau of Labor Statistics (2004). This study and the others in this section rely on the National Longitudinal Surveys.

5. This chapter uses a different longitudinal survey, the Panel Study of Income Dynamics. See http://psidonllline.isr.umich.edu.

6. U.S. Bureau of Labor Statistics (2006).

REFERENCES

AARP. 2000. American business and older employees: A summary of findings. *AARP Research Report, January.* Retrieved April 3, 2007, from www.aarp.org/research/work/issues/aresearch-import-295-D17107.html.

———. 2004. Is early retirement ending? *AARP Research Report, October.* Retrieved September 26, 2007, from www.aarp.org/research/work/retirement/is_early_retirement_ending.html.

American Management Association. 1996. *Survey on downsizing, job elimination, and job creation.* New York.

Belous, R. S. 1989. *The Contingent Economy.* Washington, DC: National Planning Association.

Bernhardt, A. D., Morris, M., Handcock, M. S., and Scott, M. A. 1999. Trends in job instability and wages for young adult men. *Journal of Labor Economics* 17 (4) Part 2 (October): S65–126.

———. 2001. *Divergent Paths: Economic Mobility in the New American Labor Market.* New York: Russell Sage Foundation.

Brooke, L. 2003. Human resource costs and benefits of maintaining a mature-age workforce. *International Journal of Manpower* 24 (3): 260–83.

Brown, C., ed. 1997. *The Competitive Semiconductor Manufacturing Human Resources Project.* Berkeley and Los Angeles: University of California.

Cappelli, P. 1993. Are skill requirements rising? Evidence from production and clerical jobs. *Industrial and Labor Relations Review* 46 (3): 515–30.

———. 1995. Is the "skills gap" really about attitudes? *California Management Review* 37 (4): 108–24.

Chauvin, K. W. 1994. Firm-specific wage growth and changes in the labor market for managers. *Managerial and Decision Economics* 15 (1): 21–37.

Conference Board. 1997. *HR Executive Review: Implementing the New Employment Contract.* New York.

EBRI. 2005. *EBRI Databook on Employee Benefits.* Available at http://www.ebri.org/publications/books/index.cfm?fa=databook.

Farber, H. S. 1997. *The Changing Face of Job Loss in the United States, 1981–1995.* Working paper. Princeton, NJ: Princeton University Industrial Relations Section.

———. 1998. *Has the Rate of Job Loss Increased in the Nineties?* Working paper (No. 394). Princeton, NJ: Princeton University Industrial Relations Section.

———. 2003. *Job Loss in the United States, 1981–2001.* National Bureau of Economic Research Working paper (No. 9707) Cambridge, MA, www.nber.org.

Fox, K. E., Tett, R. P., and Palmer, P. C. 2003. Is emotional intelligence a valid predictor of job performance? Presented at the 18th annual Society of Industrial Organizational Psychologists conference, Orlando, Florida.

Friedberg, L. 2003. The impact of technological change on older workers: Evidence from data on computer use. *Industrial and Labor Relations Review* 56 (3): 511–28.

Gottschalk, P., and Moffitt, R. 1994. Welfare dependence: Concepts, measures, and trends. *American Economic Review* 84 (2): 38–42.

Handel, M. J. 2003. Skills mismatch in the labor market. *Annual Review of Sociology* 29: 135–65.

Hipple, S. 2001. Contingent work. *Monthly Labor Review* (March): 3–27.

Hollister, M. 2006. *Occupational Stability in a Changing Economy.* Working paper. Hanover, NH: Dartmouth College Department of Sociology.

Howell, D. R., and Wolff, E. N. 1991. Trends in the growth and distribution of skills in the U.S. workplace, 1960–1985. *Industrial and Labor Relations Review* 44 (3): 486–505.

Ippolito, R. A. 1995. Toward explaining the growth of defined contribution plans. *Industrial Relations* 34 (1): 1–20.

Kambourov, G., and Manovskii, I. 2004. *Rising Occupational and Industry Mobility in the U.S., 1968–1993.* Working paper. Philadelphia: University of Pennsylvania Institute for Economic Research.

Marcotte, D. 1994. *Evidence of a Fall in the Wage Premium for Job Security.* Working paper. DeKalb, IL: Northern Illinois University, Center for Governmental Studies.

Mayer, J. D., Caruso, D. R., and Salovey, P. 1999. Emotional intelligence meets traditional standards for an intelligence. *Intelligence* 27 (4): 267–98.

Monthly Labor Review Editor's Desk. 2006, July 29. *Independent Contractors in 2005.* Retrieved September 26, 2007, from www.bls.gov/opub/ted/2005/jul/wk4/art05.htm.

Mullich, J. 2003. They don't retire them: They hire them. *Workforce Management* (December): 49–54.

Neumark, D., ed. 2000. *On the Job.* New York: Russell Sage Foundation.

Neumark, D., Polsky, D., and Hansen, D. 1999. Has job stability declined yet? New evidence for the 1990s. *Journal of Labor Economics* 17 (4): Part 2, S29–64.

Polsky, D. 1999. Changing consequences of job separation in the United States. *Industrial and Labor Relations Review* 52 (4): 565–80.

Rajan, R., and Wulf, J. 2006. The flattening firm: Evidence on the changing nature of firm hierarchies from panel data. *Review of Economics and Statistics* 88 (4): 759–73.

Ruhm, C. J. 1995. Secular changes in the work and retirement patterns of older men. *Journal of Human Resources* 30 (2): 362–85.

Schultz, K. S. 2001. The new contingent workforce: Examining the bridge employment options for mature workers. *International Journal of Organizational Theory and Behavior* 4 (3–4): 247–58.

Stevens, A. H. 2001. Changes in earnings instability and job loss. *Industrial and Labor Relations Review* 55 (1): 60–78.

Taylor, J. L., Kennedy, Q., Noda, A., and Yesavage, J. A. 2007. Pilot age and expertise predict flight simulator performance: A three-year longitudinal study. *Neurology* (February): 648–54.

U.S. Bureau of Labor Statistics. 2004, August. Number of jobs held, labor market activity, and earnings growth among younger baby boomers: Recent results from a longitudinal survey. Available from www.bls.gov/nls/nlsy79.htm.

———. 2006, September. News release. Table 6, Median years of tenure with current employer for employed wage and salary workers by occupation, selected years, 2000–6. Available at www.bls.gov/news.release/tenure.t06.htm.

U.S. Census Bureau. 2002. Census 2000 Special Reports, Series CENSR-4, *Demographic Trends in the Twentieth Century.* Washington, DC: U.S. Government Printing Office.

Valetta, R. G. 1996. Has job security in the U.S. declined? *Federal Reserve Bank of San Francisco Weekly Letter,* No. 96–97 (February 16).

Wellington, A. J. 1993. Changes in the male/female wage gap, 1976–85. *Journal of Human Resources* 28 (2): 383–411.

Wilk, S. L., and Craig, E. A. 1998. *Should I Stay or Should I Go? Occupational Matching and Internal and External Mobility.* Working paper. Philadelphia: Wharton School, Department of Management.

CHAPTER SEVEN

Telework and Older Workers

JOSEPH SHARIT, PH.D., AND SARA J. CZAJA, PH.D.

A number of trends that are taking shape argue for the need to reexamine the nature of employment opportunities for older people. One important consideration relates to workforce demographics, which in the United States as well as in other parts of the world is changing in the direction of an increasing proportion of older workers and a decreasing proportion of younger workers. This translates into fewer younger workers available to support an increasing number of people who may not be working but are likely to be living longer (Griffiths, 1999; Johnson and Steuerle, 2004).

An increasingly older population, however, may prevent many older workers from retiring or require retired people to seek employment, especially during unstable economic climates. An increasingly older population is also likely to bring about an increased caregiving burden on older individuals who are working or seeking employment (see chapter 2), which may require many of them to spend time working from home. Commuting to work is also likely to become a more significant issue with an older working population, depending on the accessibility of public transportation within the community, the proximity to one's place of employment, and the person's physical capabilities. Other considerations that may need to be addressed with an increased older working population include the preference of many older workers for part-time work and for work arrangements that enable them to accommodate other priorities (Eyster, Johnson, and Toder, 2008), especially if they have health or other personal issues to manage.

Although we can only speculate on how these issues might affect and shape the older worker population, especially in the light of other forces, such as changes in retiree health benefits, employer pension programs, and Social Security policies (see chapter 1), an emergent challenge deserves serious consideration: how can we provide employment opportunities for older people that address many of these concerns while also affording benefits to employers? An alternative work arrangement known as "telework" has the potential to meet these challenges.

Telework is a complex phenomenon that requires consideration of a number of issues. Even defining telework can be an arduous task, as the next section demonstrates. Viewing telework, for now, as a form of work that can, in principle, be performed anytime and anywhere (Buessing, 2000), there are several reasons why this type of work arrangement would be attractive to both workers and employers (Buessing, 2000; Illegems and Verbeke, 2004), as summarized in table 7.1. Some advocates of telework also point to its positive impact on the environment (Oregon Office of Energy, 1997). While cost reduction may appear to be the overriding factor governing the opportunity for telework that many firms may offer, other considerations should not be discounted. This is especially true in an economic environment in which retaining qualified workers has become more difficult (see chapter 6) and competitiveness has become fiercer. Specifically, telework can increase the prospects of keeping qualified personnel who may desire the flexibility telework affords, and it can bring about greater productivity due to more flexible and less interrupted work schedules.

Before defining and examining the concept of telework in more detail, including its implications for older workers, we should note that not every job is suitable for telework. Obviously, work activities that entail face-to-face communication or extensive team meetings or that require the use of specialized resources that are contained exclusively at the company's site cannot be performed as telework. To gain some perspective on this issue, we asked managers (as part of a telework survey discussed toward the end of this chapter) to indicate, from a list of 18 work activities, which ones could be performed successfully as telework. We found that opportunities for telework exist for a broad number of tasks, including accounting, computer programming, data entry, customer service, editing, and marketing.

This chapter examines various issues associated with telework that need to be understood for this work arrangement to be a good fit for older adults and, more generally, for promoting the employability of older workers on telework jobs. First, we present some historical background on telework, address some of the controversies surrounding how telework has been defined, and provide some information on its current status. Next, we address a number of issues associated

TABLE 7.1.
Some benefits of telework for employers and employees

Benefit for businesses	Benefit for employees
Reduces costs due to less office and parking space requirements	Reduction or elimination of the work commute
Increases productivity for many employees	Fewer distractions and improved concentration working at home
Increases the labor pool to better include people with disabilities	More relaxed at the start of the day than after a stressful commute and, generally, greater job satisfaction
Less sick leave and absenteeism	Allows people with certain disabilities to obtain employment
Improves recruitment and retention of qualified staff	Can better balance work and family or personal life

with telework from the perspectives of the worker and the manager. Finally, we discuss some of our laboratory and survey research that examined issues related to the suitability of telework for older adults. We conclude with a synthesis of the major issues and a statement of needs for ensuring the promotion of employment opportunities for older adults as teleworkers.

DEFINING TELEWORK

Telework has sometimes been referred to as mobile work or home-based work and is often used interchangeably, especially in the United States, with the term *telecommuting.* Although the idea of doing work at home is not new, the impetus for telework is generally attributed to Jack Nilles, who in the early 1970s drew attention to ways in which technology could forgo the need to rely on transportation (Nilles, Carlson, Gray, and Hanneman, 1976). Further developments in information and communication technologies (ICTs) and the consideration of a greater diversity of viewpoints on this phenomenon deriving from both academics and practitioners led to the recognition not only of additional benefits of telework but also of its potentially negative effects. This diversity of views has been primarily responsible for controversies in defining telework, since positive and negative effects of telework could not be considered, let alone understood, unless one can establish what qualifies work as telework.

At the heart of this controversy is whether technology, typically in the form of ICTs such as cell phones, handheld wireless devices, and high-speed personal computers with teleconferencing capabilities, should be the driving force that qualifies the work as telework. Another source of contention concerns the alternative site at which the work is performed. Should work performed at satellite sites, sometimes called telework centers, or at the various client sites at which sales-persons may spend the greater part of their time qualify as telework, or should the term *telework* be restricted to work performed exclusively at one's home?

Although some of the earlier work in this area made it clear that telework need not be linked to technology (Olson, 1988), others (e.g., Cross and Raizman, 1986; Nilles, 1998) have considered ICTs to be fundamental to telework. Distinctions have also been made between the terms *telework* and *telecommuting* as a means for characterizing the different types of sites or work activities considered by these alternative work arrangements. Ellison's (2004) approach is to "consider all types of work conducted outside a centrally located work space (including work done in the home) as telework" and to reserve the term *telecommuting* for "work done in the home, whether it is facilitated through broadband connection and a computer or by phone lines or by pen and paper" (2004, 18), thereby relegating telecommuting to a subset of telework.

In this chapter we will generally use the term *telework* except where other stud-ies or organizations make explicit reference to telecommuting. In addition, con-sistent with Ellison's (2004) view, telework will not be restricted to work facilitated by some form of technology but can include any kind of work, although we ac-knowledge that most opportunities today for telework involve some form of in-teraction with technology.

THE STATUS OF TELEWORK

To illustrate how a lack of consensus in the definition of telework makes it diffi-cult to gauge the extent to which this type of work exists, consider a salesperson that spends about one day a week away from the central office at a client's site. Depending on one's definition, this work description may or may not qualify as telework, telecommuting, or either of these terms. The picture becomes further confused when we consider people who work a second job from the home or run home-based businesses. In addition to generating inaccurate estimates of the number of teleworkers, the lack of a consensus in definition can also promote bi-ases in the methods used to gather data on telework. For example, individuals and organizations who have a vested interest in the findings can conduct studies based on telework criteria that could lend support to their perspectives (Ellison, 2004).

Even if definitional controversies were resolved, deriving an accurate estimate of the number of teleworkers faces staggering logistical and methodological chal-lenges due to the enormous data collection effort that would need to be undertaken. A frequently quoted estimate of the number of teleworkers in the United States, which includes individuals who work at home, at satellite offices, or are mobile workers, is 28 million (Davis and Polonko, 2001). However, even conservative annual rates of increase in telework from the time that estimate was reported would translate into a much higher current estimate.

Despite the controversies in defining telework, the feeling that telework has permeated the mindset of the work sector is inescapable, as evidenced from the various resources that have been made available to inform, regulate, and promote telework. For example, the International Telework Association and Council (2005), which was founded in 1993, provides press releases and other information related to the growth and success of telework, telework practices and statistics, and how businesses and individuals can maximize the opportunities that telework provides. The Midwest Institute for Telecommuting Education (2005) consists of a nonprofit consultant group made up of more than 50 business and government leaders who contribute their time to ensuring successful implementation of telecommuting work arrangements through their expertise in strategic planning, manager/employee training, and policy development.

Driven largely by energy and environmental concerns, the state of Oregon has produced a number of publications (e.g., Oregon Department of Energy, 1995, 1997) that highlight the various benefits of telework, including case studies of how telework can accommodate people with disabilities (and thus expand the labor pool) and improve the quality of one's life. Within the federal sector, the U.S. Office of Personnel Management (OPM) has been the catalyst for the government's efforts, which began in 1990, to promote telework. In 1996, the President's Management Council endorsed a National Telecommuting Initiative led by the U.S. Department of Transportation and the General Services Administration (GSA), whose mission was to increase the implementation of telework by U.S. employers in both the private and public work sectors. The OPM has produced a comprehensive telework manual (OPM, 2003) that provides details concerning initiating telework programs (including policy issues and training plans), selection of employees for telework, office supervision in the face of telework, and employee performance appraisal and skill development. They also have an annual survey that asks federal agencies to identify the number of employees being given the opportunity to telework (agency telework coordinators are listed on the U.S. government's GSA Web site, www.gsa.gov).

In addition to the benefits of telework noted in table 7.1, the federal government also recognizes that telework is essential in volatile situations (e.g., World

Bank/IMF mass demonstrations) and thus that it needs to be concerned, especially in the aftermath of the events of 9/11, with its ability to continue its operations and remain responsive to the nation. A similar concern has been voiced in
the private sector by AT&T (2003) with regard to how outbreaks such as SARS in
Asia have sharpened interest in telework by reinforcing the importance of business continuity planning.

Despite the perceived ubiquity of telework, however, for a vast number of organizations the decision to allow an individual to be hired, or to retain his or her
job as a teleworker, will come down to the attitudes their managers harbor about
telework, and in particular, their feelings about managing workers without the
benefit of face-to-face interaction. The next section considers some of the major
issues that arise with telework from the perspectives of both the employee and
the employer.

ISSUES WITH TELEWORK

From the perspective of the teleworker, especially one who is home-based, one
concern with telework is that the boundaries between home and work may get
blurred, which could negatively impact life in the home as well as the connection
to one's work. With ICTs, initiating work activities at home is almost too easy, and
teleworkers may frequently find themselves drifting toward overwork. Teleworkers also may feel increased pressure to be "visible" and thus resort, for example,
to frequent checking of e-mail, thereby even furthering the intrusion of work activities into the home. In the absence of frequent validation of the teleworkers's
presence, management could assume that the worker has "disappeared," which
could undermine the trust that management requires for allowing their workers
to telework. Thus, the challenge for the teleworker is to take advantage of the flexibility and focus that telework can afford, while regulating the extent to which
work infiltrates one's personal life and distractions in the home can disrupt work
activities.

Another concern of telework is that the teleworker can become insulated from
the organization. Consequently, critical organizational knowledge that is often
derived through informal or spontaneous interchanges with coworkers, support
staff, and management, which forms the basis for what is sometimes referred to
as "incidental learning" (Brown and Duguid, 2000), may become largely unat-
tainable. Acquiring knowledge about the tendencies of coworkers, which can be
essential when working on team projects (see chapter 8), may also be difficult

when teleworking. Compensatory strategies in communication on the part of the teleworker may thus be required to overcome potential gaps in knowledge.

Another factor to consider is the satisfaction that workers derive from tangible interactions with their coworkers. These interactions may fulfill important social needs that are absent in the home or difficult to satisfy elsewhere. Even if the worker can manipulate technology to maintain a socially active work life, perhaps through instant messaging, video technologies, or frequent e-mails, these devices may not serve as adequate substitutes for face-to-face interactions. Thus, an additional challenge for the teleworker is to devise patterns of communication that can simulate, as much as possible, the kinds of interactions that can best balance social and work-related information needs.

Telework also raises concerns for the possible effects of isolation on managers, since they would no longer be able to directly observe their employees. These effects are primarily twofold. First, in organizations that provide workers with the opportunity to telework, and especially to work from home, managers are likely to base their selections on the degree to which they trust these individuals (Handy, 1995). The extent of their trust may, in turn, be influenced by factors such as worker productivity, seniority, and the familiarity the manager has with the worker's job. Compromises in trust magnify the manager's supervisory tasks, which would likely jeopardize future teleworking opportunities for those workers for whom trust is not preexisting.

Second, the isolation of managers from their teleworkers shifts the burden on managers from supervising employees to supervising work (Ellison, 2004). Reynolds and Brusseau (1998) describe a software application that was used in their "virtual organization" to help identify the work to be done, monitor its progress, and manage the overall work effort and that thus could serve to facilitate the management of their teleworkers by emphasizing the management of work rather than of workers. However, in more traditional organizations that may maintain a relatively large number of their workers at company sites, this shift in emphasis from supervising employees to supervising work may impede many managers from offering telework to their employees. In some cases, for example with computer programming or data entry tasks, the work either does or does not get done, and the manager's ability to assess performance, and thus to decide whether to retain the worker in a teleworking capacity, may be straightforward. In other cases, additional procedures for detailing work processes and the satisfaction of work objectives may need to be implemented and possibly evaluated on a day-to-day basis through e-mail or videoconferencing, which could exact considerable additional pressure on supervisors.

TELEWORK AND OLDER ADULTS

A number of the issues that were raised above, particularly those that concern the possible impact of telework on the teleworkers's home and personal life, are not likely to be as applicable or as relevant to many older adults. Conversely, some of the benefits of home-based telework, such as the elimination of possibly stressful commuting and the flexibility to schedule work around obligations such as caregiving and health-management activities, will be magnified for this population. For many older people who need some additional income but have no desire to work full-time, telework can easily accommodate many part-time job opportunities such as those listed on Web sites advertising telework jobs (e.g., www .tjobs.com). In this respect, as suggested earlier, telework may represent an effective strategy for addressing a variety of concerns arising from an aging workforce.

However, there is a serious concern with employing older people as teleworkers. (Although there is no consensus regarding the age at which someone is considered an older worker, in this chapter references to older workers will generally imply workers who are 55+. We acknowledge, however, that there is a great deal of variability in cognitive capacity and employability for this broadly defined category.) Since many telework jobs are dependent—indeed, inextricably linked—to ICTs, it is essential that the older worker be both up-to-date and confident in interacting with technology (as implied in the middle block of figure 7.1). Unfortunately, the data indicate that, compared with younger adults, older people in the United States report lower use of technology (Czaja et al., 2006) and are far less likely to be users of computer technology and the Internet (UCLA Internet Report, 2003). The reduced use of technology seen in older adults may be attributed in part to anxieties about and attitudes toward technology, coupled with normative age-related declines in cognition (Park and Schwartz, 2000; Czaja et al., 2006) and changes in perceptual and psychomotor abilities that make interaction with technological systems more challenging (Kroemer, 2007)—considerations that are highlighted on the left side of figure 7.1. Although many of these problems can largely be alleviated through appropriate user-interface design and training strategies that are intended to accommodate the capabilities and limitations of older adults (Fisk et al., 2009), training presents yet another dilemma in employing older teleworkers. In particular, if training is offered online or is technologically based, employers may need to direct even greater attention to their instructional methods when targeting older adults, as indicated in the right side of figure 7.1.

Employers also need to be concerned with the older teleworkers's home work-

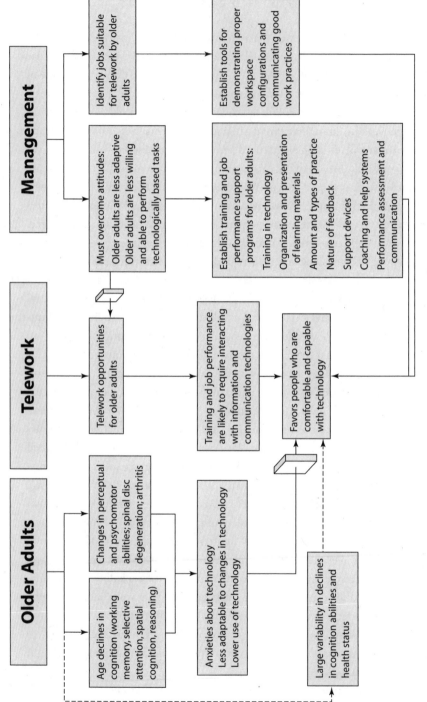

Figure 7.1. Factors that can enable or oppose telework opportunities for older adults. Dashed lines acknowledge the large variability among older people in cognitive and health declines. Blocks represent barriers and thus opposing factors.

space. A number of changes in motor skills occur with aging, including slower response times, disruptions in coordination, greater difficulty in maintaining continuous movements, and reduced flexibility in movement (Kroemer, 2007). Chronic conditions such as arthritis are also more prevalent in older individuals. Overall, these changes may make using input devices such as a mouse or keyboard or the need to manipulate hand-held devices more stressful (see chapter 15). In addition, the adoption of poor postures for extended periods of time that can result from poor seating arrangements or poor display location can, due to the reduced flexibility of the older adult's musculature system and the greater likelihood that spinal discs have undergone some degree of degeneration, produce extreme pain or discomfort and ultimately debilitate the worker. Inadequate consideration to the workspace at home could also result in unwanted glare that could impact performance, either directly by occluding visual information or indirectly by producing visual fatigue. Although these concerns are not unique to older workers, they take on added significance for them and require that employers consider strategies for communicating proper workspace arrangements and work practices for older teleworkers. For example, as implied in the right-hand side of figure 7.1, the company's Web site could be used to graphically illustrate both proper and improper workspace configurations for using a computer at home and also provide guidelines for taking breaks, depending on the nature of the work.

Despite these concerns, a great deal of variability is associated with age-related declines in cognitive abilities, and consequently there will be older adults whose performance may match or be superior to that of their younger counterparts (Czaja et al., 2001). Common myths that older people are less able and willing to work and learn are not supported in the literature (Charness, Czaja, and Sharit, 2007). In fact, studies have shown that older adults are willing and able to learn technologically based work tasks (e.g., Czaja et al., 2001; Sharit et al., 2004) but will likely learn new forms of technology more slowly and with less success than younger people (Kubeck, Delp, Haslett, and McDonald, 1996).

Whether older workers have the capability to learn and successfully perform telework tasks represents only one side of the equation. As implied earlier, there is also the need to consider the attitudes managers may have regarding employing older workers as teleworkers. The data from the literature, which indicate that older workers are not perceived as favorably as younger workers (chapter 10 of this volume; Finkelstein, Burke, and Raju, 1995; Perry, Kulik, and Bourhis, 1996; Gordon and Arvey, 2004; Kite, Stockdale, and Whitley, 2005), are consistent with perceptions of older workers as being less flexible, less adaptive, and less willing to take risks than younger workers. Many of these perceptions, however, are based on a lack of knowledge about aging, and particularly about aging and work. These perceptions are especially likely to be manifest in today's jobs, where the rapid infusion of technology into many work activities has increased the emphasis on speedy, flexible, and adaptive information processing on the part of workers. When one considers that for managers one of the primary areas of concern regarding telework is the challenge of supervising those you cannot see (Ellison, 2004), older teleworkers may be caught in a vicious cycle. Specifically, beliefs regarding the technological skills and performance capabilities of older people, which may be based on myths, undermine the heightened trust that is necessary for a manager to allow workers to engage in telework. Overall, figure 7.1 illustrates how factors associated with both the older worker and management can either enable or oppose opportunities for telework.

In summary, since opportunities for telework will often involve interacting with ICTs, a fundamental challenge in employing older workers as teleworkers is to ensure that older adults, in the face of possible declines in their cognitive abilities, are capable of handling such technologies for both learning and performing telework jobs. At the same time, organizations and managers must be willing to adjust their attitudes, policies, and supervisory strategies to accommodate the various considerations that employing older teleworkers demands. Research undertaken as part of our activities within the Center for Research and Education on Aging and Technology Enhancement (CREATE) at the University of Miami addresses these two broad concerns.

PERFORMANCE OF OLDER ADULTS
ON A SIMULATED TELEWORK TASK

An example of a job that can conceivably be performed exclusively from the home as telework and that requires interaction with technology is one in which a customer service representative processes customer queries sent via e-mail. We simulated such a job for a fictitious company that sold various media products (e.g., computers, accessories, and software) through its online store (Sharit et al., 2004). Fifty-two older participants were recruited for this study: 27 were classified as "younger-older" (50–65 years), and 25 were classified as "older-older" (66–80 years).

To respond to customer queries, the study participants accessed a database that provided information on the company's policies and procedures, its products, and its customers and their product orders. The participant's task was to sequentially open each e-mail, examine its content, navigate to the correct location within the database, and then select the information corresponding to the customer's queries. The participants were informed that a "Wizard" would construct a formal e-mail reply letter based on the information they selected, but that these reply letters could contain errors if they failed to select the appropriate information or if incorrect selections or more selections than necessary were made. To simulate different types of e-mail letters, some of the e-mails contained multiple as opposed to single queries, some required more diverse navigation through the database, and some were wordy as opposed to being succinct. A number of different task performance measures were collected as well as measures on a variety of cognitive abilities and job-related attitudinal measures such as job motivation and job satisfaction (Sharit et al., 2004).

We found that a number of the participants, but especially the older (66–80 years) participants, had problems with over-selecting information (i.e., making additional selections beyond those required for responding to the queries). In the case of the simpler e-mails, the performance of the older participants for the most part caught up with the younger (50–65 years) participants over a four-day period. However, for the more complex e-mails the over-selection error rates were higher, and there was no indication of improvement for either group, although there were some participants in each group that performed relatively well on this measure. With respect to the percentage of correct selections of information that were made in response to the queries, the older participants caught up reasonably well for both the simpler and more complex e-mails, although it took them longer to do so for the more complex e-mails. Analysis of the data indicated that some of this lag in performance by the older participants may have been due to the lesser prior experience they had with computers as compared with their younger counterparts.

Findings from exit interviews that were given to each of the participants indicated that the majority of them (39 of the 52 participants) would welcome the opportunity to perform this type of work as telework for a variety of reasons, including the flexibility and freedom it afforded and the ability to work from home and part-time. With regard to their actual experience performing this task, almost all the participants were enthusiastic about working with the computer system and the software application. However, there was dissatisfaction with workstation desks and chairs, which was voiced more frequently by the older participants.

Overall, the findings from this study indicated that the older participants were capable of learning to perform tasks that require the ability to adapt to the technologically oriented work environment and would desire performing such jobs on a telework basis. However, the findings also suggested that older adults may require increased emphasis during training on use of any task-related technologies in addition to training that would be directed toward task performance. Moreover, consideration needs to be given to performance support devices that can compensate for age declines in cognition, feedback to ensure that they understand the reasons for their errors, and workspace design factors.

THE TELEWORK SURVEY STUDY

We developed a Web-based telework survey directed at company managers that gathers information on: (1) the status of telework in the manager's company; (2) attitudes about telework; (3) work activities amenable to telework; (4) the importance of various worker attributes with respect to influencing one's decision to allow a worker to telework, and an assessment of how older workers compare to younger workers on each of these attributes; and (5) the respondent's company and level of managerial experience. To date, we have obtained 314 completed surveys. Although these are preliminary data, they reflect a broad sample of industries, with small, medium, and large organizations, as well as respondents with different levels of managerial experience, all well represented.

Of the 314 respondents, 223 indicated that their companies provided the opportunity for at least some of their workers to telework from the home. However, 120 of these respondents indicated that company or departmental policies did not exist regarding telework, compared with 84 who noted that they did exist and 19 who were not sure. The data from items addressing attitudes about telework indicated that the least favorable attributes of telework were perceived to be the friction that telework could generate among workers not given the opportunity to telework, the potential for telework to impose stress on workers in meeting performance objectives due to distractions from pressures within the home, and employer responsibility associated with home safety and other legal issues related to telework. The most favorable attributes of telework were perceived to be its ability to improve the retention and satisfaction of workers by eliminating long commutes to work and providing greater flexibility in scheduling personal activities, and to promote the hiring of part-time workers and accommodate older handicapped workers.

Table 7.2 lists some of the work activities that these managers believed could be performed as telework. Although older workers can, depending on their skills, handle any of the activities listed, jobs involving accounting, customer service, data entry, editing, and even marketing are especially amenable to part-time work

TABLE 7.2.
Number of managers in the telework survey who believed the following
work activities to be amenable to telework (N = 314)

Work activity	N	Percentage
Accounting	234	74.5
Auditing	109	34.7
Computer programming	244	77.7
Customer service	178	56.7
Health care services	50	15.9
Decision and statistical analysis	212	67.5
Data entry/documenting	261	83.1
Design of procedures	173	55.1
Design of devices	139	44.3
Editing	265	84.4
Graphics	247	78.7
Project management	108	34.4
Quality control	55	17.5
Sales	160	51.0
Inventory control	61	19.4
Human resources	80	25.5
Purchasing	146	46.5
Marketing	163	51.9

and should be well within the abilities of many older people who may want to re-join the workforce.

Table 7.3 provides ratings of importance of various worker attributes that could influence a manager's decision to allow a worker to telework. Consistent with the literature, trust was found to be an important factor. Interestingly, so was the construct of independence, which may imply that managers are inclined to let people telework who would be able to problem solve on their own rather than involve others at every turn. The importance of time management may derive from concerns managers have for workers who have a tendency to get distracted and thus miss deadlines or perform poorly, which 45.1 percent of the respondents indicated was a factor in the section of the survey that addressed attitudes about telework.

The comparisons between older and younger workers with respect to maturity, trustworthiness, and independence are especially noteworthy, given the degrees of importance the managers attributed to these worker characteristics, and overall paint a favorable picture for the employability of older teleworkers. However, the comparisons between older and younger workers on factors such as the ability to adjust, teamwork, and especially technology skills are not encouraging. These assessments are typical of characterizations of older people as being inflexible and relatively poor at interacting or keeping up with technology. Thus, there

TABLE 7.3.

Ratings of importance of employee attributes that could factor into one's decision to allow a worker to telework, and comparisons between older workers (55+) and younger workers on these attributes

Worker attribute	Ratings of importance*				Older workers are[†]		
	0–4	5–7	8–9	10	More/Better	Less/Worse	Same
Maturity	6	48	139	121	242	4	60
Trustworthiness	2	13	117	182	105	1	199
Ability to work independently	1	16	114	183	113	22	171
Time management ability	5	22	138	149	108	25	172
Writing ability	50	137	87	40	115	22	168
Verbal communication ability	38	112	109	55	88	24	193
Ability to make adjustments at work	7	98	133	76	34	141	130
Ability to work on teams	62	113	98	41	35	64	206
Technology skills	10	72	148	84	9	218	79
Health	125	124	55	10	5	187	112

*Ratings were from 0 (*no importance*) to 10 (*most important*). The data from each of these categories were based on 314 responses and collapsed into the four categories above.

[†] These comparisons were based on numbers of responses that ranged from 303 to 306.

appears to be both positive and negative forces simultaneously in operation on the side of management.

CONCLUSION

With emerging information and communication technologies that are more powerful and flexible than ever, and with organizations becoming more obsessed with cost-cutting strategies and ways to improve both worker productivity and job satisfaction, telework is receiving increased attention as an alternative work arrangement. Lost in all this attention has been the possibility for enlarging the labor pool by considering employing older people as teleworkers. However, putting this dynamic into motion faces many obstacles. Not only must older workers have the capability for negotiating the technologies that may be inherent in many types of telework jobs, but managers and organizations need to overcome negative attitudes and look past common myths concerning the abilities and tendencies of older workers. Organizations would also need to better map out the types of work activities that can be performed as telework and, especially for companies in the private sector, establish programs dedicated to creating, managing, and assessing telework. They must also provide the instructional vehicles for enabling older workers to become trained on the relevant technologies and the necessary coaching and feedback for older workers to successfully perform their jobs while working exclusively from the home. There also needs to be a means for informing older adults about telework opportunities.

Our own experimental research has revealed that many older people can learn and successfully use new technologies and are thus good candidates for telework. However, designers of telework jobs need to be aware of abilities that might decline with aging and consider interventions that can allow older people to be less affected by these declines. Greater consideration also needs to be given to workspace design factors that might hinder older more than younger workers.

Finally, while the preliminary data from our telework survey are encouraging in that they confirm the opportunities for part-time teleworkers and the importance of trustworthiness in allowing employees the opportunity to telework, they also raise a number of concerns. Specifically, an overwhelming number of managers believed that older workers had worse technology skills than younger workers and had a poorer ability to make adjustments to work. In light of the fact that many forms of telework are highly dependent on the use of communication and information technologies that are often repeatedly modified or replaced, these data suggest that organizations may not be inclined to invest in efforts to employ older teleworkers. Thus, it is essential that policies be in place at both the state and federal levels of government (see chapter 4) to promote telework opportunities for older workers, especially in the private sector. Such policies, which can be in the form of various incentives, together with a better understanding of the performance capabilities and needs of older workers, can go a long way toward ensuring the employability of older workers as teleworkers.

REFERENCES

AT&T. 2003. Remote working in the net-centric organization. *AT&T Point of View*, 7 July, 1–11.

Brown, J. S., and Duguid, P. 2000. *The Social Life of Information*. Boston: Harvard Business School Press.

Buessing, A. 2000. Telework. In *International Encyclopedia of Ergonomics and Human Factors*, ed. W. Karwowski, 1723–25. London: Taylor & Francis.

Charness, N., Czaja, S. J., and Sharit, J. 2007. Age and technology for work. In *Aging and Work in the Twenty-first Century*, ed. K. S. Shultz and G. A. Adams, 225–49. Mahwah, NJ: Erlbaum.

Cross, T. B., and Raizman, M. 1986. *Telecommuting: The Future Technology of Work*. Homewood, IL: Dow Jones-Irwin.

Czaja, S. J., Charness, N., Fisk, A. D., Hertzog, C., Nair, S. N., Rogers, W. A., et al. 2006. Factors predicting the use of technology: Findings from the Center for Research and Education on Aging and Technology Enhancement (CREATE). *Psychology and Aging* 21:333–52.

Czaja, S. J., Sharit, J., Ownby, R., Roth, D., and Nair, S. 2001. Examining age differences in performance of a complex information search and retrieval task. *Psychology and Aging* 16:564–79.

Davis, D. D., and Polonko, K. A. 2001. *Telework America 2001 Summary*. Retrieved August 12, 2003, from www.workingfromanywhere.org/telework/twa2001.htm.

Ellison, N. B. 2004. *Telework and Social Change*. Westport, CT: Praeger.

Eyster, L., Johnson, R. W., and Toder, E. 2008. *Current Strategies to Employ and Retain Older Workers*. Final Report by the Urban Institute for the U.S. Department of Labor. Washington, DC: Urban Institute.

Finkelstein, L. M., Burke, M. J., and Raju, N. S. 1995. Age discrimination in simulated employment contexts: An integrative analysis. *Journal of Applied Psychology* 80:652–63.

Fisk, A. D., Rogers, W. A., Charness, N., Czaja, S. J., and Sharit, J. 2009. *Designing for Older Adults: Principles and Creative Human Factors Approaches*, 2nd ed. Boca Raton, FL: CRC Press.

Gordon, R. A., and Arvey, R. D. 2004. Age bias in laboratory and field settings: A meta-analytic investigation. *Journal of Applied Social Psychology* 34:468–92.

Griffiths, A. 1999. Work design and management: the older worker. *Experimental Aging Research* 25:411–20.

Handy, C. 1995. Trust and the virtual organization. *Harvard Business Review* 73(3): 40–50.

Illegems, V., and Verbeke, A. 2004. Telework: What does it mean for management? *Long Range Planning* 37:319–34.

International Telework Association and Council. 2005. *Advancing Work from Anywhere.* Retrieved May 2, 2005, from www.workingfromanywhere.org.

Johnson, R. W., and Steuerle, E. 2004. Promoting work at older ages: The role of hybrid pension plans in an aging population. *Journal of Pension Economics and Finance* 3(3): 315–37.

Kite, M. E., Stockdale, G. D., and Whitley, B. E., Jr. 2005. Attitudes toward younger and older adults: An updated meta-analytic review. *Journal of Social Issues* 61:241–66.

Kroemer, K. H. E. 2007. Designing for older people. *Ergonomics in Design* 14 (4): 25–31.

Kubeck, J. E., Delp, N. D., Haslett, T. K., and McDaniel, M. A. 1996. Does job-related training performance decline with age? *Psychology and Aging* 11:92–107.

Midwest Institute for Telecommuting Education. 2005. *Small Business use of Telework: Successful Job Alternatives for Persons with Disabilities and Veterans.* Retrieved April 25, 2005, from www.mite.org.

Nilles, J. 1998. *Managing Telework: Strategies for Managing the Virtual Workforce.* New York: Wiley.

Nilles, J., Carlson, F. R., Gray, P., and Hanneman, G. 1976. *The Telecommunications-Transportation Tradeoff: Options for Tomorrow.* New York: Wiley.

Office of Personnel Management. 2003. *Telework: A Management Priority, a Guide for Managers, Supervisors, and Telework Coordinators.* Washington, DC: U.S. Office of Personnel Management.

Olson, M. H. 1988. Organizational barriers to telework. In *Telework: Present Situation and Future Development of a New Form of Work Organization,* ed. W. B. Korte, S. Robinson, and W. J. Steinle, 77–100. Amsterdam: Elsevier Science Publishers.

Oregon Department of Energy. 1995. *Telecommuting: An Option for Oregon Workers with Disabilities.* Salem, OR: Oregon Department of Energy.

Oregon Office of Energy. 1997. *Employees' Quality of Life Brings Telework into Focus.* Salem, OR: Oregon Office of Energy.

Park, D. C., and Swartz, N. 2000. *Cognitive Aging: A Primer.* Philadelphia: Taylor & Francis.

Perry, E. L., Kulik, C. T., and Bourhis, A. C. 1996. Moderating effects of personal and contextual factors in age discrimination. *Journal of Applied Psychology* 81:628–47.

Reynolds, T., and Brusseau, D. 1998. *Cyberlane Commuter.* South Pasadena, CA: iLAN Systems.

Sharit, J., Czaja, S. J., Hernandez, M., Yang, Y., Perdomo, D., Lewis, J. L., et al. 2004. An evaluation of performance by older persons on a simulated telecommuting task. *Journal of Gerontology: Psychological Sciences* 59B (6): 305–16.

UCLA Internet report. 2003. *Surveying the Digital Future.* UCLA Center for Communication Policy. Retrieved August 14, 2003, from www.ccp.ucla.edu/pdf/UCLA-Internet-Report-Year-Three.pdf.

CHAPTER EIGHT

Collaborative Work

What's Age Got to Do with It?

MICHAEL A. SMYER, PH.D.,
AND MARCIE PITT-CATSOUPHES, PH.D.

From the mundane to the monumental, today's work environment requires collaboration (see table 8.1). Three major shifts may affect the process and outcomes of collaborative work: the changing nature of work, the aging of the workforce, and the increasing importance of collaborative work. What do we know about the relationships among these trends? This chapter will focus on teams as an illustration of collaborative work. Teams are "complex, adaptive dynamic systems" (McGrath, Arrow, and Berdahl, 2000; Ilgen, Hollenbeck, Johnson, and Jundt, 2005) that are embedded in larger workforce contexts.

We begin with a brief review of the changing nature of the workplace, highlighting the "flattening" of organizations, the increasing complexity of workflow systems (e.g., Devine et al., 1999), the "flattening" world competition (Friedman, 2005), and the impact of technology on the organization of collaborations (e.g., Bell and Kozlowski, 2002; Czaja, 2001; Czaja and Moen, 2004). For more than a decade, the collaborative workplace has been touted as an important element of successful organizations (e.g., E. M. Marshall, 1995). We then review briefly the demographics of workforce participation. Although this material is covered elsewhere in this volume, we provide a synopsis of the substantial aging of the workforce in the contemporary United States and the prospects for additional change in the short term.

Most of this chapter focuses on an analysis of the relationship among these three trends. We rely on reviews of research on collaborative work highlighting

TABLE 8.1.
Examples of collaborative work

Example 1. We were at O'Hare airport on a wintry day, awaiting the arrival of a delayed flight. The airline staff member announced that the flight had landed and was making its way to our gate. We watched out the window expectantly as the plane taxied toward the Jetway, stopping about 100 feet from its destination. The reason? There was a fuel truck parked in the way. Ground crew scurried to move the truck. A burly crew member climbed in and then quickly emerged, slamming the door on his way out. Evidently, the keys were supposed to be left in the truck. He stomped across the ramp, bellowing his anger at the delay. A few minutes later another crew member emerged and sheepishly handed over the keys. The truck was moved and the jet finally "arrived," adding to the delay and possibly making many of its passengers miss their connections.

Example 2. "I have to depend on a whole bunch of people. . . . That's something you don't understand at first—that in some ways the surgeon is the least important part of the team. That's just part of the modern system." Dr. Atul Gawande, surgeon (quoted in McGrath, 2007, B1)

Example 3. "At approximately 7:00 a.m., the ice team made its second launch pad inspection. On the basis of their report, the launch time was slipped to permit a third ice inspection. At 8:30, the *Challenger* crew were strapped into their seats. At 9:00, the Mission Management Team met with all contractor and NASA representatives to assess launch readiness. They discussed the ice situation. Rockwell representatives expressed concern that the acoustics at ignition would create ice debris that would ricochet, possibly hitting the Orbiter or being aspirated into the SRBs [solid rocket boosters]. Rockwell's position was that they had not launched in conditions of that nature, they were dealing with the unknown, and they could not assure that it was safe to fly. The Mission Management Team discussed the situation and polled those present, who voted to proceed with the launch.
    A little after 11:25 a.m., the terminal countdown began. STS 51-L was launched at 11:38 EST. The ambient temperature at the launch pad was 36° F. The mission ended 73 seconds later as a fireball erupted and the *Challenger* disappeared in a huge cloud of smoke" (Vaughan, 1996, 7).

the evidence that age of the workforce has an effect on process, outcome, or both (e.g., Kozlowski and Ilgen, 2006). Because of space limitations, our review is necessarily illustrative, not exhaustive, focusing primarily on teams as an example of collaborative work units. We hope, however, that it will illuminate gaps in the empirical research base about the relationship between collaborative work and the aging of the workforce. We close with an assessment of the types of inquiry that will help to fill the gaps in the research and practice base on the impact of age on effective collaborative work approaches.

DEFINING COLLABORATIVE WORK

Often the language used to describe work groups is imprecise and does not sufficiently differentiate their important components or dimensions. Terms like *collaborative work, work group,* and *team* may be diffuse (E. M. Marshall, 1995). Before we review relevant research, it is important to clarify the meanings of the terms *collaborative work* and *teams.*

In this review, we will focus on one element of a collaborative workplace: teams. There are many, varied definitions of teams (e.g., Guzzo and Dickson, 1996). For example, Kozlowski and Ilgen suggest that "teams are complex, dynamic systems that exist in a context, develop as members interact over time, and evolve and adapt as situational demands unfold" (2006, 78). They offer a formal definition of a team: "A team can be defined as (a) two or more individuals who (b) socially interact (face-to-face or increasingly virtually); (c) possess one or more common goals; (d) are brought together to perform organizationally relevant tasks; (e) exhibit interdependencies with respect to workflow, goals, and outcomes; (f) have different roles and responsibilities; and (g) are together embedded in an encompassing organizational system, with boundaries and linkages to the broader system context and task environment" (2006, 79).

Their definition is reminiscent of Hackman's earlier definition of "real groups" as "intact social systems, complete with boundaries, interdependence among members, and differentiated member roles. . . . they have one or more tasks to perform . . . for which members have collective responsibility. . . . they operate in an organizational context . . . [which] means that the group, as a collective, manages relations with other individuals or groups in the larger social system" (1990, 4). Hackman's definition emphasizes interdependence among group members and the inter-relations of the group with other aspects of the organization. Implicit in his definition are the "four Rs" of organizations: rules, roles, responsibilities, and relationships. Each is relevant for effective team functioning, and each may also be affected by age and experience.

Both Hackman (1990) and Kozlowski and Ilgen (2006) emphasize the ecology of work groups. Both definitions remind us of the larger social context that organizations both shape and respond to. The social and economic demands of organizations affect the structure and function of teams. Formal policies and informal practices provide the context for teams' efforts. In turn, the larger social ecology affects organizations. We next turn to the larger social context that has shaped the changing workplace during the last two decades.

THE CHANGING NATURE OF THE WORKPLACE

Bluestein (2006) summarized the substantial changes that have occurred in the nature of work and their consequences for employees in the twenty-first century.[1]

Drawing on Rifkin's (1995) analysis, he points to three implications of the digital revolution in work:

- "Computers have allowed factories to increasingly turn work over to machines and robotic devices, thereby reducing jobs in numerous occupational fields and making other jobs completely obsolete." This set of events has eliminated a potential path of upward mobility for low income workers, while reducing production costs for employers.
- "Digital technology allows production to move to any part of the world and still be tightly controlled and managed from a central location." This has contributed to making the world "flat" in Friedman's (2005) now-famous phrase.
- "Automation has led to a vast decline in the need for middle-level managers, who are not as critical in managing unskilled and semi-skilled workers and in relating information between various sectors of an organization." This has led to the leaner organizational chart favored by employers and consultants alike. (Bluestein, 2006, 39)

The increased dependence on technology has affected essential processes between and among team members. Communication is increasingly computer and email-based. In addition, there is an increasing expectation of a rising standard of team members' technological literacy—an element that may be important when considering the age mix of team members. These new ways of communicating may be challenging for the current cohort of older adults who are more accustomed to more traditional forms of communication and who may not have the technical skills required by the new and emerging communication processes. In addition, employers may overlook older workers in offering training and technological upgrades, thus exacerbating the situation.

Drawing on Friedman's work (1999, 2005), Bluestein (2006) points out the underlying assumption of the pervasive spread of free market capitalism and its influence on labor markets and expectations. As a dynamic process, globalization has created a universal labor market, leaving a more competitive and less secure workplace in its wake. Berger (2005) makes clear the implications of globalization for older workers: "It's no wonder that people worry about losing their jobs. Middle-aged employees who lose work today in the United States are not likely to be reemployed at the same wages and benefits they enjoyed in the positions they once held. Too many of the new jobs in the economy pay incomes that do not move families over the federal poverty level" (287).

Of course, globalization and technological changes are closely linked. Both trends require employers to manage talent across time and space and, increasingly, across generations and age spans. As Dvorak (2007) noted, a growing number of companies in several different sectors of the economy are dividing up their work across their global talent pool. But there are several challenges for global teams: monitoring one another's progress, coordinating efforts, and sharing information. As Dvorak put it: "Engineers in the U.S. who feel their jobs are threatened by colleagues in China may hoard information rather than sharing it" (2007, B4). If older workers feel particularly threatened by the globalization or technology trends, they may be less willing or able to participate in the rapidly changing communication and collaboration processes at work.

Bluestein (2006) notes the changing expectation of lifelong employment with one employer. An older worker recently said: "These young folks come in not expecting to stay too long. They aren't willing to make a commitment to the organization. . . . But then, the organization isn't making a commitment to them."[2] This change reflects a shift from what Hall and Mirvis (1996, 21) label organizational careers to what they term "protean" careers "any kind of flexible, idiosyncratic career course, with peaks and valleys, left turns, moves from one line of work to another and so forth . . . the protean career is unique to each person" (quoted in Bluestein, 2006, 48).

The changing contract may affect both the composition of collaborative work groups and the willingness of employees to make longer-term investments in training and skills upgrading. Employees may be increasingly asking if the investment in training and skill building will have immediate and direct rewards for them as well as for their employers.

WORKFORCE DEMOGRAPHICS

Others in this volume have presented detailed analyses of the current and future demographic shifts under way in the U.S. labor force and in the world's workforce. Our purpose here is to summarize this information briefly so that later we may link this information to data on workplace perceptions and functioning.

As shown in figure 8.1, the United States is in the midst of a demographic transition to an older workforce. These data are familiar to the research community and increasingly familiar to the employer community across the nation. Several elements contribute to this pattern, including an extension of labor force participation beyond traditional retirement age by both men and women (see Quinn, 2002; Cahill, Giandrea, and Quinn, 2006) and a relatively smaller cohort of workers following the baby-boom generation: 76 million baby boom-

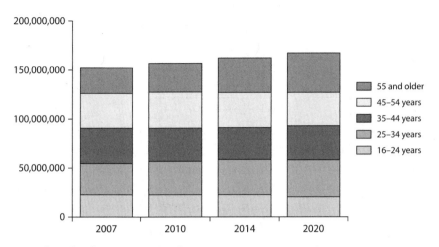

Figure 8.1. Labor force composition, by age group. *Source:* Bureau of Labor Statistics, 2007

ers are poised to retire, while only 46 million Gen Xers are entering the labor force (Eisenberg, 2002).

The generational mix of the labor force is also changing, with World War II, baby boomers, Gen X and Gen Y employees sharing the same workspace. It is important to note, though, that we should not equate generation and career stage (see Pitt-Catsouphes, Smyer, Matz-Costa, and Kane, 2007). For example, in an era of flexible work options and protean careers, a baby boomer may be an early career employee who is starting a "bridge job" or "down shifting" to remain in the paid labor force past the traditional retirement age (see Cahill et al., 2006).

Some have suggested that there may be a "crisis" because of generational differences in views of work and workplaces at a time of potential labor shortages (e.g., Dychtwald, Erickson, and Morison, 2006). More important for our consideration of team structure and function, however, is emerging information on generational perspectives of older workers and potential team members.

James, Swanberg, and McKechnie (2007) assessed employees' perception of older workers and the impact of those perceptions on older workers themselves. As part of a larger study of employees in a national retail chain, Citisales (a pseudonym), they used a measure developed by V. W. Marshall (1996) to assess perceptions of workers 55 or older. As shown in figure 8.2, members of older generations were more likely to perceive older workers more positively than were members of Generation X or Y.

James, Swanberg, and McKechnie (2007) also assessed the influence of perceived opportunities for promotion on members of different generations at work.

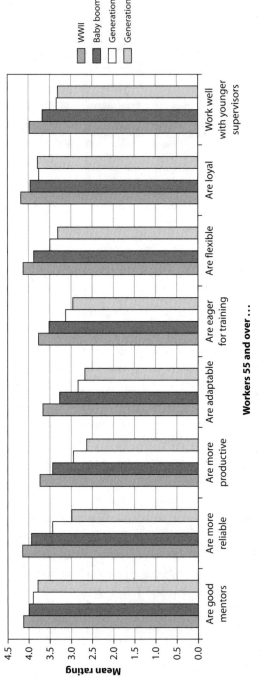

Figure 8.2. Perception of older workers by different cohorts. *Source:* Adapted from James, Swanberg, and McKechnie, 2007

Not surprisingly, they found that older workers who perceived equal opportunities for employment were significantly more engaged than those who did not. However, the results were different for the youngest generation of employees: they were less likely to be engaged if they perceived that employees 55 or older had equal opportunities for promotion. These results illustrate the complex way in which generational composition may affect individual and team functioning.

In summary, the changing age and generational mix at work poses significant challenges for employers and employees. It also suggests that age and generation may affect team functioning and the psychological elements that underlie it.

PSYCHOLOGICAL RESEARCH ON COLLABORATIVE WORK: AGING AND TEAM FUNCTIONING

Consider the following business example:

> The Boss is just over 60, seasoned and rumored to be thinking about how much longer he will be working. His second in command is a whiz kid Gen Xer with Ivy League credentials, great on strategy, but not a lot of experience in the business. Their front line manager is a baby boomer who has a lot of experience and a wry sense of humor; he's seen strategists come and go. His workforce is mainly Gen Y and Gen Xers, with a few boomers holding on. Their goals are simple: Win a world championship. Meet today's multigenerational workforce. Meet the Boston Red Sox.

In this section, we focus on the effect of aging on collaborative work. We will use teams as an example of collaborative work, drawing on Kozlowski and Ilgen's (2006) comprehensive and exhaustive meta-analysis of research on the structure and function of teams. Kozlowski and Ilgen emphasize several elements of teams that make their structure and functioning a challenge both for management and for research. They conceptualize the team as "embedded in a *multilevel system* that has individual, team, and organizational-level aspects; which focuses centrally on *task-relevant processes;* which incorporates *temporal dynamics* encompassing episodic tasks and developmental progression; and which views team processes and effectiveness as *emergent phenomena* unfolding in a proximal task—or social context that teams in part enact while also being embedded in a larger organizational system or environmental context" (2006, 80).

Two elements are important in this description: the team's embeddedness in larger organizational and social contexts, and the emergent properties of team functioning, in part in response to those contexts. The "internal pressure" of members within the team also interacts with the "external" pressure, or the system environment of the larger organization and the larger economy. The changing age composition of today's work groups could affect both the internal pressures on teams and the team's ability to respond effectively to the larger organization.

Hedge, Borman, and Lammlein (2006) focused attention on the effect of job organization and change on older workers. They noted that the increased emphasis on collaborative team work may pose significant challenges to older workers' self-management strategies: "This kind of environment can require adaptability and lead to increased stress; furthermore, these features may not be compatible with older workers' needs, preferences, or personal characteristics" (2006, 60).

Following a structure developed in earlier reviews (e.g., Kozlowski and Bell, 2003; Ilgen et al., 2005), Kozlowski and Ilgen (2006) classify team processes into three major categories: cognitive, affective/motivational, or behavioral (see table 8.2). We will briefly review each area, highlighting key themes and providing illustrations of how age might affect team functioning.

At the outset, however, we should emphasize that Kozlowski and Ilgen (2006) do not comment on the impact of age composition on team effectiveness in the cognitive, affective/motivational, or behavioral areas. Thus, our comments about aging and team work are necessarily speculative, because there are limited empirical data on this topic. We will focus on one example in each domain (cognitive, affective, and behavioral) to illustrate the potential impact of age and aging on team functioning.

TABLE 8.2.
Team processes

Cognitive	Affective/Motivational	Behavioral
Unit and team climate	Team cohesion	Team coordination, cooperation, and communication
Team mental models	Team efficacy/Group potency	Team member competencies
Transactive memory	Team affect, mood, and emotion	Team regulation, performance, dynamics, and adaptation
Team learning	Team conflict	

Source: Adapted from Kozlowski and Ilgen, 2006

Within the cognitive domain, the first element that Kozlowski and Ilgen focus on is "a collective climate that captures the strategic imperatives reflective of the core missions and objectives of an organization or unit" (2006, 82). When effective, the team climate answers the "why" question of work: Why is the team's contribution important to the overall enterprise? Kozlowski and Ilgen suggest that leadership and social interaction are the key levers for using team climate effectively. Arsenault (2004) notes the importance of generational differences in leadership style and preferences and focuses on generation, and not age, as a salient dimension.

The next cognitive domains are team mental models and transactive memory: "Cognitive structures or knowledge [are] representations that enable team members to organize and acquire information necessary to anticipate and execute actions. . . . [T]eam mental models refer to knowledge structures held in common, whereas transactive memory refers to knowledge of information distribution within a team (i.e., knowledge of who knows what)" (Kozlowski and Ilgen, 2006, 83). These elements answer the "how" question of team effectiveness: How does the team effectively distribute work and pass along the knowledge of how things get done? Kozlowski and Ilgen suggest that leadership and training are key levers for effectiveness in these domains, along with shared experience. Although some have focused on team learning (e.g., Ellis et al., 2003), the effect of age on team functioning awaits further explication.

These areas reflect the challenge of what David DeLong labeled "lost knowledge": "the decreased capacity for effective action or decision making in a specific function, team or role" (2004, 22). The organizational challenge that an aging workforce poses for team transactive memory is clear: How does a team or an organization capture the tacit knowledge acquired by its seasoned employees before they leave the setting? DeLong points out that attrition through retirement may be a significant threat to effective team performance because today's older workers have witnessed significant increases in technical and scientific knowledge as well as knowledge of integrated management and processing. DeLong suggests that the team and the organization assess the probability and seriousness of the impact of lost knowledge on team effectiveness and undertake knowledge retention strategies to prevent or remediate the effect of the aging and exiting of seasoned employees.

When Kozlowski and Ilgen turned to the affective/motivational states, they again emphasized the emergent, dynamic quality of four important phenomena that reflect the interactions among team members: "We focus on a set of constructs—*team cohesion; team efficacy and group potency; affect, mood and emotion;*

and team conflict—that capture bonding to the team and its task; confidence in members' task competencies; affective processes and reactions; and their fractures, frictions, and disagreement" (2006, 87). In reviewing this literature, Kozlowski and Ilgen conclude that there is a need for additional research in several of these areas. They note that as workforce interdependence increases, the relationship between team cohesion and performance also increases (see Gully, Devine, and Whitney, 1995; Beal, Cohen, Burke, and McLendon, 2003). Preliminary information suggests that teams with greater interpersonal cohesion and collective pride will be more effective, but the techniques for achieving cohesion and pride have not been sufficiently identified.

In assessing the effect of team efficacy and group potency, much of the literature is built upon generalizing from earlier work on the influence of individual self-efficacy (e.g., Bandura, 1977). Meta-analyses have established a link between self-efficacy and performance on both the individual (Stajkovic and Luthans, 1998) and team level (Gully, Incalcaterra, Joshi, and Baubien, 2002; Chen, Thomas, and Wallace, 2005). Again, Kozlowski and Ilgen (2006) point out that the levers for effectively developing team efficacy and group potency are not clear, although the role of leadership and team training are apparent. As Chen et al. (2005) note, there are few controlled experimental analyses of the links between team efficacy and team performance. Again, further detailed explication of the influence of age on these processes remains to be completed.

When considering team affect, mood, and emotion, Kozlowski and Ilgen (2006) note that there has been increasing interest in extending attention from individual emotional states to team functioning. However, scholars investigating individual emotions have been careful to differentiate between and among affect, moods, and emotions (e.g., Brief and Weiss, 2002; Barrett, Mesquita, Ochsner, and Gross, 2007), which differ in "specificity, duration, and the target of feelings" (Kozlowski and Ilgen, 2006, 91). Those who have been studying team affect, mood, and emotion have not been as careful. Kozlowski and Ilgen conclude that "research in the area of collective affect, mood, and emotions in work teams is in its infancy, both conceptually and empirically. Conceptually, the rising tide of interest in feeling-focused constructs at the individual level is just beginning to flow to teams. . . . However, the research base is not sufficiently well developed to provide guidance for application recommendations" (2006, 93).

Scholars and practitioners have focused on team conflict for some time. Some have argued that differences can undermine team performance and team-member satisfaction (e.g., Lau and Murnighan, 1998). Others (e.g., Janis, 1972) have suggested that conflict can avoid groupthink and can enhance the innovation and the quality of decision making (e.g., Mannix and Neale, 2005; Roberto, 2005). Again, despite interesting initial work in this area, Kozlowski and Ilgen conclude that the "research foundation is not sufficiently well developed to formulate hard recommendations for practice" (2006, 95).

One example of potential team conflict illustrates the need for additional information on the effect of aging on team functioning: intergenerational conflict between and among team members. As discussed earlier, James, Swanberg, and McKechnie (2007) documented the potential influence of generational views of competency, capacity, and likelihood for advancement within the organization. Galinsky and colleagues (Bond et al., 2002; Families and Work, 2002) noted that there are currently four generations in the workplace: the "mature" generation, ages 62 and above; the baby boomers, ages 42–61; Generation X, ages 27–41; and Generation Y, ages 18 to 26. These generations have different views of supervision, with 71 percent of the "matures" and 23 percent of the boomers reporting that their supervisor is "significantly younger." Moreover, 20 percent of the "matures" reported having "significant problems" with their younger bosses.

In the area of team action and behavioral processes, Kozlowski and Ilgen (2006) focus on three domains: coordination, cooperation, and communication; team member competencies; and team regulation and adaptation. Here they are reasonably optimistic in their summary of the literature: "Teams with better individual teamwork KSAs [knowledge, skills, and abilities], competencies and functions will be more effective. . . . [T]eams with better regulatory-process dynamics that express these competencies as synchronized individual and team action will be more effective. We conclude that factors that influence the development of self-regulation can be adapted to team regulation. . . . [T]eam leadership and team training are key leverage points for shaping the development of team regulatory-process competencies" (2006, 98). Although research has been done on each of these areas (e.g., Cohen, 1994, on self-management of teams), the effect of age on collaborative functions has not been fully explored.

Three areas for intervention emerge from Kozlowsi and Ilgen's (2006) meta-analysis: team design, team training, and team leadership. Although each area needs additional research, these are the areas that seem most promising for enhancing the performance and effectiveness of teams.

Kozlowski and Ilgen point out that team design encompasses several elements: "Team-design factors center on the structure of the team task, group composition (i.e., combination of member knowledge, skills, abilities and other characteristics [KSAOs]), and group performance norms" (2006, 99). They note that more research is needed on the most effective team composition for achieving optimal team performance, a theme echoed by Sundstrom et al. (2000). Although they do not mention it, the effect of age composition on individual and team productivity warrants further assessment.

To illustrate these themes, we will draw on information from the Boston College National Study of Business Strategy and Workforce Development (see Pitt-Catsouphes et al., 2007, for a description of the study). First, we present the employers' perspectives on age and career stage. Drawing from a sample of 578 employers, a clear sense of age- and stage-related expectations emerges. (See table 8.3.)

These data reflect employers' perceptions of individual employees. They do not convey their assumptions regarding effective team members and aging, but they give a glimpse into the employer context for aging and collaborative work. They reflect employers' perceptions of the knowledge, skills, and attributes that employees in different age/career stage categories typically bring to their team tasks.

Figure 8.3 depicts the linkage that employers see between career stage and various skills, knowledge, and abilities that are important for effective workplace functioning. Again, these employers are focused on individual employees, but they are assessing the behavioral areas of competencies that contribute to effective team functioning (e.g., skills, networks, and leadership interest). It would be useful to seek employers' assessment of the appropriate age or career stage mixture that contributes to effective team functioning in these behavioral areas.

When they turned to team training, Kozlowski and Ilgen (2006) again pointed out the limitations of the research literature. For our purposes, their summary is important: "Cross training, forms of simulation-based training, and team adaptation-coordination-CRM (Crew Resource Management) training all evidence sufficient research-based support to justify recommending them as credible and effective team-training techniques" (2006, 105). As they point out,

TABLE 8.3.
Employers' perspectives of age and career stage

Career stage	Age range	Descriptors
Early career	21–38	"New in the business," "1–3 years experience," "Still exploring interests and where they best fit"
Mid-career	31–47	"At least a decade in the business," "Family responsibilities," "Solid 8+ years experience. 1–2 employers"
Late career	46–63	"Peaked in career opportunities," "Holders of valuable knowledge and insights. . . . Getting ready to hand over the reins"

Source: Pitt-Catsouphes et al., 2007

these approaches have been developed and used chiefly in military and commercial aviation applications and, more recently, in other high-reliability areas (e.g., off-shore drilling). However, the effect of aging on these team-training techniques has not been fully explored, although there is a rich literature on the bearing of aging on learning and training effectiveness (e.g., Sterns and Doverspike, 1988, 1989; Kubeck, Delp, Haslett, and McDaniel, 1996; Warr, 2001; Hedge et al., 2006). For example, Willis and colleagues (2006) reported on the long-term (5-year) effect of a cognitive training for older adults. While their focus was on instrumental activities of daily living (IADL), their work illustrates the approach needed in the workplace: assessing the effects of age on the short- and long-term influence of training on specific tasks.

Team leadership is a key leverage point for employers seeking to enhance the effectiveness and productivity of collaborative work (Kozlowski et al., in press). Kozlowski and Ilgen (2006) review several approaches to leadership, noting that much of this literature has not focused on the most effective leadership for team processes. A significant exception is a recent meta-analysis by Burke et al. (in press). As Kozlowski and Ilgen summarized it: "The results strongly point to the conclusion that leadership in teams affects team performance by influencing the way team members work with their tasks and by influencing socio-emotional variables" (2006, 110). They note that the literature suggests that leadership affects all three types of team processes: cognitive, affective, and behavioral (Kozlowski et al., in press). Again, however, there has been little analysis of how age influences these team processes.

RESEARCH DIRECTIONS

In this section, we sketch out a framework for research on the effects of age on collaborative work processes. Salthouse (2006) suggested that five basic questions about aging form a context for considering the impact of aging. They also form a framework for considering the effect of age on collaborative work, in this case team functioning. (See table 8.4.)

As table 8.4 suggests, there are two distinctive research approaches for assessing the relationship of aging and collaborative work functioning: one approach will focus on the individual employee (e.g., Sarason, 1977); the other will focus on the context provided by the employer (e.g., Taylor and Walker, 1998). Eventually, work in both areas is necessary to answer the conditional question: Under what conditions will age affect both the employers' ability and willingness to pro-

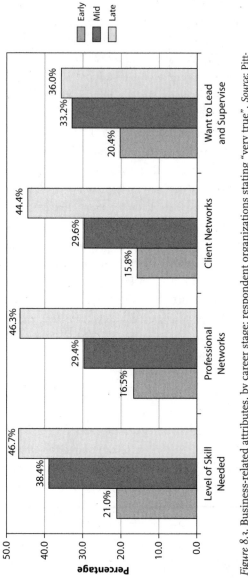

Figure 8.3. Business-related attributes, by career stage: respondent organizations stating "very true". *Source:* Pitt-Catsouphes et al., 2007

TABLE 8.4.
Pragmatic questions on aging and collaborative work

Question	Issue	Elaboration
What?	In what psychological respects do team members vary by age?	What predicts variability in individual or group functioning in cognitive, affective, or behavioral areas?
When?	At what ages do changes occur?	Are the changes influenced by age, generation, or career stage?
Where?	Which aspect of the organization or team influence the effect of aging?	Is there a cultural definition of "optimal team members"?
Why?	What is responsible for the impact of age on team functioning?	How does the larger organizational context affect collaborative work? How do we assess the collaborative person/environment fit?
How?	What mechanisms can influence the age/team functioning relationship?	Are team- and individual-focused interventions (e.g., team design, training, leadership) crafted with an aging-relevant component?

Source: Adapted from Salthouse, 2006

vide the conditions for effective collaborative work, and the employees' ability to effectively participate in a collaborative work effort?

For example, despite older workers' clear preferences for flexible work arrangements, these arrangements are not frequently used in the later years of employment (Pitt-Catsouphes and Smyer, 2006). The good news is that there are several options available to employers for improving the fit of work arrangements with their employees' desires. For the purpose of this chapter, however, it is also important to note that these are data anchored in individual perspectives. Assessing the link between flexible work options and the influence of team preferences, age composition, and employer options on collaborative work effectiveness awaits further research.

Another example from the employer perspective is employers' attempts to shape the age structure of their workforce, eventually affecting the composition of work groups and their collaborative work forces. These data from the Boston College National Study of Business Strategy and Workforce Development (Pitt-Catsouphes et al., 2007) represent employers' responses to the "how" question of table 8.4. As reflected in figure 8.4, a minority of employers are focusing on retention of older workers beyond traditional retirement age. Research on the com-

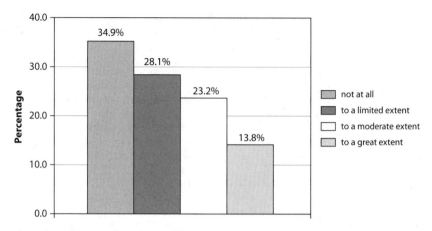

Figure 8.4. Adoption of strategies to encourage late-career employees to continue to work past typical retirement age: respondent organizations, by extent. *Source:* Pitt-Catsouphes et al., 2007

bined effect of workforce aging and collaborative work approaches may influence employers' recruitment and retention efforts. Again, research linking these elements has not yet emerged.

CONCLUSION

This chapter reviewed recent literature documenting several interacting trends: changes in the workplace requiring enhanced collaborative work; increasing scrutiny of team processes that affect productivity; increasing attention to the changing employee preferences (both older and younger employees) for workplace flexibility; and employers' perspectives on age, career stage, and the options available for their employees. Thus far, the research literature has not caught up to the realities of the workplace in exploring the intersection of aging, collaborative work, and employer options. The good news is that extensions of work from industrial/organizational psychology and from gerontological psychology may reap important benefits for both employers and employees in an aging workforce.

ACKNOWLEDGMENT

We are grateful to the Alfred P. Sloan Foundation for its support of this work through its grant to the Center on Aging and Work/Workplace Flexibility. We also appreciate the assistance of Javier Boyas and Carianne Preziosi in reviewing the literature for this chapter.

NOTES

1. Gunderson, Jones, and Scanland (2005) also offer a thoughtful synopsis of the major challenges facing employers and employees because of the converging impact of these trends.

2. Comment from a focus group on the meanings of work conducted with older workers by the Sloan Center on Aging and Work at Boston College (see Smyer and Pitt-Catsouphes, 2007).

REFERENCES

Arsenault, P. M. 2004. Validating generational differences: A legitimate diversity and leadership issue. *Leadership and Organization Development Journal* 25 (2): 124–41.

Bandura, A. 1977. Self-efficacy: Toward a unifying theory of behavioral change. *Psychological Review* 84:191–215.

Barrett, L. F., Mesquita, B., Ochsner, K. N., and Gross, J. J. 2007. The experience of emotion. *Annual Review of Psychology* 58:373–403.

Beal, D. J., Cohen, R. R., Burke, M. J., and McLendon, C. I. 2003. Cohesion and performance in groups: A meta-analytic clarification of construct relations. *Journal of Applied Psychology* 88:989–1004.

Bell, B. S., and Kozlowski, S. W. J. 2002. A typology of virtual teams: Implications for effective leadership. *Group and Organization Management* 27:14–49.

Berger, S. 2005. *How We Compete: What Companies around the World are Doing to Make It in Today's Global Economy*. New York: Doubleday.

Bluestein, D. L. 2006. *The Psychology of Working: A New Perspective for Career Development, Counseling, and Public Policy*. Mahwah, NJ: Lawrence Erlbaum Associates.

Bond, J. T., Thompson, C., Galinsky, E. and Prottas, D. 2002. *The National Study of the Changing Workforce*. New York: Families and Work Institute.

Brief, A. P., and Weiss, H. M. 2002. Organizational behavior: Affect in the workplace. *Annual Review of Psychology* 53:279–307.

Burke, C. S., Stagl, K. C., Klein, C., Goodwin, G. F., Salas, E., and Halpin, S. in press. Does leadership in teams matter? A meta-analytic integration. *Leadership Quarterly*.

Cahill, K. E., Giandrea, M. D., and Quinn, J. F. 2006. Retirement patterns from career employment. *The Gerontologist* 46(4): 514–23.

Chen, G., Thomas, B., and Wallace, J. C. 2005. A multilevel examination of the relationship among training outcomes, mediating regulatory processes, and adaptive performance. *Journal of Applied Psychology* 90 (5): 827–41.

Cohen, S. G. 1994. Designing effective self-managing work teams. In *Advances in Interdisciplinary Studies of Work Teams: Vol. 1. Theories of Self-managed Work Teams*, ed. M. M. Beyerlein, D. A. Johnson, and S. T. Beyerlein. Greenwhich, CT: JAI Press

Czaja, S. J. 2001. Technological change and the older worker. In *Handbook of the Psychology of Aging*, ed. J. E. Birren and K.W. Schaie, 547–68. San Diego: Academic Press.

Czaja, S. J., and Moen, P. 2004. Technology and employment. In *Technology for Adaptive*

Aging: Report and Papers, ed. R. Pew and S. Van Hemel, 150–78. Washington, DC: National Academies Press.

DeLong, D. 2004. *Lost knowledge: Confronting the Threat of an Aging Workforce.* New York: Oxford University Press.

Devine, D. J., Clayton, L. D., Phillips, J. L., Dunford, B. B., and Melner, S. B. 1999. Teams in organizations: Prevalence, characteristics, and effectiveness. *Small Group Research* 30:678–711.

Dvorak, P. 2007. How teams can work well together from far apart. *Wall Street Journal,* 17 September, B4.

Dychtwald, K., Erickson, T. J., and Morison, R. 2006. *Workforce Crisis: How to Beat the Coming Shortage of Skills and Talent.* Boston: Harvard Business School Press.

Eisenberg, D. 2002. The coming job boom. Time Business Web site: www.time.com/time/classroom/glenfall2002/pg30.html.

Ellis, A. P. J., Porter, C. L. H., Hollenbeck, J. R., Ilgen, D. R., West, B. J., and Moon, H. 2003. Team learning: Collectively connecting the dots. Journal of Applied Psychology 88 (5): 821–35.

Families and Work. 2002. *Generations and Gender.* New York: Families and Work Institute.

Friedman, T. L. 1999. *The Lexus and the Olive Tree: Understanding Globalization.* New York: Farrar, Strauss & Giroux.

———. 2005. *The World Is Flat: A Brief History of the Twenty-First Century.* Waterville, ME: Thorndike Press.

Gully, S. M., Devine, D. J., and Whitney, D. J. 1995. A meta-analysis of cohesion and performance: Effects of levels of analysis and task interdependence. *Small Group Research* 26:497–520.

Gully, S. M., Incalcaterra, K. A., Joshi, A., and Baubien, J. M. 2002. A meta-analysis of team-efficacy, potency, and performance: Interdependence and level of analysis as moderators of observed relationships. *Journal of Applied Psychology* 87:819–32.

Gunderson, S., Jones, R., and Scanland, K. 2005. *The Jobs Revolution: Changing How America Works.* Washington, DC: Copywriters.

Guzzo, R. A., and Dickson, M. W. 1996. Team in organizations: Recent research on performance and effectiveness. *Annual Review of Psychology* 47:307–38.

Hackman, R., ed. 1990. *Groups That Work (and Those That Don't): Creating Conditions for Effective Teamwork.* San Francisco: Jossey-Bass.

Hall, D. T., and Mirvis, P. H. 1996. The new protean career: Psychological success and the path with a heart. In *The Career Is Dead, Long Live the Career: A Relational Approach to Careers,* ed. D. T. Hall, 15–45. San Francisco: Jossey-Bass.

Hedge, J. W., Borman, W. C., and Lammlein, S. E. 2006. *The Aging Workforce: Realities, Myths, and Implications for Organizations.* Washington, DC: American Psychological Association.

Ilgen, D. R., Hollenbeck, J. R., Johnson, M., and Jundt, D. 2005. Teams in organizations: From input-process-output models to IMOI models. *Annual Review of Psychology* 56: 517–43.

James, J. B., Swanberg, J., and McKechnie, S. P. 2007. *Generational Differences in Percep-*

tions of Older Workers' Capabilities. Issue Brief. Chestnut Hill, MA: Center on Aging and Work, Boston College.

Janis, I. L. 1972. *Victims of Groupthink: A Psychological Study of Foreign-Policy Decisions and Fiascoes*. Boston: Houghton Mifflin.

Kozlowski, S. W. J., and Bell, B. S. 2003. Work groups and teams in organizations. In *Handbook of Psychology: Vol. 12. Industrial and Organizational Psychology*, ed. W. C. Borman, D. R. Ilgen, and R. J. Klimoski, 333–75. London: Wiley.

Kozlowski, S. W. J., and Ilgen, D. R. 2006. Enhancing the effectiveness of work groups and teams. *Psychological Science in the Public Interest* 7:77–124.

Kozlowski, S. W., Watola, D. J., Nowakowski, J. M., Kim, B. H., and Botero, I. C. In press. Developing adaptive teams: A theory of dynamic team leadership. In *Team Effectiveness in Complex Organizations: Cross- Disciplinary Perspectives and Approaches* (SIOP Frontiers Series), ed. E. Salas, G. F. Goodwin, and C. S. Burke, eds. Mahwah, NJ: LEA.

Kubeck, J. E., Delp, N. D., Haslett, T. K., and McDaniel, M. A. 1996. Does job-related training performance decline with age? *Psychology and Aging* 11:92–107.

Lau, D. C., and Murnighan, J. K. 1998. Demographic diversity and faultlines: The compositional dynamics of organizational groups. *Academy of Management Review* 23: 325–40.

Marshall, E. M. 1995. *Transforming the Way We Work: The Power of the Collaborative Workplace*. New York: American Management Association.

Marshall, V. W. 1996. *Issues of an Aging Workforce: A Study to Inform Human Resources Policy Development*. Toronto: Center for Studies of Aging, University of Toronto.

McGrath, C. 2007. An author rocks in the O.R. *New York Times*, 3 April, B1.

McGrath, J. E., Arrow, H., and Berdahl, J. L. 2000. The study of groups: Past, present, and future. *Personality and Social Psychology Review* 4:95–105.

Mannix, E., and Neale, M. 2005. What differences make a difference? The promise and reality of diverse teams in organizations. *Psychological Science in the Public Interest* 6: 31–55.

Pitt-Catsouphes, M., and Smyer, M. A. 2006. *One size doesn't fit all: Workplace Flexibility*. Issue Brief, 05. Chestnut Hill, MA: Center on Aging and Work/Workplace Flexibility at Boston College. Retrieved on March 27, 2007, from http://agingandwork.bc.edu/documents/IB_05_OneSizeDoesntFit_000.pdf.

Pitt-Catsouphes, M., Smyer, M. A., Matz-Costa, C., and Kane, K. 2007. The National Study Report: Part II of the National Study of Business Strategy and Workforce Development. *Research Highlight, No. 4*. Chestnut Hill, MA: Center on Aging and Work/Workplace Flexibility at Boston College. Retrieved on March 27, 2007, from http://agingandwork.bc.edu/documents/RH_04_NationalStudy_03_07_002.pdf.

Quinn, J. F. 2002. Changing retirement trends and their impact on elderly entitlement programs. In *Policies for an Aging Society*, ed. S. H. Altman and D. Shactman, 293–315. Baltimore: Johns Hopkins University Press.

Rifkin, J. 1995. *The End of Work: The Decline of the Global Labor Market Force and the Dawn of the Post-Market Era*. New York: Tarcher/Putnam.

Roberto, M. A. 2005. *Why Great Leaders Don't Take Yes for an Answer: Managing for Conflict and Consensus*. Upper Saddle River, NJ: Wharton School Publishing.

Salthouse, T. 2006. Theoretical issues in the psychology of aging. In *Handbook of the Psychology of Aging*, 6th ed., ed. J. E. Birren and K. W. Schaie, 1–13. Boston: Academic Press.

Sarason, S. 1977. *Work, Aging and Social Change: Professionals and the One Life-One Career Imperative.* New York: Free Press.

Smyer, M. A., and Pitt-Catsouphes, M. 2007. The meanings of work for older workers. *Generations* 31 (1): 23–30.

Stajkovic, A. D., and Luthans, F. 1998. Self-efficacy and work-related performance: A meta-analysis. *Psychological Bulletin* 124:240–61.

Sterns, H. L., and Doverspike, D. 1988. Training and developing the older worker: Implications for human resource management. In *Fourteen Steps in Managing an Aging Workforce*, ed. H. Dennis, ed., 97–110. Lexington, MA: Lexington Books.

———. 1989. Age and the training and learning process. In *Training and Development in Organization*, ed. I. L. Goldstein, 299–322. San Francisco: Jossey-Bass.

Sundstrom, E., McIntyre, M., Halfhill, T, and Richards, H. 2000. Work groups from the Hawthorne studies to work teams of the 1990s and beyond. *Group Dynamics: Theory, Research, and Practice* 4:44–67.

Taylor, P., and Walker, A. 1998. Employers and older workers: Attitudes and employment practices. *Ageing and Society* 18:641–58.

Vaughan, D. 1996. *The Challenger Launch Decision: Risky Technology, Culture, and Deviance at NASA.* Chicago: University of Chicago Press.

Warr, P. 2001. Age and work behaviour: Physical attributes, cognitive abilities, knowledge, personality traits and motives. *International Review of Industrial and Organizational Psychology* 16:1–36.

Willis, S. L., Tennstedt, S. L., Marsiske, M., Ball, K., Elias, J., and Koepe, K. M. 2006. Long-term effects of cognitive training on everyday functional outcomes in older adults. *JAMA* 296 (23): 2805–14.

CHAPTER NINE

The Issues and Opportunities of Entrepreneurship after Age 50

EDWARD G. ROGOFF, PH.D.

Entrepreneurship is a major force in the U.S. economy, encompassing businesses from part-time, home-based work to major enterprises backed by sophisticated venture capital funding. Although entrepreneurship has received significant and growing attention generally, it has only recently been recognized as an important activity among older Americans. While data are incomplete, the evidence is clear that entrepreneurship among older Americans is a major phenomenon. This chapter provides an overview of the field by applying accepted concepts of entrepreneurship study to an older population. The chapter also proposes steps for advancing the field academically and practically.

Research by AARP (2002) found that 69 percent of people between the ages of 45 and 74 who are still in the workforce plan to continue working in some way beyond their normal retirement. This finding was largely duplicated in a subsequent AARP (2003) study among workers ages 50 to 70, 68 percent of whom reported they plan to work in some capacity after retirement. Many of these people will likely choose entrepreneurship in the form of self-employment, business ownership, or direct investment in a small business as postretirement ventures. A 2006 nationwide survey of Americans ages 45 to 64 sponsored by Thrivent Financial, found that 71 percent believe they will lack the funds in retirement to fulfill their plans, and 43 percent plan to work either full or part-time in retirement. More specifically, 34 percent of the sample felt that it was very or somewhat likely that they would start a business following retirement from their current employment (Thrivent, 2006).

Entrepreneurship delivers many benefits, whether people consider themselves in the postretirement phase of their careers or not. Entrepreneurship is flexible, allowing individuals to design their ventures to suit their needs, whether limiting work hours, working alone or with partners, concentrating on current income or building future value, or focusing on long- or short-term goals. For older workers who prefer traditional employment, entrepreneurship becomes a choice when they encounter age discrimination, face an unwanted prospect of relocation, or find the available options unattractive because of low pay.

THE CHARACTERISTICS OF ENTREPRENEURSHIP

There is no single accepted definition of entrepreneurship. Some people think of entrepreneurship as aggressive, creative, and innovative business creation. Others define it as simply identical to self-employment. In the academic world, two definitions predominate. The first, a process-focused definition, views entrepreneurship as the process of pursuing opportunities and recruiting the resources needed to bring these ventures to reality (Stevenson and Jarillo, 1990; Ireland, Hitt, and Sirmon, 2003). The second definition is structurally oriented, and considers the legal structure used or the time commitment that a person has to the venture. The legal entity definition involves governing structure, such as a corporation or partnership, and is typified by the Census Bureau research discussed later in this chapter. The time commitment definition is usually established in hours per week of work on the venture. Major studies employing this approach have often used six hours per week as the minimum required time (Heck and Scannell, 1999).

Overall, entrepreneurship can reasonably be seen as money making through participation in any parts of the process of establishing, operating, or investing in business ventures. This definition covers self-employment, including innovative as well as more traditional businesses, and makes no requirements as to the hours spent in the business, the percentage of ownership, or legal structure; nor does it make any assumptions about the size of the financial ambitions of the entrepreneur. In fact, making money does not have to be the sole or even main goal. As discussed below, many entrepreneurs have personal or social-purpose goals as their main motivation. This broad definition suits later-life entrepreneurs because it encompasses the multitude of strategies that later-life entrepreneurs employ to achieve their varied goals through business participation.

Why Do People Become Entrepreneurs?

People become entrepreneurs because they either have to or want to. The first group includes workers who are unable to obtain wage and salary employment because of economic conditions that limit their opportunities, such as a weak labor market or discrimination due to factors such as gender, ethnicity, or age. The second group consists of people with interests and dreams they want to pursue, such as becoming commercially successful inventors or amateur chefs who hope to open restaurants. This second group includes individuals with lifestyle issues who want to be their own bosses or have more flexible work hours. The National Minority Business Owners Survey (Puryear, Rogoff, Lee, and Heck, 2003) collected data on both minority and nonminority business owners. This survey shows that entrepreneurs aged 55+ are more motivated by the opportunity to use their skills and abilities, make a contribution to society, and achieve work satisfaction than their younger counterparts. The 2006 Thrivent study revealed that about one-third of those who consider themselves somewhat or very likely to be entrepreneurs when they retire also mention starting a business as one of the three goals they most wish to accomplish in retirement. If we can generalize from this finding, then the "have-to-be" entrepreneurs represent about two-thirds of later-life entrepreneurs, while the "want-to-be" entrepreneurs represent about one-third.

The following factors seem to be among the motivators of the "have-to-be" entrepreneur:

1. *Economic conditions.* A weak overall economy or an economy that is weak in only one sector may drastically limit employment opportunities. A pilot laid off from an airline may have trouble replacing his or her job if the airline industry is suffering a general slowdown. One option for the pilot is to begin an entrepreneurial venture either within the airline industry, such as starting an air-taxi service, or in another industry entirely, such as opening a florist shop.

2. *Discrimination.* Sometimes studied under the rubric of "the theory of the disadvantaged worker" in the academic literature, discrimination holds that individuals who face prejudice often turn to entrepreneurship. Light and Rosenstein (1995), Min (1984), and Evans and Leighton (1987) provide evidence of this relationship. An immigrant who may have been an executive in a bank in his home country may find himself offered only entry-level positions at banks in the United States. Many immigrants respond to this lack of adequate employment opportunity by using their education, prior experience, and fluency in languages as tools to start or purchase a business.

3. *Lack of resources.* It is perhaps ironic that a lack of personal resources such as education, money, credit, and an established business network may actually represent a starting point for many entrepreneurs. The academic literature refers to this challenge as "the theory of liquidity constraint" and posits that individuals with a lower stock of such personal resources are generally more constrained in their employment options than in their entrepreneurial options. Among those researchers who have found evidence of this effect are Light and Rosenstein (1995), Evans and Leighton (1987), and Bates (1990).

Of course, people in this group are also limited in their entrepreneurial options. But because of the wide array of entrepreneurial opportunities, entrepreneurship can be the best available course of action for an individual whose personal resources are minimal, including low education, poor English skills, and no financial assets. Among researchers who have explored this issue are Brush (1992), and Evans and Jovanovic (1989). While a person with limited choices may begin to generate income by service work such as gardening, home cleaning, or dog walking, this is often a first step in a process that eventually leads to obtaining additional clients and hiring employees so that the business can be expanded.

Family responsibilities such as raising children, taking care of an elderly or infirm family member, or working part-time in an existing family business can also constrain an aspiring entrepreneur's ambitions (see chapter 2 of this volume).

The following are the main motivators of the "want-to-be" entrepreneur:

1. *Following the dream.* Many people harbor dreams to be involved in work that is removed from their main careers. They may yearn to be a musician or a stamp collector, to own a bed and breakfast, or start a nonprofit venture. Others may have a specific dream related to the industry in which they have worked for many years.

2. *Managing family and time constraints.* Many people who start their own businesses while still employed must face the initial time restrictions imposed by existing full-time employment. But entrepreneurs without full-time jobs also have family responsibilities, such as child or elder care, which might make starting a flexible-time, home-based business a better option than a full-time job away from home.

3. *Having a limited role.* Many entrepreneurs structure their ventures so that they have limited roles in the business, including time involved, management responsibilities, and even financial risk. By casting themselves in the role of dealmakers, entrepreneurs recruit others to participate in their ventures with mini-

mal personal risk and commitment. For example, one might purchase a business with management in place that can be operated from a distance. An extension of this is "angel investing," in which an entrepreneur invests in a business and takes an active but limited role in its management.

4. *Having flexibility over time.* A venture can be designed so that the involvement of the entrepreneur can vary over time. An antique dealer can start with a part-time commitment but become full-time when he or she retires from a full-time job.

5. *Building equity value.* Unlike regular employment, entrepreneurial ventures can create business value that can benefit the owner. If successful, a business can be sold when the entrepreneur wants to retire or begin a new venture, creating a potentially significant lump-sum payment.

6. *Being the boss.* Being your own boss is one of the most highly valued characteristics of entrepreneurship. After long careers during which they have developed clear ideas of how businesses should be run, or working for bosses whose management decisions and styles may have been frustrating and negative, entrepreneurs are highly attracted to situations in which they have the authority to make all the decisions. Palmer (1998) found this dissatisfaction with previous work to be a main motivator for late-life entrepreneurship, along with the enjoyment and satisfaction of being one's own boss.

7. *Accomplishing a social good.* Research has shown that one of the most attractive aspects of entrepreneurship is the ability to accomplish a desired political or social purpose (Lee and Rogoff, 1996). This seems to be especially true for members of certain minority groups who believe that entrepreneurship reflects positively on their ethnic group and creates employment and other economic benefits within their communities (Lee and Rogoff, 1996). By starting a business with both an economic and social purpose, such as a school or health care company, or a nonprofit organization that provides social services to members of a specific community, an entrepreneur can achieve these larger goals.

The Downsides of Entrepreneurship

Although entrepreneurs cannot be characterized as people who are attracted to risk and enjoy taking it, there is no denying that many forms of entrepreneurial activity entail risk in several ways, especially for older entrepreneurs. Many ventures involve financial risk, and older entrepreneurs have less time remaining in their employment or entrepreneurial careers to recover from losses. There is also "career risk," in that taking oneself out of the employment pool for a significant period of time to pursue entrepreneurial ambitions that may fail could leave the would-be entrepreneur disadvantaged should he or she choose to return to the workforce. Although there is no specific research on this subject, it seems likely that such a hiatus from traditional employment could have greater negative effects on older populations. Finally, potential negative effects on the family might be greater for older entrepreneurs who may have relatives who are dependent on them for financial support.

MEASURING THE PREVALENCE AND CHARACTERISTICS OF LATER-LIFE ENTREPRENEURSHIP

There is no single satisfactory measure of the prevalence of age-related entrepreneurial activity, but the conclusion from the available data is that entrepreneurship and age correlate positively. There are several ways to examine entrepreneurship, and depending on the methodology followed, the information developed and statistical descriptions can seem quite different. As discussed below, some studies sample respondents only over a certain age, some only study entrepreneurs, some look at people active in the workforce in any way, and still others use household sampling frames. Clearly, a difference in the sample being studied yields vastly different rates of entrepreneurial activity.

The most common source of data cited in this field is the U.S. Census, which employs a nomenclature that is confusing and does not reflect the reality of self-employment and business ownership. Census respondents must choose only one from a list of three employment options: being self-employed in an incorporated business, being self-employed in a non-incorporated entity, or working without pay in a family business or farm. People who report that they are self-employed in incorporated entities are, by the government's definition, employees of the corporation and are thus *not* self-employed. Because classifying someone who is employed in a corporation that he or she owns should be within the definition of entrepreneurship, the data presented below total both types of self-employment to obtain what is a more accurate measure of prevalence.

It may not be clear to census respondents that they can be self-employed in various legal entities aside from corporate forms, such as partnerships, or in no entity at all. A person with a salaried job could also have a side business during her days off and help a relative with another business occasionally. Such a person would qualify under three of the census categories, though limited to choosing only one.

One of the major shortcomings of all studies of later-life entrepreneurs to date

TABLE 9.I.
Employment status, by age

Age	Wage and salaried employees	Self-employed independents	Small business owners
18–29	84%	14%	2%
30–39	82	12	6
40–49	81	13	6
50–59	79	13	8
60+	63	26	12

Source: Data from Bond, Galinsky, Pitt-Catsouphes, and Smyer, 2005

is that this population is not segmented by their age at the time of business initiation. This is important because an entrepreneur of 70 who owns a business may have become an entrepreneur at age 69 or at age 20. It would be useful to study the population of older entrepreneurs that is segmented into subpopulations by the age at which they became entrepreneurs. Nonetheless, studies that shed light on the issues of later-life entrepreneurship can be looked at by the methodologies used to examine the issue.

Workforce Studies

While there are numerous studies of the U.S. workforce, few have collected information about entrepreneurship among older workers. Among the few that have is *The National Study of the Changing Workforce*, which has surveyed workers of various types and ages, most recently in 2002. This is a large sample that provides an in-depth look at employment issues among the working population, and it clearly reveals a strong association between age and entrepreneurship. Table 9.1 shows that while 8 percent of workers aged 50–59 are small business owners, 12 percent of workers over 60 years of age own their own businesses. Similarly, 13 percent of workers 50–59 years old are classified as self-employed independent workers, while 26 percent of workers over 60 are self-employed independent workers. Because this sample includes only those who are still in the workforce, it may actually miss entrepreneurs whose involvement may be mostly financial or who don't earn a salary or work enough hours on their ventures to be captured in studies.

Because of the central role that families play in the process of business creation and operation, an important research approach is to use the family as the research sampling unit. This approach was taken by studies by Winter et al. (1998).

TABLE 9.2.
*Self-employment rates as a proportion of all employed
and self-employed workers, 2003*

Age	Unincorporated self-employed	Incorporated self-employed	Total
16+	7.5%	3.6%	11.1%
16–19	1.5	0.2	1.7
20–24	2.0	0.4	2.4
25–34	5.3	1.9	7.2
35–44	7.8	4.1	11.9
45–54	8.7	4.8	13.5
55–64	11.7	6.1	17.8
65+	19.1	7.8	26.9

Source: Data from Hipple, 2004

Census Data

Using U.S. Census data to gain insight into the general trends regarding later-life entrepreneurship is problematic because of the limited way in which the census questionnaire defines self-employment. As discussed above, the census definitions are inadequate representations of reality. Nonetheless, the census data in table 9.2 clearly show that self-employment (for those in unincorporated entities) increases with age. For the age group 55 to 64, the total self-employment rate is 17.8 percent, and for people over 65 the total self-employment rate is 26.9 percent (Hipple, 2004.)

A FUTURE OF INCREASING OPPORTUNITIES
FOR LATER-LIFE ENTREPRENEURS

Scant data have been collected to document how changing values, technology, and business models have lowered barriers to aspiring entrepreneurs, but it seems that significant types of opportunities *are* increasing. Consider the following:

1. *Entrepreneurship has lost the stigma it once had.* Judging from fields of interests in business schools, there was a time when a long career with a large, prestigious company was seen as the most desirable professional path, while scant attention was paid to entrepreneurship in the curriculum. Today entrepreneurship is the fastest growing field of study in business schools (Katz, 2003). Large companies don't provide the security they once did, and this sector of the economy is no longer the primary engine of job creation. A white paper prepared by the Small Business Administration (1998) calculates that 69 percent of new jobs are

created by start-up firms. Business schools that once focused on preparing students for careers in major corporations have experienced major growth in the programs they offer to train entrepreneurs (Katz, 2003). All of this has combined to make later-life entrepreneurship more attractive, better understood, and highly acceptable as a career step relative to other options.

2. *Technology has made business ownership more accessible.* Until recently, the first steps in opening a new business were renting an office and hiring a staff. Working from home was regarded as unprofessional and a choice that only agoraphobes would make. Computers, cell phones, telephone answering systems, word-processing software, and the Internet have made small business start-up and operation easier, cheaper, and more professional-looking to clients.

3. *The Internet has leveled the playing field for small business.* Web sites make it easier for small firms to seem big and to service customers anywhere in the world. Companies such as eBay and Amazon.com that provide the structure for individuals and small companies to reach their markets, represent significantly lower barriers to small business operation than have existed previously. Although there are no published estimates of the number of people who use eBay as a significant income creation tool, with more than 78 million users classified as "active" by eBay in 2006 (eBay, 2006), there are clearly millions of people who earn steady incomes as entrepreneurs, buying and selling products through eBay.

4. *Knowledge-based businesses are expanding.* Later-life entrepreneurs have skills, experience, and education that represent valuable commodities. Outsourcing, once considered a bad word, is now recognized as an efficient way to do business, and later-life entrepreneurs are well-positioned to excel in this work.

5. *Franchise businesses are a growing opportunity.* For people who want to purchase a concept, operating plan, and brand name, franchises represent a "business in a box." In the United States alone, there are more than a thousand companies that franchise and more than 750,000 individual franchises (International Franchise Association, 2005). Given the greater level of wealth and access to capital that later-life entrepreneurs have, they are a good match for franchise businesses.

6. *Possible support systems.* In the United Kingdom, perhaps because of greater awareness of aging population issues, later-life entrepreneurs have already received significant attention and formalized support programs. One such program, the Prince's Initiative for Mature Enterprises (PRIME), is supported by Prince Charles and provides loans to start-up ventures owned by entrepreneurs over 50 (Hirschkorn, 2005). There are no similar age-specific programs in the United States.

FACTORS THAT INFLUENCE OUTCOMES
OF ENTREPRENEURIAL ACTIVITY

While no single agreed-upon list of factors promotes entrepreneurial success, there is general acceptance among researchers and practitioners that good strategies, combined with ample resources, in the context of a favorable economic environment promote entrepreneurial success. The general economic environment is beyond the scope of this chapter and would not, in any event, seem to be a factor influenced by the age of the entrepreneur. But strategy and resources are closely related to the entrepreneur who develops and executes the strategy and provides or recruits the resources needed to build the business. Good strategies arise from knowledge, experience, and intelligence; and their successful execution arises from the financial and other resources to bring businesses into reality. Therefore, we can examine a resource-based approach to entrepreneurship and the issues of time and risk as they vary with the age of the entrepreneur.

Businesses can be defined as the sum of their human, financial, and organizational resources. This set of resources becomes the means by which organizations develop the capacities to accomplish their goals, from building products to creating films. The greater an organization's resources and capabilities are, the more it can develop and implement a strategy to achieve its goals.

As discussed above, a good definition of entrepreneurs is those individuals who undertake ventures that require resources beyond their own control. This is certainly true for entrepreneurs, regardless of the size of their ventures. Businesses require collaborative resources such as financing, customers, raw materials, employees, partners, and space. Looking at entrepreneurship through this lens makes the process of obtaining and managing these resources the key element of success. It also makes the bundle of resources that entrepreneurs have or can obtain from others a key determinant of their success.

Grant (1991) designed a framework for strategic analysis that identifies a venture's resources and capabilities and then develops a strategy based on this analysis to establish a strong competitive advantage. This approach can also reveal gaps in resources, which, when filled, could improve the venture's capabilities and, in turn, its strategy. Later-life entrepreneurs can develop the best mix of strategy and required resources by knowing that additional resources can create additional strategic options and that different strategies define the needs for the types and amounts of required resources.

Light and Gold (2000) examined the resources that are key to the capabilities and ultimate success of ventures. They group the resources required into four types of capital: social, financial, cultural, and human. As we examine all four through the lens of age, the central question is whether the amount and quality of these resources change with the age of the entrepreneur.

Social capital is composed of personal and business networks and the entrepreneur's reputation. Making connections to others is central to obtaining all four types of resources. Older entrepreneurs generally have larger networks than younger entrepreneurs, given their years spent in both work and social situations. While age is no guarantee of a positive reputation, an older entrepreneur is probably more likely to have a greater reputation than younger entrepreneurs.

Financial capital is made up of the financial resources that entrepreneurs can deploy themselves in support of their ventures as well as the financial resources that they can obtain through family, friends, or professional sources.

Starting or buying a business requires capital. Older populations are wealthier and have better credit histories, which are critical in obtaining financing from banks and other sources. This point is made clear by the following facts: according to the 2000 U.S. Census, the median net worth for U.S. households is $46,506, while it is more than $150,824 for households headed by individuals between 55 and 64 years old, and more than $170,300 for households headed by individuals over 65. As table 9.3 shows, there is a strong correlation between age and personal financial resources as measured by net worth. For example, people over the age of 55 have tripled the net worth of people between the ages of 35 to 44. It would also seem that access to financial capital through social and professional networks or personal reputation is likely to increase with age.

TABLE 9.3.
Selected measures and components of wealth, by age

Age	Net worth	Stocks and mutual funds	Equity in business or profession	Equity in home
Under 35	5,896	6,000	7,000	22,000
35–44	33,950	14,000	6,700	40,500
45–54	68,198	20,000	10,000	60,000
55–64	100,750	36,000	10,000	78,000
65–69	107,150	32,000	25,000	85,000
70–74	118,950	44,000	24,000	90,000
75+	100,000	39,586	16,000	85,000

Source: Net Worth and Asset Ownership of Households: 1998 and 2000, Household Economic Studies, pp. 12–13, U.S. Census Bureau, May 2003 (www.census.gov/prod/2003pubs/p70-88.pdf).

Cultural capital includes the values, ethics, morals, and customs that individuals possess, usually through their ethnic, religious, family, and social backgrounds. As previous research has shown, certain ethnic and religious groups have strong business and family-oriented cultures that help them to be successful entrepreneurs even in the face of few other personal resources. Because one's personal values change little with age, age is unlikely to result in an improvement in an entrepreneur's cultural capital. However, it could be argued that experience in business will help an individual to understand the values and customs of business in various settings and with various types of other entrepreneurs.

Human capital includes the skills, knowledge, energy, and abilities that the entrepreneur possesses. Examples of these include formal and informal education, language skills, and technical skills. Research has shown that education and experience increase the probability of being an entrepreneur and the likelihood of building a successful venture (Lee and Rogoff, 1997). It makes sense that older populations have more of both (Light and Rosenstein, 1995). Researchers such as Aldrich and Cliff (2003), Larson (1991), and Dubini and Aldich (1991) have shown that, while it is possible to fly solo, almost no ventures are started entirely on one's own. Entrepreneurship is often a team sport, and entrepreneurs need lawyers, accountants, partners, investors, bankers, suppliers, and, most importantly, customers. It seems reasonable that older entrepreneurs, who are more likely to have built up work and social contacts over their lives, have more of these essential contacts than younger people, and they are able to deploy them in the pursuit of their ventures.

It also seems reasonable to assume that physical energy declines with age. Although there are no studies of this within the context of entrepreneurship, some entrepreneurial ventures, such as construction work, require great amounts of physical effort. Others, such as legal work, may require more mental exertion. Owning and operating a retail store may require a combination of the two.

The conclusion is that human capital related to many intellectual processes increases with age even while physical energy generally declines. Because many strategies readily exist for supplementing the physical energy of the entrepreneur herself, it probably should be concluded that the advantage here goes to the older entrepreneur. In fact, it seems that older entrepreneurs generally have the advantage over younger entrepreneurs because later-life entrepreneurs probably have a greater amount of three of the four types of capital required to be successful. However, as discussed below in the section on tools for building success, there are a number of strategies for entrepreneurs who may be severely resource-constrained on these four resources.

THE EFFECT OF AGE ON AN ENTREPRENEUR'S
TIME HORIZON AND RISK TOLERANCE

One quality that older entrepreneurs do not have in the same quantity as younger entrepreneurs is time. The relationship between time and business is significant. Strategies take time to execute. Mistakes take time to fix. Many successful entrepreneurs only experience a great success after spending time on previous failures. Financial returns are magnified when they are earned in a short period of time: doubling an investment in two years is a 41 percent compounded annual return, but doubling it in 15 years is about a 5 percent annual return. Trying to earn huge returns in a short period of time generally requires taking great risk. Older entrepreneurs don't have the years to execute time-consuming strategies, and they don't have the ability to withstand large risks, which limits the options for the type of entrepreneurial activity they may choose.

Successfully managing this risk requires a careful effort to identify the amount of financial and personal risk the entrepreneur can tolerate. As discussed below, later-life entrepreneurs need tools designed to address their unique situation regarding time and risk.

TOOLS FOR BUILDING SUCCESS
FOR LATER-LIFE ENTREPRENEURS

Later-life entrepreneurs need approaches that match their entrepreneurial ventures to their risk tolerance and time horizons. Because the profiles of each entrepreneur are so different vis-à-vis the resources they bring to bear on their prospective ventures, each entrepreneur must be evaluated uniquely. For example, an entrepreneur with great knowledge of an industry, a wealth of contacts, and large personal financial resources may be able to start a sizeable venture. On the other hand, an aspiring older entrepreneur may have little financial or social capital and perhaps disabilities along with the declining energy brought on by age. Even for someone with physical constraints, there are many suitable entrepreneurial strategies, such as establishing a home-based business, being part of a direct-selling network, or partnering with other entrepreneurs who have greater access to desired resources.

Table 9.4 outlines a five-step model for a program that could help later-life entrepreneurs identify viable potential ventures and strategies. To be effective, tools for later-life entrepreneurs should not only match an entrepreneur to a business strategy but also be easy to apply, be sensible, and have clear conclusions. The

TABLE 9.4.
Five-step model for creating appropriate entrepreneurial strategies
for later-life entrepreneurs

Step 1.	Identify the entrepreneur's resources	Financial resources, such as current income and expenses, network, liquid assets, current investments Social resources, such as business and personal networks and family support Cultural resources, such as ethnicity issues Human resources, such as skills, abilities, formal education degrees, relevant work experience Identify resource gaps that need to be filled
Step 2.	Develop potential venture profile	Amount that can be invested and likely sources of capital Business goals such as current income or future value Timeline for achieving these goals Industry or business type that matches the entrepreneur's abilities and desires
Step 3.	Create specific options	Develop strategy for starting a business or purchasing an existing business Identify specific options through search or business plan development
Step 4.	Judge the appropriateness of the match	Evaluate whether the business or plan is a good match with the resources as well as the time and risk profile of the entrepreneur Review whether all required resources are available either through the entrepreneur or through other strategic options such as partners, employees, or outside funding
Step 5.	Review the process of the previous four steps and take action to improve them in subsequent applications	Reevaluate searches for opportunities or plans for existing businesses that did not lead to success and revise them for subsequent efforts Continue to evaluate successful efforts in making future plans

thinking that underlies the tools can become integrated into the entrepreneur's ongoing strategic decisions.

Clinimetrics is an emerging field of practically oriented testing and tools notable for its ability to be applied quickly and easily. This ease of use results from their application by knowledgeable practitioners. Work by Feinstein (1999) and Lichtenstein and Lyons (2001) are examples of literature that have explored applied clinimetrics to issues of entrepreneurs. Clinimetric tools are administered by trained experts in the field who, through questions and discussion with the subject, arrive at conclusions about the subject on various scales. For example,

Lichtenstein and Lyons (2001) developed and have used clinimetric tools that employ experienced experts in the process of evaluating the proficiency of entrepreneurs through structured interviews. The tools lead to operational conclusions about items such as the amount of money the entrepreneur might invest, the type of business he or she should focus on, and the strategy that a particular business should pursue.

The outline of the model presented in table 9.4 begins in step 1 by evaluating the financial, social, cultural, and human resources that the entrepreneur can bring to bear on potential entrepreneurial ventures. In step 2, an ideal profile for a potential venture is created through questions and discussions of industries of interest, what the business goals are, such as earning immediate income, building value that can be harvested in the future through a sale, or achieving a social goal such as educating an underserved group. This leads to the creation of specific options in step 3, a review and evaluation of step 3, a recommendation for the recommended strategy's reasonableness and attractiveness in step 4, and the establishment of a an ongoing review process in the step 5. Through this five-step tool, an entrepreneur and an evaluator could choose the right business, the best strategy for a proposed venture, and an acceptable amount of risk in financial and personal terms for the entrepreneur to take.

CONCLUSION

The level of entrepreneurial activity among people over 50 is significant, but not nearly enough is known about this trend. Exactly what older entrepreneurs do, when they started, what their attitudes and goals are, and what they perceive as their unique challenges are not known. It is important that this knowledge gap be addressed through both longitudinal and cross-sectional research. Longitudinal research will follow later-life entrepreneurs through their endeavors in order to learn more about the process itself and the factors that influenced their success and failure. Cross-sectional studies will reveal more about prevalence, characteristics, and patterns of later-life entrepreneurship, including its effects on quality of life, family, and sense of well-being. One important goal for federal policy is to marshal its significant existing data sources, such as the U.S. Census Bureau, to reveal greater knowledge in this area.

Whether people are "have-to-be" or "want-to-be" entrepreneurs, people in later life have the ability to participate and benefit from business ownership in its many forms. Later-life entrepreneurs often have the funds necessary to start a venture or purchase one, the credit with banks to borrow money, and the network of friends, family, and colleagues to support an entrepreneurial venture. They also have the knowledge gleaned from formal education, work and life experience, and skills that are critical in supporting a successful venture. The personal and professional networks they have built can form the basis of contacts that can lead to clients, customers, and colleagues.

Whether their goal is to continue to earn income after traditional retirement, the desire to be mentally engaged in work, or the hope to follow long-held dreams, people over 50 require ways to achieve these goals. In fact, many paths to these goals exist. The ease of buying an existing business, purchasing a franchise, or starting a business from scratch are hallmarks of an American economy that has low barriers to entry for entrepreneurs, no matter how old they are. Public policy should focus on making these paths known to aspiring older entrepreneurs through training programs, Web-based resources, and public reports that will inform this population about their options.

As evidence points to longer and healthier lives, shrinking pensions, and continued personal ambitions, later-life entrepreneurship becomes a more attractive option. All of these forces combine to explain why later-life entrepreneurship is a significant element of economic vitality for older Americans and is likely to grow as the need for income and benefits among this population increase. But later-life entrepreneurs have to be especially cognizant of the need to avoid excessive risk that can cause them irreparable financial damage. Tools must be developed to help later-life entrepreneurs accomplish their specific goals. Clinimetric tools have been developed that can be easily and quickly used to help would-be entrepreneurs understand their own resource profiles, develop strategies to obtain any resources they may be missing, and match themselves to appropriate ventures that will achieve their desired goals without intolerable levels of risk.

REFERENCES

AARP. 2002. *Staying Ahead of the Curve: The AARP Work and Career Study.* Washington, DC: AARP.

———. 2003. *Staying Ahead of the Curve: The AARP Working in Retirement Study.* Washington, DC: AARP.

Aldrich, H. E., and Cliff, J. E. 2003. The pervasive effects of family on entrepreneurship: Toward a family embeddedness perspective. *Journal of Business Venturing* 18 (5): 573–77.

Bates, T. 1990. Entrepreneur human capital inputs and small business longevity. *Review of Economics and Statistics* 72 (3): 551–59.

Bond, J. T., Galinsky, E. M., Pitt-Catsouphes, M., and Smyer, M. A. 2005. *Context Matters: Insights about Older Workers from the National Study of the Changing Workforce.* Center on Aging and Work, Research Highlights: 1 (November).

Brush, C. G. 1992. Research on women: Past trends, a new perspective and future directions. *Entrepreneurship Theory and Practice* 16 (4): 5–30.

Dubini, P., and Aldrich, H. 1991. Personal and extended networks are central to the entrepreneurial process. *Journal of Business Venturing* 6:305–13.

eBay. 2006. Company press release of 2nd quarter financial results, July 19, 2006. San Jose, California.

Evans, D. S., and Jovanovic, B. 1989. An estimated model of entrepreneurial choice under liquidity constraints. *Journal of Political Economy* 97 (4): 808–27.

Evans, D. S., and Leighton, L. S. 1987. *Self-employment Election and Earnings over the Life Cycle*. Washington, DC: Government Printing Office.

Feinstein, A. R. 1999. Multi-item 'instruments' vs. Virginia Apgar's principles of clinimetrics. *Archives of Internal Medicine* 159 (1): 125–28.

Grant, R. M. 1991. The Resource-based theory of competitive advantage: Implications for strategy formulation. *California Management Review* 33 (3): 114–35.

Heck, R. K. Z., and Scannell, E. 1999. The prevalence of family business from a household sample. *Family Business Review* 12 (3): 163–87.

Hipple, S. 2004. Self-employment in the United States: An update. *Employment and Earnings-Monthly Labor Review* (July): 13–23.

Hirschkorn, J. 2005. Handyman shows how the ageists got it wrong. (London) *Daily Telegraph*, City Section, Profile column, p. 34.

International Franchise Association, 2005. *Foundation Report*, October.

Ireland, R. D., Hitt, M. A., and Sirmon, D. G. 2003. A model of strategic entrepreneurship. *Journal of Management* 29: 963–89.

Katz, J. A. 2003. The chronology and intellectual trajectory of American entrepreneurship education. *Journal of Business Venturing* 18 (2): 283–300.

Larson, A. 1991. Partner networks: Leveraging external ties to improve entrepreneurial performance. *Journal of Business Venturing* 6 (2): 173–88.

Lee, M. S., and Rogoff, E. G. 1996. Research note: Comparison of small businesses with family participation versus small businesses without family participation: An investigation of differences in goals, attitudes, and gamily/business conflict. *Family Business Review* 9 (4): 423–37.

———. 1997. A dual path model of education effects on entrepreneurship: An empirical analysis. *Journal of Business and Entrepreneurship* 9 (1): 99–115.

Lichtenstein, G. A., and Lyons, T. S. 2001. The entrepreneurial development system: Transforming business talent and community economies. *Economic Development Quarterly* 15 (1): 3–20.

Light, I., and Gold, S. 2000. *Ethnic Economies*. San Diego: Academic Press.

Light, I., and Rosenstein, C. 1995. *Race, Ethnicity and Entrepreneurship in Urban America*. New York: Aldine D. Gruyter.

Min, P. G. 1984. From white-collar occupations to small business: Korean immigrants occupational adjustment. *Sociological Quarterly* 25 (Summer): 333–52.

Palmer, S. 1998. Entrepreneurship as a new career at midlife or later: A study of the relationship between the entrepreneurial process and personal characteristics/environmental conditions in career transitions to entrepreneurship. Ph.D. diss., Case Western Reserve University.

Puryear, A. N., Rogoff, E. G., Lee, M. S, and Heck, R. K. Z. 2003. 2003 National Minority Business Owners Surveys, Whites and Blacks. Unpublished data. Lawrence N. Field Center for Entrepreneurship, Baruch College, New York.

Small Business Administration, 1998. *The New American Evolution: The Role and Impact of Small Firms.* Office of Economic Research of the U.S. Small Business Administration's Office of Advocacy. Washington, DC.

Stevenson, H. H., and Jarillo, J. C. 1990. A paradigm for entrepreneurship: Entrepreneurial management. *Strategic Management Journal* 11 (5): 17–27.

Thrivent Financial. 2006. *Thriving in Retirement Survey.* Minneapolis, Minnesota.

Winter, M., Fitzgerald, M. A., Heck, R. K. Z., Haynes, G. W., and Danes, S. M. 1998. Revisiting the study of family businesses: Methodological challenges, dilemmas, and alternative approaches. *Family Business Review* 11 (3): 239–52.

PART IV

Work Performance Issues

CHAPTER TEN

Managers' Attitudes toward Older Workers

A Review of the Evidence

RICHARD W. JOHNSON, PH.D.

The economic burden of an aging population depends partly on older adults' employment rates. If workers continue to retire at the relatively young ages that have become the norm over the past generation, then the aging of the baby boomers will reduce the ratio of working taxpayers to older retirees. However, the economy could produce more goods and services if older people worked longer, boosting living standards for both workers and nonworkers and generating additional tax revenue to fund government services.

Older people's employment depends in turn on employers' willingness to hire and retain them. Firms may be reluctant to employ older workers if managers believe they are less energetic and flexible than younger workers or lack up-to-date skills. Managers may view older workers as particularly expensive, because they demand higher salaries than younger workers or incur more health care costs. Some employers may be reluctant to train older workers because they believe they will retire soon, making it difficult for employers to recoup their training costs. The lack of training opportunities may exclude older workers from the best work assignments, hurt their chances for promotion, and depress job satisfaction and earnings growth. On the other hand, some employers may prefer older workers to their younger counterparts because they value their experience, maturity, and strong work ethic. It is not immediately obvious, then, how managers' attitudes affect employment prospects for older Americans.

This chapter reviews the literature on employers' willingness to hire and retain older workers, an increasingly important topic as the population ages. After a discussion of the benefits of delayed retirement, the current retirement landscape, and some theoretical issues in the demand for older workers, the chapter examines findings from a number of recent surveys of employer attitudes toward older workers in the United States and other countries. It then compares these attitudes to evidence on actual employer practices to better assess employment prospects for older workers. The final sections consider the apparent willingness of employers to train older workers and present conclusions.

THE BENEFITS OF DELAYED RETIREMENT

Population aging poses a serious threat to the nation's economic security. The growing size of the older population will increase the number of older Americans who qualify for publicly financed retirement and health benefits in coming years relative to the number of younger adults who typically work and pay taxes. Between 2000 and 2020, the number of working adults for every nonworking adult age 65 or older will fall from 4.5 to 3.3, if current employment patterns continue (Johnson and Steuerle, 2004). The shrinking labor pool threatens American economic growth, living standards, Social Security and Medicare financing, and funding for all other government programs. If current employment patterns persist, workers will have to pay higher taxes to support more retirees, employers will face labor shortages (particularly in selected industries), retirement benefits will likely be cut, and per capita economic output will fall.

But demographic change tells only part of the story. Future outcomes depend largely on individual employment decisions by workers and employers. Labor force participation rates for older women have been rising over the past half-century as paid employment has increased for women of all ages, and participation rates for older men have been inching upward over the past decade. Nonetheless, relatively few older adults work for pay, and older men are less likely to work today than they were 50 years ago, when health problems were more prevalent and jobs were generally more physically demanding. In 2006, for example, only 20 percent of men age 65 or older participated in the labor force, down from 47 percent in 1948 (Bureau of Labor Statistics, 2007a).

If people work longer, the economy can produce more goods and services, boosting living standards for both workers and nonworkers and generating additional tax revenue to fund all kinds of government services. For example, in 2020 if men age 55 or older worked at the same rate as they did in 1950 instead of the rate that prevailed in 2000, the ratio of working adults to nonworking older adults would rise from 3.3 to 4.1 (Johnson and Steuerle, 2004). This boost in older men's employment would eliminate about two-thirds of the expected in-crease in the old-age dependency ratio between 2000 and 2020. If every worker delayed retirement by five years, relative to retirement plans based on current work patterns, the additional revenue generated by income and payroll taxes would more than cover the Social Security trust fund deficit for the foreseeable future (Butrica, Smith, and Steuerle, 2007).

In addition to improving the economic outlook, working longer can enhance individual well-being. Those who delay retirement can raise their own retirement incomes by avoiding early retirement reductions to their Social Security and defined benefit (DB) pension benefits, accumulating more Social Security and pension credits and other savings, and reducing the number of retirement years that they must fund. By working until age 67 instead of retiring at age 62, for ex-ample, a typical worker could gain about $10,000 in annual income at age 75, net of federal income taxes and health insurance premiums (Butrica, Johnson, Smith, and Steuerle, 2004). Delaying retirement may also promote physical and emo-tional health by keeping older adults active and engaged and imbuing their lives with meaning (Calvo, 2006).

THE CHANGING LANDSCAPE OF RETIREMENT

The crucial question, then, is whether the upcoming demographic challenges will lead to higher employment rates and later retirements for older adults. A number of factors suggest that employment rates for older Americans will rise in coming years. Improved health and declines in physical job demands leave older people better able to work today than in the past (Johnson, Mermin, and Resse-ger, 2007; National Center for Health Statistics, 2006; Steuerle, Spiro, and John-son, 1999).[1] Recent changes in Social Security increase work incentives at older ages. The normal retirement age for full Social Security benefits has increased from 65 to 66 and will reach 67 for those born after 1959. Delayed retirement credits have been raised to better compensate retirees who take up benefits after the normal retirement age. And Congress repealed the earnings test past the nor-mal retirement age, which reduces Social Security benefits for employed recipi-ents who earn more than a limited amount.

Changes in employer-provided pension and retiree health benefits are also likely to encourage boomers to remain at work. Traditional DB pensions, which provide workers with lifetime retirement annuities, usually based on years of ser-vice and earnings near the end of the career, tend to discourage work at older ages (Stock and Wise, 1990). They often provide substantial subsidies for early retirement and penalize workers who remain on the job past the plan's normal retirement age, partly because workers who delay retirement by a month forfeit a month of benefits.

Over the past 30 years, however, employers have been shifting from DB pensions to defined contribution (DC) plans, which do not encourage early retirement (Pension and Welfare Benefits Administration, 1998). Employers typically make specified contributions into individual DC accounts, which workers access at retirement, generally as lump sum payments. Because contributions continue as long as plan participants remain employed and workers with a given account balance can receive the same lifetime benefit regardless of when they chose to begin collecting, DC plans do not generally penalize work at older ages. As a result, people in DC plans tend to work about two years longer than DB participants (Friedberg and Webb, 2005), and the shift to DC plans should increase the labor supply of older Americans.

Many employers that continue to offer DB plans have switched from traditional plan designs to hybrid formats, such as cash balance plans that include many features common in DC plans and do not penalize work at older ages. Employers offering cash balance plans regularly set aside a given percentage of salary for each employee and credit interest on these contributions. Interest credit rates are usually tied to a specific benchmark, such as the U.S. Treasury bill rate. Benefits are expressed as account balances, as in DC plans, even though cash balance plans are classified under the law as DB plans. Because cash balance plans tie retirement benefits to career earnings and account balances continue to grow as long as the plan participant remains employed, participants do not lose benefits if they work beyond the plan's retirement age. Moreover, many employers with cash balance plans eliminated the early retirement subsidies that their traditional plans provided (Brown et al., 2000). In 2005 one-quarter of DB-covered workers in the private sector participated in plans with cash balance or other hybrid designs (Bureau of Labor Statistics, 2007c). This share is likely to increase following the 2006 enactment of the Pension Protection Act, which affirmed that cash hybrid plans do not inherently discriminate against older workers, removing an important obstacle to plan conversions.

The erosion in employer-provided retiree health benefits is also likely to limit early retirement. Retiree health insurance, which pays health expenses for early retirees who have not reached the Medicare eligibility age of 65, discourages work by reducing retirement costs that arise from the loss of employer health benefits. Workers offered retiree health benefits by their employers retire earlier than workers who lose their health benefits (Rogowski and Karoly, 2000; Johnson,

Davidoff, and Perese, 2003). However, rising health care costs and the introduction of an accounting rule in 1993 requiring employers to recognize on their balance sheets the full liability of future retiree health costs have led many employers to terminate their retiree health plans. In 2005, only 33 percent of employers with more than 200 employees offered retiree health benefits, down from 68 percent in 1988 (Kaiser Family Foundation and Health Research Educational Trust, 2005).

Perhaps in response to these various trends, older adults are now working longer than they did about 20 years ago. Between 1985 and 2005, the share of men in the labor force increased from 46 to 53 percent at ages 62 to 64 and from 24 to 34 percent at ages 65 to 69 (Federal Interagency Forum on Aging Related Statistics, 2006). Over the same period, female labor force participation rates rose from 29 to 40 percent at ages 62 to 64 and from 14 to 24 percent at ages 65 to 69.

Several surveys also suggest that baby boomers intend to work into old age. For example, 68 percent of older workers in one recent poll said they intended to work in retirement (AARP, 2003). The mean self-reported probability of working full-time past age 65 among workers ages 51 to 56 participating in the Health and Retirement Study increased from 27 percent in 1992 to 33 percent in 2004 (Mermin, Johnson, and Murphy, 2007). Another AARP poll found that 38 percent of older workers want to gradually phase into retirement instead of leaving the labor force all together (AARP, 2005a). A recent MetLife survey found that boomers are increasingly concerned about their ability to afford an early retirement (Met Life Mature Market Institute, 2005).

THE DEMAND FOR OLDER WORKERS

Although the supply of older workers may increase in coming years, employment rates at older ages also depend on the demand for older workers. It is not clear how willing employers are to hire and retain older adults. Employment decisions hinge on perceptions of older workers' productivity and the costs of employing them. On the one hand, older workers are less likely to miss work than are younger employees (Martocchio, 1989), and older adults' long experience in the labor force may make them especially productive. On the other hand, older workers' education and skills may be outdated, and employers may view them as being less flexible than younger workers and less willing to experiment with new ways of working. Concern that increased age impairs the ability to complete physically demanding tasks may fuel employer reluctance to hire older people for strenuous work. These attitudes will likely evolve in coming years as

the workforce ages, especially if labor and skill shortages develop in certain occupations.

Managers may also view older workers as more expensive than their younger
counterparts. It is well known that wages tend to increase with age, up to about
the mid-50s (Mincer, 1974). For example, median usual weekly earnings in 2004
for full-time wage and salary workers increased from $406 at ages 20 to 24, to
$604 at ages 25 to 34, to $743 at ages 45 to 54 (table 10.1). However, wages grow
relatively slowly after the mid-30s or early-40s. Median wages in 2004 for full-
time workers was only about 4 percent higher at ages 45 to 54 than at ages 35 to
44, and they were lower at ages 55 to 64 than at ages 45 to 54. Employers likely
tolerate older workers' relatively high salaries when age-related productivity gains
cause wages to rise as workers grow older. However, managers may view older
workers as too costly at firms in which wage growth is driven by seniority pay
scales and are only loosely tied to productivity differentials, such as in unionized
settings and the public sector.[2]

Fringe benefit costs also tend to rise with age. The cost of traditional DB pension plans rises rapidly as workers approach the plan's retirement age and can
soon begin collecting benefits. Although these plans are becoming less common,
they continue to cover all federal government employees, about 90 percent of
state and local government workers (Bureau of Labor Statistics, 2000), and about
15 percent of private-sector workers (Bureau of Labor Statistics, 2007c, 2007d).
Because older workers tend to use more health services than younger workers,
the cost to employers of providing health benefits generally increases with age.
Median annual health insurance claims in 2004 for privately insured workers
were nearly twice as high at ages 45 to 54 than at ages 35 to 44 and about three
times as high at ages 55 to 64 (table 10.1). In dollar terms, however, the differences were fairly small. Median annual health insurance claims were $781 higher

TABLE 10.1.
Earnings and health insurance claims, by age, 2004

Age	Median usual weekly earnings, full-time wage and salary workers			Annual private health insurance claims, insured workers	
	All	Men	Women	Median	Mean
20–24	$406	$417	$391	$220	$983
25–34	604	639	561	278	1,500
35–44	713	804	608	396	1,560
45–54	743	857	625	715	2,388
55–64	725	843	615	1,177	2,904

Source: Bureau of Labor Statistics (2007b) and author's computations from the Medical Expenditure Panel
Survey

for workers ages 54 to 64 than those ages 35 to 44, and mean annual claims were $1,344 higher. The health insurance cost differential between workers ages 35 to 44 and those ages 55 to 64 equaled about 2 percent of annual earnings, measured in medians.

Employers may be more reluctant to hire older job applicants than to retain their older, experienced staff. Employers incur at least some recruiting, hiring, and training costs when taking on new employees, and they may have less time to recoup these costs for older hires near retirement age than for younger hires.[3] Employers do not face any of these costs, of course, by retaining existing employees. Older adults are likely to be especially costly to hire for firms with traditional DB pension plans, because older workers accumulate benefits in traditional plans much more rapidly than younger workers (Penner, Perun, and Steuerle, 2002).

Employers may also be less likely to hire older workers because they are sometimes more difficult to terminate than younger employees. Workers age 40 or older are covered by the Age Discrimination in Employment Act (ADEA), which makes it illegal for firms to discriminate unfairly against older workers in employment decisions, including hiring, firing, work assignments, and promotions. The courts can force employers who illegally fire older workers to pay monetary damages. As a result, employers may be reluctant to hire older workers out of fear that they could face legal action if they tried to terminate those that did not meet expectations. The ADEA, designed to protect older workers, may have the perverse effect of limiting opportunities for older job applicants (Adams, 2004; Lahey, 2006).

It is difficult to assess managers' willingness to employ older adults with theory alone. Employers may appreciate older workers' experience and maturity but may be reluctant to employ older people because of their relatively high compensation and limited number of remaining work years. The special legal protections that older workers receive may also deter employers from hiring them. To better evaluate older adults' employment prospects, we now examine surveys of employer attitudes and actual employer practices toward older adults.

SURVEY-BASED EVIDENCE OF EMPLOYERS' ATTITUDES

A number of recent employer surveys have attempted to measure managers' attitudes toward older workers. Most employer surveys indicate that managers generally value older workers' knowledge, experience, and work ethic. For example, a 2006 survey of 578 private-sector firms with 50 or more employees by the Center on Aging and Work at Boston College found that a majority of employers (between 50 and 54%) said it was "very true" that their late-career employees were "loyal to the company," had "a strong work ethic," were "reliable," and had "low turnover rates" (Pitt-Catsouphes, Smyer, Matz-Costa, and Kane, 2007). By comparison, fewer than one-quarter of employers said that each of these attributes applied to early-career employees. Additionally, about 47 percent of employers said it was true that late-career employees had "high levels of skills relative to what is needed for their jobs," compared with 38 percent of mid-career employees and 21 percent of early-career employees. Of course, late-career employees have many years of experience in their positions, so it is not clear from these survey results how employers view older workers with more limited experience.

Other employer surveys indicate that many managers believe that older workers benefit the firm. In a 2006 Internet-based survey of 487 organizations by Buck Consultants, Corporate Voices for Working Families, and WorldatWork, 88 percent of respondents said that mature workers' knowledge provided significant business advantages, and 74 percent said their reliability and dedication were significant advantages (Buck Consultants, 2007). Although it is not clear from the survey, these results suggest that respondents may have been referring more to professional and managerial workers than to rank-and-file workers. In another 2006 survey of 400 private-sector employers by the Center for Retirement Research at Boston College, more than four out of five managers said that older workers' "knowledge of procedures and other aspects of the job" and their "ability to interact with customers" substantially enhanced their productivity (Munnell, Sass, and Soto, 2006). An earlier 1998 employer survey conducted by AARP (2000) found that human resources executives most frequently cited "loyalty and dedication to the company," "commitment to doing quality work," "someone you can count in a crisis," and "solid performance record" as attributes that describe workers ages 50 or older.

These surveys also indicate that employers often question older workers' creativity and willingness to learn new things, however. Only about 29 percent of employers in the Center on Aging and Work survey described their late-career employees as creative, as compared with 34 percent of mid-career employees and 35 percent of early-career employees. Only one in ten employers in the Buck Consultant survey described older workers as innovative or as risk takers. (However, it is not clear whether older workers fare much worse than their younger counterparts on this dimension because the survey did not ask employers to rate younger workers.) In the Center for Retirement Research survey, more than one in five employers cited older workers' limited ability to learn new tasks quickly as an important factor in reducing their productivity. About one-third noted older workers' limited physical health and stamina, and nearly one-fifth expressed concerns about how long older workers would remain on the job. However, only 15 percent of employers in the Buck Consultants survey said that any reluctance by mature workers to learn new procedures or adapt to new technology posed significant business risks in employing them. Employers in this survey expressed more concern about the risks of integrating multiple generations of workers and of accommodating older workers' part-time and flexible schedules.

Overall, most employers appear to consider older workers to be at least as productive as younger workers. The Center for Retirement Research survey found that 56 percent of employers reported that older professionals and managers were more productive than their younger counterparts (Munnell et al., 2006). Only 6 percent of employers reported that older white-collar workers were less productive than younger ones, while 39 percent said that they were equally productive. Views toward older rank-and-file workers were not quite as positive: 41 percent said they were more productive than their younger counterparts, and 19 percent said they were less productive. Familiarity with older workers appeared to make favorable impressions on many employers. The share of employers who reported that older workers were more productive than younger ones increased with the share of their workforce age 55 or older. Survey respondents who were age 55 or older themselves were also more likely to describe older workers as especially productive.

Many American employers express concerns about the cost of employing older workers, however. In the Center for Retirement Research survey, 39 percent of employers said that older white-collar workers were more costly than their younger counterparts, and 43 percent said that older rank-and-file workers were more costly (Munnell et al., 2006), probably because older workers tend to be more experienced. Only 19 percent said that older professionals and managers were less costly than younger ones, and only 18 percent said that older rank-and-file workers were less costly. Large employers and those with DB pension plans were especially likely to view older workers as relatively expensive to employ. Employers expressed special concern about older workers' health care costs. For example, 36 percent of human resources executives in a 1991 study said that high health care costs influenced their decision about hiring and retaining older workers (Barth, McNaught, and Rizzi, 1993). In the more recent Buck Consultants survey (2007) 39 percent cited health care expenses as highly significant factors in the cost of employing older workers. (Interestingly, however, 36% said health care costs were not significant.) Overall, 62 percent of employers said the cost of transferring older workers' knowledge and skills to younger workers was highly significant.

Most employers appear to believe that the relatively high productivity of older workers offsets their relatively high costs. Two-thirds of employers surveyed by the Center for Retirement Research said an employee or prospect age 55 or older was neither more nor less attractive than a younger person capable of the same job (Munnell et al., 2006). This assessment held for both white-collar workers and rank-and-file workers. However, the survey results did indicate that older white-collar workers have better prospects for continuing their careers than rank-and-file workers. While 23 percent of employers reported that older white-collar workers were more attractive than younger ones, only 15 percent favored older rank-and-file workers over younger ones.

Although relatively few employers admit having negative views toward older workers, that does not necessarily imply that most employers are eager to hire older workers. In fact, one-quarter of employers in the Center on Aging and Work survey said that their organizations were reluctant to hire older workers (Pitt-Catsouphes et al., 2007).

Employers' Attitudes in Other Countries

Employers in other countries appear to share many of the views toward older workers that American employers hold. For example, a 2000 survey found that employers in New Zealand generally considered older workers to be more reliable and productive than younger workers and better able to work with people (McGregor and Gray, 2002). However, the survey also indicated that employers believed older workers were less flexible and harder to train than younger workers and generally failed to keep up with the latest technology. Various surveys found that Canadian managers generally held favorable views of older workers, although many expressed concerns about their ability to do heavy physical work or develop new technical skills (Marshall, 2001). Depending on region, industry, and firm size, between 25 and 43 percent of employers said they would not hire workers above certain ages, which varied between 55 and 61. A 2002 survey found that most employers in the Netherlands view older workers as more productive and reliable than younger workers but less adaptable and more resistant to innovation and technical change (Henkens, 2005). High costs of health care do not damage employment prospects for older workers outside the United States because in most other countries the government, not the employer, covers most medical expenses.

A 2005 survey found that many employers in the United Kingdom reported favoring younger workers in hiring decisions, perhaps because age discrimination in employment was not illegal in the United Kingdom until October 2006. About half of surveyed employers had a maximum recruitment age and considered potential length of service in hiring decisions (Metcalf and Meadows, 2006). More than one in five said some of their jobs were better suited for workers of certain ages. These employers generally favored prime-age workers over those older than 50 or younger than 25.

Limitations of Attitudinal Surveys

Some important limitations with employer survey data make it difficult to know how to interpret these findings. Most of these surveys collected information from only a few hundred employers, so it is not clear how well they represent all firms. Response rates tend to be quite low, with typically only about one-third of surveyed employers completing the questionnaire. Employers with relatively strong age-related policies are probably more likely than other employers to participate in the survey, potentially biasing the findings. The small number of employers sampled generally makes it impossible to examine how attitudes vary across industries. Few survey-based studies tested whether observed differences in employer attitudes toward older and younger workers were statistically significant or could instead have likely resulted from sampling variation.

How much credence to give survey responses is also unclear. Respondents may tend to understate the role of age in employment decisions (especially because age discrimination is illegal in the United States), or they might portray their policies in the best possible light, biasing the results. The respondent's position within the organization also affects survey results and how they should be interpreted. In some cases, the respondent may report the firm's policy, which may differ from actual practice. In other cases, respondents may report their personal views, which may differ from the prevailing practice within the organization. For example, as noted earlier, older survey respondents rated older workers more highly than younger respondents (Munnell et al., 2006). Finally, the surveys may fail to capture variation in attitudes and policies within establishments, particularly variation across occupations.

EMPLOYERS' PRACTICE TOWARD OLDER WORKERS

Given the difficulties of measuring and interpreting employer attitudes, a better approach might be to gauge actual employer practice. On the surface, there appears to be little direct evidence that older workers fare worse in the labor market than younger workers. As noted earlier, older workers receive higher earnings than younger workers. They also exhibit lower unemployment rates. In the first quarter of 2007, the unemployment rate was 3.4 percent at ages 55 to 64 and 3.7 percent at ages 25 to 54 (Bureau of Labor Statistics, 2007a). Additionally, job loss rates are lower for workers ages 55 to 64 than for younger workers (Farber, 2005), although the protective effect of age disappears when the analysis accounts for job tenure (Munnell, Sass, Sato, and Zhivan, 2006), suggesting that newly hired older workers face roughly the same job displacement risk as newly hired younger workers. However, Siegel, Muller, and Honig (2000) found that older workers were more likely than younger workers to lose their jobs during the early 1990s recession, reversing the age pattern that prevailed during the 1982–83 recession. And older unemployed adults experience longer unemployment spells than their younger counterparts. In 2006, 28 percent of unemployed adults ages 55 to 64 were unemployed for at least 27 weeks, compared with just 26 percent of those ages 25 to 34 and 20 percent of those ages 35 to 44 (Bureau of Labor Statistics, 2007e).

It is difficult to know what to make of these comparisons, however, because they do not control for productivity differences between younger and older workers. Labor market discrimination occurs when factors unrelated to productivity affect the employment relationship. Most economic analyses measure gender and race discrimination by differences in employment probabilities and earnings between men and women and across different racial groups that persist after controlling for observable factors that are likely to affect productivity. This approach does not work when assessing age discrimination, however, because aging per se may affect worker productivity, either positively or negatively. Thus, the assumption that older workers are equally productive after controlling for variables such as education, experience, and job tenure—the key assumption in most studies of race and sex discrimination—is not very convincing. A better approach would be to relate individual productivity measures to earnings and examine how these relationships vary by age, but individual productivity is difficult to measure.

Although national employment and earnings statistics indicate that older workers fare at least as well as their younger counterparts, many workers seem to believe that employers favor younger workers and that age discrimination is pervasive. About 16,500 age-related discrimination claims were filed with the Equal Employment Opportunity Commission in 2006, accounting for about 22 percent of all complaints (U.S. Equal Employment Opportunity Commission, 2007). By comparison, about 36 percent of all claims were based on race and 31 percent were based on sex. In a 2005 survey of 800 adults working or looking for work, 36 percent said that employers treated older workers less fairly than younger workers, and 71 percent said that older workers were more likely to be laid off (Reynolds, Ridley, and Van Horn, 2005). Overall, 60 percent of workers ages 45 to 74 responding to a 2002 survey said they felt older workers were the first to go when employers cut back their workforces (AARP, 2002). Two-thirds of the same group of respondents said they believed workers face age discrimination in the workplace, based on what they had experienced or seen.

Fewer workers said they experienced age discrimination themselves. For example, only 7 percent of employed men ages 45 to 73 reported work-related age discrimination between 1966 and 1980 (Johnson and Neumark, 1997). Only 13 percent of adult workers in a 2005 survey reported being treated unfairly by their employers because of their age (Reynolds et al., 2005).

About 18 percent of workers ages 51 to 61 participating in the 2004 Health and Retirement Study (HRS) agreed with the statement that their employers give preference to younger workers over older workers when making promotion decisions (table 10.2).[4] Men were more likely than women to agree with these sentiments, and African Americans and Hispanics were more likely than non-Hispanic whites. Men who did not complete high school were about 10 percentage points more likely than male college graduates to report that their employers favor younger workers, but these feelings did not vary much by education among women. Those who remained employed after qualifying for Social Security retirement benefits were much less likely than workers ages 51 to 61 to report that their employers discriminate against older workers, probably because those who remain employed late in life have better work experiences than those who retire early. Only 13 percent of workers ages 65 to 69 and 8 percent of workers age 70 or older reported that their employers favor younger workers. It would be informative to examine nonworkers' beliefs about age discrimination, because they may have had worse employment experiences than workers, but the HRS did not ask nonworkers about employer preferences for younger people.

It is not clear how much credence to give these discrimination claims. They are inherently subjective and difficult to document. Some survey respondents may report age discrimination when it does not exist to justify poor labor market outcomes. Nonetheless, respondents in the National Longitudinal Survey of Mature Men who reported age discrimination between 1966 and 1980 were more likely to separate subsequently from their employer and less likely to be employed later than those who did not report discrimination (Johnson and Neumark, 1997).[5] In addition, those who reported discrimination and separated from

TABLE 10.2.

Older workers reporting that their employers favor younger workers
in promotion decisions, by demographic characteristics, 2004

	All	Men	Women
Ages 51–61			
All	17.6%	20.4%	15.1%[†]
Education			
Did not complete high school	21.3	28.7	13.7[†]
High school graduate	17.6	20.5	15.3
Some college	16.5	18.8*	14.7
Four or more years of college	17.3	18.8*	15.6
Race			
Non-Hispanic white or Asian	16.5	19.3	13.9[†]
African American	21.9*	26.0	19.4*
Hispanic	23.7*	26.8	20.9
Age 51 or older			
All	16.4	18.5	14.6[†]
Age			
51–55	17.1	20.1	14.4[†]
56–61	18.2	20.7	16.0[†]
62–64	15.4	15.4	15.4
65–69	13.3*	11.6*	14.7
70+	8.3*	8.5*	8.0*

Source: Author's tabulations from the 2004 Health and Retirement Study (HRS)
   *Percentage differs significantly ($p < .05$) from the percentage in the first row of the education, race, or age group.
   [†]Percentage differs significantly ($p < .05$) from the corresponding percentage for men.

their employers suffered wage losses of about 10 percent, suggesting that self-reports of age discrimination might reflect unfair treatment.

Quasi-experimental studies provide additional evidence that some older workers face discrimination. An early study investigated how employers might treat older workers by examining how a sample of *Harvard Business Review* subscribers said they would react to hypothetical management situations (Rosen and Jerdee, 1977). The researchers mailed questionnaires to study participants, asking how they would handle different scenarios if they were managers, such as dealing with an underperforming employee, allocating training opportunities, and making promotion decisions. Rosen and Jerdee compared responses for scenarios that involved younger workers (age 32) and those that involved older workers (age 61). The results suggest that managers generally perceive older workers as less flexible and more resistant to change than younger workers and that they are reluctant to promote older workers to jobs requiring flexibility, creativity, and high motivation. Additionally, the research indicated that managers are less inclined to support career development and training for older workers. A follow-up study using similar methods (Rosen and Jerdee, 1995) also revealed managerial bias against older workers, particularly older women.

Although these results suggest that managers continue to hold negative stereo-types about older workers, there are a number of important limitations with the studies. The response rates were quite low, with only 15 percent of those contacted completing the questionnaire in 1995. Because respondents may hold different views toward older workers than nonrespondents, it is unclear how well the study participants represent the views of the underlying population of managers. Additionally, *Harvard Business Review* subscribers may differ from typical managers. Finally, managers may respond differently to hypothetical scenarios than to real-world situations.

Other experimental evidence focused on the actual hiring process. Lahey (2005) sent resumes to nearly 4,000 firms in the Boston and St. Petersburg, Florida, areas and compared responses for younger and older workers. The resumes, which were faxed in pairs in response to employment ads for entry-level jobs, were identical except for the age of the job applicant, which varied from 35 to 62. Lahey found that resumes from younger women (age 35 or 45) generated significantly more positive responses than those from older women (age 50, 55, or 62). Prospective employers in Massachusetts contacted 9.2 percent of the younger women with a positive-sounding response (but not necessarily an interview offer), compared with only 7.7 percent of the older women. They offered interviews to 5.3 percent of the younger women but only 3.8 percent of the older women. Results were similar for Florida. These findings are not necessarily evidence of age discrimination, but they do suggest that employers prefer younger women over older women in hiring decisions, at least for less-skilled entry-level jobs.

A final piece of evidence about labor market challenges at older ages comes from a study of the effects of fringe benefits on decisions to hire mature workers (Scott, Berger, and Garen, 1995). Using data from a 1991 nationwide survey of employers and 1979, 1983, 1988, and 1993 data from the Employee Benefits Supplement of the Current Population Survey, the researchers found that higher health insurance costs, in the presence of prohibitions against age discrimination and discrimination in the provision of fringe benefits, reduced employment prospects for older workers. In all five data sets over a 14-year period, the probability that a new hire was age 55 to 64 was significantly lower in firms with health care plans than in those without, and it was also significantly lower in firms with relatively costly plans than in those with less costly plans. However, neither the cost nor presence of retirement plans significantly affected hiring probabilities.

EMPLOYERS' WILLINGNESS TO TRAIN OLDER WORKERS

Training is a critical activity for an effective and efficient workforce. To remain productive, workers must continuously maintain and update their skills, especially when technology is changing rapidly. Training can provide employees with access to the best work assignments, improve their promotion chances, and promote job satisfaction and earnings growth. However, training activities are costly. Expenses include both the opportunity cost of training—employees who are being trained have less time to produce goods and services than those who are in training—and the direct cost of trainers' time and related equipment. Recent estimates suggest that U.S. employers spent between $46 and $54 billion on training in 2003 (Mikelson and Nightingale, 2004). The government spent between $3.7 billion and $6.0 billion on training in 2002, primarily at the federal level.

Training investments can be classified into two broad types. General training is investment in skills that are easily transferable to other employment situations, and specific training is investment in skills that can be used only at the current employer. Economists have noted that employees generally pay for the costs of general training themselves, through wages that are lower than the wages they could demand if they received no general training (Becker, 1975). Because employers cannot generally prevent workers from quitting, newly trained employees can move to new employers and command higher wages that reflect their enhanced skills. The former employer that provided training would lose any training investment it made. To prevent workers from extorting employers in this way, the theory goes, workers pay general training costs themselves through lower wages. Employers and employees generally share the cost of firm-specific training, because neither party can appropriate the productivity gains from training for themselves by terminating the employment relationship. Firm-specific training is forfeited when the employment relationship ends. The existing empirical evidence indicates that employers pay most training costs themselves (Parsons, 1972; Topel, 1991; Neal, 1995; Parent, 1999), suggesting that training is generally firm specific, or at least that the combination of different skills that a particular employer promotes is unique (Lazear, 2003).

Employers appear somewhat reluctant to train older workers, perhaps because firms, not employees, bear most training costs. Older employees have fewer remaining work years before retirement than younger employees, and employers may fear that they will not be able to recoup their training costs before older workers retire and leave the firm. On the other hand, older workers tend to have lower turnover rates than their younger counterparts (Farber, 1999). The evidence suggests that older workers are less likely to obtain employer-sponsored training than younger workers. A 1995 survey indicates that 51 percent of workers ages 55 or older in large and medium-sized establishments received formal employer-sponsored training during the previous 12 months, compared with 79 percent of those ages 25 to 34, 75 percent of those ages 35 to 44, and 65 percent of those ages 45 to 54 (Frazis, Gittleman, Horrigan, and Joyce, 1998). Older workers also receive less intensive training. According to the same survey, workers ages 55 and older averaged 17 hours of informal on-the-job training between May and October, 2005, compared with 30 hours for those ages 35 to 44 and 39 hours for those ages 44 to 54.[6]

CONCLUSION

Although the available evidence on employment prospects at older ages is incomplete and sometimes inconsistent, a careful review reveals that many firms have serious reservations about hiring and employing older workers. Many employers report lingering concerns about what they perceive as older workers' limited creativity and lack of willingness to learn new things, while at the same time telling surveyors that they value older workers' experience, knowledge, maturity, and work ethic. Many firms also express concern about the cost of employing older people, even though actual cost differentials by age are relatively small. Most workers believe that age discrimination in the workplace is widespread, and nearly one in five workers in their 50s reports that their own employer favors younger employees over older employees. Older workers also receive less on-the-job training than their younger counterparts. Additionally, quasi-experimental studies suggest that managers typically perceive older workers as less flexible and more resistant to change than younger workers and that they are reluctant to promote older workers to positions that require creative, highly motivated individuals.

Employment prospects at older ages may be especially bleak for rank-and-file workers and those with limited skills. Well-educated managers and professionals are more likely than less-skilled workers to accumulate the specialized knowledge that employers say they value in older workers. More employers report in surveys that older managers and professionals outperform their younger counterparts than report that older blue-collar workers perform better. Among working men in their 50s, those who did not complete high school are about 10 percentage points more likely than college graduates to report that their employers favor younger workers.

Older people appear to encounter particular difficulty when seeking employment. Recent evidence suggests that employers hiring entry-level workers prefer younger job applicants to older applicants. Employers' reluctance to hire older workers creates special problems for older people who lose their jobs, especially if they do not yet qualify for Social Security. About one in five workers ages 51 to 55 in 1992 were laid off from their jobs before they reached age 62 (Johnson, Mermin, and Murphy, 2007). Older workers displaced from their jobs are generally unemployed for long periods and suffer substantial wage losses when they become reemployed (Couch, 1998; Chan and Stevens, 2001; Johnson and Kawachi, 2007). Employers that are reluctant to hire older job applicants may be willing to keep incumbent older employees on the payroll. Many incumbent workers enjoy several advantages over job applicants. Incumbents have already proven themselves to their employers and thus are less risky than new hires; many have acquired specialized skills and knowledge that their employers value, and they do not require as much additional training as new hires.

Additional research might fill some gaps in our knowledge about the employability of older workers. New surveys should focus on a broader range of jobs, with a particular focus on low-skilled occupations, to better document any special challenges faced by particular segments of the population. Research should also concentrate on developing new survey instruments or alternative methods for gathering attitudinal measures, with sensitivity to managers' reluctance to reveal ageist preferences, especially those that could be linked to illegal discrimination. Studies are also needed that examine strategies that promote more positive attitudes among managers towards older workers.

Managers' attitudes toward older workers may improve in coming years as the population and workforce age, especially if labor and skill shortages develop in certain industries or occupations. Perceptions of older workers tend to be more favorable in workplaces with relatively high concentrations of older workers, which will become more common as the workforce ages. Similarly, older managers will likely become more prevalent in the future, and they generally have higher regard for older workers than do younger managers. Also, as younger workers become relatively more scarce in the next few decades, employers may be forced to turn more often to older workers, likely inducing new attitudes and policies. Managers' attitudes have probably not changed much yet at many companies, because most firms have not yet addressed the challenges created by the coming aging of the population (Young, 2007).

Ongoing changes in the nature of work may also make older workers more attractive to employers in the future. Although some managers question older people's physical strength and stamina, the physical demands of work have declined steadily over time. For example, between 1971 and 2006 the share of jobs involving physically demanding work declined from about 57 percent to 46 percent (Johnson, Mermin, and Resseger, 2007). As these trends continue, managers may be more likely to hire and employ older people.

In the meantime, policy makers can take steps now to soften employer attitudes toward older workers. In Arizona, for example, the governor's Advisory Council on Aging has launched a public education campaign on the value of older workers (Arizona Governor's Advisory Council on Aging, 2006). Similarly, the Arkansas Department of Workforce Services has teamed with AARP to improve awareness and appreciation of older workers by developing relationships with the public workforce system, chambers of commerce, national and local training providers, trade associations, labor unions, community organizations, policy makers, and business leaders (Arkansas Department of Workforce Services, 2007). These types of efforts, which are being duplicated around the country (NGA Center on Best Practices, 2007), can increase employment opportunities for older people and accommodate the work preferences of the growing number of boomers who say they want to delay retirement.

NOTES

1. However, there is some evidence that the trend toward better health in late midlife has ended and perhaps reversed. For example, the share of surveyed adults ages 51 to 56 reporting health problems increased between 1992 and 2004 (Soldo et al., 2006), and disability rates at ages 40 to 49 increased between 1984 and 2000 (Lakdawalla, Bhattacharya, and Goldman, 2004).

2. Wages also increase with age when employers and employees enter into implicit long-term contracts designed to encourage employees to work hard. These implicit contracts pay workers relatively little in the early stages of their careers—less than the value of the goods and services they produce—but then pay much more later in the career (Lazear, 1979; Lazear and Moore, 1984). Worker effort is often difficult to monitor and assess in the short-run, especially when employees work in teams or when extrinsic factors (such as market forces) affect their output. These implicit contracts provide employees with strong incentives to work hard, because employees who shirk their responsibilities run the risk of being fired and forfeiting future compensation premiums. These contracts are not legally binding, but employers who violate them by dismissing older workers without cause could damage their reputations and find themselves unable to offer credible implicit contracts to future generations. Although long-term employment arrangements may be less prevalent today than they used to be, they are still relatively common (Neumark, 2000).

3. Towers Perrin estimates that professional workers typically spend about 12 weeks on the job before they become fully proficient, and are about 40% less productive during that period (AARP, 2005b).

4. The HRS is a nationally representative survey of older Americans conducted by the University of Michigan with primary funding from the National Institute on Aging. Visit http://hrsonline.isr.umich.edu for additional information.

5. The analysis focused on individuals who switched from reporting no age discrimination to reporting discrimination, to attempt to net out the effects of unobserved individual differences in the propensity to report discrimination that might be correlated with labor market behavior. It also controlled for general job satisfaction to account for other negative job characteristics that might cause workers to report discrimination.

6. However, older workers may receive less training because they tend to have more experience than younger workers and thus may need less training.

REFERENCES

AARP. 2000. *American Business and Older Employees*. Washington, DC: AARP.

———. 2002. *Staying Ahead of the Curve: The AARP Work and Career Study*. Washington, DC: AARP.

———. 2003. *Staying Ahead of the Curve 2003: The AARP Working in Retirement Study*. Washington, DC: AARP.

———. 2005a. *Attitudes of Individuals Fifty and Older toward Phased Retirement*. Washington, DC: AARP.

———. 2005b. *The Business Case for Workers Age 50+*. Washington, DC: AARP.

Adams, S. J. 2004. Age discrimination legislation and the employment of older workers. *Labour Economics* 11 (2): 219–41.

Arkansas Department of Workforce Services. 2007. *Arkansas Mature Worker Initiative*. Retrieved September 24, 2007, from www.arkansas.gov/esd/General/PDF/ARMature WorkerSummary.pdf.

Arizona Governor's Advisory Council on Aging. 2006. *Arizona Mature Workforce Initiative. 2006. Year One Outcomes and Recommendations*. Retrieved September 24, 2007, from www.azgovernor.gov/aging/Documents/MWI%20Year%20One%20Report%20%20 Recs%20-%20public%20-%20April%2006.pdf.

Barth, M. C., McNaught, W., and Rizzi, P. 1993. Corporations and the Aging Workforce. In *Building the Competitive Workforce: Investing in Human Capital for Corporate Success*, ed. P. H. Mirvis, 156–200. New York: John Wiley & Sons.

Becker, G. S. 1975. *Human Capital*, 2nd ed. Chicago: University of Chicago Press.

Brown, K. N., Goodfellow, G. P., Hill, T., Joss, R. R., Luss, R., Miller, L., et al. 2000. *The Unfolding of a Predictable Surprise: A Comprehensive Analysis of the Shift from Traditional Pensions to Hybrid Plans*. Research Report. Bethesda, MD: Watson Wyatt Worldwide.

Buck Consultants. 2007. *The Real Talent Debate: Will Aging Boomers Deplete the Workforce?* Retrieved September 24, 2007, from www.cvworkingfamilies.org/downloads/Talent Debate.pdf?CFID=19353334&CFTOKEN=68992183.

Bureau of Labor Statistics. 2000. *Employee Benefits in State and Local Governments, 1998*. Retrieved September 24, 2007, from www.bls.gov/ncs/ebs/sp/ebbl0018.pdf.

———. 2007a. *Labor Force Statistics from the Current Population Survey*. Retrieved September 24, 2007, from http://data.bls.gov/PDQ/outside.jsp?survey=ln.

————. 2007b. *Median Usual Weekly Earnings of Full-Time Wage and Salary Workers by Age, Race, Hispanic or Latino Ethnicity, and Sex, Quarterly Averages, Not Seasonally Adjusted.* Retrieved September 24, 2007, from www.bls.gov/webapps/legacy/cpswktab2.htm.

————. 2007c. *National Compensation Survey: Employee Benefits in Private Industry in the United States, 2005.* Retrieved September 24, 2007, from www.bls.gov/ncs/ebs/sp/ebbl0022.pdf.

————. 2007d. *National Compensation Survey: Employee Benefits in Private Industry in the United States, March 2007.* Retrieved September 24, 2007, from www.bls.gov/ncs/ebs/sp/ebsm0006.pdf.

————. 2007e. *Unemployed Persons by Age, Sex, Race, Hispanic or Latino Ethnicity, Marital Status, and Duration of Unemployment.* Retrieved September 24, 2007, from ftp://ftp.bls.gov/pub/special.requests/lf/aat31.txt.

Butrica, B. A., Johnson, R. W., Smith, K.E., and Steuerle, C. E. 2004. *Does Work Pay at Older Ages?* Washington, DC: Urban Institute.

Butrica, B. A., Smith, K. E., and Steuerle, E. 2007. Working for a good retirement. In *Government Spending on the Elderly*, ed. D. B. Papadimitriou. New York: Palgrave Macmillan.

Calvo, E. 2006. *Does Working Longer Make People Healthier and Happier?* Work Opportunities for Older Americans Series 2. Chestnut Hill, MA: Center for Retirement Research, Boston College.

Chan, S., and Stevens, A. H. 2001. Job loss and employment patterns of older workers. *Journal of Labor Economics* 19 (2): 484–521.

Couch, K. A. 1998. Late life job displacement. *The Gerontologist* 38 (1): 7–17.

Farber, H. S. 1999. Mobility and stability: The dynamics of job change in labor markets. In *Handbook of Labor Economics, Vol. 3B*, ed. O. C. Ashenfelter and D. Card, 2439–84. Amsterdam: Elsevier.

————. 2005. *What Do We Know about Job Loss in the United States? Evidence from the Displaced Workers Survey, 1984–2004.* Working Paper No. 498. Princeton, NJ: Industrial Relations Section, Princeton University.

Federal Interagency Forum on Aging Related Statistics. 2006. *Older Americans Update, 2006: Key Indicators of Well-Being.* Washington, DC: U.S. Government Printing Office.

Frazis, H., Gittleman, M., Horrigan, M., and Joyce, M. 1998. Results from the 1995 survey of employer-provided training. *Monthly Labor Review* 121 (6): 3–13.

Friedberg, L., and Webb, A. 2005. Retirement and the evolution of pension structure. *Journal of Human Resources* 40 (2): 281–308.

Henkens, K. 2005. Stereotyping older workers and retirement: The managers' point of view. *Canadian Journal of Aging* 24 (4): 353–66.

Johnson, R. W., Davidoff, A. J., and Perese, K. 2003. Health insurance costs and early retirement decisions. *Industrial and Labor Relations Review* 56 (4): 716–29.

Johnson, R. W., and Kawachi, J. 2007. *Job Changes at Older Ages: Effects on Wages, Benefits, and Other Job Attributes.* CRR Working Paper No. 2007-04. Chestnut Hill, MA: Center for Retirement Research, Boston College. Retrieved September 24, 2007, from www.bc.edu/centers/crr/wp_2007–4.shtml.

Johnson, R. W., Mermin, G. B. T., and Murphy, D. 2007. *The Impact of Late-Career Health and Employment Shocks on Social Security and Pension Wealth.* Washington, DC: Urban Institute.

Johnson, R. W., Mermin, G. B. T., and Resseger, M. 2007. *Employment at Older Ages and the Changing Nature of Work.* Washington, DC: AARP.

Johnson, R. W., and Neumark, D. 1997. Age discrimination, job separations, and employment status of older workers: Evidence from self-reports. *Journal of Human Resources* 32 (4): 779–811.

Johnson, R. W., and Steuerle, E. 2004. Promoting work at older ages: The role of hybrid pension plans in an aging population. *Journal of Pension Economics and Finance* 3 (3): 315–37.

Kaiser Family Foundation and Health Research Educational Trust. 2005. *Employer Health Benefits: 2005 Annual Survey.* Menlo Park, CA and Chicago: Kaiser Family Foundation and Health Research Educational Trust.

Lahey, J. 2005. *Age, Women, and Hiring: An Experimental Study.* NBER Working Paper No. 11435. Cambridge, MA: National Bureau of Economic Research.

———. 2006. *State Age Protection Laws and the Age Discrimination in Employment Act.* NBER Working Paper No. 12048. Cambridge, MA: National Bureau of Economic Research.

Lakdawalla, D. N., Bhattacharya, J., and Goldman, D. P. 2004. Are the young becoming more disabled? *Health Affairs* 23 (1): 168–76.

Lazear, E. P. 1979. Why is there mandatory retirement? *Journal of Political Economy* 87 (6): 1261–84.

———. 2003. *Firm-Specific Human Capital: A Skill-Weights Approach.* NBER Working Paper 9679. Cambridge, MA: National Bureau of Economic Research.

Lazear, E. P., and Moore, R. L. 1984. Incentives, productivity, and labor contracts. *Quarterly Journal of Economics* 99 (2): 275–95.

Marshall, V. W. 2001. Canadian research on older workers. Presented at the International Association on Gerontology conference, Vancouver, B.C.

Martocchio, J. J. 1989. Age-related differences in employee absenteeism: A meta-analysis. *Psychology and Aging* 4 (4): 409–14.

McGregor, J., and Gray, L. 2002. Stereotypes and older workers: The New Zealand experience. *Social Policy Journal of New Zealand* 18:163–77.

Mermin, G. B. T., Johnson, R. W., and Murphy, D. 2007. Why do boomers plan to work longer? *Journal of Gerontology: Social Sciences* 62B (5): S286–94.

Metcalf, H., and Meadows, P. 2006. *Survey of Employers' Policies, Practices and Preferences Relating to Age.* Research Report No. 325. London: U.K. Department for Work and Pensions.

MetLife Mature Market Institute. 2005. *The MetLife Survey of American Attitudes Toward Retirement: What's Changed.* Westport, CT: MetLife Mature Market Institute.

Mickelson, K. S., and Nightingale, D. S. 2004. *Estimating Public and Private Expenditures on Occupational Training in the United States.* Washington, DC: Urban Institute.

Mincer, J. 1974. *Schooling, Experience, and Earnings.* New York: National Bureau of Economic Research.

Munnell, A. H., Sass, S. A., and Soto, M. 2006. *Employer Attitudes toward Older Workers:*

Survey Results. Work Opportunities for Older Americans Series 3. Chestnut Hill, MA: Center for Retirement Research, Boston College.

Munnell, A. H., Sass, S. A., Soto, M., and Zhivan, N. 2006. *Has the Displacement of Older Workers Increased?* CRR Working Paper No. 2006-17. Chestnut Hill, MA: Center for Retirement Research, Boston College.

National Center for Health Statistics. 2006. *Trends in Health and Aging: Respondent-Assessed Health by Age, Sex, and Race/Ethnicity.* Retrieved December 8, 2008, from http://205.207.175.393/aging/TableViewer/tableView.aspx?ReportId=457.

NGA Center on Best Practices. 2007. *NGA Center Eyes Increasing Employment and Volunteer Opportunities for Retirees.* Retrieved September 24, 2007, from www.nga.org/portal/site/nga/menuitem.6c9a8a9ebc6ae07eee28aca9501010a0/?vgnextoid=9b3a084726f b2110VgnVCM1000001a01010aRCRD.

Neal, D. 1995. Industry-specific human capital: Evidence from displaced workers. *Journal of Labor Economics* 13 (4): 653–77.

Neumark, D. 2000. Changes in job stability and job security: A collective effort to untangle, reconcile, and interpret the evidence. In *On the Job: Is Long-Term Employment a Thing of the Past?* ed. D. Neumark, 1–27. New York: Russell Sage Foundation.

Parent, D. 1999. Wages and mobility: The impact of employer-provided training. *Journal of Labor Economics* 17 (2): 298–317.

Parsons, D. O. 1972. Specific human capital: Application to quit rates and layoff rates. *Journal of Political Economy* 80 (6): 1120–43.

Penner, R. G., Perun, P., and Steuerle, E. 2002. *Legal and Institutional Impediments to Partial Retirement and Part-Time Work by Older Workers.* Washington, DC: Urban Institute.

Pension and Welfare Benefits Administration. 1998. *Private Pension Plan Bulletin: Abstract of 1994 Form 5500 Annual Reports.* Washington, DC: U.S. Department of Labor.

Pitt-Catsouphes, M., Smyer, M. A., Matz-Costa, C., and Kane, K. 2007. *The National Study Report: Phase II of the National Study of Business Strategy and Workforce Development.* Chestnut Hill, MA: Center on Aging and Work, Boston College.

Reynolds, S., Ridley, N., and Van Horn, C. E. 2005. *A Work-filled Retirement: Workers' Changing Views on Employment and Leisure.* Worktrends 8.1. Retrieved September 24, 2007, from www.heldrich.rutgers.edu/uploadedFiles/Publications/WT16.pdf.

Rogowski, J., and Karoly, L. 2000. Health insurance and retirement behavior: Evidence from the health and retirement survey. *Journal of Health Economics* 19 (4): 529–39.

Rosen, B., and Jerdee, Y. H. 1977. Too old or not too old? *Harvard Business Review* 55 (6): 97–106.

———. 1995. *The Persistence of Age and Sex Stereotypes in the 1990s: The Influence of Age and Gender in Management Decision Making.* Public Policy Institute Issue Brief No. 22. Washington, DC: AARP.

Scott, F. A., Berger, M. C., and Garen, J. E. 1995. Do health insurance and pension costs reduce the job opportunities of older workers? *Industrial and Labor Relations Review* 48 (4): 775–91.

Siegel, M., Muller, C., and Honig, M. 2000. *The Incidence of Job Loss: The Shift from Younger to Older Workers, 1981–1996.* New York: International Longevity Center—USA.

Soldo, B. J., Mitchell, O. S., Tfaily, R., and McCabe, J. F. 2006. *Cross-Cohort Differences in*

Health on the Verge of Retirement. NBER Working Paper No. 12762. Cambridge, MA: National Bureau of Economic Research.

Steuerle, C. E., Spiro, C., and Johnson, R. W. 1999. *Can Americans Work Longer?* Straight Talk on Social Security and Retirement Policy No. 5. Washington, DC: Urban Institute.

Stock, J. H., and Wise, D. A. 1990. The pension inducement to retire: An option value analysis. In *Issues in the Economics of Aging,* ed. D. A. Wise, 205–29. Chicago: University of Chicago Press.

Topel, R. 1991. Specific capital, mobility, and wages: Wages rise with job seniority. *Journal of Political Economy* 99 (1): 145–76.

U.S. Equal Employment Opportunity Commission. 2007. *Charge Statistics, FY 1997 through FY 2006.* Retrieved September 24, 2007, from www.eeoc.gov/stats/charges.html.

Young, M. 2007. No pain, no gain: Employers' responses to the aging workforce. Paper presented at the Joint Conference of the American Society on Aging and the National Council on Aging, Chicago, Illinois.

CHAPTER ELEVEN

Work and Older Adults

Motivation and Performance

RUTH KANFER, PH.D.

An organization's success critically depends on the availability of a capable and motivated workforce. Over the past decade, there has been growing organizational concern about meeting future workforce needs. The source of this concern may be traced to the confluence of two global trends. First, changes in the business environment have led to the creation of jobs and work roles that require employee knowledge, skills, and abilities (KSAs) that are substantially different from those required in the past. Second, the aging of the large baby boom cohort and the relatively smaller number of younger replacement workers in the next generation cohort has heightened organizational competition for talented younger workers (to replace retiring workers). To prevent workforce shortages and promote intergenerational knowledge transfer before retirement, many organizations are developing new programs designed to retain older workers. The success of these strategies, however, importantly depends on the motivation and performance of older workers who continue to work.

This chapter reviews recent psychological theories and research on age-related changes and how they influence work motivation and job performance. In the first section, I provide a brief description of how recent changes in the business environment and demographic trends have influenced the nature of work and the workforce. In the second section, I review findings on the relationship between chronological age and job performance and discuss why no strong relationship has been obtained. The third section focuses on job performance, including a definition of the construct, a review of theoretical developments on the person determinants of job performance, and implications for delineating the impact of age-related changes on job performance through their effects on person-job fit and motivation. The fourth section addresses the bearing of age-related changes in motives, skills, and interests on work motivation, and the implications of aging for person-job fit and its consequences. The final section summarizes major research themes in work and aging, describes current gaps in the empirical literature, and notes implications for future research, policy, and practice.

THE CHANGING WORKPLACE AND WORKER

Economic globalization has profoundly influenced the design and nature of work. In contrast to the twentieth century, when worker competencies were often closely linked to specific job *tasks* (e.g., installing auto engines, selling life insurance), the profile of desirable worker competencies in the twenty-first century has become more closely linked to evolving work *roles* (e.g., computer support specialist, sales associate; see Cascio, 1995). The transition from specific tasks to complex work roles has, in turn, influenced the profile of personal attributes that organizations value and consider when making personnel decisions. Increasingly, organizations seek to attract and retain employees who (1) possess broad job-related domain knowledge, (2) demonstrate strong learning competencies (for continuous skill updating), (3) adapt quickly to changes in the organization and work role, (4) take initiative, and (5) have interpersonal skills that promote team effectiveness and organizational success.

At the same time, demographic trends have begun to noticeably affect the pool of available workers. In most developed countries, high birth rates during the mid-twentieth century (1946–1964) led to a large baby boom worker cohort. This cohort was followed by a relatively smaller Generation X worker cohort (due to substantially lower birth rates between 1965 and 1980). Although population demographics indicate that the Millennial cohort (born 1981–2000) will be slightly larger than the Generation X cohort, a larger proportion of individuals in the Millennial cohort are expected to stay in school longer and enter the workforce at a later age than previous cohorts. As a consequence of these trends, as the baby boom cohort ages, workers aged 50 to 70 will make up the fastest-growing segment of the workforce, while the number of available workers aged 30–49 declines. From an organizational perspective, these trends indicate that older workers will likely play a critical role in meeting workforce needs for at least the next decade.

There is little disagreement among public policy makers, organizational scholars, and human resource managers on the importance of attracting, retraining, and retaining capable older workers. To accomplish this goal, many organizations are implementing new skill-training formats designed to be more attractive to older workers, compensation and benefits plans that offer workers more financial security, greater flexibility in work scheduling, and bridge retirement programs that assign older workers to work roles that promote intergenerational transfer of knowledge. Surprisingly, however, few of these programs (with the exception of programs to facilitate training) are evidence-based. That is, despite extensive study of age-related changes in personal attributes, such as cognitive abilities, personality traits, goals, and interests, relatively little research attention has been paid to understanding how these developmental changes affect worker motivation, job performance, or workforce participation. One purpose of this chapter is to describe how age-related changes in knowledge, skills, and abilities (KSAs) and other nonability person traits and characteristics influence work motivation and job performance. Delineation of these processes provides a scientific foundation from which organizations may develop programs tailored to facilitate older worker motivation and job performance more effectively.

AGE AND JOB PERFORMANCE

Many individuals maintain the general belief that older workers tend to perform more poorly than younger workers, yet a substantial body of scientific evidence shows that chronological age is not uniformly related to job performance. For example, McEvoy and Cascio (1989) conducted a meta-analytic review of the age-job performance relationship based on data taken from 65 studies conducted over 21 years. Results obtained across a range of occupations and performance rating formats showed an estimated true score correlation between age and job performance of only $r = .06$. Similar findings by Avolio and Waldman (1993) provide further evidence to contradict the notion of a universal decline in job performance as a function of age.

That is not to say, however, that age-related changes have no effect on employee performance. As Loretto and White (2006) note, although employers often deny negative bias toward older workers in general, they also believe that older workers perform better than younger workers on some dimensions (e.g., interpersonal skills) and worse than younger workers on other dimensions (e.g., skill training). These beliefs suggest that employers and managers do perceive relationships between age and work performance, the nature of which depends on the aspect of job performance under consideration. So to better understand relationships between age and job performance, one must first more carefully define job performance and then examine how age-related changes affect the behaviors that contribute to job performance.

DEFINING JOB PERFORMANCE: THE CONTENT OF PERFORMANCE AND PERSON DETERMINANTS

Job performance refers to the integrated evaluation of an individual's work behaviors and products relevant to organizational objectives. The behaviors and dimensions that make up job performance depend on the job and may include specific behaviors (e.g., counts money in the register at the end of each day) and/or general behavior patterns (e.g., acts professionally). Among customer service representatives, for example, job performance may be evaluated in terms of how well the employee handles customer grievances, the number of customers served, accuracy in keeping customer interaction records, and so on. Among computer programmers, evaluations of job performance are likely to entail ratings of how well and quickly the employee writes new programs, compiles program documentation, and resolves program errors. Although measures of job performance within a job family (e.g., clerical personnel) may include similar work behaviors, the weight that is given to a particular behavior in the overall performance evaluation usually differs across jobs.

Because different jobs involve evaluation of different behaviors, the observed lack of a relationship between age and job performance across occupations may mask a negative age-job performance relationship in jobs that demand execution of age-sensitive behaviors. Indeed, many studies find a negative relationship between age and particular aspects of performance in jobs (e.g., pilot, athlete, construction worker) that make strong demands on physical, psychomotor, or short-term memory abilities (e.g., Hardy and Parasuraman, 1997; Sharit and Czaja, 1999). But other studies investigating age-performance relations among highly skilled persons show a more gradual decline in performance with age (e.g., Krampe and Ericsson, 1996).

Changes in the nature of work over the past few decades may also partly account for the observed lack of a relationship between age and job performance. Age-related declines in physical abilities and capacities over the life span have often been assumed to contribute to lower performance in jobs that place strong demands on physical capabilities. However, fewer jobs today demand sustained physical strength (e.g., heavy lifting) than was the case fifty years ago, and these behaviors are generally not included in job performance ratings of workers in the fast-growing professional/technical and services sectors. In addition, as Hedge, Borman, and Lammlein (2006) note, the effect of age-related declines in physical and sensory abilities on performance in jobs that do make substantial physical demands may be importantly offset by changes in job design, work strategies, equipment, or employee activities that sustain functional capacity.

Still other changes in the nature of work suggest that age may play a greater role in job performance. Kubeck, Delp, Haslett, and McDaniel (1996) conducted a meta-analytic review on the relationship between age and a variety of job training outcomes. Their results indicate that among trainees learning occurs more slowly among older adults compared to younger adults. In jobs where employees must often learn new job skills to keep up with changes in technology-driven changes in work processes, older workers may take longer to learn than younger workers. When job performance ratings include this dimension, older workers are likely to show lower performance than younger workers. In contrast, research also shows a positive relationship between age and the regulation of negative emotions (Carstensen, 1998). Effective management of negative emotions is frequently cited as an important dimension of performance in customer service jobs and may also play a role in the effectiveness of team performance.

In the 1990s, Borman and Motowidlo (1993) suggested that the changing nature of work required a reevaluation of the universe of work behaviors that comprise job performance. Specifically, they proposed a two-dimensional model of job performance behaviors that included not only technical behaviors prescribed by the job description (e.g., daily register count) but also contextual behaviors that are not prescribed by the job description but rather serve to facilitate team and organizational performance (e.g., helping others). Subsequent research provides general support for this conceptualization and suggests that contextual behaviors contribute significantly to the evaluation of job performance, particularly in work team environments.

Building a Model of Job Performance

I have defined job performance in terms of the type of behaviors that are evaluated by the employer and noted that the job requirements and work role importantly determine which behaviors are included in the job performance evaluation. But such content-based descriptions of job performance are incomplete because they do not account for employee characteristics such as individual differences in KSAs that determine performance-relevant behaviors. They also neglect the key role that motivation plays in the expression of KSA-driven capabilities. To enable more precise determination of how aging affects job performance, it is necessary to delineate how these personal influences affect job performance.

Through most of the twentieth century, theories of job performance emphasized two broad personal determinants of performance: (1) KSAs, and (2) motivation. Individual differences in general cognitive abilities (intelligence) were posited to enhance job performance by facilitating the development of job knowledge and technical skills. Individual differences in motivation pertain to the individual's decision to pursue challenging and difficult work goals, to work hard, and to persist at the goal in the face of difficulties and obstacles. According to these theories, cognitive abilities and motivation operate multiplicatively to influence job performance. That is, neither motivation nor abilities alone are sufficient for effective job performance.

Recent approaches to understanding personal determinants of job performance have focused on the dynamic relationship between knowledge, skills, and abilities and the influence of the relationship between these personal characteristics and job demands on work performance. Ackerman's (1996) Process, Personality, Interests and Knowledge (PPIK) theory of adult intelligence, for example, specifies the relationship between fluid intellectual abilities (e.g., short-term memory), the role of personality and interests on the development of knowledge and skills, and their differential influence on performance across the life span. In the context of the age-job performance relationship, findings from this stream of research (e.g., Ackerman and Rolfhus, 1999; Beier and Ackerman, 2001, 2003) indicate that older persons show growth in intellectual domain knowledge over the life span. Applied to the work context, PPIK theory suggests that job performance may be maintained or improved in later years as increased job knowledge and skills serve to offset age-related decline in fluid intellectual abilities. Consistent with this view, Schmidt, Hunter, and Outerbridge (1986), for example, found that job-related knowledge provided higher predictive validities than cognitive abilities in the prediction of job performance.

A second development examines the fit between the individual's KSAs in the aggregate and the job demands. Derived from person-environment formulations and Dawis and Lofquist's (1984) Theory of Work Adjustment, person-job (PJ) fit refers to degree of correspondence between personal characteristics required for the job (demands) and the individual's KSAs. Recent meta-analytic findings by Kristof-Brown, Zimmerman, and Johnson (2005) indicate that individuals with poor PJ fit tend to perform more poorly than individuals whose KSAs are commensurate with the demands of the job. Additionally, poor PJ fit was significantly related to negative work attitudes, including job satisfaction, organizational commitment, and intentions to quit.

The influence of PJ fit on attitudes represents an important input to the final determinant of job performance, namely, motivation. As noted previously, motivation represents a key determinant of job performance and refers to the individual's motivation to allocate his or her personal resources (principally in the forms of time and effort) to a given work role. As described by Kanfer, Chen, and Pritchard (2008), motivation is a dynamic process influenced by both the person and the environment. Developmental changes in the strength of achievement, affiliative, generative, and other motives over the life course may alter allocations of time and effort to the job or reduce interest in work, depending on perceived opportunities for motive fulfillment in the work role. Perceptions of poor PJ fit may reduce job self-efficacy and also reduce work motivation. When PJ fit is poor, increased effort may compensate for insufficient knowledge, skills, and abilities relative to job demands. Decrements in motivation, however, choke off this compensatory opportunity and so further contribute to poorer job performance. Finally, an individual's allocation of personal resources to work goals is also influenced by the broader environment in which he or she functions. Nonwork demands and opportunities for motive fulfillment outside the work role may also reduce motivation for allocating time and effort to job performance.

In summary, job performance refers to the evaluation of technical and contextual work-related behaviors that contribute to the work role. During the past half-century, organizational theories on the personal determinants of job performance have evolved to consider a broader array of attributes and the pathways by which they influence job performance. As shown in figure 11.1, early conceptions of job performance emphasized individual differences in KSAs and motivation. More recent perspectives, however, emphasize the effect of a broad array of per-

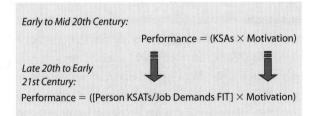

Figure 11.1. Person determinants of job performance. KSAs = knowledge, skills, and abilities; KSATs = knowledge, skills, abilities, and traits

sonal characteristics in terms of their fit to the demands of the job as well as individual differences in motivational traits such as achievement (e.g., Kanfer and Ackerman, 2000).

Using contemporary perspectives, the next section examines the effects of aging, or adult maturation, as it affects each component of the performance equation.

ADULT MATURATION, WORK MOTIVATION, AND JOB PERFORMANCE

Adult aging exerts many influences on the individual, some of which are considered positive and are welcomed, and some of which are considered negative, annoying, or even demeaning. Evidence from research in developmental and life-span psychology shows that, on average, the transition from early to late adulthood entails selective losses in cognitive, intellectual, and physical abilities; gains in job-related knowledge; gains in emotion regulation skills; and changes in the primacy of motives for action. Subjectively, these changes may be variously experienced in the context of work as increased difficulty remembering task details, greater ease in performing routine job tasks, less interpersonal conflict and fewer episodes of disruptive emotional upset over negative work events, greater interest in sharing knowledge with others and helping younger coworkers, more focus on avoiding situations that may challenge a positive work self-concept, and less interest in working long hours or taking on high workload assignments. Intra-individual changes associated with adult maturation may occur gradually over years or manifest quickly as a result of the individual's job experiences, for example, when an involuntary job layoff yields a choice between retiring from the workforce, new job skill training, or job search. On the job, the influence of intra-individual changes on job performance depends on the extent to which the individual can alter the work role to accommodate or compensate for adult development, for example, when older pilots take on supervisory or teaching responsibilities and reduce flying time.

Kanfer and Ackerman (2004) organized age-related changes that bear upon job performance along four broad maturational themes: loss, gain, reorganization, and exchange. The proposed effect of these maturational themes on job performance is shown in figure 11.2. As shown, age-sensitive changes in different aspects of intellectual development (i.e., loss and gain) that occur over the life span are posited to affect the fit between personal attributes and job demands. In con-

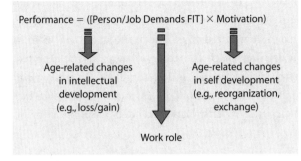

Figure 11.2. Influence of maturational themes on determinants of job performance

trast, maturational changes in self-development, or the socio-emotional, personality, and motive changes that occur over the life span (i.e., reorganization and exchange themes) are posited to affect individual differences in motivation. Each of the four themes reflect broad, normative, intra-individual changes that occur gradually, operate in concert with inter-individual differences and experiential factors, and exert subtle but distinct influences on work motivation and job performance.

Age-Related Changes in Intellectual Development and Knowledge

Theory and research in the intelligence domain provides strong evidence of age-sensitive changes in different aspects of intelligence. As described by Cattell (1943) and more recently by Ackerman (1996, 2000), two major kinds of intellectual abilities may be distinguished. Fluid intellectual abilities (termed Gf) encompass cognitive abilities involved in abstract reasoning, working memory, attention, and processing of novel information. These cognitive abilities show a pattern of gradual decline over the life span, with peak functioning generally during the second decade of life (see Kanfer and Ackerman, 2004). The maturational theme of loss pertains to the decline in these abilities over the life course.

Crystallized intellectual abilities (termed Gc) pertain to the individual's repertoire of knowledge gained through education and experiences. Gc is typically associated with general knowledge, vocabulary, and verbal comprehension. Similarly, occupational knowledge represents a form of crystallized abilities pertaining to knowledge about a work domain. In contrast to Gf, Gc, and occupational knowledge tend to show increasing levels of performance well into middle age and beyond (see Ackerman, 1996).

Age-sensitive changes in intellectual development operate in unison to affect job performance. In jobs that make high Gf demands, such as pilot, performance can be expected to show a gradual decline in late adulthood. In contrast, jobs that make high Gc demands, such as teacher or lawyer, can be expected to show sustained or improved performance in late adulthood. In many jobs, such as surgeon, task demands involve use of both Gc and Gf abilities. In these situations, age-sensitive changes in performance will depend importantly on the specific task demands of the work role.

The Impact of Age-Related Changes in Intellectual Development on Person-Job Fit

Kanfer and Ackerman (2004) propose that the effect of developmental changes that occur across the life span influence motivation through their impact on key variables involved in motivation. Using an expectancy-value formulation of work motivation (see Kanfer, 1987), Kanfer and Ackerman (2004) posit that loss and growth in intellectual abilities and knowledge over the life course may be mapped to motivation through the impact these changes have on subjective judgments of the relationship between allocations of effort and task performance (E-P function). Under conditions that motivate task effort, the E-P function can be described as a monotonically increasing "resource-limited" function, in which increases in task effort are expected to yield increases in performance. In jobs that make strong demands on Gc abilities, however, the E-P function shifts as a function of experience and is more appropriately described as "effort-insensitive" because increases in effort are perceived to have relatively little or no effects on performance. In these jobs, PJ fit is expected to decrease during later adulthood. Consistent with findings by Kristoff-Brown et al. (2005), this form of PJ misfit is expected to be associated with feelings of boredom and perceived lack of challenge. Tax accountants, for example, who perform the same work for two or more decades, have developed expertise that enables them to perform well with relatively less effort than novice tax accountants. For long-tenured mid- and late-life accountants, the work role and technical demands of the job are likely to be perceived as routine, tedious, and unexciting—conditions that may foster a motivational deficit for exerting time and effort beyond the minimal level required for satisfactory job performance.

In contrast, a different form of PJ misfit emerges among older employees who perform jobs that make strong demands on Gf abilities. In these jobs, changes in the E-P function over time operates to increase perceptions of resource limitations, as increases in effort are gradually insufficient to accomplish prior high levels of performance. Among theoretical mathematicians, for example, age-related declines in Gf abilities slowly constrain the maximal level of performance that can be achieved, even with maximal effort in late adulthood. In these situations, PJ misfit creates a gap for which the individual cannot sufficiently compensate by increasing time and effort. That is, in contrast to jobs that place high demands on Gc, individuals who perform jobs that make high and sustained demands on Gf are likely to experience frustration and increased loss of job self-efficacy as attempts to improve performance by increasing effort fall short of reducing the gap. Among older workers in this situation, the only viable solution for improving PJ fit is to change the work role so that lower demands are placed on Gf. Such work role changes are often difficult for the employee to accept, most likely due to the internal attributions made about the reason for the change and the potential threat to positive self-concept.

The impact of PJ misfit (brought about by age-related changes in intellectual abilities and job knowledge) on job performance can range from slight to severe, depending on the form of misfit, the individual's repertoire of other capabilities and interests, and the organization's flexibility with respect to making work role changes. In situations involving PJ misfit where the work role involves both Gf and Gc (e.g., lawyers, doctors), relatively minor work role changes may be made to restore job interest and motivation. For example, lawyers may take on more managerial work that emphasizes use of existing knowledge and skills, and reduce work role tasks that demand working memory, such as conducting cross-examinations. Conceptually, such changes in the work role improve work motivation by altering the subjective E-P function. Similarly, for individuals in high Gc jobs, shifts in the work role that provide opportunity for mastering new tasks using existing skills and knowledge can be expected to improve motivation by shifting perceptions regarding the value of effort for performance. Experienced tax accountants who are bored with their work role preparing individual returns may be trained to prepare estate or corporate returns, for example, or assigned to start a new individual tax return unit. Consistent with Baltes and Baltes (1990), such changes in the work role can be described in terms of age-appropriate selection and compensation. In jobs where PJ misfit stems from high Gf demands, such as air traffic controller, however, work role revision is often difficult, and accommodation through job change (frequently to an entry-level position in another field) can be discouraging and stressful.

Age-Related Changes in the Development of the Self

A second major focus in life span and aging research pertains to age-related changes in non-ability variables, including personality, motives, interests, and values. Kanfer and Ackerman (2004) suggest that two major themes characterize age-related changes in the self: reorganization and exchange. Reorganization refers to age-related changes in the primacy of motives and motivational orientations. For example, Carstensen's (1998) socio-emotional selectivity theory posits that goal orientation changes across the life span. During early adulthood, achievement goals are most prominent, and interests and activities are organized around information that promotes achievement and opportunities for the future. During mid- and late-life, goals are increasingly organized around affect. As goal orientation changes and individuals seek social interactions for the purpose of achieving emotional satisfaction, individuals tend to focus more on situations that afford such opportunities and make greater use of emotion-regulation strategies.

In a related vein, research on age-related changes in personality provides evidence for age-related mean changes in different personality traits and for the emergence of generativity motives at midlife. On the one hand, personality research (e.g., Roberts, Walton, and Viechtbauer, 2006) indicates that extraversion, neuroticism, and openness to experience all show slight mean declines with age such that older adults, on average, can be expected to be less outgoing, less anxious, and less open to new experiences than young adults. On the other hand, research by Warr, Miles, and Platts (2001) shows mean increases in conscientiousness with age. Taken together, mean changes in personality traits over the life span suggest that compared to young adults on average, older adults are more conscientious and less anxious but also less change-oriented or career motivated. Research by McAdams and colleagues (see McAdams, 2001) further suggests that generativity motives are most likely to appear at midlife. According to McAdams, these motives, pertaining to preference for activities that help others and the broader society and future generations, emerge in the context of other personality traits and may represent a discontinuity in motivational orientation for action.

The Impact of Age-Related Changes in the Self
on Motivational Processes

Kanfer and Ackerman (2004) suggest that age-related changes in the organization and primacy of non-ability traits and motives may be mapped to expectancy-value formulations of work motivation through their impact on the remaining two functions that (together with the E-P function) operate to determine an individual's work motivation, or allocation of personal resources toward task accomplishment. Associated with age-related changes in the salience of various motives, several studies show age-related changes in the salience and utility of incentives associated with performance-contingent satisfaction of instrumental motives. Warr, Miles, and Platts (2001), for example, found that older workers reported less interest than young workers in work activities and incentives associated with achieving competitive excellence, expanding work role demands, new skill learning, and external goal assignments. However, older workers reported more interest than younger workers in activities and performance-contingent incentives associated with experiential and self-protective motives, including job and salary security, opportunities to use skills, and activities that strengthen self-efficacy and sense of professional identity. These findings suggest that standard organizational incentives for improved performance, such as pay increases and promotions, may be age-sensitive and of lesser utility to older workers as compared to younger workers. To improve the perceived utility of increased performance among older adults, organizations will likely need to broaden their armada of incentives. Indeed, a growing number of organizations interested in recruiting, motivating, and retaining an older workforce have focused on contextual incentives such as teamwork, work schedule flexibility, opportunities to use skills, and intergenerational knowledge transmission (see, e.g., Dychtwald, Erickson, and Morison, 2006).

The influence of age-related changes in motives and non-ability traits is also proposed to influence the perceived utility (attractiveness) of different levels of effort (E-U function). Kanfer and Ackerman (2004) suggest that age-related changes in vitality and motivational orientation toward work contribute to an age-related downward shift in the perceived, inverted U-shaped E-U function. That is, although older individuals are assumed to maintain highest utility for moderate levels of effort expenditure, increasing interest in nonwork and health is expected to shift the function generally downward.

A substantial body of evidence provides support for two statements about the relationship between chronological age and work motivation and job performance. First, within the span of life through the seventh decade, and beyond the obvious deleterious influence of poor physical health, there is no compelling evidence to support the notion of a universal age-related decline in job performance. Rather, an individual's job performance is jointly determined by ongoing intra-individual changes in intellect, knowledge, and the self; ongoing fluctuations in specific work role demands; and the extent to which work motivation is maintained by alignment of the individual's motives and work rewards. As such, both individuals and organizations jointly contribute to job performance.

Second, there is also currently no strong evidence to support the notion of a general age-related decline in work motivation arising from some central loss in energy. Rather, it appears that motivational deficits in mid- and late-adult work reflect the consequence of different types of PJ misfit between the individual's strengths and salient interests with the demands and reward opportunities offered by the work role. Boredom and perceived lack of challenge is proposed to occur as a function of the failure to adjust work roles in light of increased knowledge and skill and changing interests. Frustration and discouragement is proposed to occur as a function of difficulties that accrue when individuals cannot sustain high levels of job performance in work roles that place strong demands on age-sensitive fluid intellectual abilities. Although both motivational deficits may reduce performance, the two forms of PJ misfit have different sources, consequences, and implications for remediation.

AGING AND WORK: FORGING A USE-INSPIRED RESEARCH AGENDA

As Stokes (1997) has argued, programmatic research inspired by practical problems potentially informs both theory and practice. The impetus for such research is often a real-world problem, in this instance the problem of promoting work engagement in an aging workforce. In this section I identify four basic areas in which use-inspired research efforts may address practical needs and scholarly gaps in our knowledge.

Motivation to Work versus Motivation for Work

Historically, work motivation refers to two related motivational processes: goal choice and goal striving. Goal choice refers to the determinants and processes underlying the decision to select a goal or course of action. In the present context, this process may be thought of in terms of the factors (e.g., motives, needs, values) that contribute to the older worker's decision to work, that is, the individual's *motivation to work*. In contrast, goal striving pertains to the determinants and mechanisms by which individuals accomplish goals. In the present context, this process reflects the personal (e.g., job self-efficacy, emotion and motivation regulation skills) and situation (e.g., PJ fit, coworker relations) factors that contribute to the older worker's allocation of time and effort in the job, that is, the individual's *motivation at work*.

The distinction between motivation *to* work and motivation *at* work was largely irrelevant for much of the twentieth century in most developed countries. In these countries, attainment of financial and social success was closely linked to successful employment, with individuals often staying in the same job or moving through a progression of jobs in the same organization for most of their working life. In addition, the workforce pool was large and generally homogenous, consisting of young males. In contrast, the twenty-first-century workforce is substantially more diverse. Nearly half of the available workforce is 40 years or older and female. Although employment remains strongly linked to financial needs for workers at all ages, younger workers change jobs more often, are less likely to stay with the same organization their entire working life, and are more likely to experience spells of unemployment across their working life span. These changes suggest that identifying what motivates older workers to participate in organized work represents a first step in understanding work and aging.

Surveys of older workers indicate that financial need and satisfaction of intrinsic motives provide the two primary motivations to work. Although these two motives to work may be similar to those expressed by younger workers, there is a potentially important age-related difference that warrants further examination. Compared to younger workers, older workers are likely to have more nonwork alternatives for satisfaction of intrinsic motives, such as avocational interests and roles within their community. In middle and late life, these activities may provide individuals with opportunities for achieving a sense of competence and identity, independent of employment. As such, for older individuals, the primary motive for work may be instrumental (e.g., to meet financial needs) rather than self-related (e.g., sense of competence and autonomy).

Alternatively, it is also reasonable that older workers employed in career jobs are motivated to work for intrinsic reasons, such as the enjoyment and sense of competence that comes from demonstrating skill expertise, the opportunity to affiliate with similar others, or the benefits associated with maintaining a strong professional identity. It is also noteworthy that older workers in these positions have typically devoted a substantial proportion of their waking life to their job and so may have developed few avocations or nonwork interests that would provide similar intrinsic satisfactions. Consistent with this notion, Mitchell et al. (2001) proposed the construct of "job embeddedness" to capture individual differences in the commitment, social integration, and benefits associated with remaining at a job.

To date, most studies investigating older worker motivation to work have been descriptive and based on reported attitudes and intentions with respect to leaving a job. Such research rarely considers the incentive value of different retirement options, or the nonmonetary reasons that persons wish to stay on the job. Additional research is needed to investigate these issues. In particular, more knowledge is needed about the relationships among an individual's work/nonwork history, employment orientation, and behavioral correlates of work intentions.

Higgins's (1998) Regulatory Focus theory may also be useful in understanding how an older worker's motivation to work relates to his or her motivation at work. Regulatory focus theory posits that an individual's motivational orientation influences motivational processing during action. According to the theory, individuals who hold a meta-motivational prevention orientation are more likely to adopt loss prevention goals and monitor their environment for threats to goal accomplishment than individuals who maintain a promotion focus that emphasizes achievement and opportunities for learning.

From the perspective of regulatory focus theory, the reasons that older workers give for continuing to work may relate to differences in meta-motivational work orientation. For example, older workers who are motivated to work for financial reasons may hold a prevention orientation that emphasizes the avoidance of loss. Motivation to work for financial reasons reflects an avoidance of loss of extrinsic rewards (pay). If working for pay represents part of a larger prevention orientation, it is reasonable to expect that this orientation would also influence motivation during work. That is, for persons with a prevention orientation, who work primarily to prevent financial difficulties, the most attractive incentives for higher levels of performance are likely to be associated with opportunities to enhance employment or work security. Similarly, a threat to work security, as often occurs in periods of organizational change, is likely to serve as a disincentive for higher levels of job effort.

In contrast, older workers who are promotion-focused can be expected to report satisfaction of intrinsic motives to be the principal reason for working. Among these individuals, work goals and incentives for high performance should be more closely associated with achievement and incentives in the form of opportunities for knowledge-transfer and use of skill. In addition, older workers who maintain a promotion-oriented employment focus are expected to be less responsive to threats to job security but more responsive to work conditions that thwart satisfaction of intrinsic motives, such as daily hassles, aversive work conditions, and the expression of age bias by coworkers. Research is needed to determine whether the validity of employment-focus orientation operates to link older worker motivation *for* work and motivation *at* work.

Resource Dynamics of Work Motivation across the Life Span

In the most general sense, work motivation refers to the application of personal resources to job tasks and objectives. Although most work motivation research focuses on resources such as attentional effort (i.e., how hard one works, or intensity) and time (i.e., how long one works, or persistence), other personal resource allocations may index motivation, such as using social support networks (e.g., calling on others for help), using time-management skills (e.g., being reliable and dependable), and being resourceful (e.g., drawing on nonwork knowledge and skills for goal accomplishment).

Investigation of other personal resources, beyond time and effort, is particularly important in the study of older worker motivation and performance. As Heckhausen and Schulz (1998) suggest, self-regulatory coping strategies represent scarce resources that may diminish over the life span and are typically used only when the environment cannot be changed. In the same vein, it seems reasonable to posit developmental changes in the use or preference for different forms of resource allocation and to conjecture that time and attentional effort are less appropriate markers of work motivation among older workers than among younger workers. As discussed previously, age-related decline in Gf implies that motivational strategies designed to increase attentional effort and encourage speed of accomplishment may be more productive for younger workers than for older workers. In terms of persistence, younger workers may also have fewer nonwork demands on their time, allowing them to work longer hours than older workers. In practical terms, if attentional effort and time are less flexible for older workers than younger workers, motivational interventions that target increased allocation of these resources may be inappropriate for older workers.

As discussed previously, gradual declines in Gf may slow new learning, and stronger nonwork demands on time and the decreased attractiveness of working longer for personal need fulfillment may reduce the effectiveness of motivational interventions directed toward intensity and persistence. However, older workers are likely to have a greater fund of job-related knowledge and more social resources than younger workers. Among older workers, motivational strategies to encourage the application of job knowledge, prior experience, and social resources to accomplish job performance may be more productive than strategies that encourage higher levels of attentional effort and longer hours. Research to investigate age-related differences in the target of work motivation strategies represents an important direction for future research.

Socio-contextual Influences on Work Motivation

Mid- and late-life workers often report that they are treated differently from younger workers in personnel decisions in ways that lead to unfavorable treatment on matters of pay raises, promotions, layoffs, and opportunities for challenging assignments (see, e.g., Gordon and Arvey, 2004, and Finkelstein and Farrell, 2007, for reviews of age bias). Findings by Panek, Staats, and Hiles (2006) also show that younger workers are more likely to view older workers as less capable than younger workers. The efficacy of interventions designed to attenuate the detrimental influence of such communications on older worker motivation is sorely needed. Specifically, research to investigate the relative efficacy of different forms of managerial training is recommended.

A second area for future investigation pertains to the determinants and consequences of intergenerational conflicts at work. Age-based cohort differences in work values, for example, may generate strained relations between younger supervisors and older workers (Smola and Sutton, 2002). As the use of team structures increases, more attention is needed to understanding the specific consequences of age-diversity on older workers' motivation and engagement. Recent findings by Wegge et al. (2008), for example, suggest that older workers may benefit from participation in complex teamwork that provides time for information exchange among age-diverse members.

Workplace Transitions: Layoffs, Retirement, and Organizational Change

Adult development may importantly affect how workers interpret and cope with destabilizing organizational events such as organizational change, mergers, and downsizing. In particular, older workers may react more negatively to such events. Caldwell, Herold, and Fedor (2004), for example, found that organizational change had a more deleterious effect on older worker than on younger worker satisfaction. Similarly, Treadway et al. (2005) found intensity of perceptions of organizational politics had a negative effect on older worker performance, but no impact on younger workers. They suggest that the detrimental impact of politics on older workers stems from their greater depletion of resources that are available for coping with work stressors. These results suggest that further research is needed to examine the extent to which the adverse effects of stressful organizational and job events among older workers (compared to younger workers) stems from resource depletion and/or age-related differences in how such events are interpreted and managed.

Training and Employee Development

Although there is a substantial literature on the benefits and disadvantages of various training formats and technologies for use with older adults, less attention has been paid to older worker motivation to learn. A number of studies indicate that older workers are more reluctant to participate in job skill training than are younger workers (see Colquitt, LePine, and Noe, 2000; Maurer, 2007). Numerous reasons have been proposed for why older workers' participation rates are lower than those of younger workers, including lack of opportunity, perceptions that the costs of training outweigh the benefits, low self-efficacy for new skill learning, and fear of looking incompetent to others. Charness, Czaja, and Sharit (2007) review a number of studies that show how training programs and technological systems may be modified to accommodate older workers, including, for example, how the use of self-paced and collaborative training formats may increase older worker training self-efficacy and enjoyment. Research by West, Thorn, and Bagwell (2003) also provides evidence for the efficacy of modified goal-setting techniques to enhance motivation and performance among older workers. The rapid growth in the use of on-line systems for all aspects of work, including job search (e.g., Monster.com), skill training (e.g., e-learning, see Beier and Kanfer, in press), and team communications suggests that future research should focus on identifying why, when, where, and how older persons use these new work systems.

CONCLUSION

Older workers represent the most rapidly growing segment of the workforce. As labor needs exceed supply and global competition increases, organizations have become increasingly concerned with the attraction, placement, and retention of older workers. Enhancing the motivation and productivity of members of this segment of the population represents a goal that may yield multiple societal benefits, including a more engaged older population and more effective intergenerational transmission of knowledge.

This chapter reviewed key adult development processes and their implications for older workers' motivation and job performance. Based on this review, future research is recommended in four areas: motivation for work, motivational dynamics at work, socio-contextual effects on motivation, and motivation for learning. Employers often assume that older workers continue to work for financial reasons or to receive health benefits. Recent studies suggest, however, that older individuals may work for other reasons as well, including task enjoyment, the opportunity to maintain important social connections, and promotion of a positive self-concept (e.g., Greller and Stroh, 1995; Kanfer and Ackerman, 2004).

Research on what motivates older individuals to work addresses a fundamental question about the forces that may shape the meaning of work across the life span. Similarly, research is also needed to better understand how adult development influences learning motivation among older workers, preferred strategies for goal pursuit, and the effects of age bias on work attitudes and performance. Advancing knowledge in each of these areas has the potential to improve our understanding of adult development as well as to enhance the well-being of older persons and the organizations that employ them.

REFERENCES

Ackerman, P. L. 1996. A theory of adult intellectual development: Process, personality, interests, and knowledge. *Intelligence* 22:229–59.

———. 2000. Domain-specific knowledge as the "dark matter" of adult intelligence: Gf/Gc, personality, and interest correlates. *Journal of Gerontology: Psychological Sciences* 55B (2): P69–84.

Ackerman, P. L., and Rolfhus, E. L. 1999. The locus of adult intelligence: Knowledge, abilities, and non-ability traits. *Psychology and Aging* 14:314–30.

Avolio, B. J., and Waldman, D. A. 1993. An examination of age and cognitive test performance across job complexity and occupational types. *Journal of Applied Psychology* 75: 43–50.

Baltes, M. M., and Baltes, P. B. 1990. Psychological perspectives on successful aging: The model of selective optimization and compensation. In *Successful Aging: Perspectives from the Behavioral Sciences*, ed. P. B. Baltes and M. M. Baltes, 1–34. New York: Cambridge University Press.

Beier, M. E., and Ackerman, P. L. 2001. Current events knowledge in adults: An investigation of age, intelligence and non-ability determinants. *Psychology and Aging* 16:615–28.

———. 2003. Determinants of health knowledge: An investigation of age, gender, abilities, personality, and interests. *Journal of Personality and Social Psychology* 84 (2): 439–48.

Beier, M. E., and Kanfer, R. In press. Motivation in training and development: A phase perspective. In *Learning, Training, and Development in Organizations*, ed. S. W. J. Kozlowski, and E. Salas. Mahwah, NJ: Erlbaum.

Borman, W. C., and Motowidlo, S. J. 1993. Expanding the criterion domain to include elements of contextual performance. In *Personnel Selection in Organizations*, ed. N. Schmitt and W. C. Borman, 78–98. San Francisco: Jossey Bass.

Caldwell, S. D., Herold, D. M., and Fedor, D. B. 2004. Toward an understanding of the relationships among organizational change, individual differences, and changes in person-environment fit: A cross-level study. *Journal of Applied Psychology* 89:868–82.

Cascio, W. F. 1995. Whither industrial and organizational psychology in a changing world of work? *American Psychologist* 50:928–39.

Carstensen, L. L. 1998. A life-span approach to social motivation. In *Motivation and Self-Regulation across the Life Span*, ed. J. Heckhausen and C. S. Dweck, 341–64. New York: Cambridge University Press.

Cattell, R. B. 1943. The measurement of adult intelligence. *Psychological Bulletin* 40:153–93.

Charness, N., Czaja, S. J., and Sharit, J. 2007. Age and technology for work. In *Aging and Work in the Twenty-first Century*, ed. K. S. Shulz and G. A. Adams, 225–50. Mahwah, NJ: Lawrence Erlbaum Associates.

Colquitt, J. A., LePine, J. A., and Noe, R. A. 2000. Toward an integrative theory of training motivation: A meta-analytic path analysis of 20 years of research. *Journal of Applied Psychology* 85:678–707.

Dawis, R. V., and Lofquist, L. H. 1984. *A Psychological Theory of Work Adjustment: An Individual Differences Model and Its Applications*. Minneapolis: University of Minnesota Press.

Dychtwald, K., Erickson, T. J., and Morison, R. 2006. *Workforce Crisis: How to Beat the Coming Shortage of Skills and Talent*. Boston: Harvard Business School Press.

Finkelstein, L. M., and Farrell, S. K. 2007. An expanded view of age bias in the workplace. In *Aging and Work in the Twenty-first Century*, ed. K. S. Shultz and G. A. Adams, 73–108. Mahwah, NJ: Lawrence Erlbaum Associates.

Gordon, R. A., and Arvey, R. D. 2004. Age bias in laboratory and field settings: A meta-analytic investigation. *Journal of Applied Social Psychology* 34:468–92.

Greller, M. M., and Stroh, L. K. 1995. Careers in midlife and beyond: A fallow field in need of substance. *Journal of Vocational Behavior* 47:232–47.

Hardy, D. J., and Parasuraman, R. 1997. Cognition and flight performance in older pilots. *Journal of Experimental Psychology: Applied* 3:313–48.

Heckhausen, J., and Schulz, R. 1998. Developmental regulation in adulthood: Selection and compensation via primary and secondary control. In *Motivation and Self-Regulation across the Life Span*, ed. J. Heckhausen and C. S. Dweck, 50–77. New York: Cambridge University Press.

Hedge, J. W., Borman, W. C., and Lammlein, S. E. 2006. *The Aging Workforce*. Washington, DC: American Psychological Association.

Higgins, E. T. 1998. Promotion and prevention: Regulatory focus as a motivational principle. In *Advances in Experimental Social Psychology*, Vol. 30, ed. M. P. Zanna, 1–46. New York: Academic Press.

Kanfer, R. 1987. Task-specific motivation: An integrative approach to issues of measurement, mechanisms, processes, and determinants. *Journal of Social and Clinical Psychology* 5:237–64.

Kanfer, R., and Ackerman, P. L. 2000. Individual differences in work motivation: Further exploration of a trait framework. *Applied Psychology: An International Review* 49:470–82.

———. 2004. Aging, adult development, and work motivation. *Academy of Management Review* 29:440–58.

Kanfer, R., Chen, G., and Pritchard, R. D. 2008. *Work Motivation: Past, Present, and Future*. Mahwah, NJ: Lawrence Erlbaum.

Kehr, H. M. 2004. Integrating implicit motives, explicit motives, and perceived abilities: The compensatory model of work motivation and volition. *Academy of Management Review* 29:479–99.

Krampe, R. T., and Ericsson, K. A. 1996. Maintaining excellence: Deliberate practice and elite performance in young and older pianists. *Journal of Experimental Psychology: General* 125:331–59.

Kristof-Brown, A. L., Zimmerman, R. D., and Johnson, E. C. 2005. Consequences of individuals' fit at work: A meta-analysis of person-job, person-organization, person-group, and person-supervisor fit. *Personnel Psychology* 58:281–342.

Kubeck, J. E., Delp, N. D., Haslett, T. K., and McDaniel, M. A. 1996. Does job-related training performance decline with age? *Psychology and Aging* 11:92–107.

Loretto, W., and White, P. 2006. Employers' attitudes, practices, and policies towards older workers. *Human Resource Management Journal* 16:313–30.

Maurer, T. J. 2007. Employee development and training issues related to the aging workforce. In *Aging and Work in the Twenty-first Century*, ed. K. S. Shultz and G. A. Adams, 163–78. Mahwah, NJ: Lawrence Erlbaum Associates.

McAdams, D. P. 2001. Generativity in midlife. In *Handbook of Midlife Development*, ed. M. E. Lachman, 395–443. New York: John Wiley & Sons.

McEvoy, G. M., and Cascio, W. F. 1989. Cumulative evidence of the relationship between employee age and job performance. *Journal of Applied Psychology* 74:11–17.

Mitchell, T. R., Holtom, B. C., Lee, T. W., Sablynski, C. J., and Erez, M. 2001. Why people stay: Using job embeddedness to predict voluntary turnover. *Academy of Management Journal* 44:1102–21.

Panek, P. E., Staats, S., and Hiles, A. 2006. College students' perceptions of job demands, recommended retirement ages, and age of optimal performance in selected occupations. *International Journal of Aging and Human Development* 62:87–115.

Roberts, B. W., Walton, K. E., and Viechtbauer, W. 2006. Patterns of mean-level change in personality traits across the life course: A meta-analysis of longitudinal studies. *Psychological Bulletin* 132:1–25.

Schmidt, F. L., Hunter, J. E., and Outerbridge, A. N. 1986. Impact of job experience and ability on job knowledge, work sample performance, and supervisory ratings of job performance. *Journal of Applied Psychology* 71:432–39.

Sharit, J., and Czaja, S. J. 1999. Performance of a computer-based troubleshooting task in the banking industry: Examining the effects of age, task experience, and cognitive abilities. *International Journal of Cognitive Ergonomics* 3:1–22.

Smola, K. W., and Sutton, C. D. 2002. Generational differences: Revisiting generational work values for the new millennium. *Journal of Organizational Behavior* 23:363–83.

Stokes, D. E. 1997. *Pasteurs Quadrant: Basic Science and Technological Innovation.* Washington, DC: Brookings Institution Press.

Treadway, D. C., Ferris, G. R., Hochwarter, W., Perrewe, P., Witt, L. A., and Goodman, J. M. 2005. The role of age in the perceptions of politics-job performance relationship: A three-study constructive replication. *Journal of Applied Psychology* 90:872–81.

Warr, P., Miles, A., and Platts, C. 2001. Age and personality in the British population between 16 and 64 years. *Journal of Occupational and Organizational Psychology* 74:165–99.

Wegge, J., Roth, C., Neubach, B., Schmidt, K. H., and Kanfer, R. 2008. Age and gender diversity as determinants of performance and health in a public organization: The role of task complexity and group size. *Journal of Applied Psychology* 93:1301–13.

West, R. L., Thorn, R. M., and Bagwell, D. K. 2003. Memory performance and beliefs as a function of goal setting and aging. *Psychology and Aging* 18:111–25.

CHAPTER TWELVE

Skill Acquisition in Older Adults

Psychological Mechanisms

NEIL CHARNESS, PH.D.

Skill acquisition can be defined as the process by which people progress from lower to higher levels of performance. That process is influenced by many factors, including age. Skill acquisition is an important topic in the context of an aging workforce. In the U.S. labor force, the median age is now about 40 years of age (e.g., Charness, 2008), and that value is projected to increase as baby boom cohorts within the workforce continue to age. A rough rule, called the 80/20 rule (Charness and Krampe, 2008), underlines the importance of developing a skilled workforce. It suggests that 80 percent of productivity is attributable to 20 percent of the workforce. That is, if one ranks individuals by performance—for instance, sales dollars—one finds that the top 20 percent of the sales force accounts for about 80 percent of all sales. Productivity is an important driver for our economy and for everyone's standard of living. The aging of the labor force is often mentioned as one potentially negative influence on productivity (e.g., Jorgenson, Ho, and Stiroh, 2004), as is the deceleration in the rate of educational attainment by the labor force. Both trends highlight the importance of skill acquisition and the development of expertise. For a current review on the topic of age and expertise, see Charness and Krampe (2008).

Experts are by definition relatively rare (Ericsson and Charness, 1994) yet are quite valuable to a society. As will be shown, the relationship between peak performance and age is curvilinear: productivity rises rapidly in young adulthood, peaks in middle adulthood, and falls thereafter. In short, on the surface, the aging of our labor force appears to be a threat to productivity. However, as some research has shown (e.g., Sparrow and Davies, 1988), it appears that declining performance with age may be attributable mostly to obsolescence of knowledge. Thus, age and education are key factors in the debate about future productivity. By acquiring new skills, our aging work force may be able to protect its longstanding tradition of providing consistent, robust productivity gains to the economy.

This chapter provides a framework for understanding the enabling conditions for skill acquisition in older adulthood. I'll review some of the motivational determinants for self-improvement. Then I'll examine some classic age-performance functions developed to describe high-level human performance. Next I'll review some individual difference factors, mainly cognitive abilities that mediate skill acquisition processes. I'll then describe some example studies of skill acquisition in both work-like and work environments. Finally, I'll provide some recommendations for how to support skill acquisition (and maintenance) by older adults.

A GENERAL FRAMEWORK FOR SKILL ACQUISITION

To understand the skill acquisition process, it is useful to have a general framework. Figure 12.1 is a relatively simplified one that indicates that the route to skill acquisition passes from somewhat more distal motivational influences to more proximal cognitive abilities, with feedback from skill acquisition to motivational influences. For more sophisticated models relating to work performance, see Ackerman (1996); Colquitt, LePine, and Noe (2000), Kanfer and Ackerman (2004), and Maurer, Weiss and Barbeite (2003).

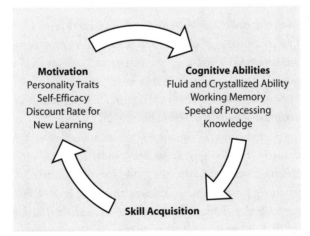

Figure 12.1. Framework for acquiring skill

Figure 12.1 indicates that the first step (left side) in the decision process to acquire a skill is being sufficiently motivated. There are individual differences in the major personality traits mediating motivation toward learning such as "openness to experience." As Kanfer and Ackerman (2004) note, openness to experience appears to diminish with age. Schaie, Dutta and Willis (1991) noted that, as they age, older adults tend to become more rigid and less flexible. Another important factor in willingness to learn is someone's sense of self-efficacy, that is, their belief that they can accomplish the task (Bandura, 1989). General self-efficacy is usually superseded by more specific forms of self-efficacy for domains. For instance, computer efficacy is a significant predictor of breadth of World Wide Web use (Czaja et al., 2006). I am proposing that these and other factors determine an individual's "discount rate for learning."

Given that one is motivated to learn, learning efficiency will depend in part on the cognitive abilities (right side), and more specifically, on speed of processing, working memory, and current knowledge base. Aging affects those processes too, mostly negatively, but in the case of knowledge, positively. Learning efficiency affects the rate of skill acquisition (bottom).

Finally, as people receive feedback on the skill acquisition process, that can in turn affect their future willingness to acquire skill. For instance, failure is likely to dampen a sense of self-efficacy, whereas success will boost it. If people find that learning is more difficult than expected, they may discount the value of future learning more steeply. I now review these factors from the perspective of aging.

Age and Motivation

Perhaps the most important initial factor in willingness to learn a new skill is the mental calculus about the cost of time and energy to be exerted versus the expected value to be gained by skill acquisition. That is, there are important prerequisites for setting the goal to engage in new learning.

A number of models are relevant to goal setting in older adulthood. Baltes and Baltes (1990) argued for *selective optimization with compensation* as a model of older adult achievement and performance. That is, in the face of diminishing resources (particularly "fluid" cognitive abilities), older adults become more selective about their time investment, narrowing the types of activities that they engage in and compensating for negative changes by investing more effort in activities where they have a better chance of succeeding. Brandstätder and Rothermund (1994) suggest that, in an attempt to maintain primary control over their life course, middle-aged and older adults reset goals to take into account diminish-

ing abilities. That is, they sometimes scale back goals that they judge are too difficult to achieve in favor of other ones that are deemed more reasonable.

Part of the dilemma for older adults in deciding how to invest their time and
resources lies in the fact that their future horizons are more limited (they have
less time to benefit from developing the new skill). In their development of socio-
emotional selectivity theory, Carstensen, Isaacowitz, and Charles (1999) note the
shift by older adults from pursuing the goal of knowledge acquisition to pursuing emotional satisfaction. Another important barrier to the skill acquisition process is the increased cost of learning. Undoubtedly because of adverse changes
in the brain with age (e.g., Head et al., 2002), older adults learn more slowly, often
taking about twice as long as young adults (e.g., Charness, Kelley, Bosman, and
Mottram, 2001).

Personality traits such as openness to experience, often viewed as enduring
sources of motivation, may show modest decline in level with age. But in general,
personality is remarkably stable over the lifetime from the adult years onward
(e.g., Costa and McCrae, 1988). There can be significant changes, particularly in
cases where salient life events such as divorce occur. A review noted that there is
probably more change in personality across time than previously appreciated
(Roberts and DelVecchio, 2000). However, personality traits are at best weak predictors of expertise level in domains such as music performance and chess (Charness, Tuffiash, and Jastrzembski, 2004). As Hunter and Schmidt (1996) noted,
cognitive abilities and knowledge account for most of the variance in job performance.

A potentially useful way to assess willingness to learn might be to estimate an
individual's *discount rate for new learning,* borrowing from the economic notion of
the future value of a good or service. Discount rates are usually investigated by
asking questions such as: "Would you rather have $100 now or $200 a year from
now?" and varying the dollar value of the second term in the comparison to determine the *temporal discount rate,* using a formula such as that employed in the
Green et al. (1996) study about age and temporal discount rate. In that study, age
and income interacted such that older lower-income adults showed less willingness to wait for a higher reward.

One of the inherent problems in this research paradigm is ensuring that the
value of the reward is internalized in the same way in different groups (i.e., has the
same subjective utility). Steeper discount rates have been interpreted in several
ways, such as evidence of the level of a personality trait such as impulsiveness, or
in terms of varying subjective values for rewards. To complicate things, older
adults appear to have steeper temporal discount rates than middle-aged adults for

the value of favorite holiday location selections under delay, perhaps moderated by health status (Melenhorst, 2002). One salient finding in the mental depreciation literature (e.g., Soman, 2001) is that time is not accounted for in the same way that money is. People seem more willing to set up a mental ledger for money purchases than for time investment, suggesting that you might expect to find different discounting rates for time investment versus resource investment.

The discount rate for new learning can undoubtedly be established by similar techniques to temporal discounting. Indirect evidence about changed willingness to learn new things is the finding that technology use diminishes with age cross-sectionally (Czaja et al., 2006). However, Melenhorst, Rogers, and Bouwhuis (2006) argue on the basis of focus group interviews that perceived benefits are more important determinants of technology adoption than costs.

One immediate form of feedback about learning cost is the degree of cognitive effort that is induced by a learning task. Are adults aware that learning requires more time and effort as they age? Sharit, Czaja, Perdomo, and Lee (2004) showed in their cost-benefit analyses for different technology devices that older adults rate learning and relearning costs more heavily in cost-benefit assessments than do younger adults, whereas monetary cost is more influential in the ratings of younger than older adults. Such findings suggest that future benefits of any new learning task will tend to be discounted more steeply by older adults, given their recognition of the greater initial (and ongoing) cognitive cost required to acquire the skill.

MOTIVATIONAL INFLUENCES FOR SKILL ACQUISITION IN WORK SETTINGS

The framework for skill acquisition stresses that the initial decision to acquire (or maintain) skill by exerting effort to learn depends on motivational factors. It takes considerable effort, termed *deliberate practice,* to reach national and international levels of skill in domains such as sports, chess, music (e.g., 1,000–10,000 hours: Charness et al., 2005; Ericsson, 2006). Deliberate practice involves organizing activities that aim at improving performance by working on weaknesses, setting appropriate goals for advancement, and using feedback to monitor progress toward those goals (Ericsson, 2006). Someone must be highly motivated to put in those long hours at activities that are usually not reported to be particularly enjoyable and that could compete with work productivity.

Maurer et al. (2003) investigated age in the context of training motivation and demonstrated that older workers need to perceive that training will benefit their performance and standing within their work place. Situational and motivational variables, rather than age, were the direct predictors of training outcome.

A paper by Judge et al. (2007) examined the relationship between personality traits, cognitive ability, self-efficacy, and job performance through meta-analysis. Although some theoretical frameworks suggested that personality and cognitive influences determine self-efficacy beliefs and that self-efficacy beliefs link tightly to job performance, these authors found that self-efficacy was a weak predictor of job performance and that direct links between cognitive abilities and work performance were much stronger than the linkage through self-efficacy. Presumably, self-efficacy for long-term job occupants is not a striking concern (else why would they have stayed in their position for so long), though it may become more of a concern for aging workers who are trying to master new technologies.

Kanfer and Ackerman (2004) argue for a somewhat more complex interplay of effort, performance, and utility functions in assessing willingness to learn new work-related tasks. Similarly, in economics, life-cycle human capital investment models predict decreased effort and performance with increased age in work settings (Diamond, 1986).

In sum, there are a variety of findings that suggest that the aging process will lead to modest changes in motivation to acquire skill. Broad theoretical work supports the notion that new learning is likely to be perceived as less rewarding than exercising old learning (selective optimization with compensation and socioemotional selectivity theories). Personality traits representing enduring motivational states are unlikely to show much change with age. Rating studies suggest that older adults perceive learning and relearning as more costly than do younger adults. Studies of learning in work environments, however, suggest that any age-related changes in motivation to engage in developmental activities are more a function of situational factors in a particular workplace.

An underlying concern implicit in many of the chapters in this volume is whether a pernicious cycle exists, wherein aging workers express the belief (overtly or covertly) that they will not benefit from training, and this in turn influences managers' beliefs and biases about older workers, leading to less access to training opportunities. This diminished access leads to obsolescence of knowledge in older workers. Beliefs do not develop in a vacuum. There is considerable evidence that human abilities change with age, particularly the ones shown in figure 12.1, though as the following brief review indicates, not all changes are negative.

AGE-RELATED CHANGES IN COGNITIVE ABILITIES
Crystallized and Fluid Abilities

In contrast to the more limited amount of research on age and motivational factors, there has been a great deal of work on age and cognitive performance. Horn
(1982) and many other investigators (e.g., Li et al., 2004) have noted that there
are markedly different developmental trends for two higher-order human abilities termed *crystallized* and *fluid* abilities. Crystallized abilities refer to the end
products of information processing, namely, the common knowledge base that
people usually acquire at a particular sociocultural period. Knowing the name of
the president of the United States, the multiplication algorithm for arithmetic,
the alphabet, and so forth is something that most members of our culture
pick up. Some pick up more knowledge than others, and knowledge is often
highly specialized within a given profession. That type of ability tends to show a
rise into adulthood and then a peak in the 50s or 60s, followed by slow decline. It
is measured by a variety of tests, such as vocabulary and general information.
Below I plot some data taken from the Center for Research and Education on
Aging and Technology Enhancement (CREATE) project (Czaja et al., 2006) that
show the trend for crystallized ability (using composite scores that are standard-
ized around a mean of 0) in a relatively large, diverse (though nonrepresentative)
sample.

The top panel of figure 12.2, using a linear regression fit line, shows that crystallized abilities rise slightly with age in this cross-sectional sample, though age
does not account for much of the variability in crystallized abilities.

Fluid abilities are thought to represent cognitive operations important in
being able to solve novel problems efficiently. A similar plot from the CREATE
data set is shown in the bottom plot of figure 12.2.

Here a pronounced decline is associated with age and a fair amount of the
variance in fluid ability is associated with age. Although crystallized and fluid
abilities are usually fairly highly correlated, in this sample that correlation is
$r(1170) = .37$. So there is a clear difference in the way in which these abilities un-
dergo change across the life span, with fluid abilities showing striking decline
and crystallized ones showing modest increase. These abilities have been shown
to be predictive of skill acquisition in new tasks (Ackerman, 1992).

Broad abilities such as crystallized and fluid abilities represent composites of
more basic abilities. Cognitive psychologists tend to describe abilities at a more
molecular level of analysis and as constructs within a specific information-processing framework. For example, they hypothesize that for someone to acquire a

A

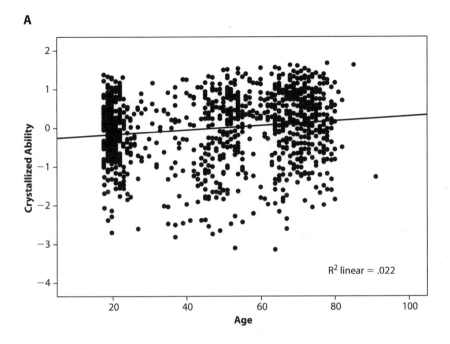

B

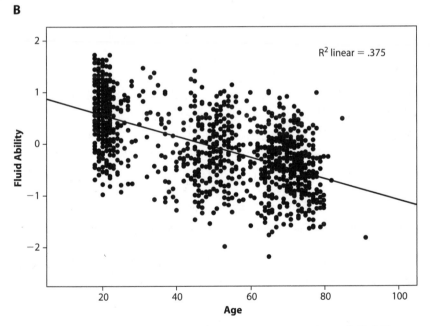

Figure 12.2. A, Crystallized ability (z-score), by age in years (*N* = 1197); *B*, Fluid ability (z-score), by age in years (*N* = 1174). *Source*: Data from the project described by Czaja et al., 2006

high-level skill, specific, domain-related knowledge structures and processes must be developed (e.g., Ericsson and Charness, 1994).

Working Memory

Many theorists have argued for the importance of working memory capacity in higher-order cognitive processing (e.g., Baddeley, 1986; Unsworth and Engle, 2007), including skilled performance. Working memory is conceptualized as a system for storing and manipulating information. Some components are seen as managing storage for different modalities of information, such as phonological representations and visuospatial representations. A limited capacity "central executive" process is believed to be responsible for coordinating and managing these subsystems. Working memory is distinguished from older concepts such as short-term memory by its emphasis on both the storage and manipulation of information. Many studies have shown that traditional short-term memory measures (passive storage measures such as forward digit span, when people are asked to recall a string of digits in the same order as they were presented) differ little as a function of adult age. However, more demanding working memory measures always show substantial decline. An example of a working memory task is alphabet span. A list of words are presented and then the person is asked to recall them in alphabetic order, necessitating holding the list information but then processing it further to rearrange and then report the items accordingly. Figure 12.3 shows plots from data discussed in Czaja et al. (2006).

Although there is a significant age-related decline in short-term memory in the top plot, it is slight. Compare this slope with the one in the Figure 12.3 bottom plot, which illustrates decline in a working memory measure, alphabet span. Unlike digit span, alphabet span requires you to remember items (words), but report them back in alphabetical order.

With alphabet span there is a substantial proportion of variance accounted for by the linear regression on age. What these two plots illustrate is that older adults have much more difficulty with working memory than with short-term memory. Any new task that requires them both to remember and to actively process large chunks of information is going to be difficult to perform. A speeded lecture on new material would fall into this category.

General Slowing Theory

Birren (1974) and Salthouse (1996) both noted that increased age is associated with slowing in the rate of information processing. Salthouse (1996) showed that

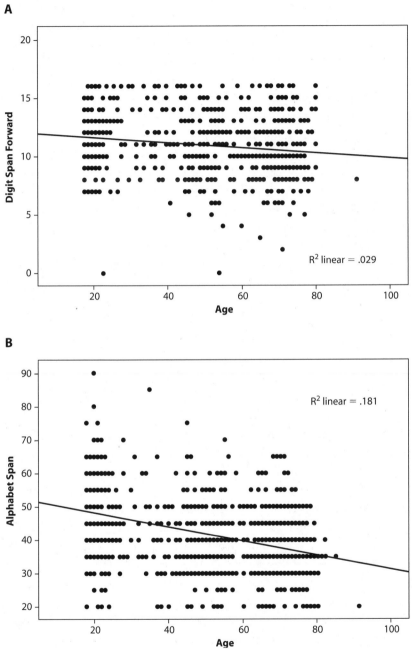

Figure 12.3. A, Digit span forward scores (*N* = 712), by age; *B*, Alphabet span scores, by age (*N* = 1202). *Source*: Data from the project described by Czaja et al., 2006

slowing in basic processes can account for much of the age-related variance in higher-order cognitive processes such as those used for reasoning and problem solving. Slowing is strikingly related to age. In fact, the fluid ability measure shown above is composed mainly from speeded tests.

A solid rule is that for most tasks, older adults will take between 50 and 100 percent longer than younger adults (e.g., Hale and Myerson, 1995). Such slowing shows up in tasks as simple as reaction time to letter stimuli and as complex as self-paced learning of word-processing software (e.g., Charness et al., 2001). Recent meta-analyses of information-processing parameters suggest that this slowing factor varies somewhat, depending on whether the task involves primarily motor processing (2.1), perceptual processing (1.8), or cognitive processing (1.7; Jastrzembski and Charness, 2007).

In sum, although knowledge tends to increase with age, processes supporting the acquisition of new knowledge tend to decrease, particularly, slowing in the speed of processing information, affecting learning rate. Changes with age in such basic cognitive processing mechanisms is expected to influence the much more complicated tasks, such as problem solving, that people perform in the workplace. About a century and a half of research on the relationship between age and peak performance (starting with Quetelet, 1842/1969) is consistent with this prediction. I now overview studies of skill acquisition and age.

SKILL ACQUISITION OVER THE LIFE SPAN

Lehman (1953) showed convincingly with a series of studies across diverse domains of human endeavor ranging from science to art that there was a characteristic function relating mankind's highest achievements to age: rapid gains in productivity in young adulthood, followed by a peak in the middle years and a decline thereafter. Simonton (1988, 1997) refined this view, developing models to understand the relationship between the peak and other parts of the curve. He also pointed out that *career age* rather than chronological age is a better indicator of performance changes. Peak age is often seen in the 30s, for instance, in chess players (Elo, 1965), although more recent analyses suggest a later peak, occurring in the mid-40s (Roring and Charness, 2007).

However, there is some indication that the shape may change when considering psychologists and their publication rates (Horner, Rushton, and Vernon, 1986). There the most productive publishers show linear decline with age from the 30s rather than showing a rising then declining performance curve. However, at all points high producers outperform low producers. As well, Roring and Charness (2007) showed with a large chess-rating data set that peak age is most likely to be found in the decade of the 40s rather than the 30s.

Given such age-performance relationships, we might expect a decline in productivity with age for older workers. However, meta-analyses that attempt to summarize relevant published cross-sectional work on the relation between age and job performance show little indication of age-related decline (Waldman and Avolio, 1986; McEvoy and Cascio, 1989), and occasionally, slight increases (Sturman, 2004). Although there are a variety of concerns in interpreting such studies (e.g., Salthouse and Maurer, 1996), the failure to find significant age-related decline suggests that most work environments do not routinely require peak performance and that most workers maintain the ability to work productively into their 50s and 60s, if not beyond.

It is worth noting that disciplines define productivity differently. In economics, productivity calculations involve consideration of inputs as well as outputs, for instance, salaries as well as worker output. The meta-analyses mentioned above are concerned solely with output measures. Salaries typically peak in the decade of the 50s for workers in the United States, meaning that older workers would need to generate greater output than younger ones to be considered as productive in economic terms.

Given the rising age of retirement for entitlement to a full Social Security pension (now age 67 in the United States for those born after 1960), U.S. society may need to find ways to prolong superior work productivity in older workers. A particularly salient trend in commerce is the increased degree of international competition, which may push the labor force closer to peak performance than usual performance. Similarly, the increasing rate of diffusion of technological innovation in the workplace (Charness and Czaja, 2005) likely will add further pressure to update skills and knowledge for all workers. The next section outlines some studies about skill-acquisition processes that may help guide effective training. First, I examine macro-level theories of skill acquisition applied to complex skill learning, and then look at some of the micro-level variables controlling effectiveness of training.

Skill-Acquisition Processes

Most models of skill acquisition (e.g., VanLehn, 1996) are described as proceeding from early to middle and late stages. The influential Fitts and Posner (1967) model called these stages the cognitive phase, the associative phase, and the autonomous phase. Later models developed more detailed understanding of the processes underlying these phases (e.g., Anderson, 1982; Taatgen et al., 2008).

The first stage is dominated by declarative learning and involves slow, consciously controlled, and relatively inefficient recall of the specific operations that are needed to perform the task. For instance, a beginning touch typist may need to think about which finger to use to strike a particular key and may have to search the keyboard visually to identify the target key. People at this stage need to monitor the environment closely and actively retrieve the relevant parts of the procedure from memory. In the second stage, compilation and proceduralization, which occurs after considerable practice with the various components of the procedure, the procedure becomes automated, and people can simply carry out the relevant activities with minimal conscious monitoring. The touch typist sees a letter, and the fingers can navigate automatically to strike the required key. Whole-word motor patterns become possible for a skilled typist. On seeing *the*, the finger movement pattern for the three keystrokes runs off automatically. In the next stage, specialization, procedures become finely tuned to specific patterns in the environment, and execution of the procedure speeds up.

As people acquire skill, they tend to speed up in a fashion known as the "power law of practice" (Newell and Rosenbloom, 1981). That is, using the simple form of the power function, if you plot performance speed against trial blocks, you find a log-linear function where:

$$\text{Response time} = aT^{-b}$$

where T represents the trial block, a is a constant representing an intercept, and b is an exponent with a value that is usually a fraction, typically 0.3. The shape of the function appears to be better fit at the individual level (rather than with group data) as an exponential or hyperbolic function (Heathcote, Brown, and Mewhort, 2000). What these functions typically reveal is that it is relatively easy to show rapid gains early in practice, but further improvements become more and more costly in terms of time and effort. Each successive unit gain in performance speed costs 10 times more effort than the prior unit gain with such log-linear functions.

Considerable theoretical work has attempted to assess skill-acquisition processes comparing younger and older adults. Charness and Campbell (1988) suggested that older adults acquire a complex mental skill (squaring two digit numbers mentally) in roughly the same way as middle-aged and younger adults. However, older adults seemed to be less efficient at the specialization process for the algorithm needed for carrying out the calculations. There was also evidence that they had more difficulty avoiding working memory errors (Campbell and Charness, 1990) even as they approached initial performance levels of young adults.

Similarly, Baltes and Kliegl (1992) suggested that age-related changes in information processing set limits for the effectiveness with which older adults could learn to use and deploy mnemonics such as the Method of Loci (Kliegl, Smith, and Baltes, 1989) to help them remember long lists of words. Even selecting people from professions skilled at using mental imagery, a component of the Method of Loci, could not override age differences after considerable practice (Lindenberger, Kliegl, and Baltes, 1992).

Using the more complex form of the power law of learning, where there are parameters to estimate initial and final intercepts, Touron, Hoyer and Cerella (2001) provide evidence that older adults may not equal the performance of younger adults at final asymptote on an alpha-arithmetic task. That is, when you train older and younger adults in a novel procedure, younger adults will continue to outperform older ones when both groups continue practicing over an extended time frame. This conclusion accords with evidence from a meta-analytic study of age and training outcome. Kubeck, Delp, Haslett, and McDaniel (1996) showed that older adults achieved less effective performance and generally took longer to train.

There is also evidence from visual search and memory search tasks that older adults may not automate their search procedure as effectively as younger adults on visual search that employs consistent mapping, though they do automate the process for memory search (Fisk and Rogers, 1991). Nonetheless, in laboratory tasks such as these, older adults, even when they have automated mental procedures, respond more slowly than young adults. That is, general slowing with age (Salthouse, 1996) tends to ensure that even expert older adults respond more slowly than equivalently skilled younger adults (e.g., Jastrzembski, Charness, and Vasyukova, 2006).

However, in many real-world situations, speed can be less important than accuracy, and both factors may pale in significance when considering training costs. McNaught and Barth (1992) argued that older adults were quite cost-effective to train as reservations agents for the Days Inns chain, given their greater longevity with the firm, despite taking longer on the phone than younger agents (though booking equivalent sales). A more recent set of analyses based on the Australian workforce shows a net cost savings for training older workers (Brooke, 2003), mainly attributable to lower turnover rates for older compared to younger workers. As in Aesop's fable of the hare and the tortoise, slow and steady appears to win the personnel training cost race.

Another important issue in skill acquisition is whether the influence of different abilities for task performance changes with continued practice. Ackerman

(1992) was one of the first to note the changing pattern for ability predictors with practice on realistic, complex tasks. He investigated skill acquisition for an air traffic control task (TRACON). Using overall performance as the criterion, he showed that some measures (reasoning, spatial ability) showed a pattern of increasing predictive power with practice, whereas others (perceptual speed, psychomotor ability) showed decreasing power to predict performance. Such work suggests that the role of abilities changes as people move from early stages of skill (declarative) to later stages (procedural).

Given the general age-related decline in some of the abilities measured by Ackerman for the TRACON task, such as speed of processing and spatial ability, one might predict that older adults would make poor job candidates. What these analyses omit, though, is consideration of the extent to which acquired skills might mitigate age-related decline in basic abilities and, more important for our purposes here, predict skill acquisition.

The Role of Knowledge in Skilled Performance and Skill Acquisition

The artificial intelligence community discovered years ago when tackling difficult problem-solving tasks that "knowledge is power" (Feigenbaum, 1989) when it comes to skilled performance. That is, general problem-solving procedures (akin to human fluid intelligence) were inefficient for searching out solutions to complex problems. Specific, domain-tailored procedures and knowledge were necessary to cut down on the exponential explosion of possibilities that occurred when searching a large problem space for a solution.

The "knowledge is power" hypothesis also holds considerable promise for understanding age and skill trade-off (e.g., Hambrick and Engle, 2002). There are several examples of how prior knowledge can partially compensate for the negative impact of age-related declines in abilities in domains ranging from chess and bridge (e.g., Charness, 1981, 1987) to typing (Bosman, 1993; Salthouse, 1984). Knowledge about arcane words is instrumental in crossword puzzle solving success in adulthood (Hambrick, Salthouse, and Meinz, 1999).

One job-related example of partial compensation was identified in research by Morrow and colleagues on aircraft pilots (e.g., Taylor, O'Hara, Mumenthaler, Rosen, and Yesavage, 2005). Older pilots can partially compensate for age-related declines in memory when doing read-back of air-traffic control messages by relying on their superior knowledge of aircraft positioning information (Morrow, Leirer, Altieri, and Fitzsimmons, 1994). They can completely compensate for age effects (seen in non-pilots for the same tasks) by taking notes (Morrow et al., 2003). We focus now on the role of knowledge in skill acquisition.

Beier and Ackerman (2005) approximated a new learning situation for younger and older adults with both an in-class video lecture and out-of-class homework assignments. The knowledge domains tapped were xerography and cardiovascular disease. Although abilities (fluid, crystallized) were predictors of performance (how much was learned), path analyses suggested that the most powerful predictor of outcome was prior knowledge.

The importance of prior knowledge for future learning was also demonstrated in a study of young, middle-aged, and older novices and experienced word processors learning new word processing software (Charness et al., 2001). Those without knowledge of word processing showed typical patterns of age-related decline in performance following several days of self-paced learning. They showed the usual pattern of slowing in performance as well. However, for those with knowledge about word processing, retraining to use a new word processor took considerably less time, and performance during and following training was virtually unrelated to age through the middle years and slightly worse for those close to retirement age. When all the groups were combined and performance was predicted using regression procedures, the most important predictors were breadth of software experience (positive) and age (negative), with the former carrying more weight. There was also an interaction between age and software experience for performance, such that knowledge of software was a more important predictor for older adults. That is, knowledge had a greater effect on the performance of older adults.

Mireles and Charness (2002) probed the trade-offs possible between knowledge and age, using neural net simulation studies of a serial recall task: memory for opening sequences of moves in chess. The results demonstrated that knowledge could directly compensate for normal aging. Aging was simulated by a variety of mechanisms. Networks that had been trained initially to high and low levels of performance experienced declining performance when these aging mechanisms were manipulated. However, the high knowledge networks were much more tolerant of such changes, whereas the performance of the low-knowledge networks declined quickly. This line of work demonstrates that knowledge is sufficient to protect performance against normal aging processes and sides with the "age is kinder to the initially more able" hypothesis.

However, all is not rosy when it comes to the role of knowledge. Salthouse (2006) argued that the evidence favors a "use it and still lose it" position. Decline in basic abilities occurs even for those who have extensive amounts of job-related experience and who practice work-related activities likely to engage such basic abilities, such as the case of spatial ability in architects. Critically, architects show the same rate of decline with age in such ability measures as those who do not exercise those abilities to the same extent (and who likely had lower levels of ability when young). Although "use it and lose it" seems to hold for basic cognitive abilities, it is doubtful whether such declines translate into poorer job-related performance as seen in the earlier meta-analyses of job performance and age. Apparently, crystallized abilities trump fluid abilities in work settings.

What might we conclude from the overview thus far about skill acquisition? First, older adults are going to be disadvantaged, relative to younger adults, when learning new skills that do not draw on their larger knowledge store. Even when the tasks do relate to prior knowledge (e.g., word processing), older adults will take more training time to reach similar levels of performance or, if training for the same amount of time, will perform at lower levels. Thus they face a steeper hill to climb when being asked to acquire a new skill and hence are likely to need stronger motivation to do so.

However, it is worth reiterating that prior knowledge and skill is the single best predictor of performance on skill-related tasks.

PRACTICAL GUIDELINES FOR IMPROVING SKILL ACQUISITION

The following sections review findings from training studies aimed at identifying best methods for helping people who are interested in acquiring skill to do so efficiently. A review of training issues is given in Charness and Czaja (2006).

Type of Training

A meta-analysis by Callahan, Kiker, and Cross (2003) reviewed studies of training methods for older adults. Although the analyses were restricted to older workers (age 40+), there were apparently no substantial interactions of age with training technique. The main techniques evaluated were: lecture, modeling, and active participation (discovery learning). All proved to be effective for older workers. Other variables examined included materials, feedback, pacing, and group size, with the latter two showing significant effects for training outcome. Self-pacing was best, as was having a smaller group size for training. Nonetheless, additional studies of such factors with middle-aged and older workers could help lead to firmer recommendations about training conditions.

Hence, a reasonable guideline is to ensure that older workers can study material at their own pace and that, where instructor support is required, instruction be provided in small group settings.

Age Composition for Groups

Given the varying rates of learning in younger and older adults, age-segregated training seems like a sensible policy when lecture-style instruction is being offered to workers and the task to be learned is unrelated to past knowledge. That being said, it is worth stressing that past knowledge is a strong predictor of new learning in older adults (Charness et al., 2001; Beier and Ackerman, 2005), as it is in younger adults. So rather than strict age-segregation, knowledge-segregation makes sense as an approach to training. Training novices, intermediates, and experts in separate groups may make for the most efficient procedure to support skill acquisition. It would likely prove advantageous if instructional techniques can draw on the probable more extensive knowledge base of older workers. Classic work on clustering techniques shows that older adults benefit differentially when information is presented in a way that makes the underlying categorical structure obvious (Hultsch, 1971).

Distributed Practice

It has long been known that spacing out practice sessions results in better skill acquisition for new information than does massing practice, and a recent meta-analysis (Cepeda et al., 2006) highlights the effectiveness of such training. Spaced retrieval practice is even successful for promoting learning in cases of brain damage due to Alzheimer disease (e.g., Bourgeois et al., 2003). Recent theory (Pavlik and Anderson, 2005) argues that the spacing effect depends on balancing two factors: the current level of activation for the to-be-learned item, and the decay rate for each boost in strength that a practice trial provides. Such research is consistent with the idea that there is a theoretically optimal schedule for practice. However, the optimal spacing of practice has not been systematically investigated for older adults, who probably have slightly different activation and decay rates for memory compared with younger adults. Thus, there is a need to pursue new studies on distributed practice.

Schedules of Practice

Another critical variable for skill acquisition is the extent to which a complex skill's components should be blocked or randomized. That is, assume that a complex task involves learning a set of sub-skills. Should these sub-skills be practiced independently or interleaved? One study by Kramer, Larish, and Strayer (1995) showed that variable priority training (varying the priority across tasks for a dual-task, such as alpha-arithmetic and monitoring gauges) promoted much better performance in younger and older adults than fixed priority training (same emphasis for the two tasks). In fact, older adult gains with variable priority training were greater than those for young adults (though they still performed more slowly).

The contextual interference effect (e.g., Lee and Magill, 1983) suggests that learning proceeds more efficiently when the subcomponents are learned independently, but transfer and retention are more effective when they are interleaved. What works best for training is worst for transfer to noncontrolled (real world) conditions, and vice versa. As an example, if you are having difficulty hitting a curve ball as a batter in baseball, you will make good progress across trials when you hit curve after curve. However, if you want to transfer effectively to a ball game where the pitcher throws curves mixed with other pitches, you are better off practicing initially hitting the curve ball as part of a mixed set of trials that include other pitch types. Your improvement on hitting curve balls during practice will be slower, but you will transfer more effectively to real game settings. This phenomenon also holds in other than motor tasks, for instance, problem solving tasks involving Boolean logic (Carlson and Yaure, 1990). Learning in context is critical to high-level performance, as has been shown with similar principles such as encoding specificity (Tulving, 1983) and part-to-whole task training (e.g., Clawson, Healy, Ericsson, and Bourne, 2001). However, too little work has been conducted thus far into the role of practice schedules in aging adults to come up with confident recommendations. That is obviously an area of research that needs further development.

RECOMMENDATIONS FOR POLICY, RESEARCH, OR INTERVENTION

Workplaces face more international competition than ever, particularly from low-labor-cost, developing countries. So maintaining a highly skilled workforce is critical for competitiveness. An accelerating rate of technology diffusion in the workplace is likely to result in even faster knowledge obsolescence for workers of all ages. Technological tools can be multiplier factors for productivity (Charness,

2008). Although one can hope that future intelligent technology systems will adapt to users rather than users being forced to adapt to technology as is true in today's situation, continuous skill acquisition is going to be a lifelong concern for most of us.

If people attempt to learn a new skill using effective techniques such as deliberate practice (Ericsson, 2006), they can usually do so. It may take them longer to achieve success as they progress across the life span past their middle-adult years. The factors most likely to interfere with successful skill acquisition are those on the left side of figure 12.1, particularly, low initial motivation to invest time in learning, probably because of the perceived high cost of the time investment coupled with a perceived poor rate of return. As well, there are potential structural impediments in the social context for older workers, including the willingness of management to include older workers in training plans and other career development activities.

One prominent structural impediment is stereotyping older workers. Negative stereotypes about older workers' learning ability have been noted in several meta-analytic attitude studies (Finkelstein, Burke, and Raju, 1995; Kite, Stockdale, Whitley, and Johnson, 2005). In the Finkelstein et al. (1995) study, though, older raters of older workers were less prone to exhibit negative stereotypes, and given that managers tend to be older, perhaps there is some reason to be optimistic that negative effects of stereotyping may not be that widespread in management. Most of the studies included in these meta-analyses are scenario-based studies in which hypothetical situations are provided to non-manager raters. Nonetheless, self-perceptions about age and aging appear to influence managers' views about promotion possibilities (Cleveland and Shore, 1992), implying that workers may signal their own uncertainty about training potential to their co-workers and managers. Negative stereotypes may be difficult to change, but education about scientific findings may help. For instance, research showing the cost-effectiveness of training older workers (Brooke, 2003) needs to be more widely recognized.

Older workers, furthermore, may need to be persuaded to change their own attitudes about the value of skill acquisition. Some of the earliest studies about older worker training have shown that even when older workers were offered the opportunity to retrain, they were less likely than younger workers to take up the offer (e.g., Belbin and Belbin, 1972). Still, it is unclear how best to intervene with managers and with older workers to ensure that they endorse processes that are supportive of skill acquisition, given the variation in implicit and explicit mental processes involved in attitude formation and change (e.g., Gawronski and Bodenhausen, 2006).

It would be helpful if management were able to increase the incentives for learning, given the greater cost of learning to older workers. Obviously, age-neutral compensation policies are needed to ensure equitable treatment. Fortunately, perceived benefits seem to be efficient motivators (Noe and Wilk, 1993).

When talking informally to HR managers about older worker issues, it quickly becomes evident that cost, rather than learning ability issues, dominates their thinking. One concern unique to the United States is health care cost, because insuring older workers is more costly than insuring younger ones. Another concern is the higher salaries that older workers typically hold. So are there ways to reduce the disincentives to retain (and train) older workers?

An admittedly radical way to ensure better economic productivity for firms would be to change lifetime salary structures. Although work output does not change much with age, salary typically does. Cross-sectional peak earning power in the United States occurs for heads-of-households in their mid-40s to mid-50s (U.S. Census Bureau, 2004). So rather than conform to the typical "underpay when young, overpay when old" lifetime contract wage pattern (e.g., Hutchens, 1986), firms could consider providing contracting arrangements that feature automatically decreasing salaries paired with decreasing job responsibilities as workers age past the 60s. Such a change could have drastic negative consequences for a defined benefit pension arrangement that overweights the last few years' wages. However, most pension plans are now defined contribution plans where pensions depend on cumulative investments that don't directly weight final years. Promoting a longer work life, even at a lower salary level, would probably be advantageous for workers and certainly would be beneficial to overstretched public pension systems. Given the high cost to both individuals and societies to acquire skills and promote skill acquisition, finding ways to amortize these skills over longer time periods of productive work is going to be an important challenge for our economy and our aging work force.

ACKNOWLEDGMENTS

This research was supported by NIA 1 PO1 AG17211-08 to the Center for Research and Education on Aging and Technology Enhancement (CREATE), and by SSHRC to Workforce Ageing in the New Economy (WANE).

REFERENCES

Ackerman, P. L. 1992. Predicting individual differences in complex skill acquisition. *Journal of Applied Psychology* 77:598–614.

————. 1996. A theory of adult intellectual development: Process, personality, interests, and knowledge. *Intelligence* 22:229–59.

Anderson, J. R. 1982. Acquisition of cognitive skill. *Psychological Review* 89:369–406.

Baddeley, A. 1986. *Working Memory*. New York: Oxford University Press.

Baltes, P. B., and Baltes, M. M. 1990. Psychological perspectives on successful aging: The model of selective optimization with compensation. In *Successful Aging: Perspectives from the Behavioral Sciences*, ed. P. B. Baltes and M. M. Baltes, 1–34. New York: Cambridge University Press.

Baltes, P. B., and Kliegl, R. 1992. Further testing of limits in cognitive plasticity: Negative age differences in a mnemonic skill are robust. *Developmental Psychology* 28:121–25.

Bandura, A. 1989. Human agency in social cognitive theory. *American Psychologist* 44: 1175–84.

Beier, M. E., and Ackerman, P. L. 2005. Age, ability, and the role of prior knowledge on the acquisition of new domain knowledge: Promising results in a real-world learning environment. *Psychology and Aging* 20:341–55.

Belbin, E., and Belbin, R. M. 1972. *Problems in Adult Retraining*. London: Heineman.

Birren, J. E. 1974. Translations in gerontology: From lab to life: Psychophysiology and speed of response. *American Psychologist* 29:808–15.

Bosman, E. A. 1993. Age-related differences in motoric aspects of transcription typing skill. *Psychology and Aging* 8:87–102.

Bourgeois, M., Camp, C., Rose, M., White, B., Malone, M., Carr, J. et al. 2003. A comparison of training strategies to enhance use of external aids by persons with dementia. *Journal of Communication Disorders* 36:361–78.

Brandstätder, J., and Rothermund, K. 1994. Self-percepts of control in middle and later adulthood: Buffering losses by rescaling goals. *Psychology and Aging* 9:265–73.

Brooke, L. 2003. Human resource costs and benefits of maintaining a mature-age workforce. *International Journal of Manpower* 24:260–83.

Callahan, J. S., Kiker, D. S., and Cross, T. 2003. Does method matter? A meta-analysis of the effects of training method on older learner training performance. *Journal of Management* 29:663–80.

Campbell, J. I. D., and Charness, N. 1990. Age-related declines in working memory skills: Evidence from a complex calculation task. *Developmental Psychology* 26:879–88.

Carlson, R. A., and Yaure, R. C. 1990. Practice schedules and the use of component skills in problem solving. *Journal of Experimental Psychology: Learning, Memory, and Cognition* 16:484–96.

Carstensen, L. L., Isaacowitz, D. M., and Charles, S. T. 1999. Taking time seriously: A theory of socioemotional selectivity. *American Psychologist* 54:165–81.

Cepeda, N. J., Pashler, H., Vul, E., Wixted, J. T., and Rohrer, D. 2006. Distributed practice in verbal recall tasks: A review and quantitative synthesis. *Psychological Bulletin* 132: 354–80.

Charness, N. 1981. Aging and skilled problem solving. *Journal of Experimental Psychology: General* 110:21–38.

————. 1987. Component processes in bridge bidding and novel problem-solving tasks. *Canadian Journal of Psychology* 41:223–43.

————. 2008. Technology as multiplier effect for an aging work force. In *Social Structures and Aging Individuals: Continuing Challenges*, ed. K. W. Schaie and R. Abeles, 167–92. New York: Springer.

Charness, N., and Campbell, J. I. D. 1988. Acquiring skill at mental calculation in adulthood: A task decomposition. *Journal of Experimental Psychology: General* 117:115–29.

Charness, N., and Czaja, S. J. 2005. Adaptation to new technologies (7.13). In *Cambridge Handbook on Age and Ageing*, ed. M. L. Johnson, 662–69. Cambridge, UK: Cambridge University Press.

————. 2006. *Older Worker Training: What We Know and Don't Know*. AARP Public Policy Institute, #2006-22. www.aarp.org/research/work/issues/2006_22_worker.html.

Charness, N., Kelley, C. L., Bosman, E. A., and Mottram, M. 2001. Word processing training and retraining: Effects of adult age, experience, and interface. *Psychology and Aging* 16:110–27.

Charness, N., and Krampe, R. Th. 2008. Expertise and Knowledge. In *Handbook on Cognitive Aging: Interdisciplinary Perspectives*, ed. D. F. Alwin and S. M. Hofer, 244–58. Thousand Oaks, CA: Sage.

Charness, N., Tuffiash, M., and Jastrzembski, T. 2004. Motivation, emotion, and expert skill acquisition. In *Motivation, Emotion, and Cognition: Integrative Perspectives*, ed. D. Dai and R. J. Sternberg, 299–319. Mahwah, NJ: Erlbaum.

Charness, N., Tuffiash, M., Krampe, R., Reingold, E. M., and Vasyukova, E. 2005. The role of deliberate practice in chess expertise. *Applied Cognitive Psychology* 19:151–65.

Clawson, D. M., Healy, A. F., Ericsson, K. A., and Bourne Jr., L. E. 2001. Retention and transfer of Morse code reception skill by novices: Part-whole training. *Journal of Experimental Psychology: Applied* 7:129–42.

Cleveland, J. N., and Shore, L. M. 1992. Self- and supervisory perspectives on age and work attitudes and performance. *Psychology and Aging* 77:469–84.

Colquitt, J. A., LePine, J. A., and Noe, R. A. 2000. Toward an integrative theory of training motivation: A meta-analytic path analysis of 20 years of research. *Journal of Applied Psychology* 85:678–707.

Costa, P. T., and McCrae, R. R. 1988. Personality in adulthood: A six-year longitudinal study of self-reports and spouse ratings on the NEO personality inventory. *Journal of Personality and Social Psychology* 54:853–63.

Czaja, S. J., Charness, N., Fisk, A. D., Hertzog, C., Nair, S. N., Rogers, W. A., et al. 2006. Factors predicting the use of technology: Findings from the Center for Research and Education on Aging and Technology Enhancement (CREATE). *Psychology and Aging* 21:333–52.

Diamond, A. M., Jr. 1986. The life-cycle research productivity of mathematicians and scientists. *Journal of Gerontology* 41:520–25.

Elo, A. E. 1965. Age changes in master chess performances. *Journal of Gerontology* 20: 289–99.

Ericsson, K. A. 2006. The Influence of experience and deliberate practice on the development of superior expert performance. In *Cambridge Handbook of Expertise and Expert Performance*, ed. K. A. Ericsson, N. Charness, P. Feltovich, and R. Hoffman, 683–704. Cambridge, UK: Cambridge University Press.

Ericsson, K. A., and Charness, N. 1994. Expert performance: Its structure and acquisition. *American Psychologist* 49:725–47.

Feigenbaum, E. A. 1989. What hath Simon wrought? In *Complex Information Processing: The Impact of Herbert A. Simon*, ed. D. Klahr and K. Kotovsky, 165–182. Hillsdale, NJ: Lawrence Erlbaum Associates.

Finkelstein, L. M., Burke, M. J., and Raju, N. S. 1995. Age discrimination in simulated employment contexts: An integrative analysis. *Journal of Applied Psychology* 80:652–63.

Fisk, A. D., and Rogers, W. 1991. Toward an understanding of age-related memory and visual search effects. *Journal of Experimental Psychology: General* 120:131–49.

Fitts, P. M., and Posner, M. I. 1967. *Human Performance*. Belmont, CA: Brooks/Cole.

Gawronski, B., and Bodenhausen, G. V. 2006. Associative and propositional processes in evaluation: An integrative review of implicit and explicit attitude change. *Psychological Bulletin* 132:692–731.

Green, L., Myerson, J., Lichtman, D., Rosen, S., and Fry, A. 1996. Temporal discounting in choice between delayed rewards: The role of age and income. *Psychology and Aging* 11: 79–84.

Hale, S., and Myerson, J. 1995. Fifty years older, fifty percent slower? Meta-analytic regression models and semantic context effects. *Aging and Cognition* 2:132–45.

Hambrick, D. Z., and Engle, R. W. 2002. Effects of domain knowledge, working memory capacity, and age on cognitive performance: An investigation of the knowledge-is-power hypothesis. *Cognitive Psychology* 44:339–87.

Hambrick, D. Z., Salthouse, T. A., and Meinz, E. J. 1999. Predictors of crossword puzzle proficiency and moderators of age-cognition relations. *Journal of Experimental Psychology: General* 128:131–64.

Head, D., Raz, N., Gunning-Dixon, F., Williamson, A., and Acker, J. D. 2002. Age-related differences in the course of cognitive skill acquisition: The role of regional cortical shrinkage and cognitive resources. *Psychology and Aging* 17:72–84

Heathcote, A., Brown, S., and Mewhort, D. J. K. 2000. The power law repealed: The case for an exponential law of practice. *Psychonomic Bulletin and Review* 7: 185–207.

Horn, J. L. 1982. The theory of fluid and crystallized intelligence in relation to concepts of cognitive psychology and aging in adulthood. In *Aging and Cognitive Processes*, ed. F. I. M. Craik, and S. Trehub, 237–78. New York: Plenum Press.

Horner, K. L., Rushton, J. P., and Vernon, P. A. 1986. Relation between aging and research productivity of academic psychologists. *Psychology and Aging* 4:319–24.

Hultsch, D. 1971. Adult age differences in free classification and free recall. *Developmental Psychology* 4:338–42.

Hunter, J. E., and Schmidt, F. L. 1996. Intelligence and job performance: Economic and social implications. *Psychology, Public Policy, and Law* 2:447–72.

Hutchens, R. 1986. Delayed payment contracts and a firm's propensity to hire older workers. *Journal of Labor Economics* 4:439–57.

Jastrzembski, T. S. & Charness, N. 2007. The Model Human Processor and the older adult: Parameter estimation and validation within a mobile phone task. *Journal of Experimental Psychology: Applied* 13:224–48.

Jastrzembski, T., Charness, N., and Vasyukova, C. 2006. Expertise and age effects on knowledge activation in chess. *Psychology and Aging* 21:401–5.

Jorgenson, D. W., Ho, M. S., and Stiroh, K. J. 2004. Will the U.S. productivity resurgence continue? *Current Issues in Economics and Finance* 10:1–7. www.ny.frb.org/research/current_issues/ci10–13.pdf.

Judge, T. A., Jackson, C. L., Shaw, J. C., Scott, B. A., and Rich, B. L. 2007. Self-efficacy and work-related performance: The integral role of individual differences. *Journal of Applied Psychology* 92:107–27.

Kanfer, R., and Ackerman, P. L. 2004. Aging, adult development, and work motivation. *Academy of Management Review* 29:440–58.

Kite, M. E., Stockdale, G. D., Whitley, B. E., Jr., and Johnson, B. T. 2005. Attitudes toward younger and older adults: An updated meta-analytic review. *Journal of Social Issues* 61: 241–66.

Kliegl, R., Smith, J., and Baltes, P. B. 1989. Testing-the-limits and the study of adult age differences in cognitive plasticity of a mnemonic skill. *Developmental Psychology* 25: 247–56.

Kramer, A. F., Larish, J. F., and Strayer, D. L. 1995. Training for attentional control in dual task settings: A comparison of young and old adults. *Journal of Experimental Psychology: Applied* 1:50–76.

Kubeck, J. E., Delp, N. D., Haslett, T. K., and McDaniel, M. A. 1996. Does job-related training performance decline with age? *Psychology and Aging* 11:92–107.

Lee, T. D., and Magill, R. A. 1983. The locus of contextual interference in motor-skill acquisition. *Journal of Experimental Psychology: Learning, Memory, and Cognition* 9:730–46.

Lehman, H. C. 1953. *Age and Achievement*. Princeton, NJ: Princeton University Press.

Li, S. –C., Lindenberger, U., Hommel, B., Aschersleben, G., Prinz, W., and Baltes, P. B. 2004. Transformations in the couplings among intellectual abilities and constituent cognitive processes across the life span. *Psychological Science* 15:155–63.

Lindenberger, U., Kliegl, R., and Baltes, P. B. 1992. Professional expertise does not eliminate age differences in imagery-based memory performance during adulthood. *Psychology and Aging* 7:585–93.

Maurer, T, Weiss, M, and Barbeite, F. 2003. A model of involvement in work-related learning and development activity: The effects of individual, situational, motivational and age variables. *Journal of Applied Psychology* 88:707–24.

McEvoy, G. M., and Cascio, W. F. 1989. Cumulative evidence of the relationship between employee age and job performance. *Journal of Applied Psychology* 74:11–17.

McNaught, W., and Barth, M. 1992. Are older workers "good buys"? A case study of Days Inns of America. *Sloan Management Review* (Spring): 53–63.

Melenhorst, A. S. 2002. Adopting communication technology in later life: The decisive role of benefits. Ph.D. thesis, Eindhoven University of Technology.

Melenhorst, A., Rogers, W. A., and Bouwhuis, D. G. 2006. Older adults' motivated choice for technological innovation: Evidence for benefit-driven selectivity. *Psychology and Aging* 21:190–95.

Mireles, D. E., and Charness, N. 2002. Computational explorations of the influence of structured knowledge on age-related cognitive decline. *Psychology and Aging* 17:245–59.

Morrow, D. G., Ridolfo, H. E., Menard, W. E., Sanborn, A., Stine-Morrow, E. A. L., Magnor, C., et al. 2003. Environmental support promotes expertise-based mitigation of age differences on pilot communication tasks. *Psychology and Aging* 18:268–84.

Morrow, D., Leirer, V., Altieri, P., and Fitzsimmons, C. 1994. When expertise reduces age differences in performance. *Psychology and Aging* 9:134–48.

Newell, A., and Rosenbloom, P. S. 1981. Mechanisms of skill acquisition and the power law of practice. In *Cognitive Skills and Their Acquisition*, ed. J. R. Anderson, 1–55. Hillsdale, NJ: Lawrence Erlbaum Associates.

Noe, R. A., and Wilk, S. L. 1993. Investigation of the factors that influence employees' participation in developmental activities. *Journal of Applied Psychology* 78:291–302

Pavlik Jr., P. I., and Anderson, J. R. 2005. Practice and forgetting effects on vocabulary memory: An activation-based model of the spacing effect. *Cognitive Science* 29:559–86.

Quetelet, L. A. J. 1969. *A Treatise on Man and the Development of His Faculties*. Gainesville, FL: Scholars' Facsimiles and Reprints. (Original work published 1842.)

Roberts, B. W., and DelVecchio, W. F. 2000. The rank-order consistency of personality traits from childhood to old age: A quantitative review of longitudinal studies. *Psychological Bulletin* 126:466–77.

Roring, R. W., and Charness, N. 2007. A multilevel model analysis of expertise in chess across the life span. *Psychology and Aging* 22:291–99.

Salthouse, T. A. 1984. Effects of age and skill in typing. *Journal of Experimental Psychology: General* 13:345–71.

———. 1996. The processing-speed theory of adult age differences in cognition. *Psychological Review* 103:403–28.

———. 2006. Mental exercise and mental aging: Evaluating the validity of the "Use It or Lose It" hypothesis. *Perspectives on Psychological Science* 1:68–87.

Salthouse, T. A., and Maurer, J. J. 1996. Aging, job performance, and career development. In *Handbook of the Psychology of Aging*, 4th ed., ed. J. E. Birren, and K. W. Schaie, 353–64. New York: Academic Press.

Schaie, K. W., Dutta, R., and Willis, S. L. 1991. The relationship between rigidity-flexibility and cognitive abilities in adulthood. *Psychology and Aging* 6:371–83.

Sharit, J., Czaja, S. J., Perdomo, D., and Lee, C. C. 2004. A cost-benefit analysis methodology for assessing product adoption by older user populations. *Applied Ergonomics* 35: 81–92.

Simonton, D. K. 1988. Age and outstanding achievement: What do we know after a century of research? *Psychological Bulletin* 104:251–67.

———. 1997. Creative productivity: A predictive and explanatory model of career trajectories and landmarks. *Psychological Review* 104:66–89.

Soman, D. 2001. The mental accounting of sunk time costs: Why time is not like money. *Journal of Behavioral Decision Making* 14:169–85.

Sparrow, P. R., and Davies, D. R. 1988. Effects of age, tenure, training, and job complexity on technical performance. *Psychology and Aging* 3:307–14.

Sturman, M. C. 2004. Searching for the inverted u-shaped relationship between time and performance: meta-analyses of the experience/performance, tenure/performance, and age/performance relationships. *Journal of Management* 29:609–40.

Taatgen, N.A., Huss, D., Dickison, D., and Anderson, J. R. 2008. The acquisition of robust and flexible skills. *Journal of Experimental Psychology: General* 137:548–65.

Taylor, J. L., O'Hara, R., Mumenthaler, M. S., Rosen, A. C., and Yesavage, J. A. 2005. Cognitive ability, expertise, and age differences in following air-traffic control instructions. *Psychology and Aging* 20:117–33.

Touron, D. R., Hoyer, W. J., and Cerella, J. 2001. Cognitive skill acquisition and transfer in younger and older adults. *Psychology and Aging* 16:555–63.

Tulving, E. 1983. *Elements of Episodic Memory.* New York: Oxford University Press.

U.S. Census Bureau. 2004. Income, poverty, and health insurance coverage in the United States: 2004, Current Population Reports, P60–229; and Internet sites: www.census .gov/prod/2005pubs/p60–229.pdf (released 30 August 2005) and http://pubdb3 .census.gov/macro/032005/hhinc/toc.htm (released 26 July 2005).

Unsworth, N., and Engle, R. W. 2007. The nature of individual differences in working memory capacity: Active maintenance in primary memory and controlled search from secondary memory. *Psychological Review* 114:104–32.

VanLehn, K. 1996. Cognitive skill acquisition. *Annual Review of Psychology* 47:513–19.

Waldman, D. A., and Avolio, B. J. 1986. A meta-analysis of age differences in job performance. *Journal of Applied Psychology* 71:33–38.

CHAPTER THIRTEEN

Preparing Organizations and Older Workers for Current and Future Employment

Training and Retraining

SARA J. CZAJA, PH.D., AND JOSEPH SHARIT, PH.D.

The aging of the baby boom cohort, coupled with changes in retirement policies, programs, and behavior and increased concerns about dwindling resources to support retirement incomes, are contributing to a renewed interest in the development of strategies to promote continued employment of older adults. It is generally recognized that the extent to which older people remain productively employed will have a large impact on business and industry, on government programs and the economy, and on the quality of life of older adults themselves. In 2002 there were about 61 million people aged 55+ in the United States; these numbers are expected to grow to 103 million by 2025, representing 30 percent of the population (U.S. General Accounting Office, 2003). A number of factors influence the extent to which this large cohort of older adults will continue to work, including financial incentives, benefits, health, employment opportunities, socialization, and ability to adapt to changes in the work environment.

Adaptation can generally be defined as the process of adjusting oneself to fit a situation or environment (Atchley, 1987). In the case of work, adaptation can be viewed as a continuous and dynamic process by which an individual seeks to establish a "fit" with his or her job, where "fit" is influenced by the degree to which the needs, values, and interests of an individual are met by the job and the knowledge/skill and ability requirements of a job are met by that individual (Yeatts, Folts, and Knapp, 1999).

To adapt successfully to the work environment of the twenty-first century and keep pace with changes in job and organizational demands, older workers will continually need to engage in activities to learn new skills and acquire new knowledge. Within the context of work, skill acquisition typically occurs through some form of job training, which generally refers to activities designed to enable an individual to learn and use new processes, procedures, equipment, and tools required in performance of the job. In today's work environments, training and retraining of older workers is becoming a fundamental component of organizational effectiveness.

This chapter (1) briefly discusses changes in work environments that have implications for job training; (2) summarizes existing data regarding job training and older adults; (3) discusses the factors and barriers that influence the participation in training activities by older workers; (4) discusses issues that are likely to affect the design of training programs in the future; and (5) outlines some needed areas of research and policy to promote successful training opportunities and productive employment for older adults.

THE CHANGING NATURE OF THE WORKPLACE

As discussed in other chapters in this volume, the work environment has undergone major changes in the last few decades, and these changes, which are expected to continue in the future, have created new knowledge, skill, and ability requirements for workers. For example, ongoing developments in technology are reshaping production processes, the task content of jobs, and the skill requirements of jobs. As shown in figure 13.1, the majority of workers use a computer, the Internet, or some other form of technology at work, and this number will continue to grow, as will the scope and sophistication of technology. In the future, the rapid pace of technological change and the transition to a knowledge-based economy is going to increase the demand for highly skilled and well-educated workers. We can anticipate that developments in technology will continue to shape what is produced, how material and labor inputs are combined to produce it, how work is organized, and the content of work (Karoly and Panis, 2004).

Thus, for many workers, existing job skills and knowledge are becoming obsolete and new knowledge and skills are required to meet the demands of today's jobs, creating enormous needs for worker training and retraining. Issues of skill obsolescence and training are especially significant for older workers because the current and upcoming cohorts of older workers (those currently in their 40s) are less likely than younger workers to have had exposure to technology such as computers (e.g., Czaja and Sharit, 1998; Czaja, et al., 2006). Recent data for the United

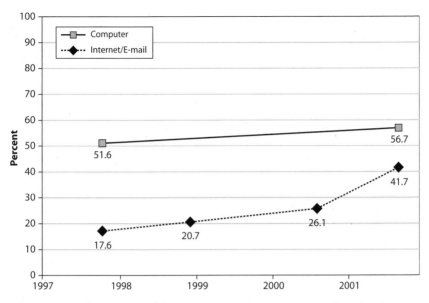

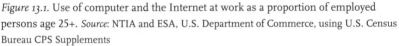

Figure 13.1. Use of computer and the Internet at work as a proportion of employed persons age 25+. *Source*: NTIA and ESA, U.S. Department of Commerce, using U.S. Census Bureau CPS Supplements

States indicate that although the use of computers and the Internet among older adults is increasing, there is still an age-based digital divide (figure 13.2).

Developments in technology and globalization are also influencing the structure of work environments. The traditional management hierarchy is disintegrating, and firms are becoming flatter and more specialized, with a focus on decentralized decision making and collaborative work. In these types of work structures, workers are often confronted with a need to learn entire processes as opposed to specific jobs and to be able to communicate effectively with diverse teams of people, usually through the use of technology, who may be in distant locations. In addition, an increased emphasis is being placed on knowledge and knowledge management as the key source of competitive advantage for businesses. Knowledge work generally places an emphasis on nonroutine cognitive skills such as abstract reasoning, problem solving, and communication. Overall, these organizational and job changes generally require that workers receive retraining to operate within new organizational structures and keep current with job requirements.

Concurrent with the changes in the structure of organizations will be an increase in the number of workers in nonstandard work arrangements such as self-

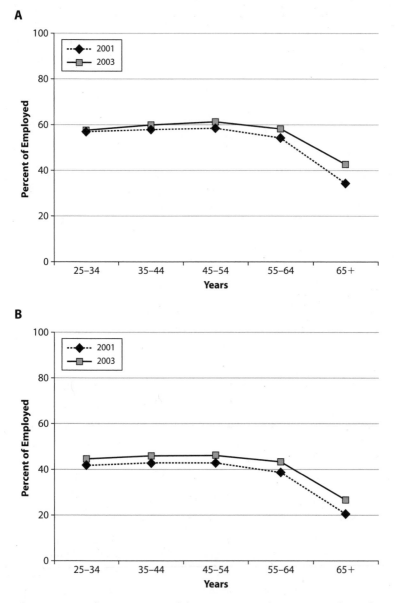

Figure 13.2. Use of computer (*A*) and the Internet (*B*) at home or at work as a function of age. *Source*: Bureau of Labor Statistics. 2005. Computer and Internet Use at Work in 2003.

employment and contract work, and the prevalence of home-based work and telecommuting is likely to increase. In 2001, about 29 million U.S. workers engaged in some form of telecommuting, and it is estimated that there could be slightly more than 40 million telecommuters by 2010 (Potter, 2003). Changes in work arrangements raise important issues with respect to how "nonstandard" workers will receive the training and education needed to update their skills.

New formats for job training such as the increased use of e-learning tools also raise a number of issues regarding the design and implementation of training programs. Current estimates from the American Society for Training and Development suggest that e-learning is used for about 30 percent of all formal organizational training programs (Sugrue and Rivera, 2005). The use of technology in training environments places new demands on learners because they not only must learn the substantive information related to the topic of interest but they also may need to acquire knowledge and skills required to use the technology. Furthermore, learning may occur in environments where there is no available technical support. As discussed later in this chapter, these demands may be especially formidable for older adults.

JOB TRAINING AND OLDER ADULTS

Successful training performance for job-related activities requires a broad range of perceptual, cognitive, and motor abilities. The literature examining the influence of age on these abilities generally suggests age-related declines. With respect to cognition, as shown in figure 13.3, many component cognitive abilities that are important to learning, such as working memory, attentional processes, and spatial cognition, show decline with age, especially under conditions of complexity or when a task represents an unfamiliar cognitive domain. Also, age-related changes in vision, audition, and perceptual/motor skills may affect on the ability of older people to learn new skills. For example, age-related declines in visual acuity may make it difficult for older people to perceive and comprehend visual information. Many older adults also experience some decline in audition and changes in motor skills, including slower response times, disruptions in coordination, loss of flexibility, and greater variability in movement (Rogers and Fisk, 2000). However, as discussed by Charness (chapter 12 of this volume), despite these age-related changes in component abilities, older adults do have cognitive plasticity, and there is a vast literature on aging and skill acquisition that generally indicates that older adults are able to learn new skills, though it typically takes them longer than younger adults and they require more practice and more

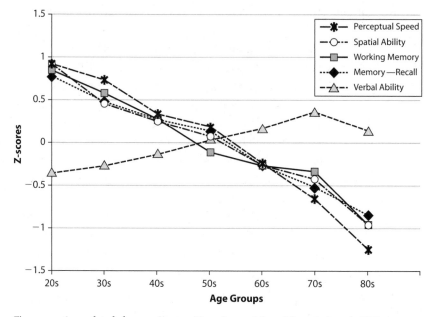

Figure 13.3. Age-related changes in cognition. *Source*: Adapted from Park et al., 2002

environmental support. Data regarding older adults and job training, though relatively sparse, generally support these findings.

Kubeck, Delp, Haslett, and McDaniel (1996) conducted a meta-analysis to examine the relationship between age and job-related training outcomes. Overall, the results showed poorer training performance for older adults. On average, older adults demonstrated less mastery of the training material and took significantly longer to train than younger adults. They also found that the age differences varied according to the nature of the task such that larger age differences were found for computer-based tasks than for noncomputer tasks. However, as noted by the authors, these findings need to be interpreted with caution, since much of the data for the meta-analysis came from experimental studies designed to emulate real-world training conditions as opposed to field studies in actual work settings. There was also variance in the effects of age on training outcomes across studies. This variance may have been due to the influence of moderating factors such as length of training, varying training measures, and training technique. They also found larger variance for older adults than younger adults on outcome measures for the majority of the studies that reported outcome measure variance by age, which suggests greater individual differences in performance in older than in younger adults. Overall, the authors concluded that there is a critical need for studies examining training methods appropriate for older workers.

In a more recent meta-analysis, Callahan, Kiker, and Cross (2003) examined the effects of three instructional methods (lecture, modeling, and active participation) and four instructional factors (materials, feedback, pacing, and group size) on the training performance of older adults. All three training methods were effective with older adults. They also determined that each method contributes independently to learning and suggest that training that integrates multiple methods could be useful when training older learners. The interaction analysis examining age and training method was not significant, suggesting that effective training techniques did not vary much with age. However, the investigation focused only on older workers and the sample only included learners' age 40+ years. With respect to instructional factors, only self-pacing and group size proved important; training that occurred in smaller groups or enabled learners to learn at their own pace was associated with higher levels of training performance. Of these two variables, self-pacing emerged as the most significant predictor.

Over the past decades, a number of studies (e.g., Elias, Elias, Robbins, and Gage, 1987; Gist, Rosen, and Schwoerer, 1988; Czaja, Hammond, Blascovich, and Swede, 1989; Charness, Schumann, and Boritz, 1992; Morrell, Park, Mayhorn, and Echt, 1995; Mead et al., 1997) have also examined the ability of older adults to learn to use technology such as computers, the Internet, and various software applications. For example, Charness and colleagues conducted a cross-sectional study of younger, middle-aged, and older adults learning to use a new word processor (an early variant of Microsoft Word; Charness, Kelley, Bosman, and Mottram, 2001). Two different groups were trained over a three-day period using self-paced training: a novice group with no word-processing experience, and an experienced group who knew a different word-processing application. For the novice users, clear age differences were evident even when the individuals could proceed at their own pace through the tutorial package. For experienced users, at the end of training, there were no real differences in performance among the three age groups and performance was better than what was achieved by young novices. However, the middle-aged and older adults also took much longer than young adults to complete the self-paced training. Several other investigators (e.g., Beier and Ackerman, 2005; Nair, Czaja, and Sharit, 2007) also showed that experience is an important factor influencing how effectively someone can learn new information. In general, if the new learning material is related to knowledge, learning will be faster than if the material is unrelated.

Mead et al. (1997) examined the effects of type of training on efficiency in a

World Wide Web search activity. The participants were trained with a "hands-on" Web navigation tutorial or a verbal description of available navigation tools. The hands-on training was found to be superior, especially, for older adults (64–81 years). Czaja et al. (1989) also found that a more active goal-oriented training approach was beneficial to older adults (55–70 years) attempting to learn text-editing (figure 13.4), and Morrell et al. (1995) found that giving procedural instructions alone was superior to using a combination of conceptual information and procedural instructions among older adults (60–89 years) and old-old (ages 75–89) adults learning to perform tasks on ELDERCOMM, a bulletin board system.

Overall, the results of training studies indicate that older adults are able to learn new job skills such as the ability to use technology and computers. However, they are typically slower to acquire new skills than younger adults. In addition, older adults generally require more help and "hands-on" practice. Also, when compared to younger adults on performance measures, older adults often achieve lower levels of performance. The results also vary according to level of experience of the learner and attitudinal variables such as self-efficacy and anxiety.

Existing data also suggest that many training techniques are effective for older adults, but there is not an adequate research database to determine whether some training techniques are consistently *differentially* beneficial for older workers. Few instances of interactions between age and training technique have been observed. Generally, it appears that what is best for the young is also best for the old if more training, practice, and support is provided. General guidelines are available (e.g., Fisk, Rogers, Charness, Czaja, and Sharit, 2004) regarding how to design training programs to facilitate the learning performance of older adults. These guidelines encompass factors such as pacing, amount and spacing of practice, feedback, training media, and general training approach (e.g., procedural versus conceptual training).

For example, it is important to allow extra time for training older adults (1.5 to 2 times the training time expected for young adults), ensure that help is available and easy to access (e.g., acquaint the person with sources of help), and that the training environment allows people to focus on the training materials. Training materials should also be well organized, irrelevant information should be kept to a minimum, and the reading level of all instructions and manuals match the abilities of the user population. Choice of instructional technique and training media should be matched to the type of material that is being presented; for example, "how to" information should be presented in a procedural step-by-step format, whereas spatial tasks are best trained using a visual medium. It is generally recommended that the learner be allowed to make errors, when safe, but timely

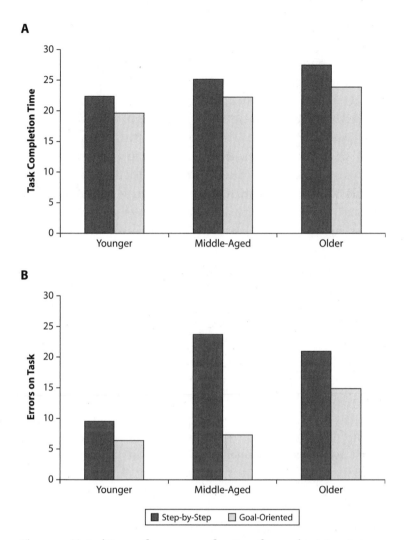

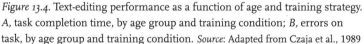

Figure 13.4. Text-editing performance as a function of age and training strategy.
A, task completion time, by age group and training condition; B, errors on
task, by age group and training condition. *Source:* Adapted from Czaja et al., 1989

feedback needs to be provided regarding how to correct mistakes. In our recent
study of telework and older adults (Sharit et al., 2004) many of our participants
commented that they would have liked more informative feedback about their
performance. Opportunities should also be created for the learner to be actively
involved in the learning process. Demands on working memory should be kept
to a minimum, and where possible, it is useful to capitalize on the learner's pre-

existing knowledge base. While these guidelines are useful as a first step in train-ing design, the design of a training program should always be based on an analy-sis of the characteristics of the trainee population, the training task, and the phys-ical and organizational environment.

As will be discussed in the next section, in addition to training program de-sign parameters, "training success" is also influenced by motivational factors, so-cial factors, and environmental factors. It is also important to note that aging is associated with substantial variability, and older adults as a group are heteroge-neous. Thus, predictions about a person's ability to learn a new skill or perform a job should be based on abilities relative to demands as opposed to chronologi-cal age. Finally, careful consideration needs to be given to the concept of "train-ing success" in terms of actual level of performance needed for a particular job.

FACTORS INFLUENCING PARTICIPATION IN TRAINING AND DEVELOPMENT PROGRAMS

One important factor influencing the ability of older workers to adapt to changes in job demands and engage in training and development activities is the extent to which training opportunities are available to them. Older adults are likely to suffer the effects of stereotypes about age-related performance declines (Kite and Johnson, 1988) which might result in negative perceptions among managers about the trainability of older adults (Sterns and Doverspike, 1989). One possible consequence of these perceptions would be the failure of management to provide appropriate incentives and training opportunities to older workers (Noe and Wilk, 1993; Rix, 1996). In fact, data indicate that attitudes held by managers are associated with a range of employment practices, such as the provision of train-ing opportunities, which affect older workers (Taylor and Walker, 1998). There are some data to suggest that employers invest less in training older workers than younger ones (Barth, McNaught, and Rizzi, 1993). The Bureau of Labor Statistics conducted a survey of training in businesses with greater than 50 employees and found that only about half of workers aged 55+ had received training in the year before the survey in contrast to 70 percent of all workers and three-fourths or more of workers between the ages of 25 and 44 (Frazis, Gittleman, Horrigan, and Joyce, 1998). In addition, older workers reported receiving substantially fewer hours of training than workers in other age groups. Recent results from the Boston College National Study of Business Strategy and Workforce Development (Center on Aging and Work Workplace Flexibility at Boston College, 2007) found that about

26 percent of employers reported that they increased training and cross-training efforts to a larger extent for younger workers than for older workers.

We recently conducted focus groups to gather insight into barriers confronting lower socioeconomic status older adults seeking employment and to gather information on training needs. The sample included 37 community dwelling adults (9 males and 28 females) ranging in age from 51 to 76 years. Most of the participants (65%) had only a high school education or less, and only 46 percent had computer experience. When asked about perceived obstacles to employment, the most common responses included age, insufficient qualifications, and lack of technical/computer skills. In fact, 100 percent of the participants indicated that they believed that their age was one of the primary reasons they were not working. The group also commented that computer and Internet training were needed to find a job (Lee, Czaja, and Sharit, 2009).

In a longitudinal study of 800 employees across the United States, Maurer, Weiss, and Barbeite (2003) found that older workers received less support for learning and development activities. Specifically, they found that chronological age had a negative relationship with nonwork support (e.g., family, friends) and perceived age had a negative relationship with work support. They also found that participation in training and development activities is influenced by individual or personal factors such as anxiety and self-efficacy as well as by perceived benefits of participation. Individuals who believed that they were capable of improving and learning new skills were more likely to participate in training activities as were those who perceived a potential benefit from participation. Overall, age was found to be negatively related to both individual and situational variables that enable participation in job development activities. However, the effects of age were relatively small, and perceived relative age was distinguishable from chronological age on the influence of the antecedents of training participation. A model depicting the general findings of this study is presented in figure 13.5 to illustrate the complex picture of training participation and subsequent training "success."

A meta-analysis of the literature on training motivation (Colquitt, LePine, and Noe, 2000) generally supports this model and indicates that both individual and situational factors influence learning-directed behaviors in actual training contexts (beyond decisions to participate in training activities) and ultimately training outcomes. Specifically, the result of this analysis showed that age was negatively related to motivation to learn, learning, and post-training self-efficacy. Consistent with Maurer et al. (2003), self-efficacy was also positively related to motivation to

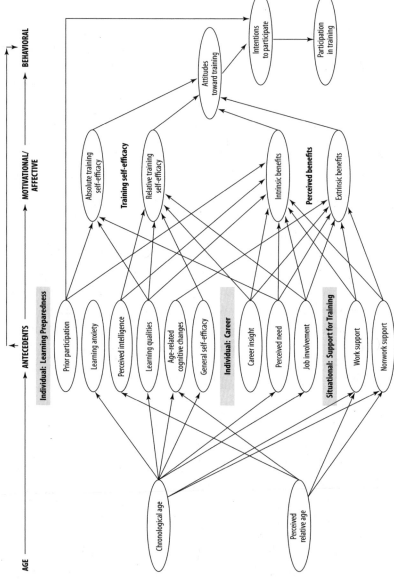

Figure 13.5. Model of participation in training. *Source:* Adapted from Maurer, Weiss, and Barbeite, 2003

learn as well as training success. The findings also showed that situational characteristics, such as support from supervisors and peers, were important to these
outcomes. In this regard, a recent report by the U.S. General Accounting Office
(2003) indicated that providers of Workforce Investment Act programs are less
likely now than in the past to have separate training programs for older workers.
The GAO recommended that program providers make adjustments to eliminate
disincentives to older worker enrollment.

Overall, it seems clear that age, though important, is not the only factor influencing involvement in training and development activities or success in these activities. Rather, both individual and situational characteristics are important before training (ability/decisions to participate), during training (involvement in
training activities), and to training success (training performance and subsequent transfer to work activities).

FUTURE CHALLENGES

Although there is a vast literature on job training (though limited on training
older workers), rapid developments in technology, dynamic changes in work environments, and current demographic trends pose some interesting challenges
for the development of future job-training programs. For example, as the number of workers in nonstandard work arrangements, such as those who work from
home or on a contractual basis, continues to increase, one important issue confronting workers will be access to traditional workplace benefits such as training.
Workers in nonstandard work arrangements will be less likely to receive structured company-sponsored training, and the responsibility of continuous learning
and job training will fall to a greater extent on the individual. It is not yet clear
how to best develop and disseminate training programs to promote lifelong
learning for these "nontraditional" workers. This issue is especially pertinent for
older workers, given that they are less likely to be provided with access to training
and development programs in traditional work environments where company-
sponsored training is available.

In this regard, technology-mediated learning or "e-learning," defined as
computer-based training, is being considered as a possible solution, since it provides opportunities for learning to occur any time and any place. The current e-
learning market is a multibillion dollar industry, and e-learning tools are quickly
emerging as preferred methods for training employees. E-learning content can
be delivered by synchronous, asynchronous, or blended formats. Asynchronous
e-learning allows the learner to complete the training on a self-paced schedule,

without live interaction with an instructor. Facilitated asynchronous training involves an instructor and group of students, but the interaction is not in real time. Synchronous training, which involves interacting with an instructor via the Web in real time, is currently a less common form of e-learning and is typically used in academic-type programs such as continuing education or college distance learning. There are strengths and limitations of both approaches (see Willis, 2004, for a more complete discussion of these issues). Overall, the key advantages of e-learning are flexibility, convenience, working at one's own pace and at any place where the requisite technology is available, and cost savings associated with commuting. Thus, this method of training is a viable option for distance learning for those who have to juggle work and caregiving responsibilities or have problems with commuting to the workplace. Disadvantages of e-learning include the lack of face-to-face interactions with instructors, lack of socialization with other students, and lack of technical support. Effective use of e-learning tools may present special challenges for many older adults who do not have technical skills or have limited access to technology or broadband Internet services. To date, there has only been limited research (e.g., Stoltz-Loike, Morrell, and Loike, 2005) examining whether mature learners can effectively learn via e-learning programs.

Recent developments in multimedia technology have resulted in an increased use of multimedia formats in on-line training programs. Multimedia makes it possible to present training content in a variety of formats, including audio, text, and video, and provides an opportunity for a more extensive representation of information than conventional graphical user interfaces. In addition, information can be presented in a synchronized, contiguous fashion. In this regard, these types of formats may be especially beneficial for learners who have some limitations in sensory/perceptual capacities or those who have low literacy. On the other hand, cognitive overload is a serious threat in multimedia environments because learners have to integrate information from a variety of sources, which may place a heavy burden on attentional resources and working memory. Age-related changes in cognition (figure 13.3) may make problems with overload especially salient for older adults. Currently, there is little empirical knowledge to guide the development of multimedia training applications, and little research has been conducted with older adult populations. A recent study that compared the effect of a multimedia condition to that of a unimodal or conventional training condition on the training performance of older and younger adults found that for both age groups the multimedia format was more efficient and resulted in less cognitive load (Van Gerven et al., 2003). However, the training task used in the study was a laboratory-based problem-solving task, and the sample size was relatively small. Although the results of this study suggest that multimedia-based instruction seems promising for older adults, the investigators cautioned that multimedia formats need to be tested on more complex and varied applications with larger and more diverse samples of older people.

Finally, consistent with demographic changes in the U.S. population as a whole, the older population is becoming more ethnically diverse. Currently about 84 percent of people aged 65+ are non-Hispanic white; this proportion will drop to about 74 percent in 2030 and 64 percent by 2050. The greatest growth will be seen among Hispanic persons, followed by non-Hispanic blacks. Currently, individuals from ethnic minority groups are less likely to own or use technologies such as computers. To promote employment opportunities for older minorities, worker training programs need to be targeted for these populations. Careful consideration needs to be given to factors such as language and technical requirements associated with training programs and cultural/ethnic differences in attitudes toward training.

CONCLUSION

Training is a critical issue confronting the twenty-first-century workforce, and successful engagement in work activities will involve continuous learning throughout working life. Inevitably, the future workplace will include many older workers. Much of the increase will be driven by the aging of the baby-boom generation. However, depending in part on the vagaries of the economy and the marked shift in the past decade from defined benefit to defined contribution retirement plans, it is also possible that a greater percentage of the generation preceding the baby boomers will also stay in the labor force or will return from retirement to perform part-time work to supplement their income. How well those (and future) older workers can adapt to the demands of the increasingly competitive labor environment is of critical importance to the productivity of the economy.

How do we equip older workers to adapt successfully to the dynamic work environment of the future? This question largely revolves around the provision of accessible and effective training and retraining programs. The development of these types of programs depends on a solid knowledge base. As noted throughout this chapter and several others in this volume, a number of changes in abilities are associated with "normal" aging. We need a clearer understanding of the implications of these changes for the design of training and instructional programs. Currently, there are many gaps in our knowledge and an enormous need for research in this area.

On the more basic research side, we need a better understanding of how age-related changes in functioning affect the ability of older adults to meet the specific skill requirements of jobs. Although there are age-related declines in most aspects of functioning, the decline is nearly always gradual, and most jobs do not demand constant performance at the level of maximal capacity. The majority of the population of older adults remains healthy and functionally able until late in life. We need a knowledge base that links age-related changes in skills and abilities to job requirements. This type of knowledge base would help identify specific components of jobs that may be limiting for older adults and help direct the development of both better selection and training strategies for older workers.

In addition, although there are well-developed models for understanding motivational antecedents such as learning self-efficacy for seeking job training (e.g., Colquitt, LePine, and Noe, 2000; Maurer et al., 2003), few studies have examined strategies that influence the antecedent conditions that control older workers' desire to train or retrain. Most of the work in this area has focused on workers in general, without distinguishing between older and younger workers. In particular, studies are needed that examine the entire path from attitudes about training or retraining to motivation within training settings and training outcomes. Understanding these issues can facilitate the development of contexts or situations that promote participation in training programs. Research is also needed to determine to what extent training and educational campaigns actually change attitudes and alter discriminatory employment practices.

Results from some research studies hint at age by training interactions, implying that some forms of training may be differentially better for older workers. The research area concerned with fine-tuning training for older workers is still poorly explored and needs significant development.

There are numerous issues to consider regarding how to best train workers who work in nonstandard work arrangements, such as those who work from home. Many of these issues are linked with questions regarding technology-mediated learning. Although on-line training is increasingly looked at as a solution to many training issues, there is little empirical evidence to guide the development of these systems; nor is there much data regarding the effectiveness of these types of programs in terms of an individual's ability to procure and successfully perform a particular job. Distance and on-line learning also has the potential to reduce opportunities for peer support and social interactions, which often provides informal support for training and learning. In addition, positive peer support can reduce anxiety and promote engagement in learning activities (figure 13.5). However, it is not clear how this lack of informal support that may evolve in a "technology-mediated world" will influence the willingness or ability of older adults to successfully engage in training and development activities.

There is also a need to identify strategies to foster lifelong learning among low-skilled and low-educated older workers who are more likely to be unemployed and have less access to formal training opportunities. A work culture where a greater emphasis is placed on individual responsibility for learning may exacerbate inequality in access to training programs. This issue is becoming especially pertinent as employers rely more on technology-mediated learning, because low-skilled workers are the least likely to have the skills needed to use technology-based training programs.

Many methodological issues need to be addressed in future training studies. Study protocols need to capture the complexity of representative job tasks, particularly the contextual elements of the work environment. These studies also need to include a wider age range of workers in order to assess potential interactions between type of training and age of worker. Many of the current studies examining age and skill acquisition are based on laboratory tasks or done in controlled environments. Overall, there is a need for the adoption of more "ecological approaches" within the realm of job training research.

Careful consideration also needs to be given to how we define and measure "training success." We need to move beyond defining success purely on the basis of achievement of statistical significance on measures such as knowledge tests, to measures that are practically significant, such as changes in the actual ability to perform a task within a work setting. Furthermore, levels of success need to be commensurate with performance requirements of jobs, that is, what qualifies as acceptable performance in work environments.

Finally, we need to examine the role of government and labor organizations in providing opportunities for job training for older workers. Despite laws preventing age discrimination in employment settings and policies, programs that foster the training of older people are not prevalent and are largely restricted to advocacy organizations for the elderly or a small number of businesses (Rix, 2004). Policies that foster partnerships between industry, academia, and the community also need to be explored.

In short, the twenty-first century will likely see an increase in the number of older workers. An important challenge confronting business and industry, public policy makers, and researchers is the development of strategies to ensure that older adults have the skills to adapt to the demands of an increasingly dynamic work environment.

REFERENCES

Atchley, R. C. 1987. *Aging: Continuity and Change.* Belmont CA: Wordsworth Publishing.

Barth, M., McNaught, W., and Rizzi, P. 1993. Corporations and the aging workforce. In *Building the Competitive Workforce: Investing Human Capital for Corporate Success,* ed. P. H. Mirvis, 156–200. New York: John Wiley & Sons.

Beier, M. E., and Ackerman, P. L. 2005. Age, ability, and the role of prior knowledge on the acquisition of new domain knowledge: Promising results in a real-world learning environment. *Psychology and Aging* 20:341–55.

Callahan, J. S., Kiker, D. S., and Cross, T. 2003. Does method matter? A meta-analysis of the effects of training method on older learner training performance. *Journal of Management* 29:663–80.

Center on Aging and Work Workplace Flexibility, Boston College. 2007. *Age Bias and Employment Discrimination.* Issue Brief 7. Boston: Author.

Charness, N., Kelley, C. L., Bosman, E. A., and Mottram, M. 2001. Word processing training and retraining: Effects of adult age, experience, and interface. *Psychology and Aging* 16:110–27.

Charness, N., Schumann, C. E., and Boritz, G. A. 1992. Training older adults in word processing: Effects of age, training technique and computer anxiety. *International Journal of Aging and Technology* 5:79–106.

Colquitt, J. A., LePine, J. A., and Noe, R. A. 2000. Toward an integrative theory of training motivation: A meta-analytic path analysis of 20 years of research. *Journal of Applied Psychology* 85:678–707.

Czaja, S. J., and Sharit, J. 1998. Ability-performance relationships as a function of age and task experience for a data entry task. *Journal of Experimental Psychology: Applied* 4:332–51.

Czaja, S. J., Charness, N., Fisk, A. D., Hertzog, C., Nair, S. N., Rogers, W. A., et al. 2006. Factors predicting the use of technology: Findings from the Center for Research and Education on Aging and Technology Enhancement (CREATE). *Psychology and Aging* 21: 333–52.

Czaja, S. J., Hammond, K., Blascovich, J., and Swede, H. 1989. Age-related differences in learning to use a text-editing system. *Behavior and Information Technology* 8:309–19.

Elias, P. K., Elias, M. F., Robbins, M. A., and Gage, P. 1987. Acquisition of word-processing skills by younger, middle-aged, and older adults. *Psychology and Aging* 2: 340–48.

Fisk, A. D., Rogers, W. A., Charness, N., Czaja, S. J., and Sharit, J. 2004. *Designing for Older Adults: Principles and Creative Human Factors Approaches.* Boca Raton: CRC Press.

Frazis, H., Gittleman, M., Horrigan, M., and Joyce, M. 1998. Results from the 1995 survey of employer-provided training, *Monthly Labor Review* 121 (6): 3–13.

Gist, M., Rosen, B., and Schwoerer, C. 1988. The influence of training method and trainee age on the acquisition of computer skills. *Personal Psychology* 41:255–65.

Karoly, L. A., and Panis, W. A. 2004. *The 21st Century at Work: Forces Shaping the Future Workforce and Workplace in the United States.* Santa Monica CA: RAND Corporation.

Kite, M. E., and Johnson, B. T. 1988. Attitudes toward younger and older adults: A meta-analysis. *Psychology and Aging* 3:233–44.

Kubeck, J. E., Delp, N. D., Haslett, T. K., and McDaniel, M. A. 1996. Does job-related training performance decline with age? *Psychology and Aging* 11:92–107.

Lee, C. C., Czaja, S. J., and Sharit, J. 2009. Training older workers for technology-based employment. *Educational Gerontology* 35:15–31.

Maurer, T. J., Weiss, E. M., and Barbeite, F. G. 2003. A model of involvement in work-related learning and development activity: The effects of individual, situational, motivational, and age variables. *Journal of Applied Psychology* 88:707–24.

Mead, S. E., Spaulding, V. A., Sit, R. A., Meyer, B., and Walker, N. 1997. Effects of age and training on World Wide Web navigation strategies. *Proceedings of the Human Factors and Ergonomics Society 41st Annual Meeting*, 152–56.

Morrell, R. W., Park, D. C., Mayhorn, C. B., and Echt, K. V. 1995. Older adults and electronic communication networks: Learning to use ELDERCOMM. Presented at the 103rd Annual Convention of the American Psychological Association, New York.

Nair, S. N., Czaja, S. J., and Sharit, J. 2007. A multilevel modeling approach to examining individual differences in skill acquisition for a computer-based task. *Journals of Gerontology* 62B (Special Issue I): 85–96.

Noe, R. A., and Wilk, S. L. 1993. Investigation of the factors that influence employees' participation in developmental activities. *Journal of Applied Psychology* 78:291–302.

Potter, E. E. 2003. Telecommuting: The future of work, corporate culture, and American society. *Journal of Labor Research* 24:73–84.

Rix, S. E. 1996. Investing in the future: What role for older worker training? In *Handbook on Employment and the Elderly*, ed. W. H. Crown, 304–23. Westport, CT: Greenwood Press.

———. 2004. *Aging and Work: A View from the United States*. Technical report. Washington, DC: American Association for Retired Persons.

Rogers, W. A., and Fisk, A. D. 2000. Human factors, applied cognition, and aging. In *The Handbook of Aging and Cognition*, ed. F. I. M., Craik, and T. A. Salthouse, 559–92. Hillsdale, NJ: Lawrence Erlbaum Associates.

Sharit, J., Czaja, S. J., Hernandez, M., Yang, Y., Perdomo, D., Lewis, J. L., et al. 2004. An evaluation of performance by older persons on a simulated telecommuting task. *Journal of Gerontology: Psychological Sciences* 59B (6): 305–16.

Sterns, H. L., and Doverspike, D. 1989. Aging and the training and learning process. In *Training and Development in Organizations*, ed. I. Goldstein, 299–332. San Francisco: Jossey-Bass.

Stoltz-Loike, M., Morrell, R. W., and Loike, J. D. 2005. Usability testing of Business Thinking—e-learning CD-roms with older adults. *Educational Gerontology* 31:765–86.

Sugrue, B., and Rivera, R. J. 2005. *State of the Industry: ASTD's Annual Review of Trends in Workplace Learning and Performance*. Alexandria, VA: ASTD.

Taylor, P., and Walker, A. 1998. Employers and older workers: Attitudes and employment practices. *Aging and Society* 18:641–58.

U.S. General Accounting Office. 2003. *Older Workers: Policies of Other Nations to Increase Labor Force Participation*. Report to the Ranking Minority Member, Special Committee on Aging. Washington, DC.

Van Gerven, P. W. M., Paas, F., Van Merrienboer, J. G. V., Hendriks, M., and Schmidt, H. G. 2003. The efficiency of multimedia learning into old age. *British Journal of Education Psychology* 73:498–505.

Willis, S. 2004. Technology and learning in current and future elder cohorts. In *Technology for Adaptive Aging*, ed. R. W. Pew and S. B. Van Hemel, 209–29. Washington, DC: National Academies Press.

Yeatts, D. E., Folts, W. E., and Knapp, J. 1999. Older workers adaptation to a changing workplace: Employment issues for the 21st century. *Educational Gerontology* 25:331–47.

CHAPTER FOURTEEN

Age and Performance Measures of Knowledge-Based Work

A Cognitive Perspective

PAMELA S. TSANG, PH.D.

This chapter examines the extent to which an aging workforce may be expected to meet the demands of today's knowledge-based jobs from a cognitive perspective. Prior job experience, cognitive plasticity of the individual, and the role of technology are likely to have a significant impact on the issue. Performance-assessment strategies needed to better assess the potential of older workers to contribute to the workforce are discussed.

AGING AND WORK PERFORMANCE

A common perception of the relationship between age and work performance is that of an inverted U-shaped function whereby performance increases with age and experience, peaks at some point, and then declines. In fact, the relationship has been found to take on many forms (Czaja, 2001). Rhodes's (1983) review found a positive, a negative, a null, and a U-shaped relationship between age and performance in approximately equal numbers of studies. Several meta-analyses revealed no relationship (Waldman and Avolio, 1986; McEvoy and Cascio, 1989), an inverted U-shaped relationship (Sturman, 2003), and a plateauing relationship (Avolio, Waldman, and McDaniel, 1990). It is now recognized that the relationship can be mediated by a host of factors. Four major mediators are described below.

How Old Is Old?

Workers of a wide range of ages have been included as "older" workers in different studies. However, different jobs have different cognitive demands, and different cognitive functions exhibit different age-related changes. For instance, many fighter pilots retire in their 40s, and air traffic controllers are required to retire at age 56; yet U.S. Supreme Court justices may serve into their 90s. Importantly, individual differences in age-related cognitive changes increase with age (e.g., Czaja, 1990; Rabbitt, 1993b; Birren and Schroots, 1996; Tsang and Voss, 1996). Grouping people of ages that could span several decades as "older" workers is likely to obfuscate the true relationship between age and work performance (Czaja and Moen, 2004).

Age and Experience Confounds

Not surprisingly, job experience and job knowledge have been found to account for significant variance in work performance (e.g., Hunter, 1986; Schmidt, Hunter, and Outerbridge, 1986; Murphy, 1989). Because job experience tends to accumulate with age, the age and job experience confound is practically unavoidable. However, the strength of the association between these two variables may not be linear and has been shown to be affected by the nature of the job demands (e.g., Sparrow and Davies, 1988; Murphy, 1989). The need to account for the interactive effects of age and experience is discussed in greater detail below (see also Murrell and Humphries, 1978; Dollinger and Hoyer, 1996; Charness, 2000).

The Nature of Job Demands

Sturman (2003) estimated job complexity based on a variation of the scale provided in the *Dictionary of Occupational Titles* (U.S. Department of Labor, 1991) and found an inverted U-shaped relationship between age and work performance only for low-complexity jobs. Sparrow and Davies (1988) noted that performance of higher complexity peaks at a more advanced age. Warr (1994) found a positive relationship between age and performance for knowledge-based jobs and a negative one for jobs that required speeded responses, but noted that most jobs have a mixture of both types of demands. Waldman and Avolio (1986) found the relationship to be more positive or less negative for professional than for nonprofessional jobs.

In all of these reviews, the nature of the job demands was considered only at a rather general level. For example, McEvoy and Cascio (1989) did not find the dichotomy of professional and nonprofessional jobs to moderate the relationship. Their professionals included engineers, scientists, managers, supervisors, and nurses. But air traffic controllers (whose job is cognitively demanding in intensive and dynamic ways) were grouped with blue-collar and sales jobs. Even graded levels of job complexity may not be sufficiently diagnostic, because different jobs can pose qualitatively different cognitive demands on the worker. It is argued below that a more fine-grained distinction of the type and intensity of job demands would provide a more useful basis for understanding the relationship between age and performance.

Measures of Work Performance

Three types of performance measures are commonly used. One is *operational performance,* such as some measure of productivity. Although operational performance would appear to be the most direct measure, it is often difficult to identify the appropriate performance variables that would provide an overall evaluation. For example, the number of publications produced by scientists does not inform about the quality or impact of the work. Another measure of operational performance is supervisory ratings, which are meant to provide an overall evaluation but could be influenced by personal biases and may be difficult to analyze quantitatively (Waldman and Avolio, 1986).

A second type of measure is *operational errors or accidents* (Kay et al., 1994; Broach and Schroeder, 2006). Accidents tend to be rare and do not lend themselves well to statistical analysis. Accident rates might be estimated differently (e.g., number of accidents per total annual flight hours or per number of takeoffs and landings) and might be based on different time spans or demarcations of age groups, making comparisons across studies or jobs difficult. Importantly, accidents tend to have multiple causes (Reason, 1990; Perrow, 1999), complicating the establishment of a causal relationship with age.

A third type of measure is *cognitive ability assessed by psychometric tests of intelligence* such as the General Aptitude Test Battery (GATB) and the Wechsler Adult Intelligence Scale-Revised (WAIS-R) or simple laboratory tasks designed to tap an isolated cognitive process (e.g., short-term memory). According to some, cognitive ability is the best predictor and correlate of work performance (Hunter and Hunter, 1984; Schmidt, 2002). Consequently, if cognitive ability tends to decline with increased age (Salthouse, 1991), one might expect a negative relationship between age and work performance. As noted above, this is by no means a uni-

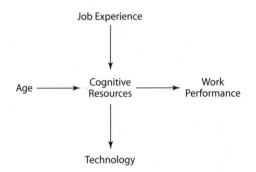

Figure 14.1. A cognitive resource model portraying the major determinants of the relationship between age and work performance

versal finding. And as discussed below, this could be because measures of cognitive abilities do not capture the contextual elements of work that might enable older workers to compensate for age-related cognitive declines with job knowledge or experience.

In short, the relationship between age and work performance is complex and is a product of a multitude of variables. Different measures may inform about different aspects of the performance. To better understand the relationship between age and work performance, a conceptual model for organizing the major variables affecting the relationship is presented in figure 14.1. Because technology will continue to play a significant role in determining the nature of the job demands, its impact on today's jobs will be considered first.

THE IMPACT OF TECHNOLOGY

Large-scale technological changes are permeating the workplace at an unprecedented pace. For example, airplane cockpits have evolved from having no instruments to having multipurpose displays and controls filling up an expansive cockpit panel. The pilot's role as a supervisory controller (monitoring and managing a multitude of automated systems) has greatly increased, whereas that of a manual controller has greatly diminished, significantly changing the nature of the job demands. More generally, computer technology has changed the process of data gathering, computing, visualizing, and communicating. There appears to be no escape from computer technology, whether one is a biochemist, an accountant, or a landscape architect.

Might older workers be disadvantaged with these sweeping technological changes? Might painstakingly acquired skills become obsolete, and would older workers have the capacity to acquire new ones? Technology does not have a categorically positive or negative impact on the relationship between age and work performance. Its impact must be considered at a finer level, distinguishing between the effect of the interface and the functionality of the technology, since they are likely to affect age-related changes differently.

Interface with Technology

Technology designed to amplify cognition or to reduce cognitive demands will benefit users only to the extent that they can interface with the technology effectively. For instance, the increased communication capability afforded by a portable cell phone certainly has the potential to increase work efficiency. However, cramped, poorly designed menus on a small display panel and fashionably small interface buttons may render the phone less useable, especially by older workers. The true impact of any technology simply cannot be determined if many of its intended functions cannot be realized as a result of a poorly designed interface.

Many interface issues directly affect the sensory and motor control processes that are particularly sensitive to age-related changes. To the extent that the quality of the input is diminished (e.g., reduced font size to conserve display space) and execution of the output is impeded (e.g., tiny buttons), cognitive demands will be affected as well. While outside the focus of this chapter, there exist extensive reviews on age-related changes in sensory and motor control processing (e.g., Schieber, 2003; Kline, 2003; Ketcham and Stelmach, 2004). In addition, a substantial body of work on human-computer interface issues has yielded many technological solutions (such as increasing the signal to noise ratio or using alternative input devices) that could address specific age-related sensory and motor control needs. Unfortunately, they have not been systematically implemented in many of today's technologies (Czaja and Lee, 2002; Fozard, 2003; Scialfa and Fernie, 2006).

The Functionality of Technology

The vision that technology could amplify cognition or lessen the cognitive demands of work has been put forth since the early days of computer technology (Bush, 1945; Licklider, 1960; Engelbart, 1963). Indeed, many of today's jobs, such as controlling a process control plant, would be impossible without computerized automation, but technology designed to enhance system capability could also add to the work demands. For example, based on his own flight career that spanned the Douglas DC-2 through the Boeing 747, Buck (1995) outlined the increasing effort needed to monitor and control the aircraft as a result of increased requirements for capability and safety. It is now recognized that automation often redistributes rather than reduces cognitive task demands (Wiener and Curry, 1980). No single function could describe the many potential impacts of technology work performance.

An organizing framework provided by Salomon and Perkins (2005) could be helpful here. They distinguished among the *effects with, effects of,* and *effects through* technology. Effects *with* technology are concerned with whether the use of technology enhances performance. Effects *of* technology are concerned with whether having used the technology enhances performance, even in the absence of the technology. Effects *through* technology are concerned with how technology fundamentally changes the way a task is performed and thought about.

Effects *with* technology emerge when there is a division of labor between the technological tool and the user. Technology could enhance performance to the extent that the user is free from "the distractions of lower-level cognitive functions or ones that simply exceed mental capacity" (Salomon and Perkins, 2005, 74). To the extent that the technology supports cognition, for example, by providing tools to compute complex flight status information or to integrate financial data, there is no basis to expect technology to affect older workers negatively.

Effects *of* technology are effects that persist after a period of using the technology. For example, practice of computer programming could enhance the user's reasoning skills that could be generalized to support other cognitively complex tasks (Salomon and Perkins, 2005). To the extent that the older workers have not lost the ability to learn and are not memory-impaired, they should be able to benefit from the effects of technology as much as the younger workers.

It is also important to consider potential confluence of the effects with and effects of technology. For instance, although the *effect with* automation (resulting in a division of labor) can lead to a reduction of cognitive demands, a possible companion *effect of* automation is the out-of-the-loop phenomenon (Wickens and Kessel, 1979; Moray, 1986; Billings, 1997). An operator used to relying on the automation may have difficulty reentering the control loop in case of an automation failure. The necessary skill may not have been practiced, or the necessary knowledge or situation awareness may not be present. Those who have worked only with the newer automated system might not have developed an understanding of the workings of the system. By contrast, the experience of the older workers who have had opportunities to operate the less-automated version of the system might help avert an adverse effect of automation.

Technology can sometimes fundamentally change how a task is performed. An example of an effect *through* technology is the flexibility afforded by Internet access, enabling new project possibilities performed by a geographically distributed team. There is little reason to expect that geographical flexibility would affect older workers more negatively than younger workers. In fact, older workers might welcome the reduced need to travel. However, these types of advantages can be realized only if an individual has the requisite skills to interact with the technical systems.

Age, Expertise, and Technology

Workers of different ages would have different degrees of exposure to the various technologies, resulting in their being affected differently by the technologies. Furthermore, an experienced worker may be better able to take advantage of certain technologies than a less-experienced one. For example, the copying and deleting functions of a word processor might help one to produce a document faster. In addition, a professional writer could make use of the ease of moving large chunks of texts back and forth to help organize thoughts. It should be clear by now that technology could affect the relationship between age and work performance at many levels. First, the effect of the interface with technology needs to be distinguished from the effect of the functionality of the technology. Second, the impact of technology may not be apparent immediately. Effects *with* technology would emerge relatively quickly, whereas effects *of* and effects *through* technology would develop over time (Salomon and Perkins, 2005). For instance, while the speed of spreadsheet data entry (effect with the new software) can be measured at the end of a training session, whether the spreadsheet helped to produce a better understanding of the financial situation (effect of) and thereby helped to instigate new ways of gathering financial data (effect through) may not be evident until much later. Consequently, using only immediately available measures may not reveal the full impact of the technology.

The next section sketches a conceptual model that serves as an overarching framework for considering the interplay of the major determinants of work performance: age, job experience, and technological implementations.

COGNITIVE AGING AND KNOWLEDGE-BASED PERFORMANCE

Age-related changes in cognitive functioning as opposed to changes in sensory and motor functioning play an especially important role in knowledge-based and technology-based performance. A better understanding of these changes not only would promote better predictions of performance but also would suggest ways of both accommodating and capitalizing on them.

Cognitive Processing Resources and Performance

Figure 14.1 portrays cognitive processing resources as the primary determinant of work performance. Cognitive resources have been conceptualized in a number of ways by different researchers. They have been referred to as cognitive ability (e.g., Schmidt, 2002), as crystallized and fluid intelligence (e.g., Beier and Ackerman, 2005), or as working memory resources (e.g., Salthouse, 1990). These conceptualizations and their associated measures are too narrowly defined to adequately account for complex work performance. For example, cognitive ability or intelligence, as assessed by psychometric tests or simple laboratory tasks, generally does not correlate well with high-level performance exhibited by experienced workers (Welford, 1986; Krampe and Ericsson, 1996; Tsang and Shaner, 1998). Complex jobs are likely to tap into both crystallized and fluid intelligence. Measures of these jobs are likely to reveal an ambiguous relationship between age and performance because fluid intelligence tends to decline with age, whereas crystallized intelligence does not (Salthouse, 1991). Last, although working memory is certainly essential for almost all complex performance, other processes such as visualizing, computing, deciding, and responding are undoubtedly involved as well (Kramer, Larish, and Strayer, 1995).

In this chapter, cognitive resources are more broadly conceptualized as *attentional processing resources* used to fuel all task processing. Performance improves monotonically with an increasing amount of resources invested in processing (Norman and Bobrow, 1975). Performance falters when task demands are not met by a sufficient supply of resources. Although attentional resources are limited, they can be modulated dynamically in graded amounts to meet task demands (Kahneman, 1973). Evidence of such modulation has been documented in both behavioral and neurophysiological data. Performance of multiple tasks has been observed to trade off as the relative demands or task priorities change (e.g., Gopher, 1993; Tsang, 2006). In addition to the activation of the various cortical regions that appear to be somewhat process specific, recent data reveal graded levels of neuronal activation as well as varying volumes of cortical region involvement as a function of task demand (Wickens, Kramer, Vanasse, and Donchin, 1983; Corbetta et al., 1990; D'Esposito, Zarahn, and Aguire, 1999; Just, Carpenter, and Miyake, 2003).

Age, Expertise, and Cognitive Processing

Particularly pertinent to the present discussion is that the *efficiency of the process-ing resources* can be modulated by both endogenous (age and skill levels) and ex-ogenous (e.g., technological support) variables. Processing efficiency has been hypothesized to be reduced with increased age (e.g., Tsang and Shaner, 1998) but increased with increased skill or experience. Expertise therefore has the potential to counteract some of the age-related effects (figure 14.1).

Although the age-related reduced efficiency hypothesis could account easily for many age-related slowing effects (Salthouse, 1991), it accounts best for difficulties associated with the higher-order cognitive functions such as those requiring dy-namic resource allocation among multiple tasks. Parallel to the empirical support from behavioral data (e.g., Kramer et al., 1995; Tsang and Shaner, 1998; Kramer, Larish, Weber, and Bardell, 1999) are neuroimaging data that reveal disproportion-ately large correlations between age and the cortical volume of the prefrontal re-gion relative to other more process-specific regions (see Kramer et al., 2004).

The increased processing efficiency associated with expertise has had consid-erable support as well. Expertise is postulated to be largely acquired through ex-tensive *deliberate practice* (Chi, Glaser, and Farr, 1988; Ericsson, 1996). Not only do experts posses a large body of domain-specific declarative (factual) and proce-dural (how-to) knowledge, but their knowledge is highly organized. This enables them to readily see meaningful patterns, frame problems, constrain search, an-ticipate future events, retrieve the appropriate course of action from memory, and respond swiftly (Glaser, 1987; Charness, 1995).

Experts also have highly developed strategies that could circumvent certain normal processing limits. For example, Ericsson and Kintsch (1995) proposed that a defining feature of advanced skill is the development of a long-term work-ing memory (LTWM) that has larger capacity and persists longer than the se-verely limited working memory. The LTWM enables experts to relate a large amount of information to their highly structured knowledge in long-term mem-ory and to devise retrieval cues for eventual access to the information (Chase and Ericsson, 1982; Horn and Masunaga, 2000). For instance, Ericsson and Kintsch (1995) reasoned that effective medical diagnosis would require a retrieval struc-ture in long-term memory that would foster accurate encoding of a large amount of patient information. Indeed, they found medical experts to be better able to re-call pertinent information at a higher conceptual level and to produce more effec-tive diagnoses than novices (see also Norman, Brooks, and Allen, 1989; Patel and Groen, 1991). Furthermore, experts have metacognitive capabilities of knowing what one knows and does not know (Druckman and Bjork, 1991). These capabilities in turn allow them to plan and to apportion their resources more effectively (Glaser, 1987). Importantly, expert-level performance has to be actively maintained through continual practice (Krampe and Charness, 2006).

The nature of expertise has important implications in the workplace. Because job expertise is a result of continual, deliberate effort to improve one's skill, it does not emerge merely as a function of the duration of job tenure. Performance is mediated by training and efforts to improve, but can training benefit older workers? Can they adapt to a workplace that is constantly shaped by technological innovations? Does cognitive plasticity extend into adulthood?

Cognitive Plasticity during Aging

A critical review provided by Kramer et al. (2004) shows that formal education received in one's early formative years (Capitani, Barbarotto and Laiacona, 1996), laboratory task training during adulthood (Schaie and Willis, 1986; Scialfa, Jenkins, Hamaluk, and Skaloud, 2000), professional experience (Sparrow and Davies, 1988; Schooler, Mulatu, and Oates, 1999), and engagement in cognitively challenging leisure activities (Hultsch, Hammer, and Small, 1993; Schooler and Mulatu, 2001; Newson and Kemps, 2006) all could affect the cognitive performance of older adults. These findings are encouraging to the extent that higher cognitive performance could translate to greater potential for an ability to acquire new skills and to benefit from training, thereby maintaining work performance at a high level.

Training

It is not surprising that training has been found to benefit older adults. However, it is noteworthy that older adults have been observed to improve on a variety of tasks (e.g., Kliegl, Smith, and Baltes, 1989; Willis and Nesselroade, 1990; Beier and Ackerman, 2005), to retain newly acquired skills for a long period of time (Saczynski, Willis, and Schaie, 2002), and even to reverse certain cognitive declines (Schaie and Willis, 1986) with relatively little training. To illustrate, three sample studies will be described.

In Rabbitt's (1993a) study, both younger (aged 50–64) and older (aged 65–80) subjects continued to improve on a visual search task for 36 sessions. The average age difference was 94 ms and the average practice effect of 232 ms; the practiced older subjects were faster than the unpracticed younger subjects. In Schaie and Willis's (1986) study, a group of subjects between the ages of 65 and 95 from the Seattle Longitudinal Study received five hours of training on either an inductive reasoning task or a spatial orientation task. Training reversed the cognitive decline that had been demonstrated reliably over a 14-year period for a subset of the subjects and enhanced the performance of those subjects whose cognitive performance had remained stable over the same period. In a study by Ball et al. (2002), 2,832 adults between the ages of 65 and 94 were included in a randomized controlled trial. Subjects received ten sessions of group training for verbal episodic memory, inductive reasoning, and speed processing in a divided attention task. Training produced immediate performance improvements that were maintained for the two-year period of the study. Results from these studies demonstrate how a relatively small amount of training could overshadow the age effects and are a strong testament to cognitive plasticity during aging.

Limitations of training benefits to older adults also have been observed, however. Studies have reported reduced magnitude of learning (Kliegl et al., 1989; Yang, Krampe, and Baltes, 2006), slower learning rates (Elias, Elias, Robbins, and Gage, 1987; Gist, Rosen, and Schwoerer, 1988; Kubeck, Delp, Haslett, and McDaniel, 1996), and failure to reduce the age difference after training (Hertzog, Williams, and Walsh, 1976; Peretti, Danion, Gierski, and Grange, 2002).

Two approaches have been effective in minimizing these limitations: a modest amount of additional training, and a training strategy that targets a cognitive function that has shown relatively large declines. For example, Shooter, Schonfield, King, and Welford (1956) examined the amount of retraining needed for ex-tram drivers between the ages of 20 and 70 to become bus drivers. The percentage of drivers who passed the retraining in three weeks declined with age; however, with six weeks or less of additional training, more than 75 percent of the older drivers (aged 61 to 67) were successfully retrained. In another study, Baron and Mattila (1989) targeted the ubiquitously observed age-related slowing by using a deadline training procedure with a memory search task. Subjects were required to constantly increase the response speed. After training, the response time difference between the younger and older groups was greatly reduced, and the two groups were equally accurate. Last, Kramer et al. (1995) and Kramer et al. (1999) targeted the age-related difficulty in flexibly allocating processing resources among multiple tasks. A variable-priority training procedure successfully reduced the age-related differences.

Professional Experience

Cognitive plasticity is also evident in the workplace. Older workers have been shown to be able to maintain a high level of performance with training and to adapt to technological changes (see Buck, 1995). In a study of service engineers between ages 25 and 55, Sparrow and Davies (1988) found that the only older engineers who performed below average were those who had not had training within the last five years. Friedberg (2003) observed that 51 percent of workers in their 50s in 1997, who were unlikely to have used a computer in college, used a computer. Friedberg also found computer skills obsolescence associated with technological changes to be related to the temporal proximity to retirement and not age. Bartel and Sicherman (1993) noted that workers in industries with a higher rate of technological changes tend to retire later, but a rapid rate of or unexpected technological change could induce earlier retirement. This suggests that older workers may be more willing to adapt to changes if given sufficient time to make the transition and opportunity to reap the benefits from the effort.

Another line of evidence for cognitive plasticity in the workplace is the effect of the mental work demand. Contradicting intuition and certain laboratory findings, both cross-sectional (e.g., Miller, Slomczynski, and Kohn, 1987) and longitudinal (e.g., Schooler et al., 1999) studies have reported that a higher degree of job complexity tends to be associated with less age-related cognitive decline. The complexity effect has been found to be greater for older workers (Schooler et al., 1999) and to hold for both the poorly and highly educated workers (Bosma, van Boxtel, Houx, and Jolles, 2003). Sturman (2003) even found a positive relationship between age and job performance for the more complex jobs. Schooler et al. (1999) proposed that workers might be motivated to develop their intellectual capacities to the degree that complex environments reward cognitive effort.

The present review shows that cognitive functioning is malleable beyond the early formative years. Furthermore, nonoptimal work performance can be a reflection of inadequate training, learning opportunities, or cognitive stimulation in the workplace as much as, or rather than, a reflection of cognitive decline. To better reveal the relationship between age and work performance, assessment approaches that take into account the limits and potential of cognitive plasticity during aging need to be used.

METHODOLOGICAL STRATEGIES TO A BETTER UNDERSTANDING OF AGING AND WORK PERFORMANCE

As figure 14.1 illustrates, age is only one of several determinants of performance. Therefore, it is not surprising that age by itself informs little. Recall that graded amounts of cognitive processing resources are needed for all information processing. Whereas aging may be associated with reduced processing efficiency, expertise is hypothesized to be associated with increased efficiency. As an analogy, the capacity of the fuel tank of an automobile is fixed and older engines may run less efficiently, but fuel efficiency could be enhanced by tactical maneuvers and strategic planning. An experienced driver with thorough route knowledge and the associated constraints could drive at a slower speed and still accomplish the mission in time by taking shortcuts and arranging stops to minimize distance. Technological innovations could affect efficiency further still. Automatic transmission lessens the demand for cognitive processing resources; talking on the cell phone has the opposite effect.

This section describes two approaches to assessing work performance that can better capture the confluence of cognitive aging, experience, and technology on work performance. First, potential limitations of some of the more traditional measures will be considered briefly.

Limitations of Traditional Measures

Many of the traditional measures would not be able to capture the confluence of the major determinants of performance in today's work environments. For example, expert-level performance is attained and sustained through deliberate practice. Experts do not necessarily possess exceptional intelligence or ability such as an extraordinarily large memory span. Psychometric measures therefore do not account well for expert-level functioning (e.g., Tsang and Shaner, 1998). Furthermore, experts use highly developed strategies to circumvent certain basic cognitive limits (e.g., LTWM), to accommodate certain age-related changes or to adapt to technological changes (e.g., Szafran, 1968). Therefore, simple laboratory tasks designed to tap an isolated elemental process in a contextually impoverished task environment are unlikely to elicit the true level of work performance (Welford, 1986).

Another common measure is job knowledge. The usefulness of this measure hinges highly on the construct of job knowledge. Factual knowledge is relatively easy to assess, but expert-level performance operates not only on factual knowledge but also on the knowledge of how to use the knowledge. For instance, knowing the laws well does not make one a good lawyer. Factual job knowledge by itself would not reveal the potential of an experienced worker.

Two other approaches to work assessment that would better reflect the confluence of the effects of age, experience, and technological changes are proposed to supplement the more traditional measures: domain-representative componential measures and global measures.

Domain-Representative Measures of Knowledge-Based Work

To better account for the advantage of experience, Kliegl and Baltes (1987), Ericsson and Charness (1997), and Horn and Masunaga (2000) advocate that expert-level performance be assessed in an environment that provides opportunities to use expertise. Ericsson and Charness reasoned that if superior performance was supported by circumventing domain-specific constraints, then representative tasks that incorporate these constraints need to be present for the natural performance of an experienced worker to be observed. The main challenge, of course, is to be able to identify the appropriate domain-representative tasks for evaluation. One approach is through a job analysis that focuses on the cognitive demands of the job (McFarland, 1973; Avolio, Barrett, and Sterns, 1984). Approaches that merely document the proportion of time that one is physically "busy," such as the time-line analysis method, would be woefully inadequate for knowledge-based performance (Sarno and Wickens, 1995). When identifying domain-representative tasks, the objective should not be physical realism but cognitive realism. This is because the cost of high physical fidelity could be exorbitant, the process of validating the simulation fidelity is equivocal, and the benefits are often dubious. Adams (1979) therefore advocates the reliance on sound psychological principles for determining whether the essential elements have been captured. For example, as elements deemed critical to the operational environment are increasingly incorporated, differentials between experts and novices should increase (Tsang, 2007), correlation with actual or simulator performance should increase (Taylor et al., 1994; Yesavage, Dolhert, and Taylor, 1994), and task performance should be predictive of operational success (Kahneman, Ben-Ishai, and Lotan, 1973; Gopher, 1982). These expectations are based on the principle that expertise is domain-specific, a principle that has had considerable empirical support from a variety of domains.

To illustrate, Gopher (1993) demonstrated that physical fidelity is not essential for positive transfer from laboratory task training to operational pilot performance. Gopher provided differential training to three groups of Israeli Air Force flight cadets. The training task was a computer game (Space Fortress) that contained multiple dynamic components identified to require attentional management skills similar to those required of a pilot. One group received training on game-specific strategies (e.g., how to control the spaceship). Another group received training on general attentional control strategies. And the third group received no strategy training. After ten hours of game practice and upon completing jet training, flight performance of the two groups that received strategy training was superior to that of the control group, demonstrating the training utility of a computer game that bore no physical resemblance to the operational task.

Global Measures

Another approach forgoes a certain degree of precision afforded by task-specific performance in exchange for more global information afforded by measures like supervisory ratings. Two other global measures that are especially suited for complex, dynamic job situations are *mental workload* and *situation awareness*. An array of performance, subjective, physiological, and analytical methods have been devised to assess these measures and comprehensive reviews are readily available in the literature (Gopher, 1994; Gawron, 2000; Vidulich, 2003; Tsang and Vidulich, 2006). This chapter focuses on the conceptual underpinnings of these measures.

Mental workload is determined by exogenous task demands such as task difficulty and task priority. It is also affected by the endogenous supply of cognitive resources for supporting information processing. As noted above, the processing efficiency of this supply can be modulated by one's age and skill level. The higher the degree of efficiency with which one works, the larger the effective resource supply or spare resource one has, the lower the workload one experiences. For example, Haier et al. (1992) found that weeks of practice with the computer game Tetris led to improved performance and reduced amount of neuronal activity as measured by positron emission tomography. Just et al. (2003) proposed that practice improved the subjects' procedural knowledge and the more efficient procedure exacted a lower level of resource.

Endsley (1990) provided a commonly adopted definition of situation awareness (SA): "the perception of the elements in the environment within a volume of time and space, the comprehension of their meaning, and the projection of their status in the near future" (1–3). The quality of SA is shaped by exogenous factors like situation complexity and uncertainty, and endogenous factors like knowledge and experience.

There is an intricate interplay between mental workload and SA. The more demanding the task and the more complex the situation, the more mental work is required to perform the task and to assess the situation. Good SA would enable more effective management of the various competing demands for processing resources. Technological implementations could reduce or add to the exogenous demands, leading to lower or higher mental workload, respectively. The development of expertise would improve processing efficiency and promote SA, potentially counteracting the reduced efficiency associated with aging. For example,

Tsang and Shaner (1994) had subjects perform a set of dual-tasks with varying task difficulties and priorities. Older nonpilots reported experiencing higher workload than younger nonpilots; experienced pilots (skilled at time-sharing multiple tasks) reported experiencing lower workload than less-experienced pilots. In another study, Pérès et al. (2000) had expert (with 3,000 flight hours and flight instructor qualifications) and novice French Air Force pilots fly a simulated flight at two speeds. Functional magnetic resonance imaging data showed dominant neuronal activation in the right hemisphere as would be expected for a visual spatial task. Novices exhibited more intense and more extensive activation than experts. At the high-speed (high workload) condition, the experts exhibited increased activation in the frontal and prefrontal cortical areas and reduced activity in visual and motor regions, suggesting that they were better able to focus their resources for the higher-level functions such as planning and attentional management. In contrast, novice pilots appeared to be engaged in nonspecific perceptual processing. (See also Bellenkes, Wickens, and Kramer, 1997.)

Other Methodological Considerations
Generalizability

The quest for establishing a single relationship between age and work performance on which reliable predictions could be made across work domains has not proven to be fruitful. The present review shows that a finer level of analysis with better-defined boundary conditions is needed. For example, the concerns for extending the professional years of healthy individuals in the workforce of knowledge-based jobs would be quite different from those of extending the professional years of soccer players. Furthermore, expertise is highly domain specific, and experienced workers do not work the same way that novices do. Several researchers have urged caution in extrapolating laboratory findings from the general population to operational competence in specific jobs (Hunt and Hertzog, 1981; Schaie, 1988; Welford, 1986; Birren and Fisher, 1995).

Performance Baseline

Currently, the bulk of the research focuses on establishing the extent of performance degradation of older subjects relative to the performance of younger subjects. For example, response time of older subjects is constantly compared to that of younger subjects. There is, however, little research on establishing the extent of performance deficiency of younger subjects relative to the performance of older subjects. Bisseret (1981) had older experienced air traffic controllers and younger inexperienced controllers perform a simulated task that required them to decide whether two aircraft would collide. Although the less experienced controllers were more sensitive to the physical separation between two aircraft, the more experienced controllers were more cautious in their decisions. Given the disastrous cost of a miss in this situation, the cautious bias is what the younger controllers should emulate. The focus should not be that the older controllers were less precise, because this particular aspect of performance is not vital for outcome success. If the minimum separation is 100 feet, knowing that there is only 90 feet of separation instead of 95 feet should not alter the collision decision. (See also Szafran, 1968.)

Another consideration is whether the peak or the satisfactory level of performance (see figure 14.1) should be the criterion against which relative decline is evaluated. Certainly, not all workers in a workplace, regardless of their age, perform at the maximum level at all times. Equating less than maximum to an unsatisfactory level of performance is likely to generate a miss rate (i.e., losing an older competent worker) so high as to be counterproductive.

Operational Significance

Statistically significant differences obtained under highly controlled laboratory conditions do not necessarily translate to operationally significant differences. For example, the reaction speediness to a simple stimulus would not make any detectable difference in most jobs. Importantly, a negative correlation between age and performance or a significant difference in the amount of training time needed between age groups by itself may not reveal the operational effect on work (Welford, 1986). Suppose a younger group requires one hour of training, whereas an older group requires two hours to produce a similar level of performance. Even though the older group requires twice the amount of training time, it amounts to only one additional hour of training. It is paramount that the cost of additional training be weighed against the cost of losing the experience of a worker that has taken years, if not decades, to build.

RESEARCH DIRECTIONS

In addition to the need for continued research on the basic processes of cognitive aging, several other research foci are needed. First, there is currently a paucity of operational performance data on which one could formulate hypotheses about aging and work performance (see Broadbent, 1971; Wickens, 2007). Few comprehensive job analyses of present-day jobs exist. Much work is needed in this effort to facilitate the identifying of domain-representative tasks for performance evaluations. Complex systems in which many of today's jobs are embedded will tap multiple cognitive functions and higher-order functions. These functions need to be assessed along with the overall level of performance (Welford, 1976; Avolio et al., 1984; Birren and Fisher, 1995). Two types of global measure have been described in this chapter, but additional approaches should be explored and specific assessment techniques will need continued development and validations.

Second, although there is ample evidence to show that cognitive plasticity continues into advanced age, certain training strategies are more effective for older adults. Only a few of these strategies have been identified and tested so far. Not only is research needed for identifying and developing training principles and methodologies that are better suited for older adults, but there also need to be opportunities in the workplace for practicing and validating these developments.

Third, there is little basis for assuming that older workers are necessarily disadvantaged by technological innovations. More concerted effort is needed to implement human-computer interface principles to better accommodate age-related changes in sensory and cognitive functioning. Much effort is also needed to exploit technological advances to support age-related changes and to incorporate these considerations early in the design of technological innovations (Graafmans and Taipale, 1998).

CONCLUSION

This chapter has identified several factors to account for the varied relationships between age and work performance reported in the literature. Central to the organizing framework presented in figure 14.1 is the efficiency of cognitive processing resources that mediates the confluence of the effects of age, job experience, and the impact of technology on performance. Increased processing efficiency associated with increased expertise or afforded by technological support could potentially ameliorate some of the reduced processing efficiency associated with increased age. Considering any one of these factors in isolation is unlikely to reveal the full picture.

This review shows that there is little basis for many of the presumed myths about aging. Supposedly ubiquitous cognitive declines such as processing speed and fluid intelligence are not always evident (Schaie and Gribben, 1975). Work performance does not inevitably decline with age. Older workers have not been found to universally reject or to be unable to adapt to technological changes. Although age-related effects certainly have been observed, they have not been shown to be nearly as incontrovertible as once believed. There is mounting evidence that older adults can continue to benefit from training. However, job expertise is subject to the availability of learning opportunities and to one's effort to improve. Importantly, assessment of training effectiveness should be criterion-based rather than time-based. Certain training strategies work better for older workers than others, and older workers may require additional training time. Because the effect of technology may not always be immediately evident, initial success or difficulties may not reveal the full impact.

Lastly, measures that do not take into account the advantage of experience, the benefits of training, and the potential support afforded by technology are likely to underestimate the potential of older workers contributing to the workforce. The methodological strategy advocated here is to supplement global measures with multiple domain-representative measures to be assessed in a contextually rich task environment. Operational performance data and job analyses needed to support this approach would require extra-laboratory efforts that would necessitate the collaboration of researchers and operational personnel. These undertakings are likely to require considerable resources in time, labor, and equipment and would be in need of financial support atypical of most basic laboratory research. Institutional and government recognition of, support for, and commitment to the necessary resources are crucial for the success of the approach.

ACKNOWLEDGMENTS

I would like to acknowledge the support from the National Institute of Aging, Grant AG 08589. I would also like to thank Michael Vidulich and the editors for their helpful comments.

REFERENCES

Adams, J. A. 1979. On the evaluation of training devices. *Human Factors* 21:711–20.

Avolio, B. J., Barrett, G. V., and Sterns, H. L. 1984. Alternatives to age for assessing occupational performance capacity. *Experimental Aging Research* 10:101–5.

Avolio, B. J., Waldman, D. A., and McDaniel, M. A. 1990. Age and work performance in nonmanagerial jobs: The effects of experience and occupational type. *Academy of Management Journal* 33:407–22.

Ball, K., Berch, D. B., Helmers, K. F., Jobe, J. B., Leveck, M. D., and Marisiske, M. 2002. Effects of cognitive training interventions with older adults: A randomized controlled trial. *Journal of the American Medical Association* 288:2271–81.

Baron, A., and Mattila, W. R. 1989. Response slowing of older adults: Effects of time-contingencies on single and dual-task performances. *Psychology and Aging* 4:66–72.

Bartel, A., and Sicherman, N. 1993. Technological change and retirement decisions of older workers. *Journal of Labor Economics* 11:162–83.

Beier, M. E., and Ackerman, P. L. 2005. Age, ability, and the role of prior knowledge on the acquisition of new domain knowledge: Promising results in a real-world learning environment. *Psychology and Aging* 20:341–55.

Bellenkes, A. H., Wickens, C. D., and Kramer, A. F. 1997. Visual scanning and pilot expertise: The role of attentional flexibility and mental model development. *Aviation, Space and Environmental Medicine* 68:569–79

Billings, C. E. 1997. *Aviation Automation: The search for a human-centered approach.* Mahwah, NJ: Erlbaum.

Birren, J. E., and Fisher, L. M. 1995. Rules and reason in the forced retirement of commercial airline pilots at age 60. *Ergonomics* 38:518–25.

Birren, J. E., and Schroots, J. J. F. 1996. History, concepts, and theory in the psychology of aging. In *Handbook of the Psychology of Aging*, 4th ed., ed. J. E. Birren and K. W. Schaie, 3–23. San Diego: Academic.

Bisseret, A. 1981. Application of signal detection theory to decision making in supervisory control: The effect of the operator's experience. *Ergonomics* 24:81–94.

Bosma, H., van Boxtel, M. P. J., Houx, P. J. H., and Jolles, J. 2003. Education and age-related cognitive decline: The contribution of mental workload. *Educational Gerontology* 29:165–73.

Broach, D., and Schroeder, D. J. 2006. Air traffic control specialist age and en route operational errors. *International Journal of Aviation Psychology* 16:363–73.

Broadbent, D. 1971. Relation between theory and application in psychology. In *Psychology at Work*, ed. P. B. Warr, 15–30. Harmondsworth, UK: Penguin.

Buck, R. N. 1995. *The Pilot's Burden: Flight Safety and the Roots of Pilot Error.* Ames: Iowa State University.

Bush, V. 1945. As we may think. *Atlantic Monthly*, July, 101–108.

Capitani, E., Barbarotto, R., and Laiacona, M. 1996. Does education influence the age-related cognitive decline? A further inquiry. *Developmental Neuropsychology* 12:231–40.

Charness, N. 1995. Expert performance and situation awareness. In *Experimental Analysis and Measurement of Situation Awareness*, ed. D. J. Garland and M. R. Endsley, 35–42. Daytona Beach, FL: Embry-Riddle Aeronautical University Press.

———. 2000. Can acquired knowledge compensate for age-related declines in cognitive efficiency? In *Psychology and the Aging Revolution: How We Adapt to Longer Life*, ed. S. H. Qualls and N. Abeles, 99–117. Washington, DC: American Psychological Association.

Chase, W. G., and Ericsson, K. A. 1982. Skill and working memory. In *The Psychology of Learning and Motivation*, Vol. 16, ed. G. H. Bower. New York: Academic.

Chi, M., Glaser, R., and Farr, M. Eds. 1988. *On the Nature of Expertise.* Hillsdale, NJ: Erlbaum.

Corbetta, M., Miezin, F. M., Dobmeyer, S., Shulman, G. L., and Petersen, S. E. 1990. Attentional modulation of neural processing of shape, color, and velocity in humans. *Science* 248:1556–59.

Czaja, S. J. 1990. *Human Factors Research Needs for an Aging Population.* Washington, DC: National Academy.

————. 2001. Technological change and the older worker. In *Handbook of the Psychology of Aging*, 5th ed., ed. J. E. Birren and K. W. Schaie, 547–68. San Diego: Academic Press.

Czaja, S. J., and Lee, C. C. 2002. Designing computer system for older adults. In *The Human-Computer Interaction Handbook*, ed. J. Jacko and A. Sears, 413–27. Mahwah, NJ: Erlbaum.

Czaja, S., J., and Moen, P. 2004. Technology and employment. In *Technology for Adaptive Aging*, ed. R. W. Pew and S. B. van Hemel, 150–78. Washington, DC: National Academies Press.

D'Esposito, M. Zarahn, E., and Aguire, G. K. 1999. Event-related functional MRI: Implications for cognitive psychology. *Psychological Bulletin* 125:155–64.

Dollinger, S. M. C., and Hoyer, W. J. 1996. Age and skill differences in the processing demands of visual inspection. *Applied Cognitive Psychology* 10:225–39.

Druckman, D., and Bjork, R. A., eds. 1991. *In the Mind's Eye: Enhancing Human Performance*, chapter 4. Washington, DC: National Academy.

Elias, P. K., Elias, M. F., Robbins, M. A., and Gage, P. 1987. Acquisition of word-processing skills by younger, middle-age, and older adults. *Psychology and Aging* 2:340–48.

Endsley, M. 1990. A methodology for the objective measurement of pilot situation awareness. In *Situation Awareness in Aerospace Operations* (AGARD-CP-478, pp. 1-1–1-9). Neuilly Sur Seine, France: AGARD.

Engelbart, D. C. 1963. A conceptual framework for the augmentation of man's intellect. In *Vistas in Information Handling*, Vol. 1, ed. P. W. Howerton and D. C. Weeks, 1–29. Washington, DC: Spartan Books.

Ericsson, K. A. 1996. The acquisition of expert performance: An introduction to some of the issues. In *The Road to Excellence*, ed. K. A. Ericsson, 1–50. Mahwah, NJ: Erlbaum.

Ericsson, K. A., and Charness, N. 1997. Cognitive and developmental factors in expert performance. In *Expertise in Context*, ed. P. J. Feltovich, K. M. Ford, and R. R. Hoffman, 3–41. Cambridge, MA: MIT.

Ericsson, K. A., and Kintsch, W. 1995. Long-term working memory. *Psychological Review* 105:211–45.

Fozard, J. L. 2003. Commentary: Using technology to lower the perceptual and cognitive hurdles of aging. In *Impact of Technology on Successful Aging*, ed. N. Charness and K. W. Schaie, 100–112. New York: Springer.

Friedberg, L. 2003. The impact of technological change on older workers: Evidence from data on computer use. *Industrial and Labor Relations Review* 56:511–29.

Gawron, V. J. 2000. *Human performance measures handbook*. Mahwah, NJ: Erlbaum.

Gist, M., Rosen, B., and Schwoerer, C. 1988. The influence of training method and trainee age on the acquisition of computer skills. *Personnel Psychology* 41:255–65.

Glaser, R. 1987. Thoughts on expertise. In *Cognitive Functioning and Social Structure over the Life Course*, ed. C. Schooler and K. W. Schaie, 81–94. Norwood, NJ: Ablex.

Gopher, D. 1982. A selective attention test as a predictor of success in flight training. *Human Factors* 24:173–84.

————. 1993. The skill of attention control: Acquisition and execution of attention strategies. In *Attention and Performance, XIV*, ed. D. Meyer and S. Kornblum, 299–322. Hillsdale, NJ: Erlbaum.

————. 1994. Analysis and measurement of mental load. In *International Perspectives on Psychological Science*, Vol. 2 of *The State of the Art*, ed. G. d'Ydewalle, P. Eelen, and P. Bertelson, 265–91. Hove, UK: Erlbaum.

Graafmans, J., and Taipale, V. 1998. Gerontechnology: A sustainable investment in the future. In *Gerontechnology: A Sustainable Investment in the Future*, ed. J. Graafmans, V. Taipale, and N. Charness, 3–6. Washington, DC: IOS Press.

Haier, R. J., Siegel, B., Tang, C., Abel, L., and Buchsbaum, M. 1992. Intelligence and changes in regional cerebral glucose metabolic rate following learning. *Intelligence* 16:415–26.

Hertzog, C. K., Williams, M. V., and Walsh, D. A. 1976. The effect of practice on age differences in central perceptual processing. *Journals of Gerontology* 48:12–17.

Horn, J. L., and Masunaga, H. 2000. New directions for research into aging and intelligence: The development of expertise. In *Models of Cognitive Aging*, ed. T. J. Perfect and E. A. Maylor, 125–59. New York: Oxford University.

Hultsch, D. F., Hammer, M., and Small, B. J. 1993. Age differences in cognitive performance in later life: Relationships to self-reported health and activity life style. *Journals of Gerontology* 48:1–11.

Hunt, E., and Hertzog, C. 1981. *Age Related Changes in Cognition During the Working Years* (Final Report). Seattle: University of Washington, Department of Psychology.

Hunter, J. E. 1986. Cognitive ability, cognitive aptitudes, job knowledge, and job performance. *Journal of Vocational Behavior* 29:340–62.

Hunter, J. E., and Hunter, R. F. 1984. Validity and utility of alternative predictors of job performance. *Psychological Bulletin* 96:72–98.

Just, M. A., Carpenter, P. A., and Miyake, A. 2003. Neuroindices of cognitive workload: Neuroimaging, pupillometric and event-related potential studies of brain work. *Theoretical Issues in Ergonomics Science* 4:56–88.

Kahneman, D. 1973. *Attention and Effort*. Englewood Cliffs, NJ: Prentice-Hall.

Kahneman, D., Ben-Ishai, R., and Lotan, M. 1973. Relation of a test of attention to motor accidents. *Journal of Applied Psychology* 58:113–15.

Kay, E. J., Hillman, D. J., Hyland, D. T., Voros, R. S., Harris, R. M., and Deimler, J. D. 1994. *Age 60 Rule Research, Part III: Consolidated Data Base Experiments Final Report* (Tech. Rep. No. DOT/FAA/AM-92-22). Washington, DC: Federal Aviation Administration, Office of Aviation Medicine.

Ketcham, C. J., and Stelmach, G. E. 2004. Movement control in the older adult. In *Technology for Adaptive Aging*, ed. R. W. Pew and S. B. van Hemel, 64–92. Washington, DC: National Academies Press.

Kliegl, R., and Baltes, P. B. 1987. Theory-guided analysis of mechanisms of development and aging through testing-the-limits and research on expertise. In *Cognitive Functioning and Social Structure over the Life Course*, ed. C. Schooler and K. W. Schaie, 95–119. Norwood, NJ: Ablex.

Kliegl, R., Smith, J., and Baltes, P. B. 1989. Testing-the-limits and the study of adult age differences in cognitive plasticity of a mnemonic skill. *Developmental Psychology* 25: 247–56.

Kline, D. W. 2003. Commentary: Aging effects on vision: Impairment, variability, self-report, and compensatory change. In *Impact of Technology on Successful Aging*, ed. N. Charness and K. W. Schaie, 85–99. New York: Springer.

Kramer, A. F., Bherer, L., Colcombe, S. J., Dong, W., and Greenough, W. T. 2004. Environmental influences on cognitive and brain plasticity during aging. *Journals of Gerontology: Medical Sciences* 59A: 940–57.

Kramer, A. F., Larish, J. F., and Strayer, D. L. 1995. Training for attentional control in dual task settings: A comparison of young and old adults. *Journal of Experimental Psychology: Applied* 1:50–76.

Kramer, A. F., Larish, J. F., Weber, T. A., and Bardell, L. 1999. Training for executive control: Task coordination strategies and aging. In *Attention and Performance XVII Cognitive Regulation of Performance: Interaction of Theory and Application*, ed. D. Gopher and A. Koriat, 617–52. Cambridge, MA: MIT.

Krampe, R., and Charness, N. 2006. Aging and expertise. In *The Cambridge Handbook of Expertise and Expert Performance*, ed. K. A. Ericsson, N. Charness, P. J. Feltovich and R. R. Hoffman, 723–42. New York: Cambridge University Press.

Krampe. R. T., and Ericsson, K. A. 1996. Maintaining excellence: Deliberate practice and elite performance in young and older pianists. *Journal of Experimental Psychology: General* 125:331–59.

Kubeck, J. E., Delp, N. D., Haslett, T. K., and McDaniel, M. A. 1996. Does job-related training performance decline with age? *Psychology and Aging* 11:92–107.

Licklider, J. C. R. 1960. Man-computer symbiosis. *Institute of Radio Engineers Transaction on Human Factors Electronics* HFE-1: 4–11.

McEvoy, G. M., and Cascio, W. F. 1989. Cumulative evidence of the relationship between employee age and job performance. *Journal of Applied Psychology* 74:11–17.

McFarland, R. A. 1973. The need for functional age measurements in industrial gerontology. *Industrial Gerontology* 19:1–19.

Miller, J., Slomczynski, K. M., and Kohn, M. L. 1987. Continuity of learning-generalization through the life-span: The effect of job on men's intellectual process in the United States and Poland. In *Cognitive Functioning and Social Structure over the Life Course*, ed. C. Shooter and K. W. Schaie, 176–202. Norwood, NJ: Ablex.

Moray, N. 1986. Monitoring behavior and supervisory control. In *Handbook of Perception and Human Performance*, Vol. 2 of *Cognitive Processes and Performance*, 40-1–40-51. New York: John Wiley & Sons.

Murphy, K. R. 1989. Is the relationship between cognitive ability and job performance stable over time? *Human Performance* 2:183–200.

Murrell, K. F. H., and Humphries, S. 1978. Age, experience, and short-term memory. In *Practical Aspects of Memory*, ed. M. M. Gruneberg, P. E. Morris, and R. N. Sykes, 363–65. London: Academic.

Newson, R. S., and Kemps, E. B. 2006. The influence of physical and cognitive activities on simple and complex cognitive tasks in older adults. *Experimental Aging Research* 32: 341–62.

Norman, D. A., and Bobrow, D. G. 1975. On data-limited and resource-limited processes. *Cognitive Psychology* 7:44–64.

Norman, G. R., Brooks, L. R., and Allen, S. W. 1989. Recall by expert medical practitioners and novices as a record of processing attention. *Journal of Experimental Psychology: Learning, Memory, and Cognition* 15:1166–74.

Patel, V. L., and Groen, G. J. 1991. The general and specific nature of medical expertise: A critical look. In *Towards a General Theory of Expertise: Prospects and Limits*, ed. K. A. Ericsson and J. Smith, 93–125. Cambridge, UK: Cambridge University.

Pérès, M., Van De Moortele, P. F., Pierard, C., Lehericy, S., Satabin, P., Le Bihan, D. et al. 2000. Functional magnetic resonance imaging of mental strategy in a simulated aviation performance task. *Aviation, Space, and Environmental Medicine* 71:1218–31.

Peretti, C-S, Danion, J. M., Gierski, F., and Grange, D. 2002. Cognitive skill learning and aging: A component process analysis. *Archives of Clinical Neuropsychology* 45:445–59.

Perrow, C. 1999. *Normal Accidents: Living with High-Risk Technologies*. New York: Basic Books.

Rabbitt, P. M. A. 1993a. Crystal quest: An examination of the concepts of 'fluid' and 'crystallised' intelligence as explanations for cognitive changes in old age. In *Attention, Selection, Awareness and Control*, ed. A. D. Baddeley and L. Weiskrantz, 188–230. New York: Clarendon Press/Oxford University.

———. 1993b. Methodological and theoretical lessons from the University of Manchester longitudinal studies of cognitive changes in normal old age. In *Aging, Health and Competence: The Next Generation of Longitudinal Research*, ed. J. J. F. Schroots, 199–219. New York: Academic.

Reason, J. 1990. The contribution of latent human failures to the breakdown of complex systems. *Philosophysical Transactions Royal Society of London B* 327:475–84.

Rhodes, S. R. 1983. Age-related differences in work attitudes and behavior: A review and conceptual analysis. *Psychological Bulletin* 93:328–67.

Saczynski, J. S., Willis, S. L., and Schaie, K. W. 2002. Strategy use in reasoning training with older adults. *Aging, Neuropsychology, and Cognition* 9:48–60.

Salomon, G., and Perkins, D. 2005. Do technologies make us smarter? Intellectual amplification with, of, and through technology. In *Intelligence and Technology: The Impact of Tools on the Nature and Development of Human Abilities*, ed. R. J. Sternberg and D. D. Preiss, 71–86. Mahwah, NJ: Erlbaum.

Salthouse, T. A. 1990. Working memory as a processing resource in cognitive aging. *Developmental Review* 10:101–24.

———. 1991. *Theoretical perspectives on cognitive aging*. Hillsdale, NJ: Erlbaum.

Sarno, K. J., and Wickens, C. D. 1995. Role of multiple resources in predicting time-sharing efficiency: Evaluation of three workload models in a multiple-task setting. *International Journal of Aviation Psychology* 5:107–30.

Schaie, K. W. 1988. The impact of research methodology on theory building in the developmental sciences. In *Emergent Theories of Aging*, ed. J. E. Birren and V. L. Bengtson, 43–57. New York: Springer.

Schaie, K. W., and Gribben, K. 1975. Adult development and aging. *Annual Review of Psychology* 26:65–96.

Schaie, K. W., and Willis, S. L. 1986. Can decline in adult intellectual functioning be reversed? *Developmental Psychology* 22:223–32.

Schieber, F. 2003. Human factors and aging: Identifying and compensating for age-related deficits in sensory and cognitive function. In *Impact of Technology on Successful Aging*, ed. N. Charness and K. W. Schaie, 42–84. New York: Springer.

Schmidt, F. L. 2002. The role of general cognitive ability and job performance: Why there cannot be a debate. *Human Performance* 15:187–210.

Schmidt, F. L., Hunter, J. E., and Outerbridge, A. N. 1986. Impact of job experience and ability on job knowledge, work sample performance, and supervisory ratings of job performance. *Journal of Applied Psychology* 71:432–39.

Schooler, C., and Mulatu, M. S. 2001. The reciprocal effects of leisure time activities and intellectual functioning in older people: A longitudinal analysis. *Psychology and Aging* 16:466–82.

Schooler, C., Mulatu, M. S., and Oates, G. 1999. The continuing effects of substantively complex work on the intellectual functioning of older workers. *Psychology and Aging* 14:483–596.

Scialfa, C. T., and Fernie, G. R. 2006. Adaptive technology. In *Handbook of the Psychology of Aging*, 6th ed., ed. J. E. Birren, and K. W. Schaie, 425–41. New York: Elsevier

Scialfa, C. T., Jenkins, L., Hamaluk, E., and Skaloud, P. 2000. Aging and the development of automaticity in conjunction search. *Journals of Gerontology: Psychological Sciences and Social Science* 55B: 27–46.

Shooter, A. M. N., Schonfield, A. E. D., King, H. F., and Welford, A. T. 1956. Some field data on the training of older people. *Occupational Psychology* 30: 204–15.

Sparrow, P. R., and Davies, D. R. 1988. Effects of age, tenure, training, and job complexity on technical performance. *Psychology and Aging* 3:307–14.

Sturman, M. C. 2003. Searching for the inverted U-shaped relationship between time and performance: Meta-analyses of the experience/performance, tenure/performance, and age/performance relationships. *Journal of Management* 29:609–40.

Szafran, J. 1968. Psychophysiological studies of aging in pilots. In *Human Aging and Behavior*, ed. G. A. Talland, 37–74. New York: Academic.

Taylor, J. L., Yesavage, J. A., Morrow, D. G., Dolhert, N., Brooks III, J. O., Poon, L. W. 1994. The effects of information load and speech rate on younger and older aircraft pilots' ability to execute simulated air-traffic controller instructions. *Journals of Gerontology* 49: 191–200.

Tsang, P. S. 2006. Regarding time-sharing with convergent operations. *Acta Psychologica* 121:137–75.

———. 2007. The dynamics of attention and aging in aviation. In *Applied Attention: From Theory to Practice*, ed. A. F. Kramer, A. Kirlik, and D. Weigman, 170–84. New York: Oxford University Press.

Tsang, P. S., and Shaner, T. L. 1994. The mental workload of time-sharing for the young and old. In *Proceedings of the 12th Congress of the International Ergonomics Association*, Vol. 6, pp. 202–204. Toronto: Human Factors Association of Canada.

———. 1998. Age, attention, expertise, and time-sharing performance. *Psychology and Aging* 13:323–47.

Tsang, P. S., and Vidulich, M. A. 2006. Mental workload and situation awareness. In *Handbook of Human Factors and Ergonomics*, 3rd ed., ed. G. Salvendy, 243–65. New York: Wiley.

Tsang, P. S., and Voss, D. T. 1996. Boundaries of cognitive performance as a function of age and piloting experience. *International Journal of Aviation Psychology* 6:359–77.

U.S. Department of Labor. 1991. *Dictionary of Occupational Titles*, 4th ed. Washington, DC: U.S. Government.

Vidulich, M.A. 2003. Mental workload and situation awareness: Essential concepts for aviation psychology practice. In *Principles and Practice of Aviation Psychology*, ed. P. S. Tsang and M. A. Vidulich, 115–46. Mahwah, NJ: Erlbaum.

Waldman, D. A., and Avolio, B. J. 1986. A meta-analysis of age differences in job performance. *Journal of Applied Psychology* 71:33–38.

Warr, P. 1994. Age and employment. In *Handbook of Industrial and Organizational Psychology*, 2nd ed., ed. H. C. Triandis, M. D., Dunnette, and L. M. Hough, 4:485–550. Palo Alto, CA: Consulting Psychologist Press.

Welford, A. T. 1976. Thirty years of psychological research on age and work. *Journal of Occupational Psychology* 49:129–38.

———. 1986. Forty years of experimental psychology in relation to age: Retrospect and prospect. *Experimental Gerontology* 21:469–81.

Wickens, C. D. 2007. Attention to attention and its applications: A concluding view. In *Attention: From Theory to Practice*, ed. A. F. Kramer, D. A. Wiegmann, and A. Kirlik, 239–49. New York: Oxford University Press.

Wickens, C. D., and Kessel, C. 1979. The effects of participatory mode and task workload on the detection of dynamic system failures. *IEEE Transactions on Systems, Man and Cybernetics* SMC-9: 24–34.

Wickens, C. D., Kramer, A. F., Vanasse, L., and Donchin, E. 1983. The performance of concurrent tasks: A psychophysiological analysis of the reciprocity of information processing resources. *Science* 221:1080–82.

Wiener, E. L. and Curry, R. E. 1980. Flight-deck automation: Promises and problems. *Ergonomics* 23:955–1011.

Willis, S. L., and Nesselroade, C. S. 1990. Long-term effects of fluid ability training in old-old age. *Developmental Psychology* 26:905–10.

Yang, L, Krampe, R. T., and Baltes, P. B. 2006. Basic forms of cognitive plasticity extended into the oldest-old: Retest learning, age and cognitive functioning. *Psychology and Aging* 21:372–78.

Yesavage, J. A., Dolhert, N., and Taylor, J. L. 1994. Flight simulator performance of younger and older aircraft pilots: Effects of age and alcohol. *Journal of the American Geriatric Society* 42:577–82.

PART V

Workplace and Ergonomic Issues

CHAPTER FIFTEEN

Ergonomic Design of Workplaces for the Aging Population

KARL H. E. KROEMER, PH.D.

Ergonomics, which is sometimes used synonymously with the terms *human factors* or *human engineering,* is the scientific discipline concerned with the understanding of interactions among humans and other elements of a system, and the profession that applies theory, principles, data, and methods to design to optimize human well-being and overall system performance (International Ergonomics Association Council, 2003). Ergonomic design strategies concern all major components of work systems. These include the human operator, work tasks and procedures, and workplaces and equipment.

Recent changes in the demographics of the aging population call for vigorous ergonomic measures to accommodate older people. This chapter (1) discusses the importance of designing workplaces for older workers; (2) highlights some important workplace design issues that need to be addressed; and (3) presents two case models of ergonomic interventions in the context of aging persons working with computers at home or in the office. The first scenario concerns improving auditory and visual conditions. The second concerns fundamental improvements of electronic devices.

OLDER PERSONS AT WORK

Other chapters in this book make it clear that noteworthy changes are taking place in the demographics of the aging population in the United States as well as in other parts of the world. They pertain, among other aspects, to the age distribution of females and males in the overall population, the increasing number of older people who are continuing to work and their reasons for still working, employment patterns and preferences of older workers, and the educational and skill levels of older workers.

Our generation, as well as future generations, can expect to work and live longer than our parents and grandparents did—yet, as our ancestors experienced, aging finally brings with it changes, usually declines, in capabilities and functions. However, there are wide variations among individuals in the aging process and in if, when, and how fast traits change. Although this fact makes a classification of capabilities by age questionable, grouping by age remains a common practice.

Although no one given year establishes the beginning of the transition into older adulthood, the U.S. age discrimination legislation calls someone of 40 or more years of age an "older" person. Many tasks become more difficult as one passes through the 40s into the 50s and on into the later years. Numerous publications (e.g., Belsky, 1990; Spence 1994; Panek, 1997; Steenbekkers and Beijsterveldt, 1998; Craik and Salthouse, 2000; Smith, Norris, and Peebles, 2000; Birren and Schaie, 2001; Rogers and Fisk, 2001; Fisk et al., 2004; Kroemer, 2006) contain detailed information about aging and physical and mental processes. Fortunately, these publications indicate that aging persons can continue most jobs successfully into their mature years. In fact, some scientific findings, and many anecdotal suggestions, indicate that many older persons may perform tasks that demand patience and experience-gained skills better than some younger people can.

The ability to keep pace is of particular importance in working with computers, which has become a key issue in modern work and lifestyle. "Computering," one of the few genuinely new tasks that developed within just a few decades, employs rapidly changing equipment and innovative procedures. Use of computers at home, en route, and in the office has become essential for work, leisure, and many kinds of communications (Czaja, 1997, 1998, 2001; Czaja and Lee, 2001, 2003). However, usability of computers by all depends to a large extent on human factors issues in the design of computers and in the related layout of workstations both on the job and at home.

For example, while working with computers as we advance in years we are likely to notice the following:

- Sight and hearing deteriorate.
- Sitting habits change for two reasons: (1) musculoskeletal alterations affect body posture and often lead to spinal problems, especially in the lumbar area; and (2) blood and lymph flow becomes less effective.

- Mobility in the joints diminishes because the smoothness of the bony surfaces in joints, the thickness of joint linings, the supply of synovial fluid, and the elasticity and resilience of joint capsules and ligaments deteriorate. This may lead to painful inflammation and arthritis.

Degenerative osteoarthritis with its associated pain is the most-cited cause for limitations in daily physical activities (Kramarow et al., 1999). When these events are combined with age-related neurological changes and proprioceptor and exteroceptor information deficits, they can lead to reduced motor capabilities with slowed and more variable coordination, affecting the afflicted older person's ability to use the computer and related mechanical and electronic equipment.

ERGONOMIC STRATEGIES TO COUNTERACT EFFECTS OF AGING

As long as age-generated difficulties remain slight, thoughtful human engineering can overcome or reduce them. Ergonomic strategies apply to the three major components of work systems noted above: work tasks and procedures, the human operator, and workplaces and equipment. For example, with respect to work tasks and procedures, a goal would be to ensure that workloads do not overly tax the person's capabilities and that appropriate training is provided. When the focus is on the human operator, ergonomic strategies may include improving auditory and visual inputs. With regard to workplaces and equipment, ergonomic interventions would include ensuring proper seating and interface designs.

Setting of work goals and tasks as well as establishing proper processes and procedures are among the responsibilities of management and engineering. These departments would need to be concerned about the strength and endurance of an elderly workforce and might need to consider, for example, replacing standing with sitting at work and using powered assistive devices. Employers can further aging employees' well-being by providing advice on health and nutrition, offering suitable food and drink in the employer's cafeteria, giving opportunity and encouragement to maintain physical and mental fitness, and offering courses to train, maintain, and enhance skills. All workers, and especially older workers, can benefit from appropriate job and shift assignments, including the ability to take work breaks as desired (Kumashiro, 1995; Haermae, 1996; Karazman et al., 1998; Cremer, 2001; Amditis, Bekiaris, Braedel, and Knauth, 2003; Sharit et al., 2004; Wegman and McGee, 2004; Knauth, 2007).

Scheduling Work

Flexible work arrangements should be considered when designing jobs for older workers. A survey cited by Penner, Perun, and Steuerle (2002) indicated that 13 percent of those who had found other jobs after their careers or left the workforce altogether would have stayed with their employer if they had been given the opportunity to work fewer hours. An approach to flexible work scheduling described by Robson (2001) involves breaking jobs into four-hour "work modules." Work times should be broken into units that are long enough to permit a worker to accomplish a set of tasks but short enough to permit the tasks to be performed over a number of work days so that older employees' scheduling needs can be accommodated. Sparks, Faragher, and Cooper (2001) found that flexible arrangements can lead to improved productivity and job satisfaction, lowered job stress, and decreased tardiness and absenteeism.

Job transfers also allow for more flexible work environments for older workers. Some organizations may move older employees to areas involving a high level of organization-specific knowledge that they have acquired over years of working at the company (Hedge, Borman, and Lammlein, 2006). This allows older workers to continue working in positions where they can function as valuable mentors for newer employees or advisors for decision makers within the organization (Beehr and Bowling, 2002). The use of a "job bank" or "skills bank," in which a company can create a pool of temporary, often skill-based jobs for older workers can also serve this purpose (Menchin, 2000). These approaches allow for flexible schedules as well as a diversity of assignments for workers and can also compensate for the loss of significant skill that results from retirements.

Job Redesign

Jobs can often be redesigned to counteract the effects of aging. Hedge et al. (2006) note a variety of recommendations in the literature on aging for design interventions that target such areas as work location, work pacing, job content, completing assigned tasks independently, the physical environment, tools, and work aids. They categorize the major areas of job redesign for the older worker as (1) physical redesign, (2) sensory redesign, (3) information processing redesign, (4) work flow and pace redesign, and (5) redesign for stress control. Within these categories, examples of redesign include designing custom workstations to complement older workers' body structures and sensory capabilities; using larger print on warning signs, better lighting, and sound amplification; using decision-making aids such as written procedures, lists, flowcharts, and menus for action; allowing older workers to perform their work at a slower pace or at one that they control; and removing stressors such as information overload, overcrowding, and noise.

Another framework for job redesign is presented by Campion and Thayer (1987), who designate the approaches as (1) mechanistic, where one seeks to increase efficiency while decreasing training time; (2) motivational, in which the aim is to maximize job involvement and satisfaction; (3) perceptual/motor, where the interest is in minimizing employees' information processing and sensory demands; and (4) biological, where the main concern is designing a job to maximize physical comfort of employees. Jex, Wang, and Zarubin (2007) point out that, of these four approaches, the mechanistic approach may not be the best for redesigning jobs for older workers because work processes may be sped up to a level that would be difficult for older workers. However, the other three methods may be beneficial for older employees, particularly the perceptual/motor and biological approaches.

The perceptual/motor approach may benefit older workers because jobs can be redesigned with consideration to the cognitive changes associated with aging. This approach can be used to reduce information processing demands or to design jobs in which older employees do not have to process information as quickly. Other examples of redesigning the work environment based on this approach are making information easier to read and reducing excessive noise to allow for a higher level of concentration.

Given the physical changes associated with aging, the biological approach to job redesign can also prove beneficial to older workers. Using this method, one should assess the ergonomics of an employee's workstation, the physical demands of the job, and also the work schedule. Redesign for the aging worker would minimize discomfort caused by such factors as repetitive motions, disparity between equipment and physical attributes of employees, and schedules that lead to fatigue and errors. This approach to redesign is especially advantageous to older workers because performing physically demanding jobs and working strenuous shifts becomes increasingly difficult due to age-related physical changes (Kawada, 2002).

Training

Training offers the possibility for offsetting both the physical and the cognitive declines that can accompany aging and thus could have many benefits for the older worker. One use of training may be to improve older workers' adjustment to changes in technology and work methods (Jex et al., 2007). While training of this nature would certainly be beneficial for employees of all ages, it is especially helpful for older employees who may have been performing their jobs in a particular way for many years.

There is disagreement in the training literature concerning what type of training is better for older workers. As noted by the National Research Council and the Institute of Medicine (2004), it is often argued that self-paced rather than forced-paced training is better for older workers, although a significant benefit for older adults compared to younger adults is not often reported. A study in training on word processing conducted by Charness, Schumann, and Boritz (1992) did, in fact, indicate an advantage of self-pacing over forced-pacing for both older and younger adults.

In contrast, a study involving the performance of data entry, file modification, and inventory management tasks indicated that there may be some benefit of forced pacing in decreasing older adults' performance variability in data entry (Czaja and Sharit, 1993). However, results also indicated that older adults felt more fatigued when performing forced-paced rather than self-paced tasks. Thus, although older workers may be more productive if forced to speed up their pace, this result may come at the expense of accumulating greater fatigue and becoming more prone to error.

When designing a training program, one must acknowledge different learning styles and special concerns of older adults (AARP, 2002). For instance, learning styles have been reported to be different between veterans (those born between 1922 and 1943) and baby boomers (those born between 1943 and 1960; Zemke, Raines, and Filipczak, 2000). While veterans tend to learn best in a classroom setting with presentations and lectures given by experts, boomers generally learn best in less structured settings. Their learning formats can include workshops, books, audiotapes, self-help guides, and videos.

A number of factors concerning the person, task, and environment should generally be considered in a training program designed for older workers (Ford and Orel, 2005). For example, personal factors in design can include developing coping strategies, establishing relevance of current tasks with previous experience, reducing anxiety about new learning situations, and providing sufficient time for repetition and rehearsal of information. Task factors to be considered in a training program include providing memory aids such as notebooks, checklists, or PDAs; providing both written and verbal cues; and allowing for the application of new learning as soon as possible after the training. Consideration should also be given to environmental factors such as organized work stations to support work flow, proper light to reduce glare, and modifications to computers to assist in operation.

Well-designed workplaces, equipment, and tools, together with instructions and training, are among the most common helpful ergonomics measures (Kroemer, Kroemer, and Kroemer-Elbert, 1997, 2003; Kroemer and Kroemer, 2001; Marquie and Volkoff, 2001; Amditis, Bekiaris, Braedel, and Knauth, 2003; Haeroe and Vaerinen, 2003). Industrial engineering and human factors handbooks provide guidance for designs that can help older persons in everyday work and life (e.g., Kumashiro, 1995; Shephard, 1995; Haermae, 1996; Fisk and Rogers, 1997; Small, 1997; Karazman et al., 1998; Konz and Johnson, 2000; ; Cremer, 2001; Hammer and Price, 2001 Kroemer and Kroemer, 2001, 2005; Chengular, Rodgers, and Bernard, 2003; Kroemer, Kroemer, and Kroemer-Elbert, 2003; Fisk et al., 2004; Wegman and McGee, 2004; Kroemer, 2006). As a rule, ergonomic measures that improve the capabilities of older people will generally benefit others, including younger people as well, without diminished capacities.

ERGONOMIC IMPROVEMENTS OF COMPUTER WORK

Computers have opened the world for many persons, especially elderly persons, who might otherwise feel shut in. Electronics allow them to communicate directly with others, to shop and bank, to get information, and to perform many other tasks. Computer technology makes long-distance interaction easy, which is especially important if it is not feasible to travel. The Internet provides an abundance of information to persons who otherwise would be isolated because of age, illness, or injury. Proper computer technology can effectively link patients, their caregivers, and medical staff (Czaja, 2001). However, computer technology can also be a challenge to many older persons. Although successful interaction with computers can enhance their self-confidence and independence, failure can be discouraging and demeaning (Goebel, Fietz, and Friedorf, 2003).

Czaja and Lee (2003) discussed how age-related deficits can make computer use difficult. A key factor is the general decline with age of a number of cognitive abilities such as attention, processing speed, memory, reasoning, and problem solving. Another set of problems relates to declines in motor skills, such as slower response time, reduced ability to maintain continuous movements, less consistency in movements, and diminished coordination and mobility, together with more frequent incidence of arthritis. Reduced motor skills particularly affect the ability to use computer input devices such as a keyboard or mouse.

The following sections address two ergonomic approaches that can ameliorate common problems with computer work. The first example provides ways to counteract aging-caused declines in individual sensory capabilities. The second example primarily addresses improvements to workstation arrangements and the usability of computers. As will become evident, these approaches overlap widely and complement each other.

Example 1: Overcoming Difficulties with Hearing and Vision

Table 15.1 provides an overview of common aging-related changes in vision and audition associated with information processing and motor skills. While these developments occur with great variability among individuals, they are nevertheless the primary functional declines in persons above 50 years of age. Many of the effects of such deficits can be reduced or even completely avoided by proper ergonomic actions, as discussed below.

Improving Hearing

With aging, the ability to hear typically decreases dramatically. Deterioration begins in one's 40s, first in the high frequencies above 10 kHz, and then extends down to about 8,000 Hz or into even lower frequencies. This impairment, presbycusis, often coincides with noise-induced hearing loss, which depends on the damaging frequencies. Estimates are that 70 percent of all individuals over 50 years of age have some kind of hearing loss; however, the deficits vary greatly among individuals (Berger et al., 2003; Casali and Gerges, 2006). Loss of hearing ability in the higher frequencies of the speech range especially reduces the understanding of consonants that have high-frequency components. This explains why older persons often cannot discriminate well between phonetically similar words, which may make it difficult to follow conversations in environments where background noise masks speech or other auditory information.

This fact leads to a simple ergonomic intervention: keeping background noise at a minimum. This improves the auditory environment so that speech and important auditory signals have sufficient penetration, which is imperative for emergency alarms. A similar ergonomic measure is to improve the clarity of auditory messages by using sound signals that are easily distinguishable by means of sufficient intensity and suitable frequency. An alternative is to provide information through other sensory channels, for instance, using flashing lights together with a wailing siren or employing vibration of a body-worn phone to indicate an arriving call. With respect to computer work, computer-generated speech must be carefully designed for easy understanding even in the presence of back-

TABLE 15.1.

Common aging-related changes in audition, vision, and related
information-processing and motor skills

Ability	Expected change
Hearing	
Sensitivity	Decreases, especially at high frequencies
Frequency discrimination	Degrades
Temporal resolution	May degrade
Understanding in noise	Dwindles
Vision	
Near vision	Deteriorates
Far vision	Deteriorates
Dynamic vision	Deteriorates
Acuity	Diminishes
Discriminable differences	Degrades
Visual field	Diminishes
Dark adaptation	Slows, more illumination required
Coping with glare	Deteriorates
Light sensitivity	Reduces
Color sensitivity	Reduces
Attention	Reduces
Short-Term Memory	
Processing	Degrades
Performance	Shows deficits especially when other information is processed at the same time
Long-Term Memory	
Episodic	Performance declines
Semantic	May slow but essentially remains
Psychomotor Skills	
Learning	Declines
Reaction time	Slows
Motion time	Slows
Movement	Slows, becomes less accurate, weakens
Mobility	
Mobility of the eyes	Declines
Mobility of head/neck and back	Declines
Mobility in shoulders, arms, and hands	Declines

Source: Adapted from Fisk et al., 2004; Kroemer, 2006; Smith, Norris, and Peebles, 2000

ground noise. The presentation of redundant information in the form of visual cues on monitors should also be considered.

Hearing aids that amplify sounds for which hearing deficiencies exist can dramatically improve a person's ability to perceive acoustic signals and words. However, one associated problem is that the amplification of sounds might also intensify unwanted background noise. Unfortunately, until recently hearing aids often looked clumsy, and many are still difficult to insert, adjust, and maintain. Also, they may malfunction or stop working just when needed, whistle annoyingly, and be bothersome to use with a telephone. Technical developments should improve these devices in the future, and built-in active noise suppression by interference is now becoming practical, at least for frequencies below 1,000 Hz.

Improving Vision

Developing deficits in basic visual functions is, for most persons, one of the accompaniments of aging. Aging-induced atrophy of the dilator muscles of the eyes reduces the size of the iris. The lens becomes yellowed and less transparent. The vitreous humor often shrinks and becomes more opaque. These and related changes usually reduce the amount of light reaching the retina of a 70-year-old to half or less of what reached there during youth. The yellowing also makes it diffi-cult to discern between hues of blue, green, and violet (Spence, 1994; Fisk and Rogers, 1997).

With aging, the movement and adjustment capabilities of our eyes generally diminish, and lenses get stiffer and often clouded by cataracts. Together with the decreased amount of light reaching the retina, near vision, depth discernment, and dynamic visual abilities all deteriorate with respect to the perception and pro-cessing of visual signals. This causes difficulties while reading small print, dis-tinguishing similar colors, coping with glare, and recognizing objects in quickly changing visual environments. Everyday examples of such problems become ap-parent while driving in dim light and working with computers.

Measures to improve an individual's vision are at the intersection of optics, bioengineering, medical surgery, and lighting engineering. Human factors engi-neering and ergonomics are involved mostly in terms of workplace solutions, as discussed below.

In the past, techniques to improve an individual's vision focused on external vision corrections in the form of either hard lenses in face-worn frames or soft lenses in direct contact with the cornea. However, there are new technological so-lutions in bioengineering and in surgery that originally dealt with cataracts. Until a few decades ago, cataracts (opacities in the lens of the eye) were among the lead-ing causes of functional blindness in aged persons. Fortunately, modern technol-ogy and surgery can remedy the impairment caused by cataracts in a 30-minute routine operation that removes the clouded and yellowed natural lens and inserts a silicon or acrylic replacement. Until recently, these intraocular lenses (IOLs) used to be all of the monofocus type, with one predetermined focus distance. At that distance, these manufactured lenses regularly provided clear vision again to the previously disabled person. Additional external lenses (framed or contact lenses) then can provide the needed sharpness for other locations. Often the surgeon inserts two dissimilar lenses into the person's eyes, each with its focus set to a different distance. With this solution, many people can automatically see clearly at both distances because the brain quickly learns to pay attention to one eye or the other. Although monofocal IOLs are widely available, are comfortable to wear, and provide crisp vision under brightly lit conditions, these lenses can reduce contrast sensitivity and create glare and halos at night. New developments of intraocular lens (IOL) technology should provide even better solutions.

Presbyopia, common in people older than about 40, makes persons unable to read and distinguish fine details at close distance. Using "reading glasses," framed or in contact with the cornea, can overcome this difficulty, and so can a newly developed class of IOLs, called presbyopics. Presbyopic lenses that have a multifocal design split the incoming light into multiple images; the brain then pays attention to the image that is in focus. Although in principle this technology can provide clear near and distant vision, not all people get crisp near vision, and midrange vision can appear blurred. Furthermore, at night glare, halos, and reduced contrast sensitivity often occur. Work is in progress to improve presbyopic IOLs, for example, by using a double lens that functions like a telescope.

Preventing Lighting-Related Visual Problems at the Computer Workplace

The use of computer displays becomes more difficult with aging when visual capabilities decline. As indicated above, impairments include loss of static and dynamic acuity; reduced accommodation; diminished contrast sensitivity; decreased dark adaptation; declines in color sensitivity, especially in the green/blue wavelengths; and increased sensitivity to glare. These eyesight problems often coincide with reductions in visual search skills and in the ability to detect targets against a complex background. The ability to see also depends, of course, on the physical lighting conditions at the site (Boyce, 2005; Howarth, 2005; Rea, 2005).

Many visual problems at the computer workplace and in other situations where viewing objects is important relate to contrast between objects, such as letters appearing on a background. Contrast is, in essence, the difference between luminances on adjacent surfaces, as the observer sees them (see below). In some office lighting environments, the contrast may be too low, making discrimination of objects difficult; under other conditions, the contrast may be too high, creating what is popularly called "glare."

Low-luminance contrast makes it difficult to distinguish features from each other, such as details on any blurry black-and-white picture on a computer display, light details on a bright backdrop, or dark letters appearing on a gray background.

The obvious solution is to provide displays or prints with higher luminance distinctions. This is particularly important for older persons, who commonly have reduced contrast perception. A related problem often occurs with color displays, for example, when several lines of similar colors, such as shades of green and blue, appear in a graphic. Their luminance contrast is low, and many people have inherent difficulties distinguishing between greenish and bluish hues: among men, about one in ten has some degree of blue/green deficiency. That problem often gets worse with aging. Again, the solution is to provide visual targets with high luminance contrast. In the example, lines in black, red, and green probably would provide better visibility than blue/green shades. However, a higher lighting level is necessary to differentiate colors as compared to white and black.

The luminance level of an object corresponds to the light energy reflected from it that passes through the eye and then falls on the retina. As we look at a printed text or a drawing on paper, we notice that a dark surface absorbs most of the incoming light (illumination), while a light surface reflects most of it. Increasing the illuminance on a drawing or text printed on paper improves our ability to read because it enhances, first, the luminance contrast, and second, the overall illumination energy that passes through the eye and strikes the retina. Both points are of importance for even young eyes, but especially so for aged eyes.

Frequently, however, there is the opposite problem of excessive contrast, called glare. In computer offices, for example, two major sources of glare are direct glare and indirect glare. In direct glare, high-intensity light sources shine directly into the eyes, as shown in figure 15.1. The sources may be sunshine, brightly lit window areas, or powerful luminaries—especially so-called task lamps located within the field of vision. Their light energy falls on the retina and there overpowers the dimmer images of the computer monitor, written text, other persons' faces, and the general surroundings. The obvious ergonomic solution to prevent direct glare is to reduce the intensity of the light sources, such as by putting a curtain in front of a window or placing task and room lights outside the field of vision.

The other high-contrast problem is "indirect glare" (or reflected glare), which occurs when we see a light source reflected in a surface at which we are looking (figure 15.2). When we work with a computer, an overhead light, a window behind us, or even a white blouse or shirt that we wear can appear brightly on the monitor and wash out what we expect to see displayed there. In fact, any bright surface, such as a picture under glass on the wall, a shiny desktop, or polished surfaces on the keyboard, may reflect glaring light. An obvious ergonomic solution to prevent indirect glare is to limit the amount of shiny surfaces.

Figure 15.1. Direct glare. *Source*: Adapted from Kroemer and Kroemer, 2005

Careful selection and placement of light sources is the basic ergonomic solution that avoids both direct and indirect glare. It is advisable to have an optical "shield" between the operator's eyes and the light source, which can easily be achieved by choosing indirect or diffuse room lighting, as illustrated in figure 15.3, instead of direct illumination. The locations of luminaires should be outside the field of vision, best overhead and to the sides of the operator, as shown in figure 15.4. Another simple solution is to position the human operator in such a way that the person does not face a light source and cannot see a reflected light. This means that one should not face a window or lamp, which cause direct glare; by the same logic, one should not have a window or light source in the back, where it could cause indirect glare. Instead, we should turn and position our workplace so that windows and bright lights sources are to our sides, or overhead. These solutions work in both the home and office; they help everybody and are especially helpful to persons with aging-related vision problems.

Figure 15.2. Indirect glare. *Source*: Adapted from Kroemer and Kroemer, 2005

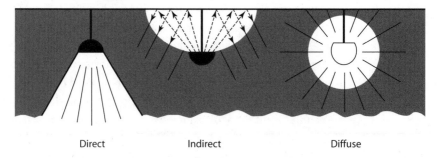

| Direct | Indirect | Diffuse |

Figure 15.3. Types of ceiling lights. *Source*: Adapted from Kroemer and Kroemer, 2001

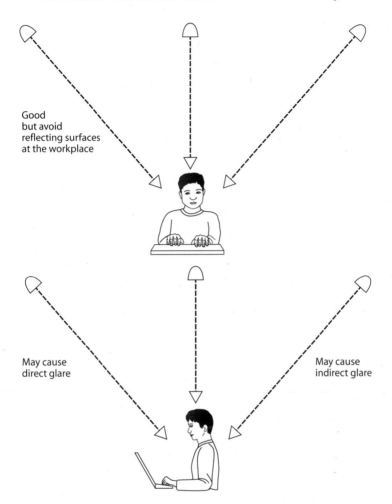

Good
but avoid
reflecting surfaces
at the workplace

May cause
direct glare

May cause
indirect glare

Figure 15.4. Placement of ceiling lights. Source: Adapted from Kroemer and Kroemer, 2001

Example 2: Issues with Computer Workstations
Sitting Postures while Interacting with Computers

Designing the computer workstation for the older user poses essentially the same challenges as setting it up for any adult computer operator but with additional concerns about aging-related special needs. These include limitations imposed on possible sitting postures by back or other musculoskeletal problems, by circulatory deficiencies, by vision requirements, and possibly by wheelchair use.

The preferred line of sight relates to the anatomical layout of the head, the placement of the eyes therein, and the adjustments natural to our visual system. In general, the preferred line of sight points "forward and down," as shown in figure 15.5. With the Ear-Eye Line as reference, the angle of the line of sight (LOSEE) is 15 degrees or more declined for distant visual targets. That angle increases as the target gets closer; for reading text in a book or on the computer screen, the LOSEE angle is generally between 30 and 45 degrees, though individual preferences are highly variable (Kroemer, 1994).

Head/neck posture, and hence the overall sitting pose, interact with the line of sight. When the head is "erect" (upright), the angle P in figure 15.5 is about 15 degrees. However, some persons may like to lean backward while sitting, whereas others hunch forward-downward. Many older persons, sitting or standing, find it difficult to raise their eyesight (by rotating their eyes up inside the skull, or by tilting the skull up; Kroemer, 1994), especially while trying to maintain a fairly short viewing distance to distinguish fine details. The binocular accommodation and vergence positions, to which the eyes return at rest, are usually not at optical infinity, as previously often assumed, but at about "arm's length" (Roscoe, 2007, 15), with wide variations from person to person. Consequently, a suitable default location of the computer display is at forearm length, with the upper edge below eye height, and with the screen at a right angle to the line of sight. Each computer user should be encouraged to adjust the monitor from that basic position to her or his most comfortable viewing height, distance, and angle, all while wearing needed reading glasses or contact lenses and sitting comfortably.

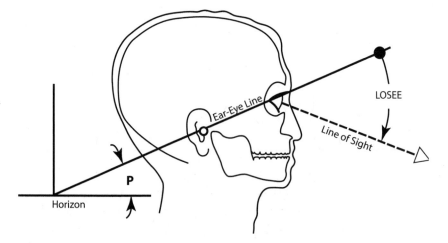

Figure 15.5. The Ear-Eye Line runs through the ear hole and the junction of the eyelids. It describes the posture of the head and serves as reference for the angle of the line of sight, or LOSEE. *Source:* Adapted from Kroemer, Kroemer, and Kroemer-Elbert, 1997

A comfortable sitting posture for older persons at the computer workstation should produce easy vision and mobility and suitable body support. Last century's recommended stiff seat, enforcing an "upright" posture, is not generally suitable. Instead, most users want to select from modern chairs that support body movements between tilting forward and leaning back (Kroemer and Kroemer, 2001; Human Factor and Ergonomics Society, 2002; Helander, 2003; Helander and Tham, 2003; Kroemer, 2006; Corlett, 2007). Given the wide variety among individually preferred postures, different chairs should be tried before one is selected.

Keyboard Issues

Table 15.1 lists reductions in motor capabilities, together with other age-related declines that are of critical importance for the use of computers because current human-computer communication predominantly depends on manual input, mostly via keyboard or mouse. The common computer keyboard, which is still essentially based on the design for the 1878 Sholes typewriter, is ergonomically flawed (Kroemer, 2001). Its major fault lies in its requirement for precise and highly repetitive motions of the hand digits, which often overstrain both older and younger operators' musculoskeletal properties (Kuorinka and Forcier, 1995; Nordin, Andersson, and Pope, 1997; National Research Council, 1999; Arndt and Putz-Anderson, 2001; National Research Council and Institute of Medicine, 2001; Marklin and Simoneau, 2004; Armstrong, 2006; Gerr, Monteilh, and Marcus, 2006; Marras and Radwin, 2006; Kroemer, 2007). Repetitive injuries such as carpal tunnel syndrome have been extensive among keyboarders, and understanding the reasons for, and the human-engineering specifics of, the historical designs of the input side of typewriters and then computers is essential for developing new ergonomic solutions.

Overcoming Keyboard-Related Difficulties.

In 1878, C. Latham Sholes obtained U.S. Patent 207,559, which included his QWERTY typewriter key layout, as shown in figure 15.6. Until that time, keyboards were components of musical instruments, especially of pianos and cembalos, and it was common knowledge that pianists were in danger of developing chronic musculoskeletal disorders (Poore, 1872, 1887). After Sholes's typewriting machine became widespread, the same "myalgia" appeared in typists as well.

Such repetition-related musculoskeletal diseases of typists have concerned physiologists and medical practitioners since the early 1900s. In 1951, Lundervold published his groundbreaking study on the involvement of individual mus-

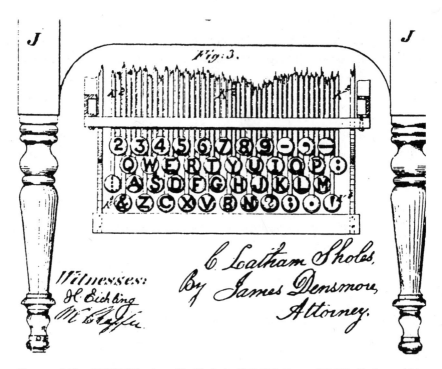

Figure 15.6. The QWERTY keyboard in Sholes's 1878 U.S. Patent 207,559. Sholes and his co-inventors obtained eight U.S. patents for "Type-Writers" with various keyboards: in 1868, Patents 79,265 and 79,868 (both with Glidden and Soulé); in 1876, Patent 182,511 (with Schwalbach); in 1878, Patents 199,382 and 200,351 (with Glidden), followed by Patents 207,557, 207,558, and 207,559. *Source*: Adapted from Kroemer, 2001

cles in typewriting that provided support for the long-held belief that repetitive typing can lead to a cumulative overexertion injury even though single keystrokes are not harmful by themselves. Partly in response to the intention of the U.S. Occupational Safety and Health Agency to establish ergonomic requirements specifically targeting repetitive injuries, in the late 1990s the (U.S.) National Research Council convened a workshop on work-related musculoskeletal disorders. In the summary of its findings, the NRC stated that musculoskeletal disorders are multifactorial because individual, social, and organizational factors can contribute to the outcome; however, the biomechanical demands of work constitute the most important risk factors (National Research Council, 1999, 59).

A major argument given since the 1950s for not changing the basic QWERTY design of the keyboard has been that an alteration of the layout would require retraining operators and hence would slow their keying performance, at least initially. This reasoning is probably true for most minor changes, such as exchanging the letter designations of certain keys, which was proposed by Dvorak in the 1930s and 1940s, or using an alphabetic layout. In these cases, carry-over confusion is indeed likely, because the new skills are similar to the old ones. However, fundamental changes in design, such as relocating whole sets of keys or employing keys that have a clearly different operational mode such as ternary keys or joysticks instead of binary keys, have seldom been tried. Such novel designs create distinctively new procedures, which, because of their dissimilarity from old practices, should not suffer from interference by crossover from these previous practices. That the human is amazingly fast in acquiring novel keyboarding skills is demonstrated by the phenomenally fast spread, across the globe, of instant text messaging with its miniature keys and keyboards and new use procedures.

Design Alternatives for Keyboards

There is no overwhelming reason for using "one keystroke for each single bit of input." The principle of allocating one key each to every character, numeral, sign, and space follows the tradition of Western writing: it is exact but also inefficient. Using fewer keys, moveable keys, virtual keys, or no keys at all would alleviate, even completely avoid, the current overexertion and posture problems caused by the requirement of "hands on keyboards." Ways to communicate with the computer without manipulating keys are of great interest for everyday use, especially to persons with physical disabilities, including older users.

We can generate inputs to the computer that do not require manual keyboarding. Voice recognition by the computer would be an obvious solution. Another solution may be "chording." Chords, traditionally used by pianists and other musicians, convey complex sound messages composed of single tones, generated by triggering keys simultaneously instead of sequentially. Chording by simultaneous activation of two or more keys was proposed repeatedly for typewriter and computer operation to replace the sequential "one-key for one character" procedure. Langley's 1988 U.S. patent is a fairly recent example for chording design, which can simplify keyboards, cut the number of keys, reduce hand digit movements from key to key, and, overall, make key input faster while relieving hand strain. However, chording transfers "knowledge in the world" (the one-to-one relationship between the symbol and the key for inputting that symbol) to "knowledge in the head" (the need to remember what the groupings of keys or "chords" signify), which could be difficult for older persons.

Another set of solutions employs recognition of body movements (McMillan, 2001; McMillan and Calhoun, 2001; Kroemer, Kroemer, and Kroemer-Elbert,

2003). Examples are using hands and fingers for sign language and gestures or for activating control devices; arms for gestures, making signs, or pressing control devices; feet for motions and gestures, stepping, moving and pressing devices; total body for distinct displacements or swaying; head for positioning; face for grimaces and other expressions; and eyes for tracking. Each of these solutions requires special sensors to recognize body motions: among these, electromagnetic pickups, cameras, force platforms, motion sensors, instrumented gloves, and similar devices are currently state-of-the-art.

Future approaches to communication may involve using surface electromyograms (EMGs) associated with muscle activations (Reddy and Gupta, 2007) or employ neural signals such as electroencephalograms (EEGs) associated with brain activities. Among the more futuristic possibilities are "nanoergonomics" (Karwowski, 2006) that may make it possible to access the human central nervous system and integrate important features of human cognition into computers, thus allowing direct interaction.

Cleverly designed software facilitates working with computers. Software can use context to distinguish between *mail* and *male, then* and *than;* it can complete words after the input of only a few first letters; it can provide a set of stock responses to given circumstances; it can anticipate the use of certain words; and it can correct spelling and grammar and insert punctuation. Currently available smart program aids include automatic adjustments of the display in size, light intensity, and contrast according to the lighting environment and following user vision preferences; provision of shortcuts to documents and electronic links; availability of optical character (written text) recognition; use of speech commands for computer functions; and transcriptions of spoken inputs. Together with future advances in artificial intelligence, the many possible software features offer seemingly unlimited opportunities for making computers easier for everybody by reducing the demands on vision, short-term memory, and manipulative skills (Czaja, 1997, 1998, 2001; Morrell and Echt, 1997; Czaja and Lee, 2001; Fisk et al., 2004) that are of particular concern to aging users.

Obviously, improvements in computer design can counteract many existing problems concerning their use. Ergonomic deficiencies in hardware and inadequacies in manuals and instructions are annoying and hamper efficient operation (Rogers 1997a, 1997b; Mead, Batsakes, Fisk, and Mykitsyshyn, 1999; Jamieson and Rogers, 2000; Mead et al., 2000). Today's electronics and perhaps tomorrow's nanotechnology allow fundamentally new solutions. We may sort these into certain categories, as has been done above; however, solutions that develop from combinations of multiple categories are most likely to succeed. A currently feasible example is a blending of traditional keys with speech recognition and smart software. However, as long as we employ the outdated Sholes keyboard with its numerous binary push keys, such design will make the job hard for most older persons and, in fact, everybody else. Abolishing the current principle of "one keystroke for one input" seems essential. Smart software should facilitate input tasks. The general acceptance of innovative mobile phones and game consoles, for example, demonstrates that the public is willing to take on, and even embrace, fundamentally new techniques in human-computer interaction, together with tech-fueled neologisms in our language.

Current mobile electronic gadgets combine telephone, text communications, Web access, and media play. For such multiple uses, there must be ways to transmit information from the human brain to the computer other than tapping one binary key for every letter, numeral, sign, and space. While simply sending neural signals is still wishful thinking, there are unexploited possibilities (Kroemer, Kroemer, and Kroemer-Elbert, 2003; Karwowski, 2006; Kroemer, 2006) that could help all operators, especially those disadvantaged by the aging process.

CONCLUSION

The goal of ergonomics in designing work environments for the older person is to ensure that work, workplaces, and work equipment are appropriately fitted to this population of workers so that tasks can be performed comfortably, safely, easily, and efficiently (table 15.2). To meet this aim, specific information about human capabilities and limitations, especially age-related changes in physical and mental capabilities, must be at hand as a basis for instituting ergonomic measures.

Two case scenarios were presented to illustrate how ergonomic measures can counteract detrimental effects of aging experienced by many computer users. The first example showed how wearing personal devices such as hearing aids,

TABLE 15.2.
Ergonomic goals when designing for elderly people

- Complex issues solved and hidden within the technical system so that its use is uncomplicated and intuitive
- Effortless, consistent, commonsense procedures
- Uniform, bright lighting of common spaces but without glare
- Easy to see, easy to hear
- No-bend, no-stretch, no-kneel
- Comfortable secure body support when sitting
- Enough space for unhindered ambulation, passage, and work
- Design for human dignity, safety, and comfort

eyeglasses, and implanted eye lenses can improve individuals' hearing and see-ing abilities. The second example concerned human engineering the details of workplace arrangements and fundamental improvements of computer systems. Our current computers suffer from well-documented complex and interdepen-dent deficiencies, especially on the input side. The most urgent task is to replace the binary keys that require one tap for each input, inherited from the 1878 type-writer keyboard, and the misuse of the numerical phone pad for text messaging. Smart software can recognize speech and other sounds, interpret body language, predict words and sentences and, possibly, respond to operators' neural signals.

Redesign of both the input and the output sides of the computer, employing new technologies and ergonomic knowledge about human abilities and limita-tions, would make using computers and evolving electronic devices easier for everyone, both young and not-so-young.

REFERENCES

Amditis, A., Bekiaris, E., Braedel, C., and Knauth, P. 2003. Dealing with the problems of elderly workforce: The RESPECT approach. In *Quality of Work and Products in Enter-prises of the Future,* ed. H. Strasser, K. Kluth, H. Rausch, and H. Bubb, 881–84. Stuttgart: Ergonomia Verlag.

AARP. 2002. *Staying Ahead of the Curve: The AARP Work and Career Study.* Washington, DC: AARP.

Armstrong, T. J. 2006. The ACGIH TLV for hand activity level. In *Fundamentals and Assess-ment Tools for Occupational Ergonomics: The Occupational Ergonomics Handbook,* 2nd ed., ed. W. S. Marras and W. Karwowski. Boca Raton, FL: CRC.

Arndt, B., and Putz-Anderson, V. 2001. *Cumulative Trauma Disorders,* 2nd ed. London: Tay-lor & Francis.

Beehr, T. A., and Bowling, N. A. 2002. Career issues facing older workers. In *Work Careers: A Developmental Perspective,* ed. D. Feldman, 214–41. San Francisco: Jossey-Bass.

Belsky, J. K. 1990. *The Psychology of Aging: Theory, Research, and Interventions.* Pacific Grove, CA: Brooks/Cole.

Berger, E. H., Royster L. H., Royster, J. D., Driscoll, D. P., and Layne, M. 2003. *The Noise Manual,* 5th ed. Fairfax, VA: American Industrial Hygiene Association.

Birren, J. E., and Schaie, K. W., eds. 2001. *Handbook of the Psychology of Aging,* 5th ed. San Diego, CA: Academic Press.

Boyce, P. R. 2005. Evaluating office lighting. In *Handbook of Human Factors and Ergonom-ics Methods,* ed. N. Stanton, A. Hedge, K. Brookhuis, E. Salas, and H. Hendrick. Boca Raton: CRC.

Campion, M. A., and Thayer, P. W. 1987. Job design: Approaches, outcomes, and tradeoffs. *Organizational Dynamics* 15:66–79.

Casali, J. G., and Gerges, S. N.Y. 2006. Protection and enhancement of hearing in noise. In

Reviews of Human Factors and Ergonomics, Vol. 2, ed. R. C. Williges. Santa Monica, CA: Human Factors and Ergonomics Society.

Charness, N., Schumann, C. E., and Boritz, G. M. 1992. Training older adults in word processing: Effects of age, training technique, and computer anxiety. *International Journal of Technology and Aging* 5:79–106.

Chengular, S. N., Rodgers, S. H., and Bernard, T. E. 2003. *Kodak's Ergonomic Design for People at Work*, 2nd ed. New York: Wiley.

Corlett, E. N. 2007. Sitting on seats, working all day. *Ergonomics in Design* 15:25–27.

Craik, F. I. M., and Salthouse, T. A., eds. 2000. *The Handbook of Aging and Cognition*, 2nd ed. Mahwah, NJ: Erlbaum.

Cremer, R. 2001. Work design: Age-related policies. In *International Encyclopedia of Ergonomics and Human Factors*, ed. W. Karwowski, 606–608. London: Taylor & Francis.

Czaja, S. J. 1997. Using technology to aid in the performance of home tasks. In *Handbook of Human Factors and the Older Adult*, ed. A. D. Fisk and W. A. Rogers. San Diego: Academic Press.

———. 1998. Gerontology case study: Designing a computer-based communication system for older adults. In *Ergonomics in Health Care and Rehabilitation*, ed. V. J. B. Rice. Boston: Butterworth-Heineman.

———. 2001. Telecommunication technology as an aid to family caregivers. In *Human Factors Interventions for the Health Care of Older Adults*, ed. W. A. Rogers and A. D. Fisk. Mahwah, NJ: Erlbaum.

Czaja, S. J., and Lee, C. C. 2001. The Internet and older adults: Design challenges and opportunities. In *Aging and Communication: Opportunities and Challenges of Technology*, ed. N. Charness, D. C. Park, and B. A. Sabel, 60–81. New York: Springer.

———. 2003. Designing computer systems for older adults. In *Handbook of Human-Computer Interaction*, ed. J. Jacko and A. Sears, 413–27. Mahwah, NJ: Erlbaum.

Czaja, S. J., and Sharit, J. 1993. Age differences in the performance of computer-based work. *Psychology and Aging* 8:59–67.

Fisk, A. D., and Rogers, W. A., eds. 1997. *Handbook of Human Factors and the Older Adult*. San Diego: Academic Press.

Fisk, A. D., Rogers, W. A., Charness, N., Czaja, S. J., and Sharit, J., eds. 2004. *Designing for Older Adults*. Boca Raton, FL: CRC.

Ford, R., and Orel, N. 2005. Older adult learners in the workforce. *Journal of Career Development* 32:139–52.

Gerr, F., Monteilh, C. P., and Marcus, M. 2006. Keyboard use and musculoskeletal outcomes among computer users. *Journal of Occupational Rehabilitation* 16:259–71.

Goebel, M., Fietz, A., and Friedorf, W. 2003. User adapted presentation of Internet information for older adults. In *Quality of Work and Products in Enterprises of the Future*, ed. H. Strasser, K. Kluth, H. Rausch, and H. Bubb, 1067–74. Stuttgart: Ergonomia Verlag.

Haermae, M. 1996. Ageing, physical fitness and shiftwork tolerance. *Applied Ergonomics* 27:25–29.

Haeroe, J. M., and Vaerinen, S. 2003. Ergonomic approach for developing products aimed at older users: Method and product cases. In *Quality of Work and Products in Enterprises of the Future,* ed. H. Strasser, K. Kluth, H. Rausch, and H. Bubb, 145–48. Stuttgart: Ergonomia Verlag.

Hammer, W., and Price, D. 2001. *Occupational Safety Management and Engineering,* 5th ed. Upper Saddle River, NJ: Prentice-Hall.

Hedge, J. W., Borman, W. C., and Lammlein, S. E. 2006. *The Aging Workforce: Realities, Myths, and Implications for Organizations.* Washington, DC: American Psychological Association.

Helander, M. G. 2003. Forget about ergonomics in chair design? Focus on aesthetics and comfort! *Ergonomics* 46:1306–19.

Helander, M. G., and Tham, M. P. 2003. Hedonomics: Affective human factors design. *Ergonomics* 46: 1269–72.

Human Factors and Ergonomics Society. 2002. *Human Factors Engineering of Computer Workstations* (BSR /HFES 100, Draft Standard for Trial Use). Santa Monica, CA: Author.

Howarth, P. A. 2005. Assessment of the visual environment. In *Evaluation of Human Work,* 3rd ed., ed. R. Wilson and N. Corlett. London: Taylor & Francis.

International Ergonomics Association. 2003. *IEA Triennial report, 200–2003.* Santa Monica, CA: IEA Press.

Jamieson, B. A., and Rogers, W. A. 2000. Age-related effects of blocked and random practice schedules on learning a new technology. *Journal of Gerontology: Psychological Sciences* 55B: 343–63.

Jex, S. M., Wang, M., and Zarubin, A. 2007. Aging and occupational health. In *Aging and Work in the Twentieth Century,* ed. K. S. Shultz and G. A. Adams, 199–223. Mahwah, NJ: Erlbaum.

Karazman, R., Kloimueller, I., Gaertner, J., Geissler, H., Hoerwein, K, and Morawetz, I. K. 1998. Participatory development of age-adjusted, optional shift time schedules in industrial workers in a plant. In *Advances in Occupational Ergonomics and Safety,* ed. S. Kumar, 139–42. Amsterdam: IOS Press.

Karwowski, W. 2006. From past to future. *Human Factors and Ergonomics Society Bulletin* 49:1–3.

Kawada, T. 2002. Effect of age on sleep onset time in rotating shift workers. *Sleep Medicine* 3:423–26.

Knauth, P. 2007. Extended work periods. *Industrial Health* 45:125–36.

Konz, S., and Johnson, S. 2000. *Work Design: Industrial Ergonomics,* 5th ed. Scottsdale, AZ: Holcomb Hathaway.

Kramarow, E., Lentzner, H., Rooks, R., Weeks, J., and Saydah, S. 1999. *Health and Aging Chart Book: Health, United States, 1999.* Hyattsville, MD: National Center for Health Statistics.

Kroemer, K. H. E. 1994. Locating the computer screen: How high, how far? *Ergonomics in Design* (January): 40.

———. 2001. Keyboards and keying: An annotated bibliography of the literature from 1878 to 1999. *International Journal of Universal Access in the Information Society* 1/2: 99–160.

———. 2006. *"Extra-ordinary" Ergonomics: How to Accommodate Small and Big Persons, the Disabled and Elderly, Expectant Mothers and Children.* Boca Raton, FL: CRC.

———. 2007 Anthropometry and biomechanics: Anthromechanics. In *Biomechanics in Ergonomics*, 2nd ed., ed. S. Kumar. Boca Raton, FL: CRC.

Kroemer, K. H. E., and Kroemer, A. D. 2001. *Office Ergonomics*. London: Taylor & Francis.

———. 2005. *Office Ergonomics*, authorized translation of *Office Ergonomics* (London: Taylor & Francis, 2001) into Korean. Seoul: Kukje.

Kroemer, K. H. E., Kroemer, H. J., and Kroemer-Elbert, K. E. 1997. *Engineering Physiology: Bases of Human Factors/Ergonomics*, 3rd ed. New York: VNR-Wiley.

———. 2003, amended reprint of *Ergonomics: How to Design for Ease and Efficiency*, 2nd ed. (2001). Upper Saddle River, NJ: Prentice-Hall / Pearson Education.

Kumashiro, M., ed. 1995. *The Paths to Productive Aging*. London: Taylor & Francis.

Kuorinka, I., and Forcier, L., eds. 1995. *Work Related Musculoskeletal Disorders: A Reference Book for Prevention*. London: Taylor & Francis.

Langley, L. W. 1988. *Ternary Chord-Type Keyboard*, Patent No. 4,775,255, U.S. Patent Office.

Lundervold, A. J. S. 1951. Electromyographic investigations of position and manner of working in typewriting. *Acta Physiologica Scandinavian* 24 Supplement 84: 1–171.

Marklin, R. W., and Simoneau, G. G. 2004. Design features of alternative computer keyboards: A review of experimental data. *Journal of Orthopaedic and Sports Physical Therapy* 34:638–49.

Marquie, J. C., and Volkoff, S. 2001. Working with age: An ergonomic approach to aging on the job. In *International Encyclopedia of Ergonomics and Human Factor*, ed. W. Karwowski, 613–16. London: Taylor & Francis.

Marras, W. S., and Radwin, R. G. 2006. Biomechanical modeling. In *Reviews of Human Factors and Ergonomics*, Vol. 1, ed. R. S. Dickerson. Santa Monica, CA: Human Factors and Ergonomics Society.

McMillan, G. R. 2001. Brain and muscle signal-based control. In *International Encyclopedia of Ergonomics and Human Factors*, ed. W. Karwowski, 379–81. London: Taylor & Francis.

McMillan, G. R., and Calhoun, G. L. 2001. Gesture-based control. In *International Encyclopedia of Ergonomics and Human Factors*, ed. W. Karwowski, 237–39. London: Taylor & Francis.

Mead, S. E., Batsakes, P., Fisk, A. D., and Mykitsyshyn, A. 1999. Application of cognitive theory to training and design solutions for age-related computer use. *International Journal of Behavioral Development* 23:553–73.

Mead, S. E., Sit, R. A., Rogers, W. A., Jamieson, B., and Rousseau, G. K. 2000. Influences of general computer experience and age on library search performance. *Behaviour and Information Technology* 19:107–23.

Menchin, R. S. 2000. *New Work Opportunities for Older Americans*. New York: iUniverse .com.

Morrell, R. W., and Echt, K. V. 1997. Designing written instructions for older adults: Learning to use computers. In *Handbook of Human Factors and the Older Adult*, ed. A. D. Fisk and W. A. Rogers. San Diego, CA: Academic Press.

National Research Council. 1999. *Work-Related Musculoskeletal Disorders: Report, Workshop Summary, and Workshop Papers*. Washington, DC: National Academies Press.

National Research Council and Institute of Medicine. 2001. *Musculoskeletal Disorders and the Workplace: Low Back and Upper Extremities.* Washington, DC: National Academies Press.

———. 2004. *Health and Safety Needs of Older Workers.* Committee on the Health and Safety Needs of Older Workers, ed. D. H. Wegman and J. P. McGee. Division of Behavioral and Social Sciences and Education. Washington, DC: National Academies Press.

Nordin, M., Andersson, G. B. J., and Pope, M. H. 1997. *Musculoskeletal Disorders in the Workplace: Principles and practices.* St. Louis: Mosby.

Panek, P. E. 1997. The older worker. In *Handbook of Human Factors and the Older Adult,* ed. A. D. Fisk, and W. A. Rogers. San Diego, CA: Academic Press.

Penner, R. G., Perun, P., and Steuerle, E. 2002. *Legal and Institutional Impediments to Partial Retirement and Part-time Work by Older Workers.* Washington, DC: Urban Institute.

Poore, G. V. 1872 "Writer's cramp": Its pathology and treatment. *Practitioner* (August): 341–50.

———. 1887. Clinical lecture on certain conditions of the hand and arm which interfere with the performance of professional acts, especially piano-playing. *British Medical Journal,* 26 February, 441–44.

Rea, M. S. 2005. Photometric characterization of the luminous environment. In *Handbook of Human Factors and Ergonomics Methods,* ed. N. Stanton, A. Hedge, K. Brookhuis, E. Salas, and H. Hendrick. Boca Raton, FL: CRC.

Reddy, N. P., and Gupta, V. 2007. Toward direct biocontrol using surface EMG signals: Control of finger and wrist joint models. *Medical Engineering and Physics* 29:398–403.

Robson, W. B. P. 2001. *Aging Populations and the Workforce: Challenges for Employers.* Winnipeg, MN: British-North American Committee.

Rogers, W.A. 1997a. Individual differences, aging, and human factors: An overview. In *Handbook of Human Factors and the Older Adult,* ed. A. D. Fisk and W. A. Rogers. San Diego, CA: Academic Press.

Rogers, W. A., ed. 1997b. *Designing for an Aging Population: Ten Years of Human Factors/ Ergonomics Research.* Santa Monica, CA: Human Factors and Ergonomics Society.

Rogers, W. A., and Fisk, A. D., eds. 2001. *Human Factors Interventions for the Health Care of Older Adults.* Mahwah, NJ: Erlbaum.

Roscoe, S. N. 2007. The gift of optometers. *Ergonomics in Design* 15:14–18.

Sharit, J., Czaja, S. J., Hernandez, M., Yang, Y., Perdomo, D., Lewis, J. E., et al. 2004. An evaluation of performance by older persons on a simulated telecommuting task. *Journal of Gerontology* 59B: 305–16.

Shephard, R. J. 1995. A personal perspective on aging and productivity, with particular reference to physically demanding work. *Ergonomics* 38:617–36.

Sholes, C. L. 1878. Improvement in Type-Writing Machines, Letter's Patent 207,559, U.S. Patent Office.

Small, A. M. 1997. Design for older people. In *Handbook of Human Factors and Ergonomics,* 2nd ed., ed. G. Salvendy, 495–504. New York: Wiley.

Smith, S., Norris, B., and Peebles, L. 2000. *Older Adult Data: The Handbook of Measurements and Capabilities of the Older Adult—Data for Design Safety* (DTI Pub 4445/3k/01/00/NP). London: Department of Trade and Industry.

Sparks, K., Faragher, B., and Cooper, C. L. 2001. Well-being and occupational health in the twenty-first-century workplace. *Journal of Occupational and Organizational Psychology* 74:489–510.

Spence, A. P. 1994. *Biology of Human Aging,* 2nd ed. Englewood Cliffs, NJ: Prentice-Hall.

Steenbekkers, L. P. A., and van Beijsterveldt, C. E.M., eds. 1998. *Design-relevant Characteristics of Ageing Users.* Delft: Delft University Press.

Wegman, D. H., and McGee, J. P. 2004. *Health and Safety Needs of Older Workers.* Washington, DC: National Academies Press.

Zemke, R., Raines, C., and Filipczak, B. 2000. *Generations at Work: Managing the Clash of Veterans, Boomers, Xers, and Nexters in Your Workplace.* New York: Amacom.

CHAPTER SIXTEEN

Safety and Health Issues for an Aging Workforce

JAMES W. GROSCH, PH.D., AND
GLENN S. PRANSKY, M.D., M.OCC.H.

In the workplace, the goal of continuing to work while remaining healthy and productive has received increasing attention in recent years (e.g., Ilmarinen, 1999; Rix, 2001; National Research Council, 2004). Much of the interest in this issue stems from the fact that the proportion of all workers who are over 55 is projected to increase twice as fast as their younger counterparts over the next decade. These older workers can be expected to spend more of their lives working due to increasing longevity and to both a decrease and a postponement of retirement benefits (Hayward, Grady, and McLaughlin, 1988). Despite much interest in maintaining older workers in the workforce, there is relatively little research on the unique health and safety issues of older workers, how they are affected by work organization, and how these issues affect occupational injury and work performance. Although older workers are more likely to have chronic health conditions and physical limitations, these factors are not directly related to decreased work performance. The causes and consequences of work injury in older persons are complex and may differ from those in younger workers (Pransky, Santosh, Lee, and Webster, 2006). Although there is considerable information on age-related differences in various types of work injuries, little is known about the most effective methods for rehabilitation and prevention of re-injury in older workers (DeZwart, Frings-Dresen, and VanDijk, 1995). This chapter reviews the state of knowledge in this area, identifies interventions that address workplace health and safety in older workers, and suggests future research directions.

AGE-RELATED CHANGES IN FUNCTIONING
AND RELATION TO WORK

A good deal of what we know about aging has come from research conducted in nonwork settings (e.g., laboratory experiments, epidemiological investigations of the general population) but has implications for worker safety and health. In terms of biological and physical functioning, it is clear that virtually every system in the body declines in functioning as we age (Masoro and Austad, 2001). This includes sensory systems (e.g., vision, hearing), pulmonary functioning, bone health, metabolism, cardiovascular ability, thermoregulation, immune functioning, musculoskeletal capacity, and skin elasticity. A complete review of these biological and physical changes is beyond the scope of this chapter, but certain fundamental features of the aging process should be noted.

Cognitive functioning, which has become increasingly important in many workplaces, also tends to decline with age. Research on what is termed "fluid" or "working" memory, which refers to the efficiency of processing information, has consistently found nearly continuous declines from early adulthood on tasks such as novel problem solving, associative learning, real-time processing, and free recall (Park, 2000). Cognitive decline is particularly evident for more complex/difficult tasks that have not been previously performed and is thought to involve reduced working memory capacity, reduced attentional resources, and slower information processing rates for older adults. One notable exception to the decline in cognitive functioning is "crystallized" intelligence, which refers to accumulated knowledge or wisdom. Research indicates that this type of cognitive ability is largely unaffected by the aging process and may even increase throughout the life course until late adulthood (Craik, 2000). Furthermore, crystallized intelligence may allow individuals to at least partially compensate for age-related declines in working memory when it comes to performance on complex tasks (e.g., typing, playing chess, flying a plane), although the degree of this compensation is subject to some debate (e.g., Charness, 1981; Salthouse, 1984; Morrow, Leirer, Alteri, and Fitzsimmons, 1994).

In terms of overall health, the past several decades have seen significant improvements for all age groups in the U.S. population. However, older adults are still more likely to develop a number of chronic health conditions such as arthritis, osteoporosis, diabetes, hypertension, respiratory disease, heart disease, stroke, Alzheimer's disease, and many forms of cancer (Federal Interagency Forum on Aging-Related Statistics, 2006). When a chronic health condition does occur, older adults are also more likely to have preexisting comorbidities that can complicate recovery. Self-rated health status and work ability tend to decline gradually with age, whereas health care utilization and expenditures and the likelihood of disability increase. There is also a trend toward increasing obesity in older workers and evidence of a strong link of obesity to work injury risk (Pollack et al., 2007). Depression and other mental health problems remain fairly stable with increasing age, with some evidence that depressive symptoms increase for those 80 years or older.

In general, age-related changes in functioning can have different rates of decline, with some evident as early as adolescence and others unnoticeable until the 70s (Rabbit, 1991). Also, changes may be discernible long before an individual notices a difference in abilities. The specific effects of aging are not always linear or generalizable, especially in nonelderly persons. Older adults tend to show greater variation in functioning than younger adults. This latter finding has been used to argue for the importance of both environmental and individual-level factors in the aging process and the possibility of reducing the rate of decline by controlling exposures, such as through the development of safer work environments or the adoption of healthy lifestyle practices (e.g., smoking cessation). It also suggests that, by itself, chronological age is a rather inadequate indicator of whether or not an individual is able to perform a given activity or task.

Given the changes outlined above, we might expect older workers to be at a substantial disadvantage when it comes to safety and health outcomes at work. For example, declining vision and hearing abilities, coupled with slower reaction time, reduced musculoskeletal capacity, and poorer working memory, might make older workers more susceptible to many types of injuries and health problems. However, there are a number of reasons why this may not necessarily be the case. Peter Warr has pointed out that older workers are at risk of being "age impaired" only when the task requirements of a job increasingly exceed a worker's abilities (Warr, 1994; Laflamme and Menckel, 1995). And for many types of jobs, an individual's physical and cognitive abilities can decline substantially before they are exceeded by the demands of the job. Age impairment, according to Warr, also requires that a worker be in a job where successful adaptation to declining abilities by relying on acquired knowledge or experience or by transferring to other activities is not possible. Yet older workers often seem to excel at making these adaptations across different work settings. As a result, it is not entirely clear how much of what is known about the aging process is generalizable to occupational contexts. Many studies on aging have been conducted in laboratory settings or focus on the very old and thus may have limited validity for working populations who by and large are not as elderly (Wegman, 1999). As age increases over 55, those who are working are more likely to represent a relatively healthy survivor population, with better health and occupational capabilities compared to the total population (Holden, 1988). Less is known about the effects of aging in middle-aged populations (those 40–64) who comprise the bulk of the working "old" (*Lancet*, 1993).

WHAT DO WE KNOW ABOUT OCCUPATIONAL SAFETY AND HEALTH OUTCOMES?

As it turns out, research on older workers presents a more complex picture of how aging can affect occupational safety and health outcomes than might be inferred from laboratory studies with older adults. This section reviews evidence from the workplace linking age to a number of selected measures of safety and health.

Nonfatal and Fatal Occupational Injuries

Over the past several decades, the link between age and workplace injury has been widely studied (e.g., Root, 1981; Laflamme and Menckel, 1995; Salminen, 2004). The most commonly reported age-related pattern is presented in figure 16.1, which shows recent data from two different sources in the United States: a national sample of hospital emergency room departments (NEISS) and the Census of Fatal Occupational Injures (CFOI), which is maintained by the Bureau of Labor Statistics (BLS). Denominator data regarding the total number of workers in each age category were calculated using estimates of employed civilian workers from the Current Population Survey (CPS).

In figure 16.1, the rate of nonfatal injuries/illnesses shows a gradual decline with age that levels off for workers 65 years or older. Although NEISS data combine work-related injuries and illnesses, this declining pattern has been frequently reported in studies that focus solely on nonfatal injuries (e.g., Mitchell, 1988). Explanations as to why nonfatal injuries decline with age include the following: (a) the compensatory benefits of experience and knowledge that older workers acquire over time; (b) reduced exposure to hazardous working conditions because of greater seniority or control over work assignments; (c) a reporting bias in which health complaints in older workers are more likely to be ascribed to the normal aging process or to age-associated chronic conditions than to a particular work-related injury; and (d) a healthy-worker or selection effect in

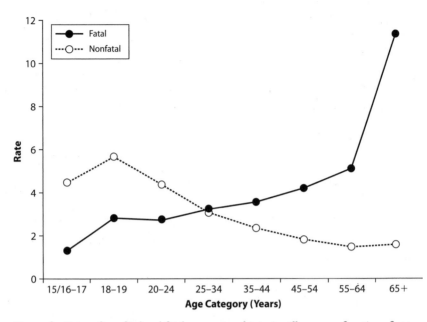

Figure 16.1. Rates of nonfatal and fatal occupational injuries/illness as a function of age. Nonfatal data are per 100 full-time equivalent workers aged ≥15 and are for nonfatal occupational injuries and illnesses among workers treated in hospital emergency departments. Fatal data are per 100,000 workers aged ≥16 and are for fatal occupational injuries. *Source:* Fatal data: National Electronic Injury Surveillance System (NEISS-Work), United States, 2004. Nonfatal data: Bureau of Labor Statistics Census of Fatal Occupational Injuries, United States, 2005.

which workers who have limitations in work capacity prematurely select out of high-risk jobs or withdraw from the workforce entirely (Holden, 1988; Laflamme, Menckel, and Lundholm, 1996; Kowalski-Trakofler, Steiner, and Schwerha, 2005). However, a declining rate is more common for men than for women, who tend to display a more level pattern with increasing age (Smith et al., 2005).

It should also be noted that a decline with age in nonfatal injuries is not a completely universal finding. Some studies focusing on specific occupations or types of injuries have reported little, if any, relationship with age (e.g., Butani, 1988) or a curvilinear relationship (e.g., Siu, Phillips, and Leung, 2003). The decline in rate may not occur for injures that are most affected by the physiological changes that accompany aging. For example, data from the 2004 NEISS on fall-related injuries indicate that the rate of falls at work for both men and women declines until the 45–54 age group and then rises for workers 65 years or older (*Morbidity and Mortality Weekly Report* [*MMWR*], 2007b). In the case of injury severity, there is clearly a positive relationship with age. For example, the likelihood of fracture tends to increase as workers reach 55 years or older (Rogers and Wiatrowski, 2005). These disparate findings suggest that the role of age in nonfatal injuries may be partly affected by the nature of the injury, the specific work activities being carried out, or other contextual factors in the workplace.

Figure 16.1 also shows that when an occupational injury does occur, it is more likely to be fatal as workers become older (see solid line). Of the 5,734 fatal injuries recorded in 2005 by CFOI, 26.4 percent occurred to workers 55 years or older, despite the fact that this group represents only 16.4 percent of the total working population. The dramatic increase in the fatality rate for workers 65 years or older has been reported in other studies (McGwin et al., 2002) and indicates that this age group is at a particularly increased risk. The higher fatality rate with age is also found when specific types of events are considered that lead to death, such as highway incidents, being struck by an object, falls to a lower level, and homicides (*MMWR*, 2007a). Age-effects in fatalities remain after controlling for industry and occupation, suggesting that this risk is not simply reflecting differences in the types of jobs younger and older workers hold (Mitchell, 1988). Possible reasons for the elevated fatality rate include greater susceptibility of older workers, lower baseline functioning, the effects of cumulative exposures, and the nature of the incident that leads to the fatality (National Research Council, 2004).

Musculoskeletal Disorders

Musculoskeletal disorders (MSDs) refer to disorders of the muscles, nerves, tendons, joints, cartilage, and spinal discs, and represent one of the most frequent and costly types of occupational injuries (Moore and Garg, 1992; National Institute for Occupational Health and Safety [NIOSH], 1999). Examples include lower back pain, carpal tunnel syndrome, rotator cuff strain, and tendonitis of the knee. MSDs are considered to be multifactorial or the result of a complex array of variables that can interact and vary over time (National Research Council, 2001). This complexity may contribute to the different findings that exist regarding how age and MSDs are related.

One common finding has been an inverted U relationship, where MSDs increase steadily with age and then decline for older age groups. For example, an analysis of worker's compensation claims in Washington State between 1996 and 2004 found that in most industries MSDs increased steadily until workers reached the 35–44 age group and then declined until the 65 or older group, at which point the rate of MSDs per 100,000 workers was similar to that for the youngest workers (SHARP, 2006). A study of the Swedish construction industry also found increasing prevalence with age that declined for the oldest age group—in this case, workers 60 or older (Holmström and Engholm, 2003). In this study, MSDs were assessed according to self-reports of discomfort during the past 12 months. The decline for workers 60 years or older occurred for MSDs in different body locations (e.g., neck, shoulder, elbow, lower back, hand) for both construction workers and foremen. A recent analysis of BLS data in the United States also suggested that MSDs seemed to be more of a problem for middle-aged workers. This analysis showed that MSDs represented a lower percentage of the overall number of nonfatal injuries and illnesses for workers 55 years or older, compared to workers 25–54 years of age (NIOSH, 2004).

However, not all studies on MSDs have found this pattern (Holness, Beaton, and House, 1998; Peek-Asa, McArthur, and Kraus, 2004). For example, a review of the literature on lower back disorders reported that only five out of twelve studies (or 42%) reported a significant association between age and reports of physical discomfort, whereas three out of four studies (or 75%) found an association between age and the actual incidence of lower back disorders (Ferguson and Marras, 1997). This suggests that the specific type of MSD and how it is measured may be a factor.

Another issue is the degree to which information about workplace exposure is taken into account. Figure 16.2 presents combined data from the 2002 and 2006 General Social Survey (GSS) in which a nationally representative sample of workers ($n = 3,431$) was asked if they had experienced back pain during the past 12 months, and whether or not their jobs required repeated lifting. When only self-reported back pain is considered (solid line), the relationship with age is fairly stable, declining slightly for the oldest age group. However, when the risk of back pain is considered, given a job that involves repeated lifting (broken line), the risk clearly increases with age. This increased risk may reflect a greater susceptibility to back pain in older workers exposed to lifting (e.g., higher prevalence of spinal stenosis or other degenerative conditions that are aggravated by heavy lifting at work), or it may reflect the cumulative effect of repeated exposures experienced over an individual's working life. In either case, older workers in physically demanding occupations may be at particularly higher risk for developing MSDs, such as back pain. Figure 16.2 also indicates that it is important to ascertain exposure information and that simple prevalence estimates may yield a different picture with regard to how MSDs and age are related.

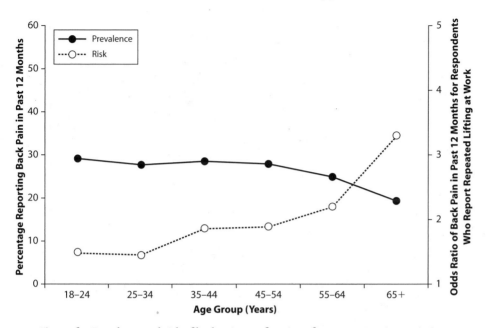

Figure 16.2. Prevalence and risk of back pain as a function of age. *Source:* Author's calculations based on General Social Survey, 2002, 2006

Return to Work

For 2005, the Bureau of Labor Statistics estimated that a total of 4.2 million nonfatal occupational injuries/illnesses occurred in U.S. private industries (BLS, 2006). Of this number, 1.2 million (or 29%) involved at least one lost work day. As shown in figure 16.3, the median number of lost days due to work-related injuries/illnesses increased from 4 in workers 16–24 years old to 12 in workers 65 years or older. This threefold increase reflects the fact that the percentage of injuries/illnesses involving long absences before returning to work (31 or more days) increased steadily with age, whereas the percentage with short absences (1–5 days) decreased. The types of injury/illness that produced the highest median number of lost work days included carpal tunnel syndrome (27 days), fractures (27 days), amputations (22 days), and tendonitis (12 days). The finding of a longer recovery time for older workers has also been reported in studies of worker's compensation (Stover et al., 2007) and studies focusing on specific types of health problems, including chronic back disorders (Mayer, Gatchel, and Evans, 2001), traumatic brain injury (Rao et al., 1990), coronary bypass surgery (Speziale et al., 1996), and lower extremity fractures (MacKenzie et al., 1998).

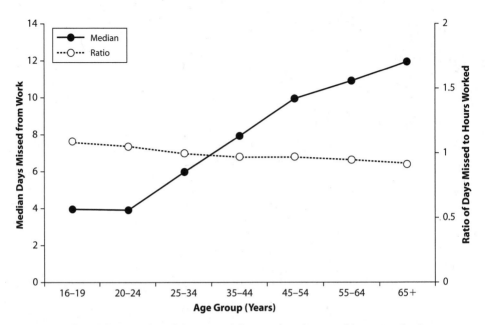

Figure 16.3. Median number of days missed from work and ratios of days missed to hours worked as a function of age, calculated as the percentage of injuries/illnesses involving missed work days divided by the percentage of total hours worked for each age category. A ratio score above 1.0 indicates that the percentage of injuries/illnesses involving missed work is greater than what could be expected from the number of hours worked. A ratio below 1.0 indicates that the percentage of injuries/illnesses is less than what would be expected from hours worked. *Source*: Bureau of Labor Statistics, 2005; Current Population Survey, 2005

The two most widely cited reasons for longer recovery in older workers are severity of injury and recuperative ability. Evidence suggests that injuries in older workers tend to be more severe in terms of the nature of the incident that occurs, for example, a fall with a fracture (Verma et al., 2007). Despite this fact, studies on return to work do not always control for this possible confound. Moreover, when an injury does occur, the body of an older worker may simply take longer to heal, even when the injury is exactly the same as that experienced by a younger worker. Additional factors that may contribute to longer recovery include: (a) older workers having less access to adequate rehabilitative services; (b) employers implicitly discouraging older workers from returning to work, particularly in jobs requiring physical effort or in occupations where a supply of younger, less costly workers is available; and (c) less attachment to a post-retirement job, or choosing to retire after an injury—all resulting in a record of prolonged post-injury work absence in BLS data (Thomas, Browning, and Greenwood, 1994; Pransky, Benjamin, and Savageau, 2005).

Figure 16.3 also presents BLS data from 2005 regarding the ratio of injuries/illnesses involving lost work days to hours worked (see broken line). This measure is an indicator of rate, and a value of 1.0 means that the percentage of injuries/illnesses involving lost work days was identical to the percentage of hours worked. As demonstrated in figure 16.3, the ratio declined gradually with age, indicating that older workers (in this case, 35 years or older) had a lower percentage of injuries/illnesses than would be expected based on hours worked. This suggests, once again, a tradeoff between severity and frequency. Although increasing age is associated with greater recovery time, it seems to also predict a reduced likelihood of experiencing an injury/illness that results in lost work days.

An important limitation of BLS data regarding older workers is that they do not capture the complexity of the return to work process and the range of variables that may play a role. Studies that have taken a more in-depth perspective have sometimes reported findings not consistent with BLS data. For example, Pransky et al. (2005) collected self-report survey data from a large sample of injured workers in New Hampshire who had reported lost work days. The surveys were completed 2–8 weeks after the injury to assess how well the return to work process had gone. Despite more severe injuries in older workers (>55 years), outcome measures such as duration of work disability, injury-related pain, decrease in work capacity, and medical care visits were similar to those of younger workers (<55 years).

Bivariate comparisons also found that older workers had significantly higher pre-injury job satisfaction, experienced more positive responses from employers after the injury, were more satisfied with the response of the worker's compensation insurer, and reported fewer problems on returning to work, perhaps as a consequence of well-established relationships in the workplace. In other words, older workers appeared to be more content and to have suffered fewer residual symptoms than younger workers. Multivariate analyses revealed only one significant association with age: injury-related financial problems were greater in younger workers. These results illustrate the need to go beyond the simple measure of "days lost" in studying return to work and strongly suggest that older workers may have certain advantages (e.g., stronger attachment to the organization, better post-injury employer support, healthy worker effect) that facilitate the return to work process.

Absenteeism and Presenteeism

Studies of absenteeism focus on days lost from work due to both work and non-work-related events. Data from the 2006 Current Population Survey (CPS), a monthly national survey of approximately 50,000 households, indicate that workers 55 years or older had a slightly higher rate for absences because of illnesses/injuries than workers 25 to 54 (3.0% versus 2.2% during the reference week) but a slightly lower rate for absences due to other reasons (e.g., personal responsibilities; 0.7% versus 1.0% during the reference week; CPS, 2007). Unfortunately, more detailed data were not available for those workers 55 years or older.

Absenteeism research conducted in a specific organizational setting has often made a distinction between absence frequency (sometimes referred to as "voluntary") and absence duration (sometimes referred to as "involuntary"). Two different meta-analyses of organizational studies both reported a modest inverse relationship between age and absence frequency, or that older workers tended to have lower rates of missing work (Martocchio, 1989; Hackett, 1990). The meta-analysis conducted by Martocchio also found an inverse relationship between age and absence duration, whereas the meta-analysis by Hackett did not. The lack of a positive relationship between age and either type of absenteeism stands in contrast to the BLS data on workplace injuries/illnesses cited earlier and suggests that how absenteeism is measured is itself an important variable. In addition, national-level administrative data such as that collected by the CPS may not always lead to the same conclusions as data collected in a specific organizational setting.

A complement to absenteeism is "presenteeism," that is, when workers are physically present but not functioning well because of illness or other health conditions, such as migraine headaches, depression, or allergies (Brouwer, Koopmanschap, and Rutten, 1999; Turpin et al., 2004). Presenteeism is a work impairment that affects a significant percentage of the workforce and reduces overall productivity. A number of studies that include age as a variable have reported a negative relationship, signifying that older workers are in general less susceptible to this phenomena than younger or middle-aged workers (e.g., Aronsson, Gustafsson, and Dallner, 2000; Burton et al., 2004; Collins et al., 2005; Musich et al., 2006). Although presenteeism research is still it its early stages, possible reasons for an inverse association with age include a healthy worker effect and more effective adaptation by older adults to health problems they may be experiencing (Turpin et al, 2004).

Health-Related Costs

Given the above data on injuries/illnesses and return to work, an important issue is whether or not the costs of work-related injuries and illness will increase significantly as the workforce continues to age. Analysis of workers compensation data in the state of Ohio suggests that the association between age and cost of injury depends on a number of factors, including the type of injury and the industry in which the worker is employed (Dunning, Jewell, Lockey, and Shuklah, 2004). For example, medical costs were found to be higher in older workers who experienced lumbar sprain and knee internal derangement, but lower when the work-related injury involved shoulder tendonitis or carpal tunnel syndrome. In a study of workers compensation claims in eight major states, Tattrie, Gotz, and Liu (2000) estimated that between 1995 and 2020 total costs will be .07 percent *lower* than they would have been if the age of the workforce had remained the same. Furthermore, they note that the impact of age should have been greater in the 1970s, 80s, and 90s, when the baby boom generation was moving into middle-age. Because costs per claim differ only slightly between middle-aged and older workers (as compared with younger versus middle-aged workers), the overall effect of aging on future overall costs is expected to be small. This general conclusion is supported by Restrepo, Sobel, and Shuford (2006), who argued that most of the impact of aging on workers' compensation has already occurred. However, it should also be noted that workers' compensation policies can vary greatly across states, so there may be situations in which age has a larger effect than reported in these two industry-based reports.

A different type of health benefit is employee health insurance for nonoccupational conditions. Employer policies vary considerably regarding what types of health condition are covered and the extent of coverage. Even so, there is a consistent finding that the cost of health insurance increases steadily with a worker's age. For example, using data from the 2002 Medical Expenditures Panel Survey, Johnson, Mermin, and Steuerle (2006) reported that covered workers in their early 60s incurred an annual average of $3,579 worth of insured health expenses. This compared with only $1,301 for covered workers in their early 30s. This type of age-related difference has been reported by other researchers, and evidence exists that health insurance costs can provide a disincentive for hiring older workers, particularly when these costs are high (Scott, Berger, and Garen, 1995; Lahey, 2007).

The Impact of Changes in Work Organization

A macro-level variable that can significantly affect occupational safety and health is work organization, which refers to the work process and the organizational practices that influence job design, including how jobs and human resource policies are structured (Sauter et al., 2002). Recent changes in work organization include flatter management structures and greater reliance on teams, organizational restructuring (often downsizing) in which all but core functions are outsourced, nontraditional employment arrangements that depend on temporary or contingent workers and lean production technologies such as just-in-time manufacturing. Many of these changes, while focused on improving organizational efficiency, can also produce stressful working conditions such as increased workload and greater job insecurity.

The impact of recent changes in work organization is only beginning to be understood, and research focusing specifically on older workers is limited. However, it is clear that older workers are more likely than younger workers to be found in nontraditional employment settings such as being self-employed, working part-time or from home, working in a small business with fewer than ten employees, and working as independent contractors (Karoly and Zissimopoulos, 2004; Grosch, 2006; Johnson and Kawachi, 2007). For older workers, this type of employment may have the advantage of providing greater flexibility in balancing work and non-work demands, but it also makes monitoring and improving the safety and health of older workers more challenging.

Although older workers typically report slightly higher levels of job satisfaction than younger workers (e.g., Janson and Martin, 1982; see also chapter 17 for additional data on age-related differences in quality of work life), some research suggests that older workers may be disproportionately affected by certain aspects of work organization. For example, research on involuntary job loss, such as that resulting from downsizing, has found that older workers often have greater trouble finding reemployment, and when they do, it is often at a significantly lower salary (Kivimäki et al., 2003). Displaced older workers can also experience significant declines in physical functioning and mental health, with an elevated risk for health problems such as stroke and musculoskeletal disorders, compared to displaced younger workers (Vahtera, Kivimäki, and Pentti, 1997; Gallo, Bradley, Siegel, and Kasl, 2000; Gallo et al., 2004). These differences tend to persist even after controlling for baseline differences in health and sociodemographic factors.

When it comes to work schedules, research suggests that workers over the age of 40 have greater difficulty tolerating shift work than do younger workers and are more susceptible to some of the health problems often associated with shift work, such as digestive, cardiovascular, and psychological disorders (Tepas, Duchon, and Gersten, 1993; Härmä and Ilmarinen, 1999). Older workers also appear to have greater difficulty tolerating situations involving tight time constraints and assembly line work (Molinié and Volkoff, 1994), and there is evidence of a differential physiological response to job strain. For example, Schnall et al. (1992) reported that ambulatory blood pressure was increased more by job strain in men aged 51–60 and 41–50 than among those 31–40 years old. Some studies have found a similar pattern when cardiovascular disease is the outcome variable (Johnson, Hall, and Theorell, 1989), while other studies have reported greater susceptibility among younger workers (Theorell et al., 1998). Additional variables related to work organization that have been discussed as possibly interacting with age are social support, training opportunities, work demands, and lack of professional development (Griffiths, 1997), although systematic empirical research is currently lacking. As the workplace continues to become more technologically complex with newer forms of work organization, understanding the role of these variables for older workers will become increasingly important.

RESEARCH DIRECTIONS

Our growing understanding of the link between age and occupational health has led to many suggestions for future research. This section highlights three general areas of research that we consider to be especially important: at-risk older workers, longitudinal/in-depth studies of aging, and intervention research.

At-Risk Older Workers

In most studies, older workers are treated as a single, homogeneous group. However, more research is needed on specific subgroups of older workers who may be at increased risk for experiencing adverse safety and health outcomes. For example, older workers who remain in jobs with high physical demands may become increasingly susceptible to the workplace exposures they experience, particularly when job demands exceed declining work capacity. In one of the rare longitudinal studies on this topic, older workers in physically demanding jobs showed a more rapid decline in self-reported work ability (a significant predictor of disability) over an 11-year period, compared to older workers in mentally demanding or mixed jobs (Ilmarinen, Tuomi, and Klockars, 1997). These findings raise the issue of what factors are responsible for increased susceptibility, and why it seems to occur for physical exposures but apparently not for mental ones.

Another dimension on which older workers differ is socioeconomic status (SES), a variable that has long been associated with many types of occupational health disparities (e.g., Marmot and Shipley, 1996; Marmot et al., 1997). Low-SES jobs have characteristics that can affect a worker's safety and health, such as low levels of autonomy, moderately high levels of physical demands and hazardous working conditions, little impact of work within an organization, low skill level, high job insecurity, and limited interpersonal contacts (Bernstein and Gittleman, 2003). Only a few empirical studies of low-SES workers have been conducted (e.g., Lee, Teng, Lim, and Gallo, 2005), and much remains to be learned about the different pathways through which SES influences safety and health.

A related dimension involves older workers who remain in their jobs because they have no other choice, often due to financial necessity or in order to obtain some form of health care coverage. This "job lock" phenomenon has been found to affect slightly more than 50 percent of injured older workers and is associated with poorer health and mental functions, lower job satisfaction, declining work performance and increased work absences, and incomplete recovery after a work-related injury (Benjamin, Pransky, and Savageau, 2008). Feeling locked into one's job, however, is not limited to low-SES workers but can extend to higher-SES workers with significant financial responsibilities or prior existing health conditions that require treatment. In either case, more research is needed to understand the long-term health effects of job lock and to develop workplace accommodations that can ameliorate these effects.

Finally, more knowledge is needed regarding the role of gender differences in work-related safety and health outcomes, especially given the increasing number of older women in the workplace over the past 25 years (Federal Interagency Forum on Aging-Related Statistics, 2006). In the study on job lock cited above, women were more likely than men to report job lock (56% versus 51%). Older female workers are also more likely to be widowed, have limited work experience, and have fewer financial resources in terms of pension and retirement benefits. These factors (and others) may affect the types of employment older female workers choose as well as the health risks they experience and the availability of resources in the workplace (e.g., training opportunities) for dealing with these risks.

Longitudinal and More In-Depth Studies

A limitation of many studies on older workers is a reliance on cross-sectional samples that make it extremely difficult to disentangle true aging effects from cohort and selection effects. For instance, the finding that reports of back pain decrease slightly with age (see figure 16.2) may be confounded by the fact that workers who do experience back pain are more likely to change occupations or leave the labor force entirely, thereby creating a survivor group of workers that becomes relatively more healthy with age. Longitudinal datasets have the advantage of comparing workers to themselves over time and can often provide a much different picture of the changes associated with aging. A few national longitudinal datasets do exist (e.g., Health and Retirement Study, National Longitudinal Surveys of Youth, Panel Study of Income Dynamics), but these have tended to be underused by occupational health researchers, perhaps because work-related injuries and illnesses were not the main focus and data on the relationship between health and work were limited. Sorely needed are new longitudinal datasets that contain detailed information about workers' employment histories, workplace exposures and risks, and work-related health outcomes (see National Research Council, 2004, for additional recommendations on this topic).

A related issue is that some studies have focused on relatively simple outcome measures (e.g., percentage who return to work) that are easy to quantify but may not capture the complexity of the interrelationships between aging, work, and health. Research on topics such as musculoskeletal disorders and return to work suggests that a more in-depth, multilevel (e.g., individual, job, organizational) approach is needed if we are to resolve contradictory findings and gain a more complete picture of the experiences workers go through. As part of this approach, a greater reliance on qualitative research methods may help broaden the range of variables that are considered to be important.

Intervention Research

Although age-related increases in risk for occupational and nonoccupational conditions are well documented, development of interventions or best practices to improve occupational safety and health outcomes is at an early stage. Few programs specifically addressing the unique needs of older workers have been evaluated and reported in the scientific literature. Clearly, this is a priority area for future intervention research. However, based on the limited evidence available and results from programs designed to address safety and health of the entire workforce, some suggestions for interventions and future research can be offered.

Interventions can be categorized as primary (designed to prevent loss of work capacity or work injury), secondary (designed to prevent disability if illness or injury occurs), and tertiary (designed to restore function and work ability after injury or illness). Many of the interventions that might prevent work injury (such as decreasing maximum physical job demands) would also affect disability prevention and return to work. They can be organized by target area—workplace, individual, health care system, benefits system. Table 16.1 lists target areas and possible interventions.

Most of these interventions are essentially recommendations that have yet to be systematically studied. For example, ergonomic modifications may be an important pathway that enable older workers to stay on the job, to avoid injury, and to facilitate return after illness of injury. Suggestions include slower and more self-paced work, more rest breaks, less repetitive tasks, avoidance of static postures, better illumination, less glare, and more adjustable seating (Thomas et al., 1994; Chaffin and Ashton-Miller, 1991). For workers with chronic illness, flexible work schedules may be important to accommodate medical care and periods of decreased work ability. Flexible hours may be the most important accommodation for those who need periodic visits to health care providers (Mitchell, 1990). However, many with serious chronic illnesses require at most minimal accommodations; thus an individualized, not diagnosis-specific approach is necessary. Older workers often have the best experience and knowledge needed to design optimal accommodations and modifications, and some of the most effective accommodations are those arranged informally by workers and their co-workers and supervisors (Daly and Bound, 1996). These changes are often inexpensive and tailored to meet the specific needs of an older worker with a unique set of abilities and limitations. Unfortunately, worker input is often neglected in typical disability management systems that rely primarily on a medically deterministic model (Pransky, Shaw, Franche, and Clarke, 2004).

In addition to the interventions presented in table 16.1, many strategies have been proposed from a public policy perspective for recruiting older workers and encouraging continued labor force participation (e.g., Walker 1997; General Accounting Office, 2007). Examples include redesigning pension plans, increasing the age for Social Security benefits, and providing tax incentives to employers as a way of motivating them to hire older workers. Although these and other strategies hold promise, few are ever evaluated in terms of their potential impact on worker safety and health. Increasing the retirement age, for instance, may affect

TABLE 16.1.
Target areas and possible interventions

Target area	Intervention
Workplace	
Physical job demands	Ergonomic modification, rest breaks, worker input for job changes
Psychological job demands	Evaluate worker-job fit; consider changes in assignment/schedule
Shift schedule	Evaluate shift tolerance; reduce shift work
Low decision latitude	Job enlargement
Limited advancement opportunity	Retraining/transfer to jobs where experience is important
Age discrimination	Employer/employee education
Workers	
Poor health behaviors	Age-tailored wellness programs
Decreased physical capacity	Exercise and regular evaluation of job fit
Chronic illness	Proactive disease management—focus on maintaining employment; greater flexibility in work hours, assignment
Age-related cognitive changes	Evaluate job-person fit; tailored training
Visual changes	Adjust lighting and contrast; glasses
Limited skills	Senior worker-specific training programs
Tendency not to report occupational injury	Worker and management education
More severe work injury	Customized post-absence follow-up
Higher fracture risk	Focus on preventing slips and falls
Longer recovery	Maintain workplace connection; effective return-to-work programs
Lower attachment to part-time job	Maintain post-illness/injury job contact
Health care system	
Poor recognition of work issues	Provider education about older workers
Need for longer recovery	Provider-workplace communication; recognize/address comorbidity
Illness/workplace interaction	Provider education/recognition
Age-appropriate rehabilitation	Age-specific systems and protocols; gerontology input in program design
Benefits system	
Inadequate retirement savings	Support advance/realistic planning
Higher health care costs	Adapt insurance plan to older workers' needs

labor force participation, but it may also place certain groups of older workers at increased risk for disability and other unintended health problems (e.g., Choi, 2000). As the discussion about programs and policies for an aging workforce continues, it is important that the protection of worker health and well-being remain a primary objective.

CONCLUSION

When it comes to occupational safety and health, age matters. However, the associations between age and health do not necessarily follow directly from laboratory studies or research conducted with elderly, nonworking populations. Some associations reviewed in this chapter suggest that older workers are at a relative disadvantage compared to younger workers (e.g., severity of injury), while other associations suggest a relative advantage (e.g., frequency of injury). There are also health outcomes (e.g., absenteeism, back pain) in which the role of age appears small or even inconsistent across studies and may be overshadowed by a number of other factors in the workplace (e.g., job attachment, physical job demands, and decision latitude). The result is a complex picture of the safety and health issues that will emerge as workers in the United States and other industrial countries continue to age. Clearly, more research is warranted to better understand these issues and to identify cost-effective interventions that can both protect and promote the safety and health of older workers.

NOTES

The findings and conclusions of this report are those of the authors and do not necessarily represent the views of the National Institute for Occupational Safety and Health or the Liberty Mutual Research Institute for Safety.

REFERENCES

Aronsson, G., Gustafsson, K., and Dallner, M. 2000. Sick but yet at work: An empirical study of sickness presenteeism. *Journal of Epidemiology and Community Health* 54: 502–509.

Benjamin, K. L., Pransky, G., and Savageau, J. A. 2008. Factors associated with retirement-related job lock in a cohort of workers with recent occupational injury. *Disability and Rehabilitation* 23:1–8.

Bernstein, J., and Gittleman, M. 2003. Exploring low-wage labor with the National Compensation Survey. *Monthly Labor Review* 126:3–12.

Brouwer, W. B. F., Koopmanschap, M. A., and Rutten, F. F. H. 1999. Productivity losses without absence: Measurement validation and empirical evidence. *Health Policy* 48: 13–27.

Bureau of Labor Statistics. 2006. Nonfatal occupational injuries and illnesses requiring days away from work, 2005. USDL 06-1982. Washington, DC: U.S. Department of Labor.

Burton, W. N., Pransky, G. S., Conti, D. J., Chen, C. Y., and Edington, D. W. 2004. The association of medical conditions and presenteeism. *Journal of Occupational and Environmental Medicine* 46:S38–45.

Butani, S. J. 1988. Relative risk analysis of injuries in coal mining by age and experience at present company. *Journal of Occupational Accidents* 10:209–16.

Chaffin, D. B., and Ashton-Miller, J. A. 1991. Biomechanical aspects of low-back pain in the older worker. *Experimental Aging Research* 17:177–87.

Charness, N. 1981. Search in chess: Age and skill differences. *Journal of Experimental Psychology: Human Perception and Performance* 7:467–76.

Choi, N. G. 2000. Potential consequences of raising the Social Security eligibility age on low-income older workers. *Journal of Aging and Social Policy* 11:15–38.

Collins, J. J, Baase, C. M., Sharda, C. E., Ozminkowski, R. J., Nicholson, S., Billotti, G. M., et al. 2005. The assessment of chronic health conditions on work performance, absence, and total economic impact for employers. *Journal of Occupational and Environmental Medicine* 47:547–57.

Current Population Survey. 2007. Table 46: Absences from work of employed full-time wage and salary workers by age and sex. Retrieved on October 22, 2007, from www.bls .gov/cps/cpsaat46.pdf.

Craik, F. I. 2000. Age-related changes in human memory. In *Cognitive Aging: A Primer,* ed. D. Park and N. Schwartz, 75–92. Philadelphia: Taylor & Francis.

Daly, M. C., and Bound, J. 1996. Worker adaptation and employer accommodation following the onset of a health impairment. *Journal of Gerontology* 51B: S53–60.

DeZwart, B. C. H., Frings-Dresen, M. H. W., and VanDijk, F. J. H. 1995. Physical workload and the aging worker: A review of the literature. *International Archives of Occupational and Environmental Health* 68:1–12.

Dunning, K., Jewell, G., Lockey, J., and Shuklah, R. 2004. Injuries among older workers: Diagnoses, treatment and disability. Presentation given as part of a research program on workers' compensation at the University of Cincinnati, Cincinnati, Ohio.

Federal Interagency Forum on Aging-Related Statistics. 2006. *Older Americans Update, 2006: Key Indicators of Well-being.* Washington, DC: U.S. Government Printing Office.

Ferguson, S., and Marras, W. 1997. A literature review of low back disorder assessment measures and risk factors. *Clinical Biomechanics* 12:211–26.

Gallo, W. T., Bradley, E. H., Galba, T. A., Dubin, J. A., Cramer, L. D., Bogardus Jr., S. T., et al. 2004. Involuntary job loss as a risk factor for subsequent myocardial infarction and stroke: Findings from the Health and Retirement Survey. *American Journal of Industrial Medicine* 45:408–16.

Gallo, W. T., Bradley, E. H., Siegel, M., and Kasl, S. V. 2000. Health effects of involuntary job loss among older workers: Findings from the Health and Retirement Survey. *Journal of Gerontology* 55B: S131–40.

General Accounting Office. 2007. *Highlights of a GAO Forum. Engaging and Retaining Older Workers.* GAO-07-438SP. Washington, DC:

Griffiths, A. 1997. Ageing, health and productivity: A challenge for the new millennium. *Work and Stress* 11:197–214.

Grosch, J. W. 2006. Older workers in the U.S.: National data regarding working conditions and health. Paper presented at the 28th International Congress on Occupational Health Conference, Milan, Italy.

Hackett, R. D. 1990. Age, tenure, and employee absenteeism. *Human Relations* 43:601–19.

Härmä, M. I., and Ilmarinen, J. E. 1999. Towards the 24-hour society: New approaches for aging shift workers? *Scandinavian Journal of Work, Environment, and Health* 25:610–15.

Hayward, M. D., Grady, W. R., and McLaughlin, S. D. 1988. Recent changes in mortality and labor force behavior among older Americans. *Journal of Gerontology* 43:S194–99.

Holden, K. C. 1988. Employment characteristics of older women, 1988. *Monthly Labor Review* 111:3–12.

Holmström, E., and Engholm, G. 2003. Musculoskeletal disorders in relation to age and occupation in Swedish construction workers. *American Journal of Industrial Medicine* 44:377–84.

Holness, D. L., Beaton, D., and House, R. A. 1998. Prevalence of upper extremity symptoms and possible risk factors in workers handling paper currency. *Occupational Medicine* 48:231–36.

Ilmarinen, J. 1999. *Ageing Workers in the European Union: Status and Promotion of Work Ability, Employability and Employment.* Helsinki: Finnish Institute of Occupational Health.

Ilmarinen, J., Tuomi, K, and Klockars, M. 1997. Changes in the work ability of active employees over an 11-year period. *Scandinavian Journal of Work, Environment, and Health* 23 (Supplement 1): 49–57.

Janson, P., and Martin, J. K. 1982. Job satisfaction and age: A test of two views. *Social Forces* 60:1089–1102.

Johnson, J. V., Hall, E. M., and Theorell, T. 1989. Combined effects of job strain and social isolation on cardiovascular disease morbidity and mortality in a random sample of the Swedish male working population. *Scandinavian Journal of Work, Environment and Health* 15:271–79.

Johnson, R. W., and Kawachi, J. 2007. *Job Changes at Older Ages: Effects on Wages, Benefits, and Other Job Attributes.* Washington, DC: Urban Institute.

Johnson, R. W., Mermin, G., and Steuerle, C. E. 2006. *Work Impediments at Older Ages.* Washington, DC: Urban Institute.

Karoly, L. A., and Zissimopoulos, J. 2004. Self-employment among older U.S. workers. *Monthly Labor Review* 127:24–47.

Kivimäki, M., Vahtera, J., Elovainio, M., Pentti, J., and Virtanen, M. 2003. Human costs of organizational downsizing: Comparing health trends between leavers and stayers. *American Journal of Community Psychology* 32:57–67.

Kowalski-Trakofler, K. M., Steiner, L. J., and Schwerha, D. J. 2005. Safety considerations for the aging workforce. *Safety Science* 43:779–93.

Laflamme, L., and Menckel, E. 1995. Aging and occupational accidents: A review of the literature of the last three decades. *Safety Science* 21:145–61.

Laflamme, L., Menckel, E., and Lundholm, L. 1996. The age-related risk of occupational accidents: The case of Swedish iron-ore miners. *Accident Analysis and Prevention* 28: 349–57.

Lahey, J. 2007. Does health insurance affect the employment of older workers? Issue Brief 08. Center on Aging and Work, Boston College.

Lancet editorial. 1993. Aging at work: Consequences for industry and individual. *Lancet* 240:87–88.

Lee, Y. G., Teng, H.-M., Lim, S.-H., and Gallo, W. T. 2005. Older workers: Who are the working poor in the U.S.? *Hallym International Journal of Aging* 7:95–113.

MacKenzie, E. J., Morris Jr., J. A., Jurkovich, G. J., Yasui, Y., Cushi, B. M., DeLateur, et al. 1998. Return to work following injury: The role of economic, job-related factors. *American Journal of Public Health* 88:1630–37.

Marmot, M. G., and Shipley, M. J. 1996. Do socioeconomic differences persist after retirement? 25-year follow of civil servants from the first White Study. *British Medical Journal* 313:1177–80.

Marmot, M. G., Bosma, H., Hemingway, H. J., Brunner, E., and Stansfeld, S. 1997. Contribution of job control and other risk factors to social variations in coronary heart disease incidence. *Lancet* 350:235–39.

Martocchio, J. J. 1989. Age-related differences in employee absenteeism: A meta-analysis. *Psychology and Aging* 4:409–14.

Masoro, E. J., and Austad, S. N., eds. 2001. *Handbook of the Biology of Aging*, 5th ed. San Diego, CA: Academic Press.

Mayer, T., Gatchel, R. J., and Evans, T. 2001. Effect of age on outcomes of tertiary rehabilitation for chronic disabling spinal disorders. *Spine* 26:1378–84.

McGwin, G., Jr., Valent, F., Taylor, A. J., Howard, H. J., Davis, G. G., Brissie, R. M., et al. 2002. Epidemiology of fatal occupational injuries in Jefferson County, Alabama. *Southern Medical Journal* 95:1300–1311.

Mitchell, O. S. 1988. The relation of age to workplace injuries. *Monthly Labor Review* 111: 8–13.

———. 1990. Aging, job satisfaction, and job performance. In *The Aging of the American Workforce: Problems, Programs, Policies*, ed. I. Bluestone, R. J. V. Montgomery, and J. D. Owen, 242–72. Detroit: Wayne State University Press.

Molinié, A. F., and Volkoff, S. 1994. Working conditions: Problems ahead for workers over the age of 40. In *Work and Aging: A European Perspective*, ed. J. Snel and R. Cremer, 214–23. London: Taylor & Francis.

Moore, J. S., and Garg, A., eds. 1992. Ergonomics: Low-back pain, carpal tunnel syndrome, and upper extremity disorders in the workplace. *Occupational Medicine: State of the Art Reviews* 7:593–790.

Morbidity and Mortality Weekly Report. 2007a. Fatal occupational injuries, United States, 2005. *MMWR* 56:297–301.

———. 2007b. Nonfatal occupational injuries and illnesses, United States, 2004. *MMWR* 56:393–97.

Morrow, D., Leirer, V., Alteri, P., and Fitzsimmons, C. 1994. When expertise reduces age differences in performance. *Psychology and Aging* 9:134–48.

Musich, S., Hook, D., Baaner, S., Spooner, M., and Edington, D. W. 2006. The association of corporate work environment factors, health risks, and medical conditions with presenteeism among Australian employees. *American Journal of Health Promotion* 21:127–36.

National Research Council. 2001. *Musculoskeletal Disorders and the Workplace: Low Back and Upper Extremities.* Panel on Musculoskeletal Disorders and the Workplace, Division of the Behavioral and Social Sciences and Education. Washington, DC: National Academy Press.

———. 2004. *Health and Safety Needs of Older Workers.* Committee on the Health and Safety Needs of Older Workers, Board on Behavioral, Cognitive, and Sensory Sciences, Division of the Behavioral and Social Sciences and Education. Washington, DC: National Academy Press.

National Institute for Occupational Safety and Health (NIOSH). 1999. *Musculoskeletal Disorders and Workplace Factors: A Critical Review of Epidemiologic Evidence for Work-Related Musculoskeletal Disorders of the Neck, Upper Extremity, and Lower Back.* Pub. No. 97-141. Washington, DC: Author.

———. 2004. *Worker Health Chartbook, 2004.* Publication No. 2004-146. Washington, DC: Author.

Park, D. 2000. The basic mechanisms accounting for age-related decline in cognitive function. In *Cognitive Aging: A Primer,* ed. D. Park and N. Schwartz, 3–22. Philadelphia: Taylor & Francis.

Peek-Asa, C., McArthur, D. L., and Kraus, J. F. 2004. Incidence of acute low-back injury among older workers in a cohort of material handlers. *Journal of Occupational and Environmental Hygiene* 1:551–57.

Pollack, K. M., Sorock, G. S., Slade, M. D., Cantley, L., Sircar, K., Taiwo, O., et al. 2007. Association between body mass index and acute traumatic workplace injury in hourly manufacturing employees. *American Journal of Epidemiology* 166:204–11.

Pransky, G. S., Benjamin, K. L., and Savageau, J. A. 2005. Early retirement due to occupational injury: Who is at risk? *American Journal of Industrial Medicine* 47:285–95.

Pransky, G. S., Benjamin, K. L., Savageau, J. A., Currivan, D., and Fletcher, K. 2005. Outcomes in work-related injuries: A comparison of older and younger workers. *American Journal of Industrial Medicine* 47:104–12.

Pransky, G. S., Santosh, V., Lee, O., and Webster, B. 2006. Length of disability prognosis in acute occupational low back pain: Development and testing of a practical approach. *Spine* 31:690–97.

Pransky, G. S., Shaw, W. S., Franche, R. L., and Clarke, A. 2004. Disability prevention and communication among workers, physicians, employers, and insurers: Current models and opportunities for improvement. *Disability and Rehabilitation* 26:625–34.

Rabbit, P. 1991. Management of the working population. *Ergonomics* 34:775–90.

Rao, N., Rosehthal, M., Cronin-Stubbs, D., Lambert, R., Barnes, P., and Swanson, B. 1990. Return to work after rehabilitation following traumatic brain injury. *Brain Injury* 4:49–56.

Restrepo, T., Sobel, S., and Shuford, H. 2006. *Age as a Driver of Frequency and Severity.* National Council on Compensation Insurance (Research Brief).

Rix, S. 2001. *Health and Safety Issues in an Aging Workforce.* Publication ID: IB49. Washington, DC: AARP.

Rogers, E., and Wiatrowski, W. J. 2005. Injuries, illnesses, and fatalities among older workers. *Monthly Labor Review* 128:24–30.

Root, N. 1981. Injuries at work are fewer among older employees. *Monthly Labor Review* 104:30–34.

Salminen, S. 2004. Have young workers more injuries than older ones? An international literature review. *Journal of Safety Research* 35:513–21.

Salthouse, T. A. 1984. Effects of age and skill in typing. *Journal of Experimental Psychology: General* 13:345–71.

Sauter, S. L., Brightwell, W. S., Colligan, M. J., Hurrell, J. J.J r., Katz, T. M., LeGrande, D. E., et al. 2002. *The Changing Organization of Work and the Safety and Health of Working People: Knowledge Gaps and Research Directions.* Publication No. 2002-116. Washington, DC: Department of Health and Human Services (NIOSH).

Schnall, P. I., Schwartz, J. E., Landsbergis, P. A., Warren, K., and Pickering, T. G. 1992. Relation between job strain, alcohol, and ambulatory blood pressure. *Hypertension* 19:488–94.

Scott, F. A., Berger, M. C., and Garen, J. E. 1995. Do health insurance and pension costs reduce the job opportunities of older workers? *Industrial and Labor Relations Review* 48: 775–91.

SHARP. 2006. *Work-Related Musculoskeletal Disorders in the Neck, Back, and Upper Extremity in Washington Sate, 1996–2004.* Technical Report Number 40-10a-2006. Olympia, WA: SHARP Program, Washington State Department of Labor and Industries.

Siu, O. L., Phillips, D. R., and Leung, T. W. 2003. Age differences in safety attitudes and safety performance in Hong Kong construction workers. *Journal of Safety Research* 34:199–205.

Smith, G. S., Wellman, H. M., Sorock, G. S., Warner, M., Courtney, T. K., Pransky, G. S., et al. 2005. Injuries at work in the U.S. adult population: Contributions to the total injury burden. *American Journal of Public Health* 95:1213–19.

Speziale, G., Bilotta, F., Ruvolo, G., Fattouch, K., and Marino, B. 1996. Return to work and quality of life measurement in coronary artery bypass grafting. *European Journal of Cardio-Thoracic Surgery* 10:852–58.

Stover, B., Wickizer, T. M., Zimmerman, F., Fulton-Kehoe, D., and Franklin, G. 2007. Prognostic factors of long-term disability in a workers' compensation system. *Journal of Occupational and Environmental Medicine* 49:31–40.

Tattrie, D., Gotz, G., and Liu, T-C. 2000. *Workers' Compensation and the Changing Age of the Workforce.* Cambridge, MA: Workers Compensation Research Institute

Tepas, D. I., Duchon, J. C., and Gersten, A. H. 1993. Shiftwork and the older worker. *Experimental Aging Research* 19:295–320.

Theorell, T., Tsutsumi, A., Hallquist, J., Reuterwall, C. Hogstdet, C., Fredlund, P., et al. 1998. Decision latitude, job strain, and myocardial infarction: A study of working men in Stockholm. SHEEP Study Group. Stockholm Heart epidemiology Program. *American Journal of Public Health* 88:382–88.

Thomas, S. A., Browning, C. J., and Greenwood, K. M. 1994. Rehabilitation of the older worker. *Disability and Rehabilitation* 16:162–70.

Turpin, R. S., Ozminkowski, R. J., Sharda, C. E., Collins, J. J., Berger, M. L., Billotti, G.M., et al. 2004. Reliability and validity of the Stanford Presenteeism Scale. *Journal of Occupational and Environmental Medicine* 46:1123–33.

Vahtera, J., Kivimäki, M, and Pentti, J. 1997. Effect of organizational downsizing on health of employees. *Lancet* 350:1124–28.

Verma, S. K., Sorock, G. S., Pransky, G. S., Courtney, T. K., and Smith, G. S. 2007. Occupational physical demands and same-level falls resulting in fracture in female workers: An analysis of workers' compensation claims. *Injury Prevention* 13:32–36.

Walker, A. 1997. *Combating Age Barriers in Employment: European Research Report*. Dublin, European Foundation for the Improvement of Living and Working conditions.

Warr, P. 1994. Age and employment. In *Handbook of Industrial and Organizational Psychology*, 2nd ed., Vol. 4, ed. H. C. Triandis, M. D. Dunnette, and L. M Hough, 485–550. Palo Alto, CA: Consulting Psychologists Press.

Wegman, D. 1999. Older workers. In H. Frumkin, and G. Pransky, eds., *State of the Art Reviews: Special Populations* 14:537–58.

CHAPTER SEVENTEEN

Work Organization and Health in an Aging Workforce

Observations from the NIOSH Quality of Work Life Survey

STEVEN L. SAUTER, PH.D., JESSICA M. STREIT, M.S., AND DENNIS J. HANSEMAN, PH.D.

The aging of populations in postindustrial countries is now a well-understood phenomenon. This trend has raised a variety of concerns such as the sustainability of the workforce, long-term care needs and costs for elderly people, and the viability of social insurance programs and pension systems.

Labor force demographics mirror this trend in population aging. In the United States, the long-term decline in labor force participation rates for individuals of ages 55 or older reversed in the early 1990s (Mosisa and Hipple, 2006), fueled mainly by the aging of the baby boom cohort and by economic incentives for workers to delay retirement. In the period 2005–2020, the age 55 or older segment of the workforce is expected to increase from just over 24 million workers to nearly 40 million workers. This represents an annual growth rate of 4.2 percent—more than five times the annual growth rate for the overall workforce (0.76%) and 21 times faster than the annual growth rate (0.2%) for workers in the 25–54 year age group (Toosi, 2006).

In contrast to the extensive public discussion surrounding economic and health care-related issues in the aging population, comparatively little attention has been given to occupational safety and health aspects of the aging workforce. In 2002, the National Institute for Occupational Safety and Health (NIOSH), the National Institute on Aging, and the Archstone Foundation asked the National Research Council (NRC) and the Institute of Medicine to convene a scientific committee to consider these health and safety aspects in more detail. The committee issued a report in 2004 discussing research issues that needed to be addressed regarding the health and safety of older workers (Wegman and McGee, 2004). Of special relevance in relation to the focus of this chapter, this report gives considerable attention to the role that work organization might play in affecting the health and safety of aging workers. The topic of work organization also appears quite prominently in other recent reviews on age, work, and health (Robertson and Tracy, 1998; Barnes-Farrell, 2005; Kowalski-Trakofler, Steiner, and Schwerha, 2005; Griffiths, 2007). However, apart from pioneering studies by Ilmarinen and colleagues at the Finnish Institute of Occupational Health, empirical research on work organization and health and safety among aging workers is surprisingly scarce.

In an 11-year prospective study to investigate "workability" (referring to the capacity to perform work, including physical, mental, and social functions) and the health of aging workers, Finnish researchers observed a relationship between decreased workability and disease symptoms, disability retirements, and mortality before retirement. Declines in workability were attributed both to high physical demands and to changes in work organization and the social environment at work (Tuomi et al., 1997a, 1997b). Role conflicts, unsatisfactory supervision, time pressure, and lack of influence over work were just some of the work organization factors linked to these outcomes.

This chapter goes beyond the issue addressed by Finnish investigators (i.e., effects of work organization on work capacity and health in aging workers) to focus on an issue that is equally important from the standpoint of work design and health protection for older workers: Do older workers differ somehow from younger workers in terms of risks posed by work organization factors? Two possibilities exist, and neither has been subjected to systematic study. First is the idea that work organization exposures may vary as a function of age, creating different risk profiles for older and younger workers. Second is the vulnerability hypothesis: that older workers may differ from younger workers in their capacity to respond to stressful situations related to work. This latter possibility is aptly framed by Griffiths (2007, 34), who commented that "key to our concerns for older workers, is that there may be specific characteristics of work design and management that are experienced as particularly problematic by older workers and therefore are likely to be particularly stressful for them."

This chapter examines these two possibilities further. We begin with a summary of findings from the literature on comparative levels of subjective well-being, including job stress, between older and younger workers. Age differences

in these outcomes might indicate age differences in risks posed by the organization of work. Next, we report on findings from the much smaller body of research
that directly investigates both age gradients in work organization exposures and
age differentials in the effects of work organization on health and safety outcomes. We then describe the results of new analyses we have conducted using
a nationally representative workforce sample to further explore these types of effects, including analyses of (1) age differences in a variety of health-related outcomes, (2) age differences in work organization exposures and work-life balance
indicators, and (3) age differences in the relationship of these exposure and balance factors with health-related outcomes.

AGE DIFFERENCES IN THE SUBJECTIVE WELL-BEING OF OLDER WORKERS

A substantial body of research on age gradients in various facets of subjective
well-being suggests a rather optimistic picture for older workers. For example,
the weight of the evidence suggests that older workers experience similar or even
reduced levels of job stress and improvements in overall mental health and job
satisfaction in comparison to younger workers.

Job Stress

Both occupation-specific investigations and results from large representative surveys find moderating levels of job stress among older workers. In a study of work
experiences of middle-aged (30–53 years) and preretirement-aged (54–72 years)
white collar workers, Remondet and Hansson (1991) found significantly reduced
job tension/stress and reduced generalized stress in the older workers. Similarly,
age-related reductions in stress have been reported among physicians (Swanson,
Power, and Simpson, 1996).

A trend toward reduced stress is also evident across the three strata of older
workers in the 2004 wave of the University of Michigan Health and Retirement
Survey (HRS). Agreement with the survey item "my job involves a lot of stress"
declined from 63 percent for workers aged 51–64 years, to 39 percent for workers aged 65–74 years, to 27 percent for workers older than 74.[1] Smith (2001) observed a modest inverted U-shaped trend between age and stress in a large
sample of employees from the Bristol (UK) electoral register. Workers aged
41–50 years in this sample were the most likely (21%) to report they felt "very" or

"extremely" stressed at work. By comparison, just 17 percent of workers more than 50 years old reported such high levels of stress, a rate closer to the prevalence for workers aged 18–32 years (16%).

One departure from this trend toward reduced stress among older workers is found in data on illness, disability, and physical problems from the British Labour Force Survey. As described by Griffiths (2007), results from the British survey in 2004–2005 showed that stress, depression, and anxiety together represented one of the two most populated categories of work-related illness, and that these conditions were more prevalent among older (aged 45 years to retirement) than among younger workers. However, this age differential in symptoms is not reflected at the broader European Union (EU) level in data from the year 2000 Third European Survey of Working Conditions that captured data from nearly 16,000 workers. Ilmarinen (2005) reported that data from this survey fail to show EU15-wide differences between workers under and over 45 years of age in the prevalence of work-related "psychosomatic syndrome" (affirmative response to one or more items pertaining to stress and tension, general fatigue, sleeping disorders, anxiety, irritability, or mental trauma) and in the prevalence of "stress syndrome" (affirmative response to one or more items denoting head and stomach ache, stress, general fatigue, or tension).

Mental Health

Evidence of age-related improvements in subjective well-being is stronger for mental health outcomes than for stress outcomes. A study of Hong Kong managers by Siu, Spector, Cooper, and Donald (2001) found older workers to exhibit improved mental well-being as measured on the Occupational Stress Indicator-2 (Williams and Cooper, 1996), and several other studies showed declines in depression and anxiety among older workers. The Remondet and Hansson (1991) study of white collar workers, for example, found significantly lower scores on the Center for Epidemiologic Studies Depression Scale (CES-D) in the older cohort. Frone, Russell, and Barnes (1996) also reported significant negative correlations between age and CES-D scores among employed parents in two studies of work-family conflict that used data from large community samples. Additionally, 2004 HRS data show a higher 12-month prevalence of two or more weeks of feeling sad, blue, or depressed among workers aged 51–64 years (22%) than for workers aged 65–74 years (7%). However, unlike the continuing decline for job stress, the prevalence of these states then increases among workers older than 74 years (17%).[2]

Similar to the curvilinear age-stress relationship observed by Smith (2001), Warr (1992) found an inverted U-shaped relationship between age and both anxiety and depression measures in a large sample of employed British adults. Although the quadratic effect became nonsignificant when possible explanatory (mediating) variables were added to the analysis, significant negative linear relationships remained. However, analysis of General Health Questionnaire scores from more than 5,000 employed participants in the 1991 British Household Panel Study revealed a curvilinear effect with improved context-free mental health among young and older participants that remained significant after adjustments for 80 control variables (Clark, Oswald, and Warr, 1996).

Job Satisfaction

Finally, studies looking at the relationship between age and job satisfaction show that older workers are favored. In the Remondet and Hansson (1991) study of white collar workers, significantly higher levels of job satisfaction were found in the older group (54–72 years) than in the middle-aged group (30–53 years). Most recently, Conference Board data from a sample of 5,000 U.S. households revealed a similar trend. Nearly half of workers aged 55 years or older reported they were satisfied with their jobs—a greater proportion than in any other age group (Conference Board, 2007). Data from the 2004 wave of the Health and Retirement Survey extend this trend to the very old. Twenty-eight percent of workers aged 51–64 years strongly agreed that they "really enjoy" going to work, and the level of agreement increased to 34 percent among workers aged 65–74 years and to 46 percent among workers more than 74 years old.[3]

This trend toward age-related improvements in job satisfaction is sustained in several large U.S., U.K., and multinational studies that implemented more extensive controls for demographic factors, dispositional factors (positive/negative affectivity and general mental health, work values and rewards), and job-related factors (salary, firm size, occupation, tenure, supervisory status, working hours, and job autonomy) that might otherwise explain the age effect. Analyzing data from the International Social Survey, Clark (2005) found age-related improvements in job satisfaction, and Rode (2004) reported similar findings with data from the University of Michigan Americans' Changing Lives Survey. One exception to this general pattern is found in the Siu et al. (2001) study of a smaller sample of managers in Hong Kong. A correlation of .36 between age and job satisfaction became nonsignificant when work-related explanatory variables were incorporated in the analyses.

Several other studies reported higher-order effects, suggesting a robust curvilinear relationship between age and job satisfaction that favors both younger and older workers. Using data from the 1972–1973 U.S. Quality of Employment Survey, Kalleberg and Loscocco (1983) found both a significant linear trend toward increased satisfaction among older workers, and significant curvilinear trends depicting reduced satisfaction in middle age characteristic of the pattern of increased dysphoria in middle age seen in some studies of age gradients in job stress and mental health (e.g., Clark et al., 1996; Smith, 2001). Significant linear and quadratic trends of this general nature were also found in analyses by Clark et al. (1996) of age and job satisfaction data in the British Household Panel Study. A similar quadratic trend was reported in a U.S. study of 2,200 university employees (Hochwarter, Ferris, and Perrewé, 2001), although a linear trend was absent.

AGE DIFFERENCES IN WORK ORGANIZATION EXPOSURES

Improvements in subjective well-being among older workers might suggest reduced exposures to stressful forms of work organization or reduced sensitivity to these stressors among older workers. Extant literature, however, provides little basis for judging these possibilities. Studies of such effects are scarce, and findings reported in the literature are commonly based on fairly simple descriptive analyses.

Using data from the year 2000 administration of the European Survey of Working Conditions, Ilmarinen (2005) and Molinié (2003) conducted the most comprehensive analyses of age differentials in exposures to work organization factors. Results of these analyses suggest that age is generally protective with regard to these exposures. Workers over 45 years of age reported greater opportunity to take breaks at will; greater control over work tasks, work methods, and workloads; greater skill match with job requirements; reduced work pace and less repetitive work; and less shift work (although working hours were greater). Older women also reported greater task complexity.

Trends seen in the data from the European Survey of Working Conditions, particularly between age and control, find support in prior research. Fewer threats to control among older workers, along with increased job involvement and less disruption of performance, were reported in the Remondet and Hansson (1991) study of white-collar workers. Greater internal locus of work control, together with reduced total sources of stress, were reported for older workers in the Hong Kong study of managers (Siu et al., 2001). Data presented in the Warr

(1992) report of aging and well-being among British adults also showed a significant association of age with control (decision latitude), and also an association of age with job demands. However, in this case, only the quadratic function was significant, and control was reduced for both younger and older workers (as was demands), similar to the curvilinear functions commonly seen in studies of age and subjective well-being.

Evidence of more favorable working conditions among older workers comes also from more general studies of population aging. Steady reductions across age strata in the 2004 HRS are seen for agreement that "the job requires me to do more difficult things than it used to": 51–64 years (49% agree); 64–74 years (27% agree); >74 years (16% agree). Also, steady age-related increases occur in the proportion of workers reporting ability to reduce working hours: 51–64 years (33% able to reduce); 64–74 (54% able to reduce); >74 years (60% able to reduce).[4] Likewise, the prevalence of "work problems" is substantially reduced in late midlife in a study of over 1,000 Boston men (Aldwin, Sutton, Chiara, and Spiro, 1996), and recent work-related crises and threats of job loss similarly decline with age in an Australian community study of age and psychological distress by Jorm et al. (2005).

Several sources, however, suggest countervailing trends with regard to supervisory interactions and opportunities for development at work. Data from the European Survey of Working Conditions show reductions in training and learning opportunities among older workers, and fewer proactive and problem-solving discussions with supervisors (Ilmarinen, 2005). Warr and Birdi (1998) similarly found reduced participation in voluntary development activities among older workers in a study of 1,800 employees of a vehicle manufacturing company. Additionally, supervisory support and encouragement were reduced among workers aged 46–55 years, and learning and development opportunities were reduced for workers aged 56–65 years in a large representative Swedish sample (Aronsson, Gustafsson, and Dallner, 2002).

AGE DIFFERENCES IN THE EFFECTS
OF WORK ORGANIZATION EXPOSURES

Although evidence suggests that older workers may experience no greater (perhaps even less) exposure to stressful working conditions than younger workers, they may still be at disproportionate risk of adverse health effects from these exposures. Reviews of knowledge on health and safety aspects of an aging workforce document certain physical and cognitive decrements associated with aging, such as a decline in fluid cognitive abilities (Robertson and Tracy, 1998; Wegman and McGee, 2004; Barnes-Farrell, 2005; Kowalski-Trakofler et al., 2005). Conceivably, these decrements might increase the vulnerability of older workers to stressful work organization exposures (Barnes-Farrell, 2005; Griffiths, 2007). Alternatively, these losses may be offset by functional improvements associated with the accrued experience and skill possessed by older workers or by compensatory strategies they may employ, thereby protecting them from increased risk (Wegman and McGee, 2004; Kowalski-Trakofler et al., 2005; Griffiths, 2007). Additionally, literature on aging and subjective well-being suggests that older workers may possess psychological characteristics that would serve to protect them from taxing workplace exposures by essentially short-circuiting the stress process. These mechanisms might include age-related alterations in job values and expectations that serve to reduce the salience for older workers of stress factors that operate for younger workers (Kalleberg and Loscocco, 1983; Warr, 1992; Aldwin et al., 1996; Clark et al., 1996), down-regulation of emotional response and improved emotional control among older workers (Hansson, Robson, and Limas, 2001; Barnes-Farrell, 2005; Jorm et al., 2005; Warr, 2007), and more effective coping strategies among older workers (Folkman, Lazarus, Pimley, and Novacek, 1987; Aldwin et al., 1996; Hansson et al., 2001).

Little systematic study of any of these possibilities and conjectures is evident in the literature, however. With regard to the premise that effects of work organization exposures may differ for older and younger workers, Warr (2007, 314) comments, in reference to subjective well-being, that "issues of statistical moderation, contrasting the correlations between job features and well-being observed for younger and older workers, have apparently not been examined at all." The NRC review (Wegman and McGee, 2004) also considered the possibility of age differences in health effects of work organization; however, few studies were identified and the effects were mixed.

OBSERVATIONS FROM THE NIOSH QUALITY OF WORK LIFE SURVEY

We used data from the NIOSH Quality of Work Life Survey (QWL) to further explore the age-related effects discussed in the foregoing overview. We began by examining the relationship between age and a variety of health, safety, and well-being outcomes. Next, we looked at the association of age with exposures to various facets of work organization and work-life balance. Both linear and curvilinear effects were evaluated. Finally, we investigated the influence of age in moderating the relationship between these exposures and outcomes. In all of these analyses, statistical controls were implemented for demographic factors (e.g., tenure) and major work arrangements (e.g., full- or part-time work) that might otherwise confound the effects of age.

Methods and Materials

The QWL survey was administered in 2002 as a module of the General Social Survey (GSS). Administered biannually by the National Opinion Research Center, the GSS captures information on a wide range of social issues in the United States (see www.norc.org/projects/General+Social+Survey.htm). A "core" set of demographic and attitudinal questions are asked of all respondents. Subsets of respondents receive special topic modules, such as the 76-item QWL (www.cdc .gov/niosh/topics/stress/qwlquest.html), which is designed to assess a broad range of factors relating to the organization of work and worker safety and health. The GSS is conducted as a personal interview survey and employs a multistage probability design that yields a representative sample of the civilian, noninstitutionalized, U.S. adult (aged 18 years or older) population.

In 2002 the GSS was completed by 2,765 individuals, for a response rate of 70 percent. The QWL was administered to all respondents who were employed for pay either full- or part-time during the week before the survey or who were temporarily not working for various reasons such as vacation, illness, etc. ($n = 1,777$). The present analyses were further limited to respondents working at least 20 hours per week ($n = 1,620$). This sample was 75 percent non-Hispanic white, evenly split by gender and nearly so by marital status (48% currently married), and ranged in age from 18–86 years ($M = 41$, $SD = 12.4$). Notably, the age distribution of the sample conformed closely to norms for the civilian workforce (see Toosi, 2005), although it was slightly overweighted for ages 25–34 years and slightly underweighted for younger workers. Fifty-six percent of the sample had some postsecondary education, and 61 percent were employed in white-collar jobs. Tenure in the current job ranged from less than one year to 50 years ($M = 6.9$, $SD = 8.3$).

Table 17.1 lists all measures (boldface text) employed in the current analyses, including demographic measures; measures of major work arrangements and more specific job attributes (job exposures); measures of work-life balance; and measures of health, safety, and well-being outcomes. For ten of the measures (mainly demographic measures), corresponding questionnaire items were drawn from the GSS Core. The QWL was the source of questionnaire items for all other

TABLE 17.1.
Study measures

Demographics	Social environment
Gender (male, female)*	*Supervisory support (α = .74)*
*Age**	Supervisor is helpful + Concerned
Race (non-Hispanic white, other)*	about employee
Marital status (married, not married)*	*Co-workers are helpful*
Highest degree (< high school,	*Co-workers take personal interest*
graduate)*	**Climate**
Occupation (white collar, other)*	*Organizational climate (α = .71)*
Tenure	Treated with respect + Trust in
Major work arrangements	management
Self-employment (yes, no)*	*Safety climate (α = .88)*
Multiple job-holding (yes, no)	Safety is priority + No safety shortcuts
Part- versus full-time (part, full)*	+ Managers and workers collaborate
Work at home (never, mainly)	on safety
Job attributes	**Security/benefits/development**
Work time/schedule	*Job security is good*
Hours worked weekly (20–48, >48)*	*Fair salary*
Days per month extra hours worked	*Fringe benefits good*
(0–5, >5)	*Promotion chances good*
Shift work (day shift, other shift)	*Sufficient training opportunities*
Flexible start-stop time	**Work-life balance**
Job task/job content	*Work interferes with family*
Autonomy (α = .61)	*Family interferes with work*
Lot of say on job + Freedom on how	*Hours to relax after work*
to do work	*Easy to take time off*
Complexity (α = .64)	**Health, safety, and well-being**
Do numerous things + Job requires	Subjective well-being
learning	*Satisfaction with job*
Skill Use (α = .61)	*Work is stressful**
Opportunity to develop skills +	*Feel used up*
Use skills	Health
Participation	*Self-rated general health*
Participate in decision making +	Health-related quality of life
Set way things done	Days in last month (0–13, >13) . . .
Role clarity/conflict	*Mental health not good*
Know what's expected	*Physical health not good*
Free from conflicting demands	*Mental or physical health not good*
Workload/pressure	*Activity limitation due to poor*
Too much to do	*health*
Enough time	Experience of injury
Enough staff	*Hurt at work last year* (0, >0)

*Item taken from General Social Survey core module; all others taken from Quality of Work Life module

measures, half of which were taken directly from the 1977 Quality of Employment Survey (Quinn and Staines, 1978). Items for the remaining measures were selected from published research on work organization and health or developed by NIOSH to represent job conditions of interest in recent years. The health-related quality of life measures have been used extensively in public health research by the Centers for Disease Control and Prevention (www.cdc.gov/hrqol/monograph.htm).

With the exception of some measures of job attributes consisting of two- to three-item scales, all of the study measures were single-item measures. Scales were formed a priori as guided by theory and practice in the work organization and health literature and then subjected to confirmatory factor analysis. Although measures of internal consistency (Cronbach's alpha) were somewhat low for some of the two-item job task/content scales (α = 0.61–0.64), inter-item correlations for these scales were similar to inter-item correlations for three-item scales yielding more acceptable alphas (e.g., $\geq$ 0.7). Item names in table 17.1 were abstracted from the actual GSS and QWL survey items to connote the construct of interest and to enable easy reference to the full GSS items (Davis and Smith, 2002) and QWL items (www.cdc.gov/niosh/topics/stress/qwlquest.html).

For many of the survey items, responses were rescaled to the (usually dichotomous) format shown in table 17.1 to facilitate logistic regression analyses. All of the items in table 17.1 for which response scales are not shown were rated using four- or five-point Likert scales (e.g., often to never, strongly agree to strongly disagree, excellent to poor, etc.), and then re-scored as dichotomous scales. To help with interpretation of analyses, "0" was assigned to desirable states and "1" to undesirable states (whenever survey items allowed such determinations) for all survey items with dichotomous scales, regardless of the wording of the item. Thus, for the job stress item (in which the item wording implies a negative condition), a score of "0" connotes a desirable state (low levels of stress), and a score of "1" connotes an undesirable state (high levels of stress). Following this same logic, for the job satisfaction item (in which the wording implies a positive condition), a score of "0" connotes a desirable state (high levels of satisfaction) and a response of "1" connotes an undesirable state (low levels of satisfaction).

Three sets of exploratory analyses were conducted. Multiple logistic regression techniques (SAS Version 9.1) were used to explore: (1) relationships of age with health, safety, and well-being outcomes; (2) relationships of age with job exposures and work-life balance; and (3) the moderating effects of age on the relationship of job exposure and balance measures with health, safety, and well-being outcomes. Analyses proceeded in stages according to the general hierarchical process illustrated in figure 17.1. For exploratory purposes, significance was set at $p < .10$ and stepwise procedures were used at each stage of analysis. However, in the results we report only effects that are significant at $p < .05$.

To investigate the effects of age on health, safety, and well-being outcomes, a regression model for each health and safety outcome was first developed from

STAGE 1		STAGE 2		STAGE 3	
Demographics (individual)	+	Demographics (work-related)	+	Major Work Arrangements	⟶ Outcomes
Gender		Tenure		Self-employment	Health, safety &
Age		Occupation		Work at home	well-being
Race				Multiple job holding	Job exposures
Marital status				Part- vs. full-time	Work-life balance
Highest degree					

Figure 17.1. Hierarchical regression approach

the age and other demographic variables. At the second stage of analysis, the demographic factors surviving stage one were combined with the tenure and occupation measures to compute a more elaborate model. Finally, surviving factors from stages one and two were combined with the work arrangement measures to establish a "base" model for each outcome. (This yielded nine base models, one for each of the nine health, safety, and well-being outcomes.) To investigate nonlinear effects of age, subsequent models were tested in which a quadratic age term was added to each base model. When the linear age term was also not in the base model, both the linear and quadratic age terms were added.

To investigate the effects of age on job exposures and work-life balance, including nonlinear effects of age, this same procedure was followed. First a base model was developed for prediction of each of the job attribute (exposure) and work-life balance measures, following the general hierarchical procedure described above. Then subsequent models were tested in which the quadratic age term was added.

To investigate whether or not age moderated the relationship of job exposures and work-life balance with health, safety, and well-being outcomes, analyses proceeded as follows. Interaction terms between age and each of the job attribute (exposure) and work-life measures were developed. One of these interaction terms was then added to each of the nine base models predicting safety and health outcomes. Age (linear term) was also included if not already in the base model. The job attribute or work-life term comprising the interaction with age was also added. The nine base models were then recomputed. This process was repeated for every interaction term.

Finally, we carried the analyses of interactions one step further by analyzing interactions of age and the major work arrangement variables for each of the health, safety, and well-being outcomes. A similar procedure was followed as for the analysis of job exposure and work-life balance interactions with age. However, because there were only four work arrangement terms, all four age by work arrangement interaction terms were entered as a group into each of the nine base models.

Results
Age Differences in Health, Safety, and Well-being

The results of analyses examining the relationship of age with the various health, safety, and well-being outcomes are summarized in table 17.2 (only effects of the age variable are shown). The column labeled "Linear Effects Model" shows age effects for the base regression models that included only the linear term for age. The column labeled "Quadratic Model" shows the effects of the quadratic form of the age term that was included in subsequent models that tested for curvilinear effects of age.

As shown, efforts to discern linear effects of age resulted in significant findings for six of the nine outcomes—all of the subjective well-being outcomes (job satisfaction, work stress, and feeling used-up); the two health-related quality of life outcomes that captured mental health (days of poor mental health in the last month, days of poor mental or physical health in the last month); and the injury outcome measure. Odds ratios (odds of adverse health states for older persons

TABLE 17.2.
Effects of age on health, safety, and well-being outcomes

Outcome variables	Linear effects model (odds ratio / p-values for age)*	Quadratic model (p-values for age-squared term)
Subjective well-being		
Satisfaction with job	.842 / .033	—
Work is stressful	.854 / .003	—
Feel used up	.823 / .000	—
Health		
Self-rated general health	—	—
Health-related quality of life		
Days in last month . . .		
Mental health not good	.786 / .004	—
Physical health not good	—	—
Mental or physical health not good	.830 / .001	—
Activity limitation due to poor health	—	—
Experience of injury		
Hurt at work last year	.822 / .005	—

*Odds ratio for 10-year change in age
  — = Nonsignificant effect

relative to odds for younger persons) were less than 1.0 in all cases, indicating a protective effect of increasing age. (Odds ratios show effects for 10-year increments of age.)

Increasing age was neither predictive of self-rated general health nor the only indicator of strictly physical health (days of poor physical health in the last month); nor was age predictive of days of activity limitation in the last month. Also, in contrast to the abundant evidence of monotonic improvement in health with increasing age in these analyses, the quadratic effect of age was not significant for any of the outcomes.

Age Differences in Job Exposures and Work-Life Balance

The results of analyses examining the relationship of age with job exposures and work-life balance indicators are summarized in table 17.3, which is formatted the same as table 17.2 with respect to linear and curvilinear effects. For reasons of economy, only variables exhibiting significant age effects are included. Because odds ratios vary as a function of age for non-linear effects, the column denoting quadratic effects of age gives significance levels only.

As shown in table 17.3, significant findings appear for 8 of the 23 job exposure measures (well above chance expectations) and for all 4 of the work-life balance indicators. For the job exposures, initial efforts to model linear effects of age resulted in significant findings for just three exposure measures. However, inclusion of age quadratic terms in subsequent regression models resulted in curvilinear trends for five additional exposure measures. For the work-life balance indicators, linear effects were observed for all indicators and curvilinear effects occurred in all but one case.

No particular pattern or clustering of age effects is evident for the job exposures. Effects of age were rather evenly distributed across five of the seven major categories of job attributes that were investigated. No effects of age were found for exposure to job task/content factors or aspects of the social environment.

With respect to linear effects of age, the results are similar to the findings for health-related outcomes—increases in age were protective in all but one case. As indicated by the odds ratios in the left column, older workers in comparison to younger workers experienced less shift work, better organizational climate, less work-to-family conflict, less family-to-work conflict, greater ease in taking time off from work for family reasons, and more hours to relax after work. Only in one instance were older workers disadvantaged: they reported fewer promotional opportunities than do younger workers.

To examine curvilinear effects, we used regression coefficients from the logis-

TABLE 17.3.

Effects of age on job exposures and work-life balance

Exposure and balance variables*	Linear effects model (odds ratio / p-values for age)†	Quadratic model (p-values for age-squared term)
Job attributes		
Work time/schedule		
Days/month extra hours worked	—	.020
Shift work	.895 / .040	—
Role clarity		
Free from conflicting demands	—	.019
Workload/pressure		
Too much to do	—	.047
Enough staff	—	.004
Climate		
Organizational climate	.759 / .001	—
Security/benefits/development		
Job security is good	—	.034
Promotion chances good	1.266 / .000	—
Work-life balance		
Work interferes with family	.779 / .000	.001
Family interferes with work	.776 / .000	.001
Easy to take time off	.902 / .033	—
Hours to relax after work	.815 / .000	.001

*Only exposure and balance variables with significant main effects and/or quadratic effects of age are included in the table

†Odds ratio for 10-year change in age

— = Nonsignificant effect

tic regression models where the quadratic form of the age term was significant to estimate and plot the probability of adverse exposures and work-life imbalance at each decade of age from age 20 to age 70. Significant quadratic effects of age on job exposures are shown in panels A–D of figure 17.2. All of these effects exhibit a common pattern. The probability of adverse exposures (more long workdays, more conflicting demands, excessive workload, insufficient staffing, and job insecurity) increased from early adulthood through the middle years and declined thereafter. (Remember that, regardless of the label given to the plot, which corresponds to the name of the exposure measure from table 17.1, increases in the value of the ordinate signify an increased probability of an *adverse* exposure.) Similar curvilinear effects were seen for the work-life balance indicators (figure 17.2, panel E). The probability of work-to-family interference, family-to-work interference, and fewer hours of relaxation after work first increased and then decreased across the age span. However, the age at which risk of these outcomes

Figure 17.2. Curvilinear relationships of age with job exposures and work-life balance.
A, work/time schedule; B, role clarity/conflict; C, workload/pressure; D, security
benefits/development; E, work-life balance

begin to decline tended to occur about a decade earlier than the age at which improvements in job exposures are first seen.

Age Differences in the Effects of Job Exposures and Work-Life Balance
on Health-related Outcomes

Table 17.4 shows the results of analyses to investigate interactions of age with job
exposures and work-life balance indicators in the prediction of health, safety, and
well-being outcomes. Effects of age interactions with work arrangements are also
shown. Age interaction terms found to be nonsignificant are excluded from the

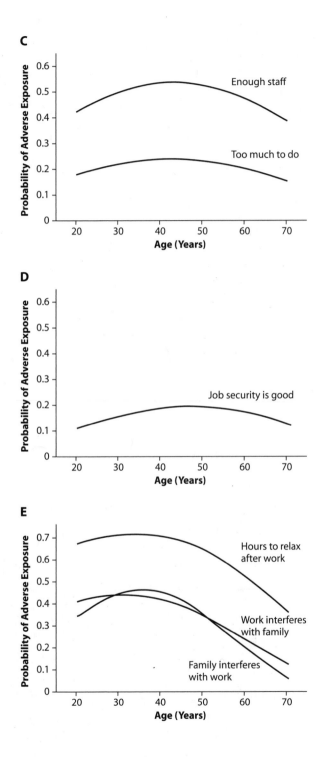

TABLE 17.4.

Interactions of age (with job exposure and work-life balance) on health, safety, and well-being outcomes*

	Satisfaction with job	Work is stressful	Feel used up	Self-rated general health	Days in last month			
					Mental health not good	Physical health not good	Mental or physical health not good	Activity limitation due to poor health
Major work arrangements								
Age × Part- versus full-time	.046	—	—	—	—	—	—	—
Age × Work at home	—	—	.035	—	—	—	—	—
Job attributes								
Role clarity/conflict								
Age × Know what's expected	—	—	—	—	—	—	.031	—
Social environment								
Age × Co-workers are helpful	—	—	—	—	—	—	.024	.001
Age × Co-workers take personal interest	.005	.021	.019	—	—	—	—	—
Climate								
Age × Organizational climate	.043	—	—	—	.036	—	.034	—
Age × Safety climate	—	—	.027	—	—	—	—	—
Security/benefits/development								
Age × Fringe benefits good	—	.019	—	—	—	—	.041	—
Age × Fair salary	—	—	—	.018	—	.036	—	.011
Work-life balance								
Age × Family interferes with work	—	—	—	—	—	—	—	.027
Age × Work interferes with family	.020	—	—	—	—	—	—	—

*Only exposure and balance variables with significant age interactions are included. "Hurt at work last year" is not included because no age interactions were significant for this health outcome.

— = Nonsignificant effect

table. Because none of the age interactions were predictive of the injury outcome, we have also omitted this outcome from table 17.4.

The number of age interactions investigated in these analyses was substantial (nearly 300). Table 17.4 shows that only 20 of these interaction terms were significant—a rate only slightly exceeding chance expectations. However, it is notable that the significant interactions were not widely disbursed across work arrangement, exposure, and balance variables. Instead, these effects tended to be nested within just a few classes of variables. Five of the interactions were specific to the two co-worker support variables, four were specific to the two climate variables, and six were specific to the two variables pertaining to financial circumstances (salary and benefits). Interactions were also found for each of the work-family interference variables.

To investigate the form of these interaction effects, we predicted and plotted probabilities of an adverse health or well-being outcome for each level of the interacting variable at ages 20 and 70 using regression coefficients from the logistic regression models.[5] Plots for the four clusters of interaction effects are shown in Figures 17.3 through 17.6. Even though age is the moderating variable in these analyses, we have retained age along the abscissa to better visualize the effects of differential exposures on health across the age continuum.

Figures 17.3 and 17.4 illustrate, respectively, the interactive effects of age with co-worker support variables and workplace climate variables. A common feature across these interaction effects is that, with few exceptions, differential exposures were of little consequence for young workers. However, as workers aged, adverse exposures were associated with increasing risk of adverse health-related outcome and positive exposures with increasingly protective effects. As shown in figure 17.3, panels A–C, increasing age was associated with increased job satisfaction, reduced stress, and reduced fatigue (feeling used up) when co-workers express interest in one another, but all of these outcomes worsened with age when coworker interest was lacking. Panels D and E of figure 17.3 show similar trends in two health-related quality of life measures in relation to the helpfulness of co-workers—quality improved (fewer days poor mental or physical health; fewer days of activity limitation) with age when co-workers were helpful and deteriorated with age when co-workers were not helpful. This general pattern held for interactive effects of age and climate variables (figure 17.4). Age-related improvement in job satisfaction and health-related quality of life (fewer days of poor mental health; fewer days of poor mental or physical health) occurred in the presence of a positive organizational climate (panels A–C), but age-related reversals in these trends occurred when the climate was poor. Similarly, fatigue declined with age when the climate was positive (panel D) but increased when the safety climate was poor.

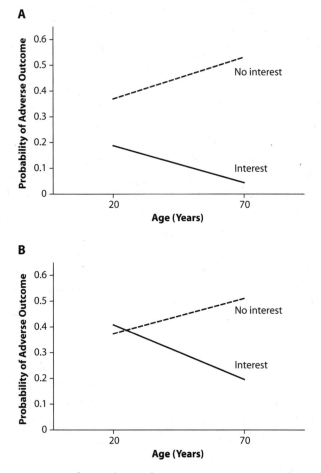

Figure 17.3. Interactions of age with coworker support. *A*, Age × Co-workers take personal interest (satisfaction with job); *B*, Age × Co-workers take personal interest (work is stressful); *C*, Age × Co-workers take personal interest (feel used up); *D*, Age × Co-workers are helpful (days mental and physical health not good); *E*, Age × Co-workers are helpful (days of activity limitation due to poor health)

Unlike the interactions of age with support and climate variables that predicted poorer health among older workers under conditions of adverse exposures, the effects of age interactions with the salary and benefit variables showed younger workers to suffer most noticeably from adverse exposures. Figure 17.5, panels A and B, show that poor fringe benefits were associated with a sizeable increase in stress and reduced health-related quality of life (more days of poor mental or physical health) among young workers. However, this elevated response for

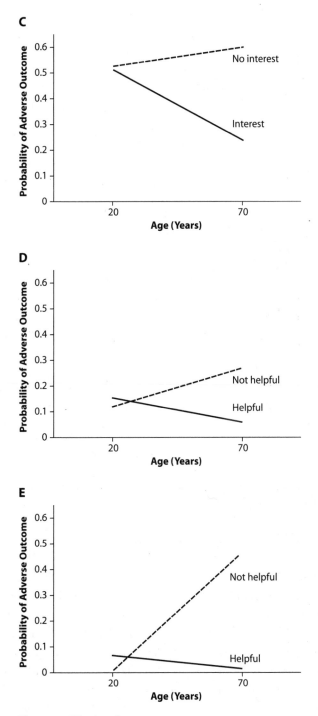

Figure 17.3. (*Continued*)

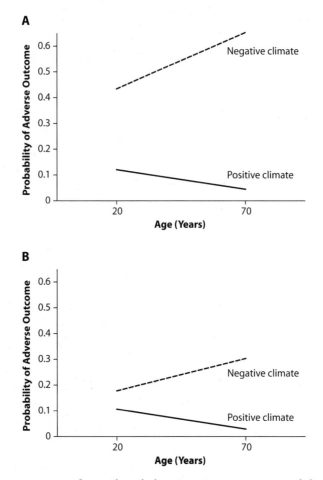

Figure 17.4. Interactions of age with work climate. *A*, Age × Organizational climate (satisfaction with job); *B*, Age × Organizational climate (days mental health is not good); *C*, Age × Organizational climate (days mental or physical health not good); *D*, Age × Safety climate (feeling used up)

young workers diminished rapidly with age. Age interacted with salary ratings in a similar fashion. Panels C–E of figure 17.5 show that unfair salary was associated with poorer self-rated health and reduced health-related quality of life (more days of poor physical health and activity limitation) for younger workers, but again, this differential between unfair and fair salaries is reduced with age.

Finally, interference between work and family also appeared to be more of a strain for younger workers than for older workers. Figure 17.6, panel A, shows that work-to-family inference was associated with reduced job satisfaction among

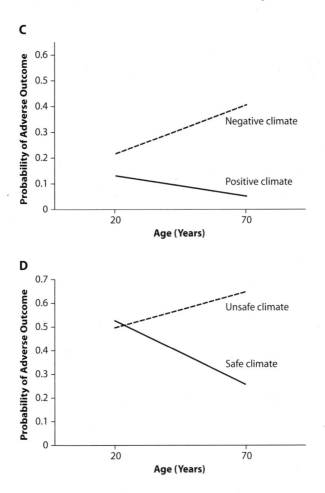

young workers, but this effect was diminished with age. As shown in panel B, the interaction of age with family-to-work interference had an almost identical influence on health-related activity limitation—interference is associated with more days of activity limitation among young workers, but there is little effect of interference among older workers.

Discussion
Age Differences in Health, Safety, and Well-Being

Evidence of age-related reductions in stress and fatigue and improvements in job satisfaction in the present study agrees with a substantial body of prior research on age trends in these outcomes (Kalleberg and Loscocco, 1983; Remondet and

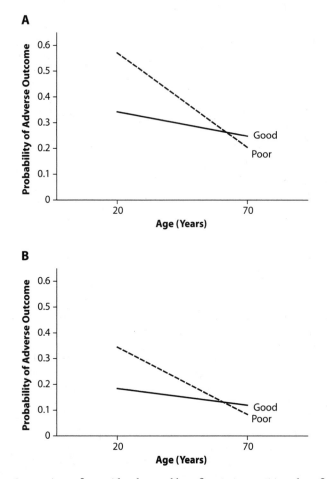

Figure 17.5. Interactions of age with salary and benefits. *A,* Age × Fringe benefits good (work is stressful); *B,* Age × Fringe benefits good (days mental or physical health not good); *C,* Age × Fair salary (self-rated general health); *D,* Age × Fair salary (days physical health is not good); *E,* Age × Fair salary (days of activity limitation due to poor health).

Hansson, 1991; Clark et al., 1996; Swanson et al., 1996; Hochwarter et al., 2001; Smith, 2001; Rode, 2004; Clark, 2005; Conference Board, 2007). In the context of these findings and prior work showing improvement in mental health among older workers (Remondet and Hansson, 1991; Warr, 1992; Clark et al., 1996; Frone et al., 1996; Williams and Cooper, 1996; Siu et al., 2001), our novel finding of age-related improvements in health-related quality of life indicators denoting mental health (days of poor mental health; days of poor mental or physical health) is not surprising.

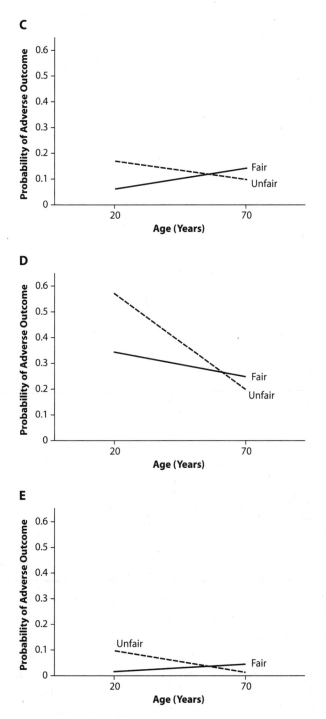

Figure 17.5. (Continued)

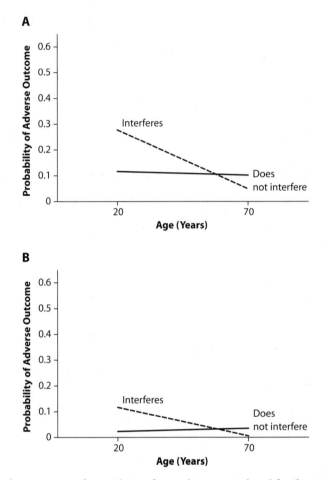

Figure 17.6. Interactions of age with interference between work and family. *A*, Age × Work interferes with family (satisfaction with job); *B*, Age × Family interferes with work (days of activity limitation due to poor health)

It is noteworthy that curvilinear effects were observed in several prior studies of age and subjective well-being showing reduced stress, better mental health, and more job satisfaction for younger and older workers in comparison to workers in middle adulthood (Kalleberg and Loscocco, 1983; Warr, 1992; Clark et al., 1996; Hochwarter et al., 2001; Smith, 2001). Yet the present analyses yielded only linear effects for these outcomes. Speculating that dichotomous outcome scores may have constrained our analyses, we conducted follow-up analyses using multiple linear regression to model the effects of linear and quadratic age terms only on all nine of the health, safety, and well-being outcomes, using their original response scales. However, this effort was met with only limited success. Quadratic effects of age similar to findings in prior studies appeared for only the stress and fatigue (used-up) outcomes.

In contrast to age-related improvement in subjective well-being, we failed to find significant age gradients in either self-rated general health or the health-related quality of life outcome specific to physical health (days of poor physical health). These null effects differ from trends in the general population, which show age-related declines in these two outcomes (CDC, 2007; Zahran et al., 2005). Possible attrition of unhealthy older workers from the workforce may have contributed to our findings, and it is also possible that the scoring convention we employed for these outcomes contributed. However, as noted, modeling self-rated general health with multiple regression using the original 5-point response scale failed to show a significant effect of either the linear or quadratic age terms, and the same was true for the health-related quality of life outcome specific to physical health.

We also failed to find evidence of age gradients in activity limitation due to poor health in the present sample. Evidence of age gradients in this measure in the general population is mixed. Data from the CDC Behavioral Risk Factor Surveillance System show rather pronounced increases in health-related activity limitation with age (Zahran et al., 2005), but a clear age trend of this nature is not evident in 2001–2002 NHANES data (Zahran et al., 2005).

Finally, the decline in injury risk among older workers in our sample replicates a well-established trend in the literature (Root, 1981; Mitchell, 1988; Rogers and Wiatrowski, 2005). Mitchell found, however, that this age effect did not hold after adjustment for occupation and industry. Industry effects were not investigated in the present study, but like Mitchell, we found a strong effect of occupation (blue-collar vs. white-collar) reflecting less injury risk among white-collar workers (OR = 3.2, CI = 2.2–4.7). Of interest, however, our data show a significant decline in injury experience among older workers even after adjustment for the effects of occupation.

While our data provide new and confirmatory evidence of improved subjective well-being and reduced injury risk among older workers, there remains little clarity regarding mechanisms that may underlie these trends. Several possible sources for these effects have been raised in the literature, including, most prominently, (1) migration and transition of older workers to better jobs; (2) job socialization and "molding" of the job among older and more seasoned workers to improve the job-person fit; (3) age-related improvements in job skill and coping; (4) sample composition issues (e.g., healthy worker effects); (5) spillover from age-related improvements in context-free subjective well-being; (6) cohort effects that may manifest in cross-sectional studies; and (7) developmental processes, including age-related changes in work values, attitudes, and expectations. Further discussion of these mechanisms and results of studies investigating their effects are found in Warr (2007), and in other sources cited in this chapter (e.g., Kalleberg and Loscocco, 1983; Folkman et al., 1987; Clark et al., 1996; Semmer and Schallberger, 1996; Hansson et al., 2001; Hochwarter et al., 2001; Jorm et al., 2005).

Age Differences in Job Exposures and Work-Life Balance

The present analyses also reveal associations between age and job exposures. However, evidence of main effects distinguishing older and younger workers was limited and lends little support to findings of either positive or negative relationships between age and job quality reported in the small body of prior research on this topic. Our analyses show a monotonic decline in shift work with age, confirming effects reported in Ilmarinen's (2005) analysis of data from the European Survey of Working Conditions. However, there are few other similarities with prior findings. Earlier studies reported reduced opportunities for training, learning, or development among older workers (Aronsson et al., 2002; Ilmarinen, 2005) and reduced participation in training among older workers (Warr and Birdi, 1998). In contrast, we found no age differences in availability of training opportunities. Furthermore, we found no age differences in our job complexity measure, which incorporated an item on learning demands. However, consistent with reduced developmental opportunities seen in prior work, the present analyses do show reduced promotion potential among older workers.

Statistical approaches may explain some of the differences between present and earlier findings. Simple correlations and bivariate analyses in several prior studies suggest increased levels of job control or similar constructs among older workers (Remondet and Hansson, 1991; Siu et al., 2001; Ilmarinen, 2005). Simple comparisons by Ilmarinen (2005) also show increased use of skills among older workers. We similarly found age-related increases in autonomy (lot of say on job + freedom on how to do work) and in use of skills in simple bivariate regressions. However, neither of these effects was significant in the final multiple regression models.

More prominently featured in our results are novel findings of curvilinear relationships between age and job exposures, showing improvements in job quality for both older and younger workers. In contrast to workers in middle adulthood, both younger and older workers reported fewer workdays with long hours, reduced workload and improved staffing, fewer conflicting demands, and improved job security. There is little basis for comparison of these findings in the literature. Ilmarinen's (2005) analyses showed reduced time pressure among older workers (but, paradoxically, more working hours per week) and as described above, our analyses of HRS data found declining job difficulty among older workers—but these effects were monotonic. Warr (1992), however, presented data showing a significant correlation between demands and a quadratic age term that resembles the pattern of reduced demands in both younger and older workers seen in our data.

Taken together, the present findings of increases in working hours, work loads, and conflicting demands through middle adulthood would seem consistent with the growing demands that are commonplace for workers who are advancing through the early stages of their careers, and the ensuing decline in these exposures seems consistent with opportunities for more senior workers to assume higher-quality jobs. The curvilinear relationship between age and job security, showing steady reductions in security until age 50 and improving security thereafter, is also reasonably consistent with the age trend in rates of job displacement among longer-tenured (> 3 years) workers in the U.S. workforce (Helwig, 2001).

Our analyses also reveal a significant curvilinear relationship between age and work-life balance indicators, showing erosion in balance until the third decade, with improvement thereafter that is so pronounced that strong linear trends were evident as well. Trends of this nature have been reported previously in national survey data on work-family conflict (Bellavia and Frone, 2005). Because the presence of children under 18 years of age in the household is an important predictor of family-to-work conflict (Bellavia and Frone, 2005), increasing parenting demands in early adulthood and the abatement of these demands beginning in middle adulthood is a plausible explanation for the increase and decline in family-to-work interference observed here. Also, attribution of the rise and fall in work-to-family interference to spillover from job demands is tempting, considering the striking similarity between the curvilinear trends for the hours to relax after work measure and work-to-family interference (figure 17.2, panel E). Trends for the work load and pressure indicators and other exposures (figure 17.2) are curvilinear as well, although less congruent with the work-to-family interference trend.

Despite the appeal of these suggested explanations for the present trends in job exposures and work-life balance, influence from other sources cited as possible explanatory mechanisms for health-related effects cannot be ruled out. In this regard, the results of a Finnish study comparing workers' ratings of workplace quality (mainly physical attributes) with independent ratings by the research team are of interest (Räsänen, Laitinen, and Rasa, 1997). The study found that younger and older workers rated their work environments as more satisfactory than did middle-aged workers, but this curvilinear trend was less evident in ratings by researchers. The study concluded that "the younger worker's assessments were more realistic . . . whereas the other age groups seemed to be over-satisfied compared to the real situation" (518).

Age Differences in the Effects of Job Exposures and Work-Life Balance on Health-Related Outcomes

The present analyses provide little evidence of disproportionate threat to older workers from stressful job exposures. Relatively few interactions of age with job exposures were found. Unlike earlier findings that showed shift work and tight time constraints to be more problematic for older workers (Molinié and Volkoff, 1994; Härmä, 1996), age did not interact with any of our work time and schedule measures or the work load and pressure measures in prediction of any of the health, safety, or well-being outcomes.

For the few age interactions that were significant, most clustered within a few categories of exposures (co-worker help and interest, organizational and safety climate, salary and benefits, interference between work and family), suggesting that these effects are not chance events. First impressions of the interactions of age with the co-worker help and interest (support) measures and the climate measures (figures 17.3 and 17.4) might suggest that older workers have a heightened sensitivity to the workplace climate and social environment. However, an unavoidable limitation of cross-sectional research on age and exposure is that age is entangled with exposure history. In the absence of ready theory to explain age differences in the effects of climate and coworker support, it is plausible that the more favorable effects seen for older workers when the climate and social environment are positive, and the less favorable effects seen when the climate and social environment are negative, are more reflective of the influence of cumulative exposure to these conditions than differential sensitivity to these conditions.

Age interactions with salary and benefit measures (figure 17.5) actually shift the focus of concern away from older workers to younger workers. These interactions suggest that it is younger workers, not older workers, who are at disproportionate risk when compensation is judged to be inadequate. There is some consistency between this interpretation and the results of earlier analyses of 1972–1973 Quality of Employment Survey data by Wright and Hamilton (1978) and Kalleberg and Loscocco (1983) showing that financial rewards are more highly valued by younger workers than by older workers. Although the interaction of age with part- and full-time work is not plotted here, the nature of this interaction complements the present stream of logic. Part-time work, which rarely

provides the level of compensation and benefits associated with full-time positions, was more dissatisfying for young workers than was full-time work. However, no difference in job satisfaction was evident between part- and full-time
work for older workers.

Finally, we also found effects of interference between work and family among
younger workers (increased job dissatisfaction and health-related activity limitation) that were absent for older workers (figure 17.6). Insight to understanding
this difference is hampered by the lack of attention to older workers in research
on work-family conflict. Mechanisms raised in foregoing explanations of salutary
effects among older workers (e.g., improved coping strategies) might explain the
improved situation. Alternatively, sources of conflict may be different and less
aversive for older workers. Clearly, this is topic in need of further study.

CONCLUSION

The present analyses provide confirmatory evidence of age-related improvements in subjective well-being reported in prior studies of worker samples and
extend these effects to health outcomes not previously investigated. The results
also build on the limited base of research investigating age differences in exposures to work-related stressors, providing evidence of curvilinear effects favoring
both younger and older workers. Finally, our findings provide little support for
the vulnerability hypothesis—age differentials in the effects of work organization
exposures were largely absent.

Taken at face value and in the context of an aging workforce, these findings
are encouraging, suggesting that older and younger workers differ little or not at
all in risks posed by the organization of work. However, because of study limitations, some caution in interpreting these findings is warranted. As an exploratory
study, a substantial number of analyses were undertaken, creating the potential
for type 1 error. Also, many of the effects observed, though significant, were not
especially strong. Possible sample composition problems resulting in healthy
worker effects is perhaps the greatest concern. Although labor force participation
rates for older workers have been increasing for two decades, these rates (2005
estimates) still fall dramatically for older workers—dropping from 83 percent for
workers aged 25–54, to 63 percent for workers aged 55–64, and to just 22 percent
for workers aged 65–74 (Toosi, 2006). To the extent that declining health contributes to early withdrawal from the labor force, it is possible that the favorable
age-health relationships observed here are biased by the presence of a surviving
pool of uncharacteristically healthy older workers in the study. Finnish data linking decreased workability to disease and early retirement on disability pension

lends support to this possibility (Tuomi et al., 1997b). Healthier older workers may also be more capable of withstanding adverse job exposures, perhaps rating these exposures more favorably and responding less strongly. Such effects could bias the age-exposure trends we observed and contribute to the scarcity of age-exposure interactions in our results.

On the other hand, our analyses reveal age-related improvements in subjective well-being, health-related quality of life, and some job exposures that are linear in nature and thus manifest before labor force participation rates begin to decline. Even for the age-exposure relationships that are curvilinear in nature, midlife improvements in job ratings for several exposures are evident during a period (ages 40–50 years) when labor force participation rates are highly stable. Work-family balance begins to improve even earlier.

Because of the exploratory nature of this study and uncertainties in interpretation of findings, there is clearly need for further, theory-driven research to investigate the type of effects targeted in the present analyses. However, it is unlikely that much progress can be made in the absence of longitudinal data systems that capture information needed to more reliably chart the health and safety of workers across the life span and to disentangle various factors that might contribute to age-related effects. Notably, this is the primary recommendation of the NRC for research to better under understand health and safety needs of older workers (Wegman and McGee, 2004).

NOTES

The findings and conclusions in this report are those of the authors and do not necessarily represent the view of the National Institute for Occupational Safety and Health.

1. Results of analyses of 2004 HRS data by the present authors.
2. Ibid.
3. Ibid.
4. Ibid.
5. For ease of expression in describing these effects, we describe these effects in terms of adverse or positive changes in the outcome measures themselves even though, as noted, the actual metric (ordinate value) is probability of an adverse outcome.

REFERENCES

Aldwin, C. M., Sutton, K. J., Chiara, G., and Spiro, A. III. 1996. Age differences in stress, coping, and appraisal: Findings from the normative aging study. *Journal of Gerontology: Psychological Sciences* 51B (4): 179–88.

Aronsson, G., Gustafsson, K., and Dallner, M. 2002. Work environment and health in different types of temporary jobs. *European Journal of Work and Organizational Psychology* 11(2): 151–75.

Barnes-Farrell, J. L. 2005. Older workers. In *Handbook of Work Stress*, ed. J. Barling, K. Kelloway, and M. Frone, 431–54. Thousand Oaks, CA: Sage Publications.

Bellavia, G. M., and Frone, M. R. 2005. Work-family conflict. In *Handbook of Work Stress*, ed. J. Barling, E. K. Kelloway, and M. R. Frone, 113–48. Thousand Oaks, CA: Sage Publications.

Centers for Disease Control and Prevention (CDC). 2007. *Summary Health Statistics for the US Population: National Health Interview Survey, 2005.* Hyattsville, MD: U.S. Department of Health and Human Services.

Clark, A. E. 2005. Your money or your life: Changing job quality in OECD countries. *British Journal of Industrial Relations* 43 (3): 377–400.

Clark, A., Oswald, A., and Warr, P. 1996. Is job satisfaction U-shaped in age? *Journal of Occupational and Organizational Psychology* 69:57–81.

Conference Board. 2007, February. *US job satisfaction declines.* Retrieved May 23, 2007, from www.conference-board.org.

Davis, J. A., and Smith, T. W. 2002. *General Social Surveys, 1972–2002: Cumulative Codebook (NORC Ed.).* Chicago: National Opinion Research Center.

Folkman, S., Lazarus, R. S., Pimley, S., and Novacek, J. 1987. Age differences in stress and coping processes. *Psychology and Aging* 2 (2): 171–84.

Frone, M. R., Russell, M., and Barnes, G. M. 1996. Work-family conflict, gender, and health-related outcomes: A study of employed parents in two community samples. *Journal of Occupational Health Psychology* 1 (1): 57–69.

Griffiths, A. 2007. Healthy work for older workers: Work design and management factors. In *The Future for Older Workers: New Perspectives*, ed. W. Loretto, S. Vickerstaff, and P. White, 125–41. Bristol, UK: Policy Press.

Härmä, M. 1996. Ageing, physical fitness and shiftwork tolerance. *Applied Ergonomics* 27 (1): 25–29.

Hansson, R. O., Robson, S. M., and Limas, M. J. 2001. Stress and coping among older workers. *Work* 17:247–56.

Health and Retirement Study—HRS 2004 Core [Public use dataset]. Ann Arbor: University of Michigan with funding from the National Institute on Aging (grant number NIA U01AG009740; 2004).

Helwig, R. T. 2001. Worker displacement in a strong labor market. *Monthly Labor Review* 124 (6): 13–28.

Hochwarter, W. A., Ferris, G. R., and Perrewé, P. L. 2001. A note on the nonlinearity of the age-job-satisfaction relationship. *Journal of Applied Social Psychology* 31 (6): 1223–37.

Ilmarinen, J. 2005. *Towards a Longer Worklife! Ageing and the Quality of Worklife in the European Union.* Helsinki: Finnish Institute of Occupational Health.

Jorm, A. F., Windsor, T. D., Dear, K. B. G., Anstey, K. J., Christensen, H., and Rodgers, B. 2005. Age group differences in psychological distress: The role of psychosocial risk factors that vary with age. *Psychological Medicine* 35:1253–63.

Kalleberg, A. L., and Loscocco, K. A. 1983. Aging, values, and rewards: Explaining age differences in job satisfaction. *American Sociological Review* 48 (1): 78–90.

Kowalski-Trakofler, K. M., Steiner, L. J., and Schwerha, D. J. 2005. Safety considerations for the aging workforce. *Safety Science* 43:779–93.

Mitchell, O. S. 1988. The relation of age to workplace injuries. *Monthly Labor Review* 111 (7): 8–13.

Molinié, A.-F. 2003. Age and working conditions in the European Union. Ireland: European Foundation for the Improvement of Living and Working Conditions. Retrieved April 24, 2007, from www.eurofound.eu.int/publications/files/EF02107EN.pdf.

Molinié, A.-F., and Volkoff, S. 1994. Working conditions: Problems ahead for workers over the age of 40. In *Work and Aging: A European Perspective,* ed. J. Snel and R. Cremer, 214–23. London: Taylor & Francis.

Mosisa A., and Hipple, S. 2006. Trends in labor force participation in the United States. *Monthly Labor Review* 129 (10): 35–57.

Quinn, R. B., and Staines, G. L. 1978. *The 1977 Quality of Employment Survey: Descriptive Statistics with Comparison Data from the 1969–1970 and 1972–1973 Surveys.* Ann Arbor: University of Michigan Research Center, Institute for Social Research.

Räsänen, T., Laitenen, H., and Rasa, P-L. 1997. The effect of age on subjective assessment of work environment. In *Proceedings of the 13th Triennial Congress of the International Ergonomics Association, Vol. 5, From Experience to Innovation,* ed. P. Seppälä, T. Luopajärvi, C-H. Nygård, and M. Mattila, 516–18. Helsinki: Finnish Institute of Occupational Health.

Remondet, J. H., and Hansson, R. O. 1991. Job-related threats to control among older employees. *Journal of Social Issues* 47 (4): 129–41.

Robertson, A., and Tracy, C. S. 1998. Health and productivity of older workers. *Scandinavian Journal of Work, Environment, and Health* 24 (2): 85–97.

Rode, J. C. 2004. Job satisfaction and life satisfaction revisited: A longitudinal test of an integrated model. *Human Relations* 57 (9): 1205–30.

Rogers, E., and Wiatrowski, W. J. 2005. Injuries, illnesses, and fatalities among older workers. *Monthly Labor Review* 128 (10): 24–30.

Root, N. 1981. Injuries at work are fewer among older employees. *Monthly Labor Review* 104 (3): 30–34.

Semmer, N., and Schallberger, U. 1996. Selection, socialization, and mutual adaptation: Resolving discrepancies between people and work. *Applied Psychology: An International Review* 45 (3): 263–88.

Siu, O., Spector, P. E., Cooper, C. L., and Donald, I. 2001. Age differences in coping and locus of control: A study of managerial stress in Hong Kong. *Psychology and Aging* 16 (4): 707–10.

Smith, A. 2001. Perceptions of stress at work. *Human Resource Management Journal* 11: 74–86.

Swanson, V., Power, K., and Simpson, R. 1996. A comparison of stress and job satisfaction in females and male GPs and consultants. *Stress Medicine* 12:17–26.

Toosi, M. 2005. Labor force projections to 2014: Retiring boomers. *Monthly Labor Review* 128 (11): 25–44.

———. 2006. A new look at long-term labor force projections to 2050. *Monthly Labor Review* 129 (11): 19–39.

Tuomi, K., Ilmarinen, J., Martikainen, R., Aalto, L., and Klockars, M. 1997a. Aging, work, life-style and work ability among Finnish municipal workers in 1981–1992. *Scandinavian Journal of Work Environment and Health* 23 (suppl. 1): 58–65.

Tuomi, K., Ilmarinen, J., Seitsamo, J., Huuhtanen, P., Martikaininen, R., Nygård, C., et al. 1997b. Summary of the Finnish research project (1981–1992) to promote the health and work ability of aging workers. *Scandinavian Journal of Work Environment and Health* 23 (suppl. 1): 66–71.

Warr, P. 1992. Age and occupational well-being. *Psychology and Aging* 7 (1): 37–45.

———. 2007. *Work, Happiness, and Unhappiness.* Mahwah, NJ: Lawrence Erlbaum.

Warr, P., and Birdi, K. 1998. Employee age and voluntary development activity. *International Journal of Training and Development* 2 (3): 190–204.

Wegman, D. H., and McGee, J. P. eds. 2004. *Health and Safety Needs of Older Workers.* Washington, DC: National Academies Press.

Williams, S., and Cooper, C. L. 1996. *Occupational Stress Indicator, Version 2.* Harrogate, North Yorkshire: RAD, Ltd.

Wright, J. D., and Hamilton, R. F. 1978. Work satisfaction and age: Some evidence for the "job change" hypothesis. *Social Forces* 56:1140–58.

Zahran, H. S., Kobau, R., Moriarty, D. G., Zack, M. M., Holt, J., and Donchoo, R. 2005. Health-related quality of life surveillance—United States, 1993–2002. *Morbidity and Mortality Weekly Report* Surveillance Summary 54 (SS-4). Washington, DC: Centers for Disease Control and Prevention.

CHAPTER EIGHTEEN

Health Promotion and Wellness Programs for Older Workers

ROBERT B. WALLACE, M.D.,
AND GWENITH G. FISHER, PH.D.

Health promotion and wellness programs have been in the workplace for many years. However, a review of the relevant historical literature reveals that little specific attention has been given to the preventive needs of older workers. There are probably several reasons for this: in the past, the number and proportion of older workers was relatively smaller; older workers were thought able to participate in the wellness programs aimed at all adults; and the special preventive needs of older workers and older persons were not well appreciated. For example, few if any workplace programs assisted with early degenerative arthritis, medication management, or changes in learning abilities. Furthermore, the evidence base dictating effective health-promotion and disease-prevention practices intended for older persons has always lagged behind that for young and middle-aged adults, and the structure of special programs was not well defined. However, as documented elsewhere in this volume, the number of older workers is increasing, and while the nature of the work that they are performing also may be changing, most would agree that the workplace continues to offer an important potential venue for applying health-promotional activities.

The primary goal for promoting health and preventing disease in the workplace must always be to minimize or avoid illness and injury related to the workplace environment. The environmental risks associated with the workplace vary dramatically and may have physical, mechanical, chemical, social and behavioral dimensions that require substantial education and training (Institute of Medicine, 2000). Also, the origins of work-related adverse health outcomes may often extend beyond the literal worksite, including the risks of commuting and forced changes in company organization, such as downsizing, upsizing, and closure (Schecter, 2007). Promoting worksite health and safety is always challenging, and this includes the special issues of older workers (National Research Council, 2004).

Beyond protecting the health and safety of workers, promoting the general health of the workforce may be enhanced in several ways. Employers can provide employee health insurance benefits that cover effective clinical health promotion and disease prevention interventions such as cancer screening, routine immunization, and smoking cessation programs. A more healthful workplace environment can be encouraged by maintaining cigarette smoking restrictions and providing walking paths and low-fat cafeteria menus—interventions that may be effective without direct worker participation. Employers can also actively provide direct health promotional programs such as health education classes or programs on exercise, disease screening, substance abuse management, or even chronic disease management. These latter health promotion programs overlap with activities that may be provided through employee assistance programs (EAPs)—a series of services varying widely in content and worker access but frequently including emergency consultation for acute health matters, incident stress management, health assessment and referral, risk management consultation, short-term family counseling, and assistance in returning to work after prolonged illness or other absence (Fitzgerald, Hammond, and Harder, 1989).

Employers provide a substantial menu of services under the rubric of EAPs that address many health issues in addition to wellness and health promotion. Reviewing this range of services is not feasible here, but table 18.1 shows a list of current EAP training courses that are part of the Federal Occupational Health program as offered by the Department of Health and Human Services. This table is revealing in several respects. First, the list is dominated by issues aimed to improve organizational management, with many of the offerings aimed at managers and supervisors. These issues emphasize the interrelation of management and worker benefits. Next, many of the courses are related to human behavior, and wellness programs represent only a small proportion of the available curriculum. Review of the range of EAPs offered nationally also reveals that there is no "standard" set of services and that even within an organization, access to services may be position-dependent. However, in recent years worksite health programs have increased in scope and sophistication, and along with EAPs, they are now sometimes referred to as health and productivity management (HPM) programs

TABLE 18.1.
Employee assistance program courses, Federal Occupational Health, March 2007

Organizational planning and change	Transitions in the workplace—coping with change
	Transitions in the workplace—for employees
	Managing change
	Coping with downsizing and job loss
Organizational readiness	Prevention of violence in the workplace
	Critical incident stress debriefing and management services
	"Be prepared, not scared" (preparing for emotional reactions to terrorist acts). Program for federal leaders
	"Be prepared, not scared." Program for federal employees
Employee relations and conflict management	Mediation
	Conflict resolution—dealing positively with difficult people—for supervisors
	Conflict resolution—for employees
	Conflict management—alternative dispute resolution
	Cultural diversity—understanding our differences and similarities
	Men and women on the job—gender-related issues
	Communication skills
	Respect and positive interaction in the workplace
	Working well
	Anger management
	Dealing with difficult people
	Sexual harassment—for supervisors
	Sexual harassment—for employees
	Understanding domestic violence
Worksite wellness	Healthy lifestyle and wellness
	Stress management
	Time management
	Becoming a wise health consumer
	Coping with depression
	Ups and downs for the holiday season
	Loneliness from loss
Financial management and retirement	Preretirement planning workshop
Employee Assistance Program orientation	EAP program orientation—supervisors
	EAP program orientation—employees
Substance abuse and addiction	Substance abuse—the supervisor's role
	Substance abuse—increasing awareness—employees
	Gambling
Balancing work and life	Effective parenting
	Elder care
	Balancing work and family
	Enriching relationships: communication skills
	Enriching relationships: differing needs
	Enriching relationships: lasting commitment
	Enriching relationships: common pitfalls

Source: Adapted from the Federal Occupational Health Program, offered by the U.S. Department of Health and Human Services. www.foh.dhhs.gov/Public/WhatWe/Do/Training/EAPtrainings.asp

(Goetzel et al., 2007). While HPM programs have been studied, ongoing surveys of their prevalence, nature, and scope at the national level do not exist.

This chapter addresses issues related to the delivery and effectiveness of this spectrum of occupational health promotion and wellness programs, with special emphasis on older workers, and suggests directions for further research and programs relevant to this age group. The emphasis will be on the promotion of general health, but many issues also apply to preventing illness and promoting work-related safety. The terms *health promotion* and *wellness* will be used interchangeably. Disease prevention will be addressed separately but is often subsumed under the health promotion rubric.

WORKPLACE HEALTH PROMOTION PROGRAMS: RATIONALE AND ISSUES
Why Should Workplace Health Promotion Be Provided?

When health promotion and disease prevention professionals seek efficient ways to deliver their services, they often seek venues where large numbers of persons may participate, making workplaces with many employees promising locales. An explicit goal of Healthy People 2010 is for 75 percent of employers to offer comprehensive health promotional programs and 75 percent of workers receive them (U.S. Department of Health and Human Services, 2007). The majority of American adults aged 20–60 years are full-time employees, and a substantial portion of waking hours are spent at the workplace or commuting to it. Many meals are taken there, and there are often substantial opportunities for social interaction, information exchange, and both formal and informal educational programs. There is evidence that most employees view workplace health promotion in a positive light, although participation is often far less than complete. Employers may see these programs as a way of improving productivity by reducing risks to health, improving employee health status, improving morale, and decreasing absenteeism. In regions where certain types of workers are in short supply, workplace health promotional programs may also improve employee retention. Employers are likely also motivated by rapidly increasing costs of health insurance and may hope to reduce their premium rates.

While it is beyond the scope of this report, it is not well known whether a "return on investment" is realized from workplace wellness programs, EAPs, and HPMs, but there is at least some suggestion of small gains in certain disease management programs (Goetzel, Ozminkowski, Villagra, and Duffy, 2005). An association between mitigating modifiable disease risk factors and subsequent health care expenditures has been suggested (Anderson et al., 2000). Some preventive and health promotional interventions, like immunization, were shown to save money and produce "health"; however, while many preventive interventions were efficacious in randomized trials, it is often difficult to determine whether they actually save money for the health care payer or the patient (Phillips and Holtgrave, 1997).

General Issues for Delivering Wellness, EAP, and HPM Programs

Several general issues and challenges are associated with delivering workplace wellness, EAP, and HPM programs at the worksite. Because workforce populations are generally healthier than the general population, from a public health perspective those who might benefit most from these activities may have limited access. However, such programs may have a multiplier effect in the community, not merely to the families of workers but also to others interacting with the workers or those exposed to the electronic communications, bulletin boards, newsletters, or community-based meetings (Tiede et al., 2007). Another issue is whether screening programs at entry to a particular company may prevent some people with certain health risks from achieving employment. An important example is routine testing of employees for illegal drug use (Carpenter, 2007). Also, many workers may not avail themselves of voluntary wellness programs for various reasons, such as fear of revealing various conditions to employers, lack of experience with wellness activities, and medical or mental health comorbidity associated with high-risk behaviors. For example, persons with a history of current serious mental illness are more than twice as likely to smoke cigarettes and to be overweight (Compton, Daumit, and Druss, 2006).

Another important issue is that U.S. workers are changing jobs more frequently than in the past, raising concerns on the continuity, duration, and thus efficacy of health-promotional programs. In addition, many people are self-employed or work for small businesses in which the resources, expertise, and economies that support wellness programs and HPMs may be meager or nonexistent. Even large companies that can offer HPMs may contract out a substantial proportion of tasks to smaller subcontractors, who in turn are ill-equipped to deliver workplace wellness. While there has been an effort to bring wellness programs to small companies, substantial challenges remain. Goetzel et al. (2007) explored factors that may lead to successful HPMs: (1) integrating programs into management operations; (2) simultaneously addressing individual, environmental, policy, and cultural factors affecting health and productivity; (3) targeting several health issues; (4) tailoring programs to address specific needs; (5) attaining high participation; (6) rigorously evaluating programs; and (7) communicating successful outcomes to key stakeholders.

DELIVERING WORKPLACE WELLNESS TO OLDER PEOPLE

The tremendous diversity in the types and demands of workplaces are directly relevant to HPMs and wellness programs. While many worksites are typical "white-collar" office facilities, where such programs are perhaps most easily offered, others have complex and challenging characteristics such as being outdoors (agriculture, utilities), underground (mining), within active transportation settings (trucking, aviation), or sustaining complicated indoor manufacturing processes. Some industries employ a large number of teleworkers (who work at home) or mobile workers. These situations require special methods to deliver HPMs. While many workplace environmental hazards are now controlled better than in the past and some of the more dangerous workplaces have been "exported" to developing countries, many hazardous worksites remain that require safety and worker protection efforts that may overwhelm wellness programs. These problems, of course, apply to older workers as well.

As workers age, they tend to migrate out of the most demanding jobs, selecting jobs that are perceived as easier to perform. These changes may challenge the delivery of wellness programs that require continuity to be effective. Each change may require some reevaluation to provide optimal work conditions and appropriate worksite interventions and wellness programs. It is unclear whether today's older workers behave more like their age cohort or more like today's younger workers, who change jobs more frequently, but the assumption of multiple late careers ("bridge jobs") after retirement from a major life's career described in the nationally representative Health and Retirement Study (Cahill, Giandrea, and Quinn, 2006) makes it likely that older workers may share the job-change issue with younger workers. How more frequent bridge jobs among older workers alter health promotional needs will require further investigation.

What Types of Wellness Program Do Older Workers Want?

An important issue in providing EAPs, HPMs, and wellness programs is ascertaining what workers actually want from these programs. As in all complex health services, workers may not have the health literacy to understand how to use such sophisticated services and thus may need to be made aware of the options. Such options may be presented by several sources, such as employers, unions, health plans, and other, more informal directions. Workers' interests and needs vary greatly, depending on the characteristics of the company, industry, demographics of the employees, and available fiscal resources; but few studies have surveyed worker perceptions and interests.

Jinks and Daniels (1999) conducted qualitative interviews of 27 British health care workers and found that perceived health needs were generally subsidiary to problems associated with the workplace such as an inhospitable work environment, inadequate staffing levels, excessive work volume, and work tasks that were deemed inappropriate. The United Kingdom has universal access to health care, so although assistance with health matters might be less emphasized than in the United States, this study showed that worker wellness programs are considered important tools for addressing health issues like substance abuse, diet, and exercise. In general, workers had a positive view of workplace wellness programs.

A Finnish survey of workers over 45 years old asked for opinions of wellness programs in the workplace (Naumanen, 2006). This survey showed that workers overwhelmingly endorsed promoting healthy behaviors, but they placed an equally high value on promoting a healthy workplace environment through tailoring of jobs to individual needs and capacities and providing a good workplace atmosphere, access to health checks, counseling, and nursing. Workers also emphasized the important role of management in approaching them with a positive attitude and providing specific programs to support their well-being.

Under any circumstances, some workers will disagree with or show indifference to the content of worker wellness programs (Crump, Earp, Kozma, and Hertz-Picciotto, 1996; Sorensen et al., 1998), making it inevitable that programs be continuously reevaluated, redirected, and enhanced. Concepts of health and well-being change with age (Kronenfeld, 2006) and in part alter acceptance of well-intended health promotion programs. Older people have different health-related goals and valuations of health status. In addition, the social context of the workplace is a crucial consideration when designing effective wellness programs. The social context includes workers' organizations, particularly union locals, safety representatives, and shop stewards; corporate policies; management; regulations and practices on occupational and other health hazards; material resources and funding potential; industrial hygiene monitoring and interventions; safety committees and safety personnel; community health programs and organizations; insurance systems; local leadership; workers' families; and other factors (Peltomaki et al., 2003). Pragmatic considerations, like physical proximity to programs and ancillary program charges, also influence whether workers will accept wellness programs.

Health Promotion for Older People: Assessing the Evidence

Assessing the effectiveness of worksite wellness programs for older persons requires an evidence-based framework with two basic components: the intervention's efficacy under general circumstances, and its efficacy when delivered in the workplace. With regard to the former, a basic tenet of health promotional interventions, including those for older people, is that their efficacy and safety be clearly established. This requires evidence as "proof-of-principle," and it includes the demonstration of safety and efficacy for all targeted demographic groups and in the presence of a general range of environmental threats. Many potentially attractive interventions, such as the use of antioxidant vitamins for preventing mortality from chronic illnesses, simply do not have an adequate evidence base (Bjelakovic et al., 2007) and should not be considered as components of worker wellness programs. While assessing evidence itself is an art and different bodies may come to different conclusions, evidence-based practice focuses scarce resources on proven interventions, both to promote wellness and to clinically manage existing conditions.

A general problem for health-promotional interventions targeting older people is that the evidence base is much less secure than for young and middle-aged adults. For example, there is no randomized trial of mammographic screening that enrolled a substantial number of women over age 70 years, nor are studies of cholesterol-lowering interventions as complete for those in their 80s and 90s as for younger people. This may not be a big problem for many older workers, because most are not working after they are 70 years old. However, the number at that age who do continue to work in traditional settings is increasing, and in the future this may become a more serious concern. One potentially important use of worksite health promotion programs may be to develop personal health habits that carry over into retirement, when the programs courses and supports are not available. This is important because, with the exception of blood pressure and cholesterol screening, it appears that one-third to two-thirds of Medicare recipients do not receive recommended preventive interventions (Ozminkowski et al., 2006). Wellness programs for older workers may provide enhanced value by teaching recipients how to promote healthful behaviors outside the workplace in preparation for retirement. An excellent general evaluation of preventive and health promotional interventions can be found in the guidelines promulgated by the U.S. Preventive Services Task Force (see www.ahrq.gov).

The other element of an evidence-based framework for worker wellness programs is their effective delivery in the workplace. Here the evidence is less secure than for the general population, and a decline in rigorous research on this topic has been noted (Pelletier, 2005). While some worksite wellness programs have succeeded (e.g., see Sorensen et al., 1998), the great variation in workplaces, employees, and available resources may not allow easy generalization. A key issue is whether workers will accept and join various programs. An additional problem is that some workplace interventions may be effective individually, but not when delivered as a "bundle" of multiple offerings. From the employers' perspective, the appropriate outcomes for evidence-based studies may not always be clear. Such outcomes may be short-term (e.g., increased organizational morale, higher productivity, decreased absenteeism) or longer term (e.g., increased survivorship, decreased morbidity, decreased health care costs, including insurance premiums). For many common wellness programs, not all of these outcomes are known, largely because the critical studies have not been performed; however, the general presumption is that there is a positive impact from both fiscal and health perspectives (Reidel et al., 2001). A good example of the complexity of invoking effective worksite wellness programs is found in the report on strategies for preventing and controlling overweight and obesity at the worksite (Katz et al., 2005).

Another approach for assessing workplace health and wellness programs is general population surveying. One survey that can address some of the outcomes of this program is the Health and Retirement Study (HRS), a representative sample of about 20,000 Americans age 51 years or older (available at www .hrsonline.umich.edu). The HRS emphasizes the health, labor, economic, and social status of older people. We conducted one preliminary descriptive analysis of a single preventive measure, influenza immunization, according to work status (see tables 18.2 through 18.4).

Tables 18.2 and 18.3 show the proportions of men and women, respectively, reporting receipt of the "flu shot" in the two years before the 2004 survey. Differences according to work status were generally small, but nonworking men age 51–59 were a bit more likely to get immunized, whereas the reverse was true for women in the same age group. Beyond that, there were few differences between workers and nonworkers. Table 18.4 shows immunization rates for men and women workers according to work status. These work categories are not mutually exclusive, but they do evaluate potential differences among them. Until age 70, those reporting themselves to be self-employed have lower immunization rates. These data require substantial additional analyses, for example, accounting

TABLE 18.2.
Influenza immunization status among men,
by work status and age group

Age group (years)	Workers	Nonworkers
51–54	34.1%	40.8%
55–59	45.1	50.9
60–64	52.1	52.5
65–69	62.3	65.1
70–74	73.9	74.1
75+	80.4	82.9

TABLE 18.3.
Influenza immunization status among women,
by work status and age group

Age group (years)	Workers	Nonworkers
51–54	45.4%	39.9%
55–59	47.7	53.2
60–64	57.4	58.5
65–69	62.7	71.3
70–74	68.8	74.9
75+	75.3	78.3

TABLE 18.4.
Influenza immunization among workers (men and women combined),
by work status

Age group (years)	Full-time	Part-time	Self-employed
51–54	40.8%	36.9%	29.8%
55–59	46.5	44.5	39.1
60–64	53.1	56.8	47.3
65–69	61.2	63.9	53.9
70–74	69.2	72.6	69.9
75+	73.9	80.5	80.8

for insurance status and job type. However, they suggest that population approaches can add information not available from worksite surveys.

Secondary Prevention Programs at the Worksite: Disease Screening and Management

If primary disease prevention and health promotion attempt to avoid the onset of important illnesses such as coronary disease, cancer, or diabetes, then secondary prevention is equally important for older workers seeking to prevent the consequences of medical conditions that have already occurred. This is performed in two ways: screening (early disease detection), and disease management (chronic management of the risk factors or conditions).

Screening may be conducted at the worksite, particularly if it does not require substantial medical facilities. Thus, workers can be screened for hypertension, diabetes, or skin tumors, but not for breast cancer (mammography) or colon cancer (colonoscopy). At entry, workers may be screened using structured questionnaires generally known as health hazard appraisals or health risk appraisals (HRAs) that assess health conditions and related social problems as well as job suitability and placement. Some HRAs may be completed online (Kashima, 2006). These tools can generate an extensive profile of worker risk status, assuming that the respondent is competent and motivated to complete the appraisal. There is evidence that these instruments can predict worker health and productivity outcomes (Yen, Schultz, Schneuringer, and Edington, 2006). However, even if certain conditions are identified, not all workers may wish to commit to a comprehensive disease management program (Hudson and Pope, 2006). HRAs have been developed for older persons (Stuck et al., 2007), although whether these have been applied to work settings is not known.

The other element of secondary prevention applied to the workplace is disease management. This could be clinically managing health problems at the worksite, or providing relevant educational programs to assist in self-care, or interaction with the community health system. While many clinical problems have been addressed, much of the emphasis here is on workers with specific chronic conditions or risk factors such as hypertension, type II diabetes, substance abuse, chronic depression, recurrent musculoskeletal injuries or disabilities, and asthma. Presumably, such programs will minimize suffering and improve both the quality of life and the long-term risk of disease occurrence or progression. As noted above, the evidence that such programs are consistently effective is sometimes unclear; but successes, such as convincing workers to quit smoking (Moher, Hey, and

Lancaster, 2005), have occurred. Finally, paramount for success in any clinical management and education program is that workers are able to understand the program's goals and activities (Bouchard, 2007).

The Content of Wellness Programs for Older Workers

The content and efficacy of EAPs, HPMs, and wellness programs for older workers has not been intensively studied. Overall, older workers should enjoy the benefits of programs aimed at all age groups, such as moderate exercise, low-fat diet, substance abuse abatement, and stress management programs. Even here, however, there may important differences in how such programs should be presented to recipients of different ages. Tailoring educational formats to different age groups can increase a program's effectiveness. The formats chosen must take into account variations in sensory perceptive abilities or cognitive demands, and intergenerational tastes in diet, recreational practices, and behavioral styles should govern age-specific program presentations. (For example, some 60-year-olds might be uncomfortable in an exercise class with 25-year-olds.) Also, in the future, technological literacy may be key for successfully delivering wellness programs to older workers.

Many EAPs aimed at older workers attend to family social and health situations rather than to the needs of the worker themselves. These situations include dealing with disabled adult children or parents with dementia or physical impairments, for example, nursing home insurance, issues in Medicare or Medicaid, advanced directives, and assisted living. While these are all undoubtedly valuable services, they may not address the changing needs of the older worker him- or herself. In addition to wellness programs with a general health promotion mission, two additional domains of wellness programs should be considered for older workers: preventing specific health problems, and managing those that have already occurred.

Older people have increasing levels of risk for medical conditions, physiological changes, and functional losses; and to some extent, these may be preventable or subject to effective clinical or social interventions. At the very least, many specific conditions can be mitigated or deferred. New areas or conditions where interventions may be useful for older workers *at the worksite* include the following:

— *Degenerative arthritis.* Specific exercise interventions can enhance mobility and decrease pain.

— *Incontinence*. Interventions can ease the burdens of this dysfunction and allow greater worker productivity.

— *Hypercholesterolemia and other dyslipidemias*. These are conditions for which population levels increase until the eighth decade of life.

— *Sleep disorders*. These are common and may be disabling for older people.

— *Systolic hypertension*. This condition is already being addressed in worker wellness programs. It becomes more common with age, and the special problems of managing it in older people still need attention.

— *Glucose intolerance*. This becomes more common with advancing age, but evidence now shows that type II diabetes can be prevented with lifestyle modification, especially among older persons (Diabetes Prevention Research Group, 2006).

— *Colon cancer*. This disease receives less attention in the workplace because screening for it is only recommended after age 50.

— *Polypharmacy*. Pharmaceutical management programs can remedy this problem.

— *Hearing and visual loss*. In many instances this can be corrected, so substantial attention is already given to this area. Increasing emphasis on age-related hearing loss and visual conditions such as cataracts and macular degeneration may be useful.

— *Abuse and bullying of older adults*. This can be addressed both at the worksite and in the general community.

— *Vaccines for older adults*. Examples include those aimed at preventing pneumonia, influenza, and shingles.

— *Cognitive decline*. New randomized trial evidence shows that the functional consequences of age-related cognitive change can be deterred (Willis et al., 2006), and the worksite may provide an opportunity to explore such programs.

— *Caregiver stress*. New trial evidence suggests that various tailored interventions improved the quality of life in an ethnically diverse group of dementia caregivers (Belle et al., 2006).

An important issue for potential worksite interventions is how to coordinate programs with the worker's regular medical care. Because the sources of medical care are not well coordinated, it is critical that various care sources notify each other of ongoing interventions and programs in order to avoid duplicating or omitting services. It may be valuable for the older worker to maintain copies of all of appropriate medical records. However, situations have been reported where workers fear that medical records in the hands of companies may lead to discrimination and job loss, and thus some may not participate in voluntary worksite programs for that reason (Heikkinen, Wickstrom, and Leino-Kilpi, 2006).

RESEARCH DIRECTIONS

This review of wellness programs, EAPs, and HPMs for older workers leads to several suggestions for research directions. Many of these areas have been recognized, and some important work has been accomplished; however, most would agree that much more needs to be done:

1. *Bridge jobs and late career paths.* To determine the nature of later career exposures and hazards for older workers, patterns of bridge jobs need further study, particularly with respect to rates of change and risk of workplace hazards.

2. *Health risk appraisal.* Health risk appraisals that are used at job entry and periodically thereafter need to be tailored to older workers, who have special health problems, conceptions of health, and preventive needs that are different from younger workers. This includes the special issues related to bridge and other late-career jobs. Evaluating the health status of older workers may require other modes, such as personal interviews, health testing procedures, or acquisition of medical records.

3. *Effectiveness of worksite interventions for older workers.* There have been many important studies of workplace interventions, and more general work needs to be done. It is likely that an ongoing effort on this front will be needed, in part because the nature of work and the characteristics of workers will continuously evolve. However, older workers have special and common health problems that require intervention research to determine whether worksite programs will prevent the progression of these special health and social problems. This evaluation and demonstration research must harness the growing number of new studies suggesting the general feasibility of intervention and include cost-effectiveness analyses.

4. *Communicating with older workers.* The special problem of communicating with older persons effectively is critical when delivering workplace health, safety, and education programs. Research is needed to determine the most effective programmatic structures and barriers, in order to maintain workers' general and health literacy.

5. *Assessing older workers' preferences and needs*. There is a dearth of survey information concerning older workers' perceived health needs and preferences with regard to workplace wellness programs. Such information would be critical for defining health policies and programs both nationally and within specific industries and companies.

CONCLUSION

Providing workplace wellness and health promotion programs that directly benefit older workers is all but unexplored. Expanded research and demonstration programs in this area may yield activities that not only improve the health and productivity of older persons in the workplace but also enhance their quality of life in the years after retirement.

REFERENCES

Anderson, D. R., Whitmer, R. W., Goetzel, R., Ozminkowski, R. J., Dunn, R. L., Wasserman, J., et al. 2000. The relationship between modifiable health risks and group-level health care expenditures. Health Enhancement Research Organization Research Committee. *American Journal of Health Promotion* 15:45–52.

Belle, S. H., Burgio, L., Burns, R., Coon, D., Czaja, S. J., Gallagher-Thompson, D., et al. 2006. Enhancing the quality of life of dementia caregivers from different ethnic or racial groups: A randomized, controlled trial. *Annals of Internal Medicine* 145:727–38.

Bjelakovic, G., Nikolova, D., Gluud, L. L., Simonetti, R. G., and Gluud, C. 2007. Mortality in randomized trials of anti-oxidant vitamin supplements for primary and secondary prevention: Systematic review and meta-analysis. *JAMA* 297:842–57.

Bouchard, C. 2007. Literacy and hazard communication: Ensuring that workers understand the information they receive. *American Association of Occupational Health Nurses Journal* 55:18–25.

Cahill, K. E., Giandrea, M. D., and Quinn, J. F. 2006. Retirement patterns from career employment. *The Gerontologist* 46:514–23.

Carpenter, C. S. 2007. Workplace drug testing and worker drug use. *Health Services Research* 42:795–810.

Compton, M. T., Daumit, G. L., and Druss, B. G. 2006. Cigarette smoking and overweight/obesity among individuals with serious mental illness. *Harvard Review of Psychiatry* 14:212–22.

Crump, C. E., Earp, J. A. L., Kozma, C. M., and Hertz-Picciotto, I. 1996. Effect of organizational level variables on differential employee participation in 10 federal worksite health promotion programmes. *Health Education Quarterly* 23:202–24.

Diabetes Prevention Research Group: Crandell, J., Schade, D., Ma, Y., Fujimoto, W. Y., Barrett-Connor, E., Fowler, S., et al. 2006. The influence of age on the effects of lifestyle and metformin on the prevention of diabetes. *Journal of Gerontology Series A: Biological Sciences and Medical Sciences* 61:1075–81.

Fitzgerald, S. T., Hammond, S. C., and Harder, K. A. 1989. Role of the employee assistance program in helping the troubled worker. *Occupational Medicine* 4 (2): 233–43.

Goetzel, R. Z., Ozminkowski, R. J., Villagra, V. G., and Duffy, J. 2005. Return on investment in disease management: A review. *Health Care Financing Review* 26:1–19.

Goetzel, R. Z., Shechter, D., Ozminkowski, R. J., Marmet, P. F., Tabrizi, M. J., and Roemer, E. C. 2007. Promising practices in employer health and productivity management efforts: Finding from a benchmarking study. *Journal of Occupational and Environmental Medicine* 49:110–30.

Heikkinen, A., Wickstrom, G., and Leino-Kilpi, H. 2006. Understanding privacy in occupational health services. *Nursing Ethics* 13:510–30.

Hudson, L. R., and Pope, J. E. 2006. The role of health risk appraisal in disease management. *Managed Care Interface* 19:41–42.

Institute of Medicine. 2000. *Safe Work in the Twenty-first Century*. Washington, DC: National Academies Press.

Jinks, A. M., and Daniels, R. 1999. Workplace health concerns: A focus group study. *Journal of Management in Medicine* 13:95–104.

Kashima, S. R. 2006. Transitioning from a pen-and-paper health risk appraisal to an online health risk appraisal at a petroleum company. *Health Promotion Practice* 7:450–58.

Katz, D. L., O'Connell, M., Yeh, M. C., Nawaz, H., Njike, V., Anderson, L. M., et al. 2005. Public health strategies for preventing and controlling overweight and obesity on school and worksite settings: A report on the recommendations of the Task Force on Community Preventive Services. *MMWR Recommendation Report* 54 (RR-10): 1–12.

Kronenfeld, J. J. 2006. Changing conceptions of health and life course concepts. *Health* 10:501–17.

Moher, M., Hey, K., and Lancaster, T. 2005. Workplace interventions for smoking cessation. *Cochrane Database of Systematic Reviews* 18 (2): CD003440.

National Research Council. 2004. *Health and Safety Needs of Older Workers*. Washington, DC: National Academies Press.

Naumanen, P. 2006. Opinions of ageing workers on relative importance of health promotion. *International Journal of Nursing Practice* 12:352–58.

Ozminkowski, R. J., Goetzel, R. Z., Shechter, D., Stapleton, D. C., Baser, O., and Lapin, P. 2006. Predictors of preventive service use among Medicare beneficiaries. *Health Care Financing Review* 27:5–23.

Pelletier, K. R. 2005. A review and analysis of the clinical and cost-effectiveness studies of comprehensive health promotion and disease management programs at the worksite: Update VI 2000–2004. *Journal of Occupational and Environmental Medicine* 47:1051–58.

Peltomaki, P., Johansson, M., Ahrens, W., Sala, M., Wesseling, C., Brenes F., et al. 2003. Social context in workplace health promotion. *Health Promotion International* 18:115–26.

Phillips, K. A., and Holtgrave, D. R. 1997. Using cost-effectiveness/cost-benefit analysis to allocate health resources: A level playing field for prevention? *Abstract Book Association Health Services Research Meeting* 14:32–33.

Reidel, J. E., Lynch, W., Baase, C., Hymel, P., and Peterson, K. W. 2001. The effect of disease prevention and health promotion on workplace productivity: A literature review. *America Journal of Health Promotion* 15:167–91.

Schecter, A. 2007. Occupational and environmental health. In *Public Health and Preventive Medicine*, ed. R. B. Wallace, section 3. New York: McGraw-Hill.

Sorensen, G., Stoddard, A., Hunt, M. K., Hebert, J. R., Ockene, J. K., Avrunin, J. K., et al. 1998. The effects of a health promotion-health protection intervention on behavioral change: The WellWorks Study. *America Journal Public Health* 88:1685–90.

Stuck, A. E., Kharicha, K., Dapp, U., Anders, J., von Rentein-Kruse, W., Meier-Baumgartner, H. P., et al. 2007. Development, feasibility and performance of a health risk appraisal questionnaire for older persons. *BMC Medical Research Methodology* 7:1.

Tiede, L. P., Hennrikus, D. J., Cohen, B. B., Hilgers, D. L., Madsen, R., and Lando, H. A. 2007. Feasibility of promoting smoking cessation in small worksites: An exploratory study. *Nicotine and Tobacco Research* 9 (Suppl 1): S83–90.

U.S. Department of Health and Human Services. 2007. *Healthy People 2010.* Retrieved March 24, 2007, from www.healthypeople.gov/Implementation/.

Willis, S. L., Tennstedt, S. L., Marsiske, M., Ball, K., Elias, J., Koepke, K. M., et al. 2006. Long-term effects of cognitive training on everyday functional outcomes in older adults. *JAMA* 296:2805–14.

Yen, L., Schultz, A., Schneuringer, E., and Edington, D. W. 2006. Financial costs due to excess health risks among active employees of a utility company. *Journal of Occupational and Environmental Medicine* 48:896–905.

Conclusion

Synthesis and Future Directions

SARA J. CZAJA, PH.D., AND JOSEPH SHARIT, PH.D.

The book addresses the complex issue of aging and work from a broad and multidisciplinary perspective, with the goal of summarizing current and future issues confronting industry, society, and the workforce in the twenty-first century. Topics covered include demographic and societal trends, changes in work organizations and practices, health and safety, training, attitudinal and motivational issues, and unique concerns such as telework, working caregivers, and entrepreneurship as a life transition. These topics are covered from the perspectives of both academics and representatives from government, business, and industry. Fair coverage of the topic of aging and work requires a multidisciplinary approach and inclusion of a broad array of issues.

One of the major themes that emerges throughout this book and that underscores its relevance concerns the convergence of a number of social, demographic, policy, and industry trends into the "making of a perfect storm" with respect to work and the aging of the population. Unless we develop strategies to extend working life, current employment patterns that favor early retirement, coupled with the shrinking labor pool, threaten future economic growth, pension and health benefits, and living standards for a large segment of the population. We hope that this book provides important insights into the critical issues regarding work and aging that are confronting our society. This chapter summarizes the major points and themes discussed by our authors and outlines some key directions for future research, policy, and work organizations.

The first section discusses important demographic and social trends that are shaping work and work organizations. All three chapters highlight the elements of this perfect storm, though from different perspectives, and in doing so set the tone for the remaining chapters. Richard Burkhauser begins the discussion by pointing out that the aging of the population and the change in the age structure of the population that we are currently witnessing will be permanent since fertility rates are likely to continue to decline and life expectancies will continue to increase. If this prediction is correct, current pension and health insurance programs that support older adults will erode because they are dependent on contributions from a shrinking younger workforce. Burkhauser maintains that traditional solutions, such as raising taxes or reducing benefits for future generations, are not optimal solutions and that instead what is required are changes in social structures and in the private sector that encourage people to work longer. He points out that we are currently experiencing structural lags in our society because our existing social structures are not being modified at a pace commensurate with demographic trends. In particular, a structural lag between the increased work capacity of older adults because of increases in health, lifestyle preferences, and changes in work demands due to technology, and a retirement system that continues to discourage work at older ages is still very much in place. Burkhauser argues that major policy changes are needed to reduce incentives for early retirement. Changes such as increasing the value of individual contributions to pension income are also needed in the private sector to encourage people to work longer.

Richard Schulz and Lynn Martire continue the discussion of the idea of structural lags within the context of the increasingly important topic of work and caregiving. As these authors note, traditional models of family life are eroding as more women enter the labor market. This is happening at the same time that the demands for elder care are increasing and resources for formal care are decreasing. Schulz and Martire point out that a major crisis may evolve if we do not develop plans to maximize our ability to combine caregiving and work. Achieving this goal requires the development of programs that support caregivers at work and policies that provide economic support for caregivers that are cost effective for industry. They caution, however, that the development of programs and policies for working caregivers must be based on data from large-scale representative samples regarding how work impacts caregiving and caregiving impacts work, especially for nontraditional families. We also need accurate data on the prevalence of working caregivers, especially for older caregivers. The authors also suggest that the potential role of technology in providing support for working caregivers is a fruitful area for research.

In chapter 3, Juhani Ilmarinen provides an overview of trends in aging and work from an international perspective with a focus on the European Union. He points out that the issues regarding the aging of the work force and supporting social structures are a prominent concern throughout the European Union and that a major goal for the EU countries is to increase the employment rate of people aged 55 to 64 years in the upcoming decades. Ilmarinen argues that achievement of this goal requires mutual changes at the individual, organizational, and societal levels that include better management of changes in work organization and work structures, an increased focus on the well-being of workers, elimination of age biases, better integration of work, family, and societal roles, and changes in views about retirement. He discusses new paradigms of aging and work that are evolving in the European Union to capture changes in work, and the needs of different generations. Ilmarinen also presents the concept of work ability, a holistic approach to human potential in worklife, and provides examples of how this approach has been successfully used in Finland and other countries in the European Union. He concludes with a series of recommendations for future research and policy that include the need for new conceptualizations of aging and retirement, changes in work structures and work hours to accommodate the abilities and preferences of mature workers, and programs that foster the promotion of lifelong learning.

Part II provides insights into the topic of older adults from a public policy and business/industry perspective. Fernando Torres-Gil expresses concern about the employment and financial security of older adults that may result from an unwillingness or inability of the government and public policy to take on the challenges of an aging workforce. He suggests that emerging demographic trends may not, in fact, increase employment opportunities for older people and that policies may need to be enforced to promote work and financial security for older adults. Specifically, he suggests that challenges confronting older workers include globalization of the economy and practices such as outsourcing and lower pay scales in foreign countries, skill obsolescence, declines in the power of labor unions, increased diversity of older adults, and continued discrimination by managers toward older workers. He argues that in the United States we have a legacy of using legislation, regulations, and tax incentives and disincentives to promote or inhibit employment among older adults, yet historically these public policy responses have been fragmented and largely influenced by one major program, Social Security. He maintains that overarching and comprehensive public policies are needed that are explicitly designed to oversee or influence the nature of work and aging. He also maintains that there is a strong need for the government to step in and work in partnership with the private sector to accommodate older persons who need to work.

Vicki Hanson and Eric Lesser compliment Torres-Gil's comments and provide an illuminating discussion of the implications of changing workforce demographics on business and industry. The authors indicate that many industries, such as the health care and the electric utility industries, are confronting skill level shortages due to increased turnover of mature, experienced workers whose skills and expertise are critical to productivity and organizational effectiveness. They discuss four integrated strategies that companies are beginning to employ to mitigate risks associated with the changing demographics and remain competitive in today's economy. They suggest that many companies are beginning to view using older workers to fill labor shortages as a valuable option and as such are providing incentives such as flexible work arrangements and financial packages to both attract and retain older workers. As noted by the authors, an important first step that is often overlooked in these efforts is an analysis of company needs to identify positions that are most vulnerable within an organization. At the same time, the needs and preferences of workers are often overlooked. Hanson and Lesser also highlight the importance of preserving the knowledge of older workers, and they provide examples of techniques to foster knowledge transfer between seasoned and novice employees. They also point out that opportunities must be provided to ensure that older workers themselves are provided with opportunities to update their skills, especially for technology-mediated work. The authors conclude that there are enormous opportunities for research within these areas that would benefit industry and suggest that collaborations between business and academia represent a valuable approach for gaining needed knowledge.

Part III moves to a discussion of some of the changes in work environments and jobs that will likely have an impact on employment opportunities for older workers. In chapter 6, Peter Cappelli provides an overview of some changes in work roles and job demands and the potential implications for an aging workforce. He emphasizes the virtual end of the lifetime employment that characterized work for most of the twentieth century and the subsequent emergence of job insecurity. Cappelli views the move away from lifetime employment to shorter tenures, and in particular contingent work (part-time, temporary, and seasonal work), as positive trends for older workers because these types of work arrangements may serve as a bridge or transition between full-time work and retirement. These work arrangements also offer more flexibility, which is attractive to older workers and represents another theme that emerges throughout many of our chapters. Cappelli also notes that there is a greater shift toward jobs requiring higher skills such as cognitive and interpersonal skills, resident knowledge, and more mature attitudes. This presents a mixed bag for older adults because although older adults are typically the keepers of resident knowledge and have better attitudes about work and work responsibilities, cognitive skills tend to decline with age, as discussed in detail in Charness's chapter. Another trend mentioned by Capelli that may bode well for older workers is the flattening of organizations and the increased need for workers to operate in teams. Capelli is optimistic about the current trends in the nature of organizations for the employability of older workers since he believes that today's work environment affords many opportunities for their skills and qualities.

In our chapter on telework, we expand on Capelli's discussion of the changing nature of work and focus on telework, where work is performed outside of the traditional work situation and oftentimes in the home. As discussed throughout the chapter, telework offers a number of advantages for older workers, given the flexibility it affords. However, there are also challenges associated with telework, such as employee supervision, work scheduling, training, and limited opportunities for social interaction. For example, one issue with home-based telework is achieving a balance between work and home responsibilities; other issues include lack of a "presence" within the organization and isolation from coworkers. The extent to which these issues are problematic naturally depends on the specific needs and characteristics of the worker. From a management point of view, potential problems with telework include selection of employees who are suitable for telework and development of strategies for supervision and assessment of work output. With respect to older workers, unique challenges include potential problems with technology adoption, since in many instances telework involves the use of information technologies, and methods for training. Another important consideration is negative biases management may have about older workers, which may limit the opportunities for these workers to engage in telework. Recent data from our lab suggests that older people are receptive to telework arrangements but also that ensuring provision of adequate training and performance feedback and guidelines for safe and comfortable workplace design is of paramount importance. Data from our survey study with managers suggests that while telework is common in many organizations, organizational guidelines for telework jobs are less common. We conclude with some recommendations for needed research in this area, such as information to help organizations assess the types of jobs that are most suited to telework and discovery of the optimal methods for training teleworkers. In addition to research, policies are needed to promote telework for older people, especially in the private sector.

Michael Smyer and Marcie Pitt-Catsouphes present an interesting discussion of another emerging trend—collaborative work. They focus their discussion on one element of the collaborative workplace that has particular relevance to older workers: work teams. To explain why team work has particular relevance for older adults, the authors provide an overview of some of the larger social and organizational factors that are shaping today's work teams. Not surprisingly, one of these factors is technology, which is changing essential processes among team members. For example, communication within the work setting is increasingly computer and Internet based, and there are rising expectations about technology literacy within the work environment. These expectations may be challenging for the current and immediate next cohort of older adults who are accustomed to more traditional communication formats.

Closely linked to technology is the emphasis on a globalized economy, which also increases demands for collaborative efforts among people with different backgrounds and skill sets and among those who work at different locations and time zones. Work groups will also be diverse with respect to the age mix of group members. Thus, strategies must be developed to ensure that workers of different ages are comfortable with each other and that their skills are maximized. In fact, this presents a wonderful opportunity for knowledge transfer from older to younger workers on issues related to expertise and organizational culture, and from younger to older workers on issues related to emerging technologies. Team work is obviously an important area of investigation. We know little about the impact of aging on team functioning or on how intergenerational conflicts among team members influence work outcomes. Smyer and Pitt-Catsouphes suggest that there are two distinctive research approaches for assessing the relationship of aging and collaborative work functioning. One approach focuses on the individual employee, and the other on the work context. Research in both areas is necessary to understand how age influences the willingness and ability of employees to effectively participate in collaborative work efforts and what conditions are optimal for maximizing collaboration and output among team members.

Edward Rogoff discusses another emerging trend—the increased number of older adults who are pursuing entrepreneurship through self-employment, business ownership, or direct investment in a small business. He claims that it is only recently that entrepreneurship is being recognized as an important activity among older Americans and that many older adults are pursuing entrepreneurial activities because of advances in health, shrinking pensions, age discrimination, and continued personal ambitions. Interestingly, he points out that many older adults are also considering these work options as they reach a point in their lives where they are unwilling to relocate to pursue work activities. In this regard he makes an important distinction between the "have-to-be entrepreneurs" and the "want-to-be entrepreneurs"; however, he notes that in either case entrepreneurship provides an interesting option for older workers since it offers greater flexibility than traditional work.

Rogoff astutely observes that entrepreneurial ventures present some unique concerns for older adults because they often entail risk and the ability to bounce back from loss, and older people do not have the same quantity of time as younger people to rectify mistakes. Furthermore, absence from the traditional employment pool could have more negative implications for older people. He maintains that we need tools to help older people identify and manage risks associated with these activities. In doing so, he outlines a five-step model for programs that could help support later-life entrepreneurs. He concludes that we have limited empirical knowledge about entrepreneurship for people aged 50+ and that there is a vast need for research in this area. Rogoff also states that it is important for policies to evolve that make paths to successful entrepreneurship easily available to older people.

Part IV begins to address some of the more specific topics that influence the work ability and work performance of older people. Richard Johnson's chapter focuses on the influence of managerial attitudes on continued employment opportunities for older people. He states that demographics only tell part of the story and argues that future outcomes depend to a large extent on the willingness of employers to hire and retain older workers. He agrees with Hanson and Lesser that employers may appreciate older workers' experience and maturity. However, he cautions that managers may be reluctant to employ older people because they typically cost more and have limited remaining years of work, skills that may not be current, and, to some extent, special legal protections. Johnson provides a nice summary of current survey-based evidence about employer attitudes and indicates that managers generally value older worker's knowledge, experience, and work ethic and consider them to be at least as productive as younger workers. However, at the same time many express concerns about older workers' creativity and willingness to learn new things along with the costs of employing older workers. Complimenting Ilmarinen's chapter, he includes a section on employer attitudes in other countries and indicates that to a large extent they share many of the views that American employers hold.

Johnson discusses the limitations of survey data and suggests that a better approach is to gauge actual employer practices. He asserts that on the surface there appears to be limited evidence to suggest that older workers fare worse than younger workers since they receive higher wages and exhibit lower unemployment rates. Yet as he points out, it is difficult to truly understand age group comparisons on these variables because they do not control for productivity differences between older and younger workers or differences in job tenure. In addition, many older workers feel that age discrimination is pervasive throughout the workplace. Overall, Johnson is less optimistic than Capelli. He concludes that generally many firms have serious reservations about hiring and employing older workers and that employment prospects at older ages may be especially bleak for workers with limited skills. He notes, however, that better attitudes concerning employing older workers may evolve if labor shortages continue in certain industries or occupations. Johnson recommends that avenues for future research include development of new surveys or alternative methods for assessing employer attitudes and organizational climates, and development of strategies to promote more positive attitudes toward older employees.

Ruth Kanfer discusses the important topic of worker motivation and describes how age-related changes in knowledge, skills, and abilities (KSAs) and other "nonability person traits" influence work motivation and job performance. She begins with a definition of work performance and correctly notes that many descriptions of jobs and subsequent metrics of performance evaluation are content-based and overlook the important role that motivation plays in job performance. In contrast, current perspectives on job performance emphasize that performance is influenced by a broad array of personal characteristics in terms of their fit to job demands as well as individual differences in motivational traits. In this regard, she contends that age-related changes that bear upon job performance can be organized along four broad maturational themes: changes in intellectual development (loss and growth) that occur over the lifespan, the fit between personal attributes and job demands, maturational changes in self-development, and motive changes that affect individual changes in motivation.

Importantly, Kanfer emphasizes that there is no universal evidence to support the notion of a universal age-related decline in job performance, but rather, job performance is jointly determined by ongoing intra-individual changes in intellect, knowledge, and the self, and ongoing fluctuations in work role demands and work motivation. In addition, she notes that there is no strong evidence of an age-related decline in work motivation because of some central loss of energy but that declines in motivation result from misfits that arise between a person's strengths and salient interests and the demands and reward opportunities offered by the work role. In this regard, Kanfer suggests that to foster employment opportunities among older people it is important to identify what motivates older adults to participate in organized work and how intrinsic motives for work differ between older and younger people. She notes in particular that investigation of other personal resources, beyond time and effort, is important in the study of older worker motivation and performance. Another area for future investigation discussed by Kanfer is the determinants and consequences of intergenerational conflicts at work that might arise from differences in work values. She also suggests that more information is needed about how workplace transitions such as layoffs and organizational changes are differentially handled by younger and older workers and influence decisions about participation in work activities.

In his chapter on changes in job demands, Peter Capelli notes that current and future jobs will place an emphasis on knowledge and cognitive skills. Neil Charness concurs with this observation and provides a timely and thorough review of what is known about aging, cognition, and skill acquisition. Charness presents a model of the skill acquisition process that depicts the broad array of factors that influence one's ability to learn new skills. He introduces the concept of "discount rate for new learning," suggesting that the cost-benefit analysis of engaging in learning activities may vary for people of different ages and that older people may be less willing to incur the time and effort costs that new learning requires because they may not perceive the same long-term rewards as younger people. Charness concludes that because of cognitive declines, older people are going to be at a disadvantage when learning new skills when compared to younger people, especially if the skill in question does not draw on their knowledge store. Thus, older adults may need greater incentives to engage in work development activities. He points out that situational factors in the workplace such as negative stereotyping of older workers present a strong disincentive for older people. But he also provides strong evidence that use of effective training techniques enhances the likelihood of learning success for workers of all ages. Charness agrees with Richard Johnson about the need for the development of programs for HR managers concerning older worker issues and the value of older workers. He also indicates that there is a need for programs that increase incentives for older adults to engage in work development activities and that amortize the skills of older people over longer periods of productive work.

In our chapter on training, we continue the discussion introduced by Charness regarding the critical need for workers to continually engage in learning and training activities to successfully adapt to the work environment of the twenty-first century. We echo the comments of many of our colleagues about the dynamic nature of work. Factors that point to the need for workers to engage in learning activities include the rapid diffusion of technology into the workplace, the flattening of organizations, and increased demand for knowledge and skilled workers. We also note that in general the available evidence clearly indicates that older adults can learn new skills and adapt to new work situations; however, when compared to younger adults, they may take longer and require more assistance and support. As noted by both Charness and Kanfer, learning is a complex process and is influenced by motivational factors, social factors, and environmental factors. One common impingement on the ability of older adults to participate in training programs is the availability of training opportunities. Because of negative stereotypes about aging, employers are often less willing to invest in older workers. With respect to the future, a number of challenges need to be addressed. Because of the increased prevalence of nonstandard work arrangements, the responsibility of continuous learning and job training will fall to a greater extent on the individual. Strategies need to be developed to facilitate and promote training and retraining opportunities for "nontraditional" workers. Much work needs to be done in the area of e-learning. There is little empirical knowledge to guide the development of multimedia applications, especially for older learners. Another area that requires serious attention is identifying strategies to foster lifelong learning among low-skilled and low-educated older workers who are more likely to be unemployed and have less access to training opportunities. Clearly, worker training is one of the key issues that the government, organizations, and employees will need to invest in to ensure that the workforce is able to adapt to the changing landscape of the workplace.

In her chapter, Pamela Tsang discusses the need for measures of work performance that adequately assess performance on today's knowledge-based jobs. She argues that a more thorough analysis of the type and intensity of the cognitive demands associated with these work activities would allow for more accurate performance assessments and a clearer understanding of the relationship between age and performance. Tsang provides a conceptual model for organizing the variables that influence the relationship between age and job performance as a platform for discussing assessment approaches. She expands upon this model by discussing the impact of technology on current job demands and makes the keen observation that technology can amplify or lessen the cognitive demands of jobs and subsequently affect the relationship between age and work performance in a variety of ways. Ultimately, the impact of technology depends on the type and the design of the technology, how it is used, and the worker's expertise. Tsang stresses that age is only part of the work performance equation and that new measures of work performance are needed to capture this complexity. To expand on this issue, she discusses the limitations of traditional performance measures. As noted by Tsang, a shortcoming of traditional measures such as psychometric measures or measures of job knowledge is that they only tell part of the story. She argues that two other approaches to work assessment are more promising: domain-representative componential measures, and global measures. However, she cautions that few comprehensive job analyses exist for present-day jobs and that much work is needed to facilitate the process of identifying domain-representative tasks for performance evaluations. An interesting area of future research identified by Tsang is investigating how technological advances can be used to support age-related ability changes.

Part V discusses addresses issues related to worker health and workplace design. Karl Kroemer provides a classic discussion of the importance of ergonomic considerations to the health and productivity of older workers. Although the point has been made by many of the authors that the physical demands of work are decreasing, greatly enhancing the employability of older workers, there is a still a need to address ergonomic issues. It is well established that violation of "good" design practices leads to poorer performance and possible adverse health effects. Given the broad umbrella that ergonomics covers, Kroemer's approach is to provide an overview of well-known interventions such as work scheduling, redesigning the workplace, and training, which have proven to benefit older workers. He then discusses two main issues in more depth: auditory and visual aspects of work, and design of the computer keyboard. These issues are extremely relevant for two reasons. One, given the emphasis on information processing and communication in today's workplace, normative age-related declines in vision and hearing could greatly handicap many older workers. Likewise, the emphasis on interacting with software applications places burdens on keyboard entry that may also compromise the health and comfort of older workers, given age-related declines in psychomotor skills and a greater propensity among older people to develop chronic conditions such as arthritis. Kroemer suggests the need to consider a number of alternatives to conventional computer interfaces that collectively could reduce demands on vision, hearing, memory, and manipulative skills. Overall, his message is that employers will need to become more sensitized to age-related decrements and ways to accommodate these decrements through ergonomic interventions if we are going to be successful in our attempt to accommodate the growing number of older workers.

James Grosch and Glenn Pransky continue the discussion of worker well-being in their chapter on safety and health issues for older workers. They begin with the observation that despite the recent interest in maintaining older people in the workforce, there is relatively little knowledge about the unique health and safety issues of older workers, how health and safety is influenced by work organization, and how these issues affect occupational injury and work performance. They reiterate that aging is associated with tremendous variability and that while age is associated with declines in physical functioning and enhanced likelihood of chronic disease, age by itself is a poor indicator of whether someone is able to perform a given task. To illustrate these points, they provide a thorough review of evidence from the workplace linking age to a number of standard measures of safety and health. They conclude that while age matters, for some variables, such as injury severity, older workers are at a relative disadvantage as compared to younger workers, while for others, such as injury frequency, they have a relative advantage. There are also other outcomes, such as absenteeism, where the influence of age is relatively small and inconsistent. These authors note that much of the existing data does not capture other factors in the workplace such as the nature of job activities and contextual factors.

An important message imparted by Grosch and Pransky is that work processes and organizational practices can significantly affect occupational safety and health and that in today's changing labor market older workers are more likely to be found in nontraditional employment settings such as being self-employed or working from home. This trend makes the monitoring of worker health and safety and the development of interventions to protect and enhance worker well-being even more challenging. The authors highlight several important gaps in knowledge, including data on specific subgroups of older workers, such as low-SES workers, who may be at increased risk for experiencing adverse safety and health outcomes; data on gender differences in health outcomes; and longitudinal data that contains detailed information about workers' employment histories, workplace exposures and risks, and work-related health outcomes. Another much-needed area of research is the development of interventions or best practices to improve safety and health that specifically address the unique needs of older workers.

Steven Sauter, Jessica Streit, and Dennis Hanseman continue with this theme but with a focus on stress and health. Of particular relevance is the role that work organizations might play in affecting health and safety of older works. To illustrate this point, the authors summarize recent data from the Finnish Institute of Occupational Health that indicates that high physical demands of jobs, and organization and social factors (e.g., role conflicts, time pressure) contribute to declines in work ability. In their chapter they take the next step and examine whether older workers differ from younger workers in terms of risks posed by work organization factors. They postulate two possibilities: that work organization exposures vary as a function of age, and thus older and younger workers have different risk profiles; and that older workers differ from younger workers in their capacity to respond to stressful situations related to work. Initially, they provide a review of the literature regarding age, job stress, and mental health outcomes. They shed further light on this issue by presenting some new data from the NIOSH Quality of Work Life Survey (QWL) based on responses from 1,620 adults who worked at least 20 hours per week. Overall, these data are encouraging and demonstrate a protective effect of increasing age on subjective well-being measures (e.g., job satisfaction, work stress) and health-related quality of life outcomes that captured mental health. Similar results were found for job exposure (e.g., organizational climate) and work-life balance outcomes, except for work opportunities, where older workers reported fewer opportunities for promotion.

Interesting and important findings from these new analyses relate to the interactions between age and co-worker support and organizational climate variables. For older workers, adverse exposure (e.g., lack of co-worker helpfulness) was associated with increasing risk of adverse health and well-being outcomes, and positive exposure was associated with increasing protective effects. These findings were not evident for younger workers. Contrary to expectations, the data did not indicate age-related declines in self-rated health or health-related quality of life. The authors hypothesize that this might be the effect of attrition of unhealthy older workers from the workforce. Overall, the data support the authors' assertion about the importance of contextual and organizational factors to worker health and safety. They concur with Grosch and Pransky that to clearly understand the influence of workplace factors on older workers' health there is a need for longitudinal data systems that capture the complexity of the work situation.

Health promotion and injury prevention is a key component of maintaining a healthy and productive workforce. In many respects, the workplace is an ideal forum for health promotion activities because the majority of adults work and spend a substantial amount of time at the workplace or in the engagement of work activities. Robert Wallace and Gwenith Fisher provide an overview of issues related to the delivery and effectiveness of workplace health promotion and wellness programs. They stress that although health and wellness programs have been in the workplace for many years, little specific attention has been given to the needs of older workers. Importantly, they note that in addition to general wellness, two other domains of wellness promotion for older workers are preventing specific health problems and managing those that have already occurred. Wellness programs for older workers might also have enhanced value by teaching recipients how to maintain personal health habits into retirement when formal support might not be available. Topics that have special relevance to older people include sleep disorders, arthritis, sensory and memory problems, hypertension, and caregiving.

Wallace and Fisher emphasize that there may be important differences in how wellness programs should be presented to workers of different ages and that tailoring educational programs to participant needs and characteristics can increase program effectiveness. The authors underscore that development of effective programs requires a solid evidence base regarding "what works" and "for whom"; however, the current evidence-base for wellness programs is sketchy, especially for older workers. They highlight several important areas of research that are needed to foster the development of effective older-worker wellness programs, including assessment of older workers' perceived health needs and preferences with respect to wellness programs, understanding exposures and health risks associated with bridge jobs and alternative work arrangements, and barriers that prevent workers from participating in and benefiting from wellness and health promotion activities. Clearly, much work needs to be done in this area, which represents an extremely valuable mechanism for enhancing productivity and the health and well-being of workers and their families.

This volume presents a comprehensive assessment of the state of aging and work, a complex and pressing issue that is at the forefront of work and productivity in the twenty-first century. It seems clear that traditional models of retirement are no longer adequate and that people can expect to work longer in the future. It is also clear that with globalization and rapid developments in technology the work environment is changing dramatically and will continue to do so in the coming decades. So what can we conclude? First, there is little reason to believe that workers who are older cannot continue to make important contributions to work and productivity. Older workers represent a valuable resource that has yet to be mined. Second, older workers themselves are complex, and chronological age tells us little about a worker's knowledge, skills, or abilities. How well one performs one's jobs is dependent on a myriad of individual and environment factors. Another theme that emerges throughout this volume is that technology will continue to have a significant impact on jobs, skill requirements, communication processes, and work locations. The influence of technology will be far-reaching and will affect workers of all ages, but it has special significance for older people because it creates a need for lifelong learning. In fact, most of the authors underscore the importance of development of worker training and re-training programs. Finally, it is evident that successfully accommodating an aging workforce will require efforts on the part of the government, private industry, the research community, and individual employees.

Index